S0-AKK-246

trees
and man

trees and man
·the forest in the middle ages·

·roland bechmann·

· Translated by Katharyn Dunham ·

Paragon House
New York

The paper used in this publication meets the minimum requirements of
American National Standard for Information Sciences—Permanence of Paper
for Printed Library Materials, ANSI Z39.48-1984.

First edition, 1990

Published in the United States by

Paragon House
90 Fifth Avenue
New York, NY 10011

Copyright © 1984 by Éditions Flammarion
Copyright © 1990 by Paragon House

All rights reserved. No part of this book may be
reproduced, in any form, without written permission
from the publishers, unless by a reviewer who wishes
to quote brief passages.

Originally published in French under the titles
Des arbres et des hommes: La forêt au moyen-âge.
This edition has been revised and updated by the author.

Library of Congress Cataloging-in-Publication Data

Bechmann, Roland.
    [Des arbres et des hommes. English]
    Trees and man : the forest in the Middle Ages / Roland Bechmann ;
translated by Katharyn Dunham.— 1st ed.
      p. cm.
    Translation of: Des arbres et des hommes.
    ISBN 1-55778-034-X
    1. Forests and forestry—Europe—History. 2. Europe—
History—476-1492. I. Title.
SD177.B4313   1990
333.75'094'0902—dc20
                                        89-3357
                                          CIP

Manufactured in the United States

table of contents

introduction

THE FOREST OCCUPIES A FUNDAMENTAL PLACE in the history of mankind. The ancient relations between man and forest are a mixture of attraction and fear, love and repulsion.

The forest was Man's birthplace. When, four million years ago, temperatures fell all around the world and the ice cap grew extensively, the intertropical forests were replaced by grasslands, and our distant ancestors, in order to survive, had to adapt their behavior to their new environment. As trees no longer guaranteed their security and helped them move about, our ancestors stood up: they adopted the standing position which allowed them to see further so they could find their food and spot their enemies. Paleontologists seem to agree that this passage to the standing position occurred under these circumstances. The change was important for the development of the brain: it grew from 450 cubic centimeters three million years ago to 1200 cubic centimeters, one and a half million years ago. The standing position also allowed a specialized use of the hands and, eventually, the use of tools that the *homo habilis*, first true human of the lineage, made for the first time intentionally.

So, the determining factor in man's development was that he had to get out of the forest and was forced to survive outside of that protective shelter.

There remains in our subconscious an attraction mixed with fear for the original environment from which our species emerged. At all times, it is in the forest that man has sought refuge when he was in danger. It is from the forest that, for a long time, he drew most of his resources. From it he obtained the fuel that gave him fire, allowing him to dominate the other species; he picked its fruits; he gathered its diverse products; he hunted its animals; there his domestic animals grazed; there he found the all-purpose material with which he built houses, raised fences, made tools, vehicles, and ships.

Our purpose here is to examine the multiple interrelations—in a given region at a specific time in history, the Middle Ages—between this original environment already greatly transformed through the years—the forest—and the people of that time. We will study the forms and diverse functions of the forest, determine its place in the civilization of that time and follow its evolution.

In the history of the forest in western Europe, the Middle Ages was a crucial period. Until then, in that region, man had not managed to appreciably diminish this force of nature even though for thousands of years he had attacked, exploited, and ravaged it. The forest always grew back, apparently inexhaustible. But during the Middle Ages man discovered the forest's limits. He began to realize not only that it was necessary to preserve the capital by using only the usufruct of the forest, but also that the forest occupied an essential place in the balance of society's life environment.

Through numerous, painful experiences the western European people discovered between the tenth and the twentieth century that they could no longer abuse the forest. Abuse deprived them of material that had taken a long time to form and of the living wealth produced by the forest. They also found that the forest is an essential and permanent factor in the climate, the water cycle, and earth conservation. Many prestigious civilizations were ruined because of the degradation of the forests, prelude to the disappearance of cropland.

During the Middle Ages, people learned about the necessity of long-term planning, which goes beyond immediate profit and takes into account the needs of future generations. Through their inter-action with the forest, people discovered the responsibility of human communities toward their heirs. It is during the Middle Ages that the idea of prospective planning and economical use of natural re-sources was gradually conceived by men who remained close to the land. This concept paved the way for ecology, an accepted science which shows that it is absolutely necessary for man—faced with his own proliferation—to maintain the forest's place around the world.[1]

1 · the forest ecosystem ·

The Forest: A Complex System

a FOREST IS NOT SIMPLY a group of trees. It is a complex system: it includes the soil with its geological substratum, its humus inherited from successive generations, and its microbic flora, the vegetation, and also the fauna, from the burrowing, underground insects to the birds, which fly above the tree tops. Four layers of vegetation are generally distinguished in the forest: the layer of mosses and lichens, the layer of grasses, the layer of shrubs and the layer of trees. To these must be added the underground layer, which includes the roots and tubers as well as the humus with all the microorganisms that play an important role in the vegetation process.

It is impossible to consider the vegetation without taking into account the living beings—insects, reptiles, batrachians, herbivores, carnivores, and birds—that populate the forest and live in close interdependent relation with the plants. For example, the central European beech forest contains over ten thousand live species, some of which include a large number of individuals. One can imagine the infinite complexity of the exchanges and interactions among all the forest's elements.

If the climate doesn't change, the climax—balanced ecosystem —survives because its biogeochemical cycle is closed and can repeat itself indefinitely in the absence of any perturbing intervention, such as man. Most everywhere in western Europe this cycle has been modified by human intervention.

But the experiment of nonintervention has been made in a few forests. The earliest example is the forest of Bialowicza, in Poland, which King Jagellon declared in the fourteenth century to be a reserve for dying species of wild animals (bison, auroch, and tarpan or wild horse). In Yugoslavia, a primitive oak forest was maintained in the Miljet National Park in Croatia; others exist in Bosnia.

Sometimes, the conservation of such relic forests is due to exceptional circumstances. For example, in Switzerland, in Derborance (Valais), a hanging valley remained separated for centuries from the rest of the canton by a huge landslide. The result is quite different from what we expect a western European forest to be. Between trees of all heights, the ground is littered with fallen trunks, most of them rotten and, between these, bushes grow irregularly. The growth of new trees is hampered by the existing ones, and the trees are too close to each other to develop harmoniously. Curiously, there are sharp alignments of trees on several dozens of yards: it would appear that, as the giant trees fell, they cleared the ground and then, as they rotted, created an area repulsive for certain species but favorable to the development of some plants whose seeds, elsewhere, would have been choked by the low vegetation.

One of the reasons why trees can colonize the ground is that they create a shaded area, and in doing so gradually eliminate the competition not adapted to the shade. A hectare (2.47 acres) of forest stores each year about 5 tons of carbon (approx. *50m³* of wood). Light allows for direct assimilation of the carbon in the air: the tree is thus a solar pump that extracts carbon from the air and fixes it in the wood where it constitutes an energy reserve. Among the trees, the species of "light" grow more easily, since they can develop without the others' shade and, if necessary, can start the ground colonization (pines, birches, larches, and acacias). The "shade" species (beeches, firs) need shelter at the outset and, for a long time, live at the shrub level.

Different tree species can develop only in specific climate and temperature conditions. They bloom more or less frequently depending on the temperature and the climate: thus, oaks have acorns about every year in Italy, but only every six years at the latitude of Paris, and in the Ardennes every ten or fifteen years. Northern country trees might grow much slower then those of southern countries but their wood is of much better quality. Trees also regulate the hydrological system by pumping water through their roots, by absorbing it through their leaves and by returning it to the atmosphere by evapotranspiration. The trees' shade also prevents the soil from drying up.

As forests are thicker and denser when the climate is more humid, mountains (on which rain is often more abundant than on the plains) are frequently a favored location for forests. Consequently, there is a certain assimilation between the words for "mountain" and for "tree" in different languages. Also, in some regions, the name given to the mountains evokes the darkness of the forest (particularly in the case of coniferous forests, frequent at high altitudes). The following qualifiers are found in different languages: *noir, maure, morena, nègre, schwartz*, black, *tcherna*. The following places, among others, can be found in Europe: the *Montagne Noire*, the *Morvan*, the *Noirmont*, the *Bois Noirs*, the *Maures* in France, the *Sierra Morena* in Spain*, the Black Forest (*Schwarzwald*) in Germany, the Black Mounts in Great Britain, and the *Tchernagora* (or *Montenegro*) in Yugoslavia. Many other places use this qualifier to evoke the forests that characterize or used to characterize them: *Noirmoutier, Noiretable, Noirfontaine, Noirlieu, Noirlac*, Blackpool, Blackburn, *Schwarzbach*, etc.

Few soils are hostile to trees, provided they are sufficiently irrigated. Nonetheless, even in lands favored by rain, some grounds are naturally untimbered, such as boggy soils or loess soils, choice spots for grasses. Although the forest can manage in poor grounds that have little vegetational soil, whether calcareous, gritty or sandy,

♦ ♦ ♦

* However, the Saracens' occupation of these last two massifs might lead to other hypotheses on the origin of their names.

it grows better and more rapidly on deeper and richer soils. It is most often man who pushed it back, confining it to grounds less fertile or less accessible. The forest is able to colonize poor soils because it makes up its own soil, particularly when it consists of leafy trees, which produce a very rich humus. The lower layers—grasses, bushes, shrubs, lichens, mosses, and mushrooms—also contribute to the slow production of the forest humus.

In western Europe, the excessive exploitation of the forest resources at times of population growth—during the Gallo-Roman and the Carolingian periods, and later, during the twelfth-thirteenth centuries and the sixteenth-seventeenth centuries—encouraged, particularly in the South, the disappearance or degradation of the forests, which in the Gallic period covered three-quarters of the territory. This evolution included in many cases the replacement of leafy species—such as oak or beech—by conifers, a change to which man contributed a lot, especially since the fifteenth century. But in places where the forest had already been degraded by man, nature reinforced the movement because, while the oak's acorns fall straight down, the pine seeds, light and winged, are blown away, sometimes quite far. Thus, when the primitive forest has been destroyed, nature favors the extension of pine trees to the detriment of species such as oak. Other trees, such as maples, also have winged seeds but, as they are shade species, they cannot develop in the open as pine trees do.

The forests' edges are particularly rich areas. Just as the shore of a pond where three environments—air, water and ground—meet has a very numerous and varied population, vegetation and microflore, so the edge of the forest is an interface, a privileged area of exchanges and life. Light species and shade species grow together, creating an environment that is much more varied than the deep forest or the open space. There, almost all species that live in both environments meet, confront each other and mix as they search for their food—vegetal or animal.

This variety, productive of wealth, is also found to a certain extent near those linear forests formed by hedges, wooded slopes and windbreakers that create a frequent landscape in many French regions, which, rich in trees, are nonetheless poor in forests. The cultivated fields are crisscrossed by stretches planted with trees and bushes. This network of living fences demarcates clearings, helps rotate the crops and organize the grazing, and provides the peasants with almost everything that a real forest would.

Plant Interactions

In the late thirteenth century, Pietro dei Crescenzi, better known in France as Pierre de Crescence, wrote in his Latin agricultural treatise (translated into French at the request of Charles V): *"Le noyer est dict de nuyre pour ce que son ombre nuist auz autres arbres."*[1] [Lit.: The walnut tree is so called because its shade is harmful to other trees.] This amusing statement, only understandable in French and which at first may appear as a simple play of words, is, in fact, confirmed by modern etymologists who attribute the origin of the word *noyer* (walnut) to the Latin word *nocere*, which means "to be harmful." However, modern research has determined that it is not the shade that prevents other species from growing near this tree but a chemical substance, a toxic volatile product released by the walnut tree's roots. Incidentally, popular wisdom advises that one should not rest or sleep under a walnut tree.

Other trees also release substances that eliminate competing species. So called "dominant" species supplant the others totally; others merely hinder or slow down the development of nearby trees, without totally suppressing them. Rainwater, dew, and microorganisms can contribute to releasing or spreading these substances, and the nature of the soil in which they spread can modify their diffusion or even their composition. The effects of the substances can remain in the soil for a long time.

Some tree leaves as well as some herbaceous plants prevent the germination of certain species' seeds. Thus, the *Pinus taeda* cannot grow near the andropogon grass which prevents the action of the bacteria that fix nitrogen in the soil.

The action of certain substances may vary depending on the state of their carrier: beech leaves contain a product that is detrimental to young spruces, but the dead leaves are no longer harmful. While the robina false acacia prevents the development of certain pine trees, it favors the growth of several oak species. This also happens between fir and spruce, by a sort of reciprocity.

But trees don't limit their action to other trees. Species such as ash, spruce, and alder protect themselves by releasing in the ground products that repel certain mushrooms or pathogenic germs that make their roots rot. On the other hand, some mushrooms encourage the trees' growth by providing them with elements such as phosphorus. The toxins produced by the roots of plants—such as heather—are harmful to mushrooms that are essential to the growth of various trees such as spruce, Norway pine, and white birch. These properties, which certain plants have, to inhibit, hinder, prevent or favor the development of other species, oppose or facilitate species' associations or successions.

In the Middle Ages, Pierre de Crescence wrote with a certain foreknowledge of ecology: "Although plants often prevent each other . . . however, we often see different grasses coming together and growing, as in meadows and in other places, and it is not often that nature makes only one kind of grass when it is left to its natural movement."

Soils lose their fertility for a variety of reasons and often neither farming practices nor fertilizing can help. It can be due, for example, to the incorporation of plant residue into the ground (leaves, straw or manure), to the existence of large quantities of organic matter left after logging, to certain characteristics of the layers of dead leaves (as oak leaves, which prevent the decay of the litter because of the tannin they contain), or to the previous existence of certain herbaceous plants that remained there for a certain length of time.[2]

All these characteristics of the action of plants can explain the lack of success of certain attempts to clear and cultivate. In some cases, they can also explain the phenomenon of the so-called "repulsive" lands alluded to by historians of the Middle Ages.

From Microorganisms to Pastures

The soil's microscopic organisms are extremely important for the forest vegetation as well as for cultivation in general; in particular, the symbiotic bacteria that are able to fix the nitrogen of the air caught in the soils. These bacteria live on the roots of leguminous plants where they form bacterial nodules as well as on the roots of certain tree species such as the robina false acacia (a light specie that doesn't need shade to develop and is able to colonize unproductive soils).

Other species, too, possess symbiotic bacteria: sallow-thorn, Bohemian olive tree, cammock, alder, white willow, goat willow, etc. As these species enrich the ground in nitrogen, they modify the environment. On poor acid soils, grasses grow under the robinas and are a perfect feed for the big herbivores.

In forests of light foliage, for example in certain coniferous forests such as forests of Norway pines when they are scattered, and particularly in forests of larch trees with deciduous foliage, the ground gets quite a bit of light and the grass layer can develop. In addition, the animals can find shade under trees that is important to their digestion.

Beech forests, where the foliage creates a continuous shelter for six to eight months of the year, are not favorable to the development of grass, and few bushes, except holly, can stand this dark and humid atmosphere in which the young beeches thrive. Oaks do not mind open space; the foliage of large oaks lets through quite a bit of light and solar heat. Consequently, bushes such as aspen, birch, and mountain ash proliferate, as does grass if the brambles don't prevent its development.

In the forests of the Middle Ages, the big herbivores included both wild species—red deer, fallow deer—and domestic animals—bovines, caprines, ovines, and equines. Other animals, such as wild boars and pigs, fed on seeds or fallen fruits—such as beechnuts, acorns, hazelnuts, and apples—or on tubers that they dug out. Acorns, especially, are the traditional feed for pigs whose meat constituted a basic element of human food in the Middle Ages, as it already did among the Gauls and the Germans. So oak was privileged to the detriment of other tree species—all the more since its wood was the most appreciated for construction and most common uses.

It must be noted, too, that if the herbaceous layer is too thick, the trees' seedlings cannot succeed. By reducing it and airing it, grazing can be favorable to the seedlings' growth.

Vegetarian animals modify the forest mainly at two levels: grass and bush. At the herbaceous level, the species that the animals do not consume start to dominate and the ones that they eat start to disappear. At the bush level, there might be a quasi-destruction—especially with caprines (goat, deer)—if the bushes are not sufficiently protected and if the animals don't find plenty of more attractive food. In this case, even mature trees have their bark grazed and die; the ligneous capital stagnates, grows poorer and runs out as it cannot renew itself.

Pigs and wild boars, who eat mainly tubers, fallen fruits, and seeds (especially acorns), do less damage than herbivores provided they are not too numerous. It is even said that they often bury seeds, acorns or beechnuts, and so help the future growth.

In a "climax" forest ecosystem, in the absence of man, the big carnivores, by eating the herbivorous population, prevent it from becoming too numerous and thus contribute to maintaining the forest cover. Hunting can upset this balance. Man also hunts the noncarnivores such as deer, aurochs, bisons, and wild boars, but in a much less selective and regular way than the carnivores, as they are not motivated only by the need for food.

Once man eliminated the animals from the forest that might have been a danger to his domestic herds, he brought his livestock to the forest pasture. But in order to prevent damage to the forest, he was forced to organize the grazing in a rigorous and controlled manner, and not overstep the threshold of tolerance.

That is why, quite rationally, in the Middle Ages, man appraised forests not by their surface but by the number of animals that they could feed.

Soils' Vocation and Man's Action

One might wonder what determines the sites of forests through the years and what are the principal factors of this localization. One might think that the forest is determined above all by the soil, the climate, the exposure; in other words, the natural factors. It becomes apparent, however, independently of the climate's variations, that the forests are not always a given of geography. In western Europe, other factors, mainly man's actions, were determinants.

Since man, in the Neolithic Age, came out of the forest and became a farmer, he struggled incessantly with the forest to obtain cropland. Open spaces, savannas or grasslands—grounds not very favorable to trees—have always existed but were relatively rare in western Europe. Priority was long given to cultivated space when a numerous population needed to be fed.

Geology as well as the nature of the superficial soil, which is even more important for the vegetation, are important factors but are far from being determinants in the forests' localization. "The soil's fertility clearly appears," writes J. F. Stevens, "as the result of a process of production and reproduction of fertility and not any more as a free gift of nature."[3]

Indeed, man's work is at any given time an essential element of the soil's composition, an element that is even more important for cultivated land than for the forest. Soil is a resultant: the work of successive generations of men is written into it. On sharp slopes men maintained the ground for centuries. Patiently, they carried up again the soil washed down by the precipitations; they built support walls to hold it back. Elsewhere, they planted trees and created hedges, ditches, and embankments, organized windbreakers, drained the soils that were too wet, diverted rivers and streams to irrigate the fields, brought manure and conditioners to improve and maintain the land's fertility. In other places, they provoked erosion by inconsiderately clearing the land or by letting too many animals graze. In many places they let their predecessors' work—embankments, ditches, hedges, support walls, drainages, and canalizations—fall into disrepair; or, by lack of understanding, negligence, mere absence, or just because they weren't numerous enough, tore them down, destroyed them, let them collapse or become lost.

It is these changes of the land in man's hands that the farmer or forester takes into account when, today, he discusses a regrouping, an exchange, or a sale. Without knowing the history, he experiences the result in the quality, the thickness, the texture, the composition, and the productions of every lot, each of which, even on identical soil, will, in fact, be different. Thus, field or forest, the soil is first a given of nature but, mostly, it is what man made it throughout history. The will, choice, and constraints of men are dominant. But where men fail to recognize the essential natural factors, their attempts to extend cultivated land often end in deceiving results, failures, and withdrawals.

Where man had no absolute need to cling to a soil unfavorable to farming, forests remained or developed. Often, in order to survive, he had to cultivate land that did not lend itself to cultivation. Sometimes, for historical reasons, either by man's will or by lack of demographic pressure, land that would have lent itself perfectly to culture remained covered by forest.

Of course, many forests are situated on poor soils that would not be suitable for farming or that, in a given territory, would be less suitable than the nearby lots. This results from the conclusions, drawn from centuries of experience, that showed the farmers which soils were best suited to cultivation—this varied with the period's agricultural means—and were the ones that the forest was satisfied with and could even improve by its slow deposits of humus.

The soil's composition, in turn, is modified by the vegetational cover that has existed there for many decades or even centuries. The forest can maintain the same type of vegetational cover without exhausting the ground; it is a characteristic of this plant formation. But to maintain the fertility of cultivated soils, either different species must succeed each other on the same piece of land or there must be external dressings of fertilizers and conditioners.

To a natural equilibrium, a climax vegetation, man—guided in the past by empiricism and experience and today by scientific knowledge—has substituted a treatment whose medium- and long-term effects are difficult to foresee.

Because the human factor is determining in the set of possibilities, constraints, and limiting factors of nature, it is not surprising that forests are not always situated where, logically, geologically, and pedologically, they would be thought to be and, furthermore, that through the years, many forests moved, and others appeared or disappeared.

So, in general, the forest is not at all confined to the worst soils. Nonetheless, when the demographic pressure has not been too strong in a given area, the experience of the successive generations has sometimes selected and effected the forest to the less fertile soils, the worst exposed, the most uneven, or those which have the least vegetational soil. This result can be obtained only by a strong collective organization, able to impose a distribution of the different land categories and, eventually, even maintain them for common usage. This collective organization existed traditionally among the so-called "barbarous" people who invaded the Roman Empire and whose customs permeated forest uses in most of France.

The localization of the wooded areas in a region also results from the fact that the farmers pushed back the forest to the limits of the fields, whether the houses were grouped in a village surrounded by its fields, or dispersed. Indeed, the site of the cultivated fields, in which men work often and year-round, should not force the peasant to long, time-consuming journeys. While some of the various forest products are exploited at different seasons, wood is exploited at specific times of the year. And as the forest became less a varied and permanent resource and more a wood culture, it became increasingly logical to push it back to the territory's periphery. The layout became particularly systematic in certain Norman villages and is also found in the agricultural colonization lots in the Quebec province of Canada: the farms and the cultivated zones border the access road, and at the end of the lots is the forest, more or less penetrated by each farmer within his lot's lateral limits, which go deep into the forest. Today, in Normandy, there still are such linear villages, maintained since the Middle Ages.

Among the natural factors, the soil is not always the most important; sometimes it is the exposure to the sun, or to the wind, or the relief, which leads to a first selection rather than the soil's composition and quality. Thus, in mountain valleys oriented from east to west, it is not the soil which determines the predominance of forest on one side and of meadows and fields on the other; it is the exposure to the sun with the more-or-less precocious vegetation that results from it. It is this exposure which, in the Alps, defines the mountain sides: the "ubac" on one side, the "adret" on the other. These local terms have been adopted by geographers to define, in all cases, this situation. Furthermore, on these mountain sides, man has often taken advantage of the slightest irregularity of the ground, the slightest counterslope oriented differently, the slightest microclimate, to establish fields or pastures when he needed them.

In other places, lands that could have been good for culture, or even that have been cultivated, have become unsuitable by man's fault because he thoughtlessly provoked the soil's degradation and thus the erosion of the layer of soil that could have been farmed. There, even the forest, although less demanding, cannot start over.

So, although a certain number of soils have been dedicated all along either to the forest or to farming, alternating different utilizations of land is frequent. Human factors have always been dominant—whether historical, social or technical—and have taken precedence over the ecological factors and the alleged "vocation" of the soils. There is no lack of examples either of good soils left to the forest or of mediocre or poor soils used as cropland.

First of all, since any territory at the time needed to include wooded land to be self-sufficient and viable, often, in a sector where all the soils were of good quality, the forest was *de facto* on plots that could just as well have been cultivated. Man made the choices and distributed the soil's utilization without constraints.

It has been noted that forests in northern France are often situated on good soils. They remained there for historical, real estate, and economic reasons and, in spite of periods when they were overexploited (particularly for metallurgy and later to extract mining timber), they included no degraded plant formations; this is due to the forest's vigor, and is a consequence of the soil quality.[4]

The main valleys, sometimes easily flooded, have alluvium soils that are considered today as choice cropland, but in the Middle Ages were often covered with forests. Those lands started to be farmed only after they were protected by dikes, as the "turcies" of the Loire River, which transformed that valley at the initiative of the Plantagenet. In addition, those deep and heavy soils could not be cultivated until the farmer's tools—plow, harnessing and traction system—allowed him to do so. It was only in the fifteenth and sixteenth centuries that this became possible thanks to the progress of agricultural techniques.

The forest's presence can often be explained by historical reasons: maintenance or creation of a hunting territory, owner's will, defense or isolation purposes, and low density of population. Many plain forests were kept as hunting grounds for the nobles without considering the nature of the soil. Some forests were created: for example, the New Forest in Hampshire, England, was deliberately planted on land previously lived on and cultivated. Elsewhere, the proximity of a capital or of a royal or noble residence was the reason for the conservation of certain forests, as for example, around Paris. This is also the case near Brussels where the forest of Soignes grows on perfectly good cropland, and in Brabant, for the wood of Houtain-le-Mont.[5]

In many regions some forests were maintained for strategic purposes, without concern for the soil's nature, but because of the position of frontiers and sometimes because of the terrain. They formed barriers, "hedges," that social groups voluntarily allowed to subsist and sometimes even purposefully planned in order to isolate their territory, constitute a protection, and facilitate the control or prohibition of passage. This aspect of the use of the forests in the Middle Ages will be further developed.

In western and northern Europe, all the regions close to the rivers were exposed to the raids of the Normans for a long time. As the forest was both a barrier and a less attractive zone than cultivated farmland, people maintained a wooded strip as large and as dense as possible along the river. Later, this localization was sometimes maintained by a political decision: to make it easier to float the wood or transport it by boat. That is why rather wide strips of forests were protected for centuries along the Seine River.

Of Words and Things: Woods and Forests

The French word *forêt* (*foresta*) appeared at the Merovingian period. The term *forêt* in the *Diplômes de Childebert*, the Law of the Longobards and the Capitularies of Charlemagne applied only to royal forests. Soon the texts also mentioned forest rangers (*forestarius*) who were the stewards in charge of the forests.

Certain authors have suggested that "forest" (*forêt*) might come from *forum*, which in Latin designates a closed space, a market, and from which derives the French word *for* designating a jurisdiction. It is also frequently used in the Middle Ages to designate the customs of a region or a town, particularly in Navarre. The use of this term became limited in French to the expression *le for intérieur* [Lit., the interior space, the conscience]. Its counterpart the *for extérieur* [Lit., the exterior space] was still used in the eighteenth century, among others by Diderot. However, as the adjunction of a suffix "esta" or "est" is not explained, this origin is very doubtful.

There exists in low Latin a verb *forestare* and a noun *foresticus* (cited by the grammarian Placidus) that mean "exterior" and gave derivatives in Provençal and in Sicilian. *Forestare* comes from the Latin word *foris* meaning "outside, outwards" that is found in French words such as *forclos* (set out), *forain* (from outside, stranger), in Italian in *forestiere* (stranger, man from outside), and in English in "foreign" and "foreigner." Any Frenchman knows François I's famous phrase: "*Tout est perdu, fors l'honneur*" (Everything is lost except honor). In Latin *forestare* meant "to banish, exclude." Littré explains that "the forest was originally a space on which a 'ban' had been pronounced, a proscription of farming and living in the interest of the noble's hunting." Guillaume Le Roux established such a "ban" in Hampsphire when he created the New Forest on lands that were inhabited and cultivated.

Those spaces were generally wooded or, if originally they were not, trees grew rapidly as the land was not cultivated. From there might come the present meaning of the word *forêt*, which replaced the Latin word *nemus*.

For a long time the word *nemus* was used in deeds of the Middle Ages; like today's word "wood" it also designated the ligneous matter. *Nemus* has left in French only the scholarly term *némoral* cited by Littré but no longer used. *Nemus* might be linked to *nemo* (nobody) as the forest, in Roman times, was generally if not *res nullius* (object not taken into account), at least *locus neminis*, a place that belonged to nobody, public land.

The Latin word *boscus* has given the French word *bois*, designating the material wood as well as spaces covered with trees, but smaller than forests; the latter term is reserved today for larger areas. Today the French words *forêt, bois, bosquet* and *boqueteau* evoke, respectively, smaller and smaller groupings of trees.

So, what originally was defined by the word forest was not a closed space (as if the word had been derived from *forum*) but the legal delimitation, the prohibition, the reserved usage. From its origin, the word evokes a decision, a human option, a zoning choice; it is a space whose vocation was imposed, not a natural fact; it is due to planning.

2 · natural RESOURCES of the forest ·

Edible Plant Resources

I N FRANCE, DURING THE EARLY MIDDLE AGES, the "natural space," or more precisely the space where the vegetation was not cultivated, covered more surface than the cultivated areas. It included genuine forests, bush formations that were less dense, grasslands, and wild mountain slopes that were sometimes unreachable. The cultivated areas were like clearings that were more-or-less spacious and surrounded the inhabited sites. The limits of these clearings fluctuated but, except in Provence and Narbonne, which were the oldest Roman provinces in Gaul, the agricultural space was always surrounded by the forest, encircled and crisscrossed by wooded zones.

The clearing of some wooded lots could be temporary: after a few years of crops, the ground was abandoned to the forest to recover its fertility. The rotation period was sometimes very long and allowed the forest to reinstall itself; it could not, however, develop totally as long as the system persisted and periodically destroyed it.

Forest and cultivated space were not absolute opposites in the Middle Ages. The forest was dense and impenetrable—as we imagine it today—only where man wanted it to be so or in certain sparsely inhabited mountains. Generally broken up by cultivated clearings, it was almost everywhere a much-visited forest, if not always by the right people. A whole population lived there and made use of the natural produce. Outlaws took refuge in the forest and so did the country people when they were threatened by army incursions. Many people came for the products—wood, food, etc. —and all travelers at one time or another had to go through it. So the forest remained all around the countryside. Some provinces even systematically maintained around them a protective forest zone that travelers had to cross.

The forest was quite often sparse and penetrable not because it was, as some of today's woods, maintained by rangers, but as a consequence of the pasturing of pigs and cattle in the underwood. This also resulted from the traffic created by all the people who came into the forest to hunt, fish, pick berries or mushrooms, and feed their animals. The pigs found acorns, the sheep found grass, and the goats attacked the leaves and smaller branches of the trees when they didn't like the undergrowth.

This aspect of the forest appears in the period's literature. Chrétien de Troyes describes Perceval: "He enters into the forest and his heart rejoices because of the mild weather and the singing of so many birds. He likes all these things. Because of the sweetness of the day, he takes the bit off his horse and lets him graze the fresh green grass."[1]

Further on the author describes the forest with the preciseness of someone who lives in a world where it is a familiar environment. The trees seem to be rather small, their lower branches at the height of the riders; it is not a majestic forest where one can ride at ease among tall tree trunks.

◆ *He hears now five armed knights come by.*
Their weapons clang against the branches of the oaks and
    hornbeams.
Their hauberks quiver. Their lances bang the shields.

*The forest resounds with the clash of the iron of the shields and
the hauberks.* ♦

The forest, thinned by periodical clearings or just by frequent cuttings, allowed the growth of a low vegetation that liked light and
in which the grazing herds prevented the development of brambles.
Farther out, beyond the limits of where the peasants brought their
animals, the forest was denser but nonetheless crisscrossed with
trails. Its vegetation must have been much more varied than it is
today, after centuries of exploitation and planning. As man has
favored the development of certain species that were more needed,
variety has therefore been slowly reduced. People of the time were
familiar with this variety and knew how to turn it to good account
by harvesting all the wild produce.

Evoking the Golden Age, the poet Jean de Meung describes an
enchanting time when men neither farmed nor hunted and ate the
wild produce of the land, in particular the forest's fruits: "For bread,
meat and fish, they gathered acorns in the woods, they searched in
the bushes of the plains, valleys and mountains for apples, pears,
walnuts and hazelnuts, rosehips, blackberries, sloes, raspberries,
strawberries, and haws."[2]

Behind the myth appears the reality of the Middle Ages as a time
when the forest's natural resources played an important role, especially for food. Other literary works of the time depict heroes who,
having taken refuge in the forest, find everything they need to live.
Such is the case of Tristan and Iseult: "Already it was Sainte Croix
of September, and there was abundance of hazelnuts, cornel berries,
cress, crab-apples, sloes, service-berries and sorb-apples on the
bushes . . ."[2] Tristan and Iseult are not vegetarians as were the men
of the Golden Age, evoked by Jean de Meung. Tristan finds a bow
and arrows as well as something to make fires, and soon hare and
deer are added to the diet of the two lovers and their servant. They
even barter the game for bread, the traditional basis of alimentation
that they sorely miss.

What were the wild plants that people in the Middle Ages could
eat in western Europe?[3]

Little is said in the chronicles and the novels that were written

for members of the upper classes who were not compelled to use all
the resources—including those of less nutritional value—of their
environment. For these privileged people, the only important foods
were bread, meat, condiments and spices to improve their taste and
finally, wine or beer. But the peasants and the lower classes, who
lived in or near the forest, could find in it many precious food
resources that were not just extras.

First of all, there were mushrooms: Gaul was already famous under
the Romans for the abundance of its mushrooms. At the end of the
winter, mushrooms such as morels and *pesis* appear under the pine
trees. Other edible mushrooms appear at different seasons: in summer, the *roussettes* and the chanterelles grow under the beeches; *cèpes*
and Caesar's mushrooms can be found under the oaks. In the fall,
boletuses, St. George's agarics, *nébulaires* and *clitocybes* grow in the
dead leaves.

Edible products were also found below ground level: it wasn't
only in times of shortages that people ate "roots." Today, the French
word *racines* is still used in the region of Lyons to mean carrots. The
poor hermits who were reduced to eating "roots" were therefore
greatly pitied. In fact, just as the peasants, they knew how to use
the natural resources and needed—only occasionally—to resort to
meat; so, they might not have eaten as badly as we may imagine.

Many roots, bulbs, rhizomes or tubers of forest plants are edible:
the tubers of the so-called *noix de terre* (earth nuts; *burnium bulbo
castanum*) and the *genottes*); the roots of rampions (whose leaves can
also be eaten) and burdocks; the bulbs of *dents de chien* (or *erythronium*);
the roots of the *cirse potager* that tastes like artichoke and whose
leaves, stem and receptacle are also eaten; wild garlic; the rhizomes
of Solomon's seals so common in European forests; and truffles, which
today are a luxury.

The rhizomes of ferns are rich in glucides and starch. With fern
leaves and ground rhizomes it is possible to make a bread that was
still eaten in periods of famine in the eighteenth century.

> ♦ "Sire, this is the bread that your people are eating,"
> said an intendant (regional administrator) to Louis XV,
> showing him a piece of fern bread. ♦

But on the one hand, people looked for the most nourishing elements: cultivated cereals, the result of selections, were more nour-

ishing than wild plants. On the other hand, the tendency is always to try and follow the diet of the ruling and privileged class. What has become a mere social tendency (and has no absolute physiological necessity) was much more justified in an era when the rich appropriated the most substantial foods by exacting dues paid in kind or by looting and brutal plundering. Wild or cultivated foods that were important in the past and sometimes still are in less-developed countries, have thus been supplanted by more nourishing or more appealing species, often of exotic origin. Many of today's common vegetables and fruits are of foreign origin.

If we continue this survey of the natural plant products above ground level—that man of the Middle ages could gather in the forest—we find countless plants that generally do not provide many calories in small volume but could constitute an important food resource, procure precious vitamins or improve the taste or aroma of recipes. Sometimes caution bred by experience was necessary. For example, marsh marigold and clematis have young shoots and leaves that can be eaten after they have been cooked, but are toxic when they are raw. Other plants, however, do not present the same risks: cooked nettle that makes an excellent soup, starwort or chickweed, violets, primrose whose leaves and flowers make succulent salads and can also be eaten cooked, as well as cress, oxalis (or wood sorrel), goutweed, angelica, comfrey, white laurel, lungwort, white and yellow laurels, *épiaire*, plantain and ribgrass, ruscus, veronica (or speedwell), rampions, wall lettuce, and black bryony. The tender young shoots of many of these plants can be eaten as well.

Many plants were also picked for their aroma as seasoning or to flavor drinks: hops (used for beer from the ninth century on), woodruff, *aillière*, a cruciferous with a garlic taste, cardamine, broom buds, furzes, ground ivy, wild mint, oregano, wild garlic, and finally so-called "urban" avens, which can be found only in the forest.

Trees, too, frequently provide edible products: leaves, young shoots, fruits, seeds, bark, and even sometimes sap. Ash leaves were fed to animals but the plant was also used to make *frênette* (a fermented drink made from leaves that are attacked by aphids that concentrate the sap in the excoriations of which bees and ants are also fond). The male cornel has red fruit that can be eaten raw or can be pickled or preserved when it is still green. Some kinds of European maple trees produce sugar but the product cannot be compared to that of the sugar maple of the northern countries (which needs a specific climate of very cold nights and very hot days). Birch sap, which contains 2 percent sugar, is still used nowadays in certain countries: for example, in the USSR to make a drink.

Pierre de Crescence indicates in his treatise that beech marrow is edible, at least by animals: "The marrow is appreciated by mice. It is eaten by several animals and is very good for pigeons and other birds. It feeds them well and their meat is good for cooking."

Wild fruits and berries are much better known today than the various forest vegetables that were just mentioned. Nevertheless, some of them, which in the past constituted an important element of the forest food resources, have fallen into disuse. Among the berries are the brambles (blackberries and loganberries), currants, cranberries and bilberries, the *raisins d'ours* that grow in the mountains, the moorberries (in the northern peat bog areas), and hawthorns (the hawthorn fruit, farinaceous and nutritious, is eaten dried, ground into flour and cooked but its young leaves can also be eaten). Wild strawberries that include several species were, in the Middle Ages, the only ones known.

Wild pear, apple, medlar, service, and sorb-trees bore small fruits that were eaten only when they were overripe. The French word *blet* (overripe) gave them their generic name of *blessons*—that is found in the literature of the Middle Ages. Those fruits could also be used to make wine or cider. All these trees have been cultivated at one time or another, but only a few still are today, generally as improved species: the apples and pears that we eat today are four times bigger than those of our ancestors (some were found in Neolithic sites) and can be eaten raw.

Cherry, wild cherry, wild plum trees and blackthorn yielded, like today, fruits that could be eaten right off the tree. But the cultivated plum tree, as well as almond, peach and apricot trees, appeared after the Middle Ages and came from the Orient. The *viorne lentane*, a kind of viburnum whose black fruits are eaten raw, and the *viorne obiée*, whose raw fruits are toxic but can be eaten cooked, are plants that today are forgotten.

In addition to the fruits, various tree seeds were eaten. Some of them still exist today, such as beechnuts from which an oil can be made (contrary to walnut oil, it improves with age) and that are also eaten ground into meal.

Certain resinous trees have edible seeds, such as pine kernels that are still eaten today as a delicacy in Eastern countries or the seed of the *arolles* ("cembro" pine) in the Alps. The young shoots of pine trees, and sometimes even the resin, are edible. The fruits of the yew tree are excellent but their seeds are toxic and can even be deadly.

Oak acorns were eaten by man all through ancient times and still are in certain European regions. Sweet acorns can be ground to meal and eaten without special care; bitter acorns must first be cooked to eliminate the tannin (which remains in the skin and the cooking water). These seeds, however, were especially important for domestic animals since they were the pigs' main feed.

Chestnuts were the basic food in various regions, for example, Castaniccia in Corsica or certain parts of the Cévennes. Although the chestnut tree likes heat and sun it also used to grow in the Parisian basin as witnessed by the toponymy. Today in France, most of the chestnuts are not picked but the local industry still treats and sells imported fruits.

Walnuts are not forest fruits. Walnut trees are sometimes found at the edge of the forest or in hedges but mostly along roads, in gardens and in fields. The walnut tree area and the chestnut tree area have moved North since the Middle Ages.

The juniper tree bears a fruit used to make beer and jam. The hazel tree is an aboriginal species of which the fruits have an important nutritive value.

The study of pollens has shown that in England in the prehistoric era, there were many hazel trees that constituted an important food resource.

The customs, which regulated the users' rights and which, after a long oral existence, were written down in the sixteenth century, mention several forest fruits considered for regular consumption. Sainct Yon, in his compilation *"Les Édits et Ordonnances . . . des Roys"* mentions the medlar, quince, pear, apple, service, nettle, cornel, walnut, sorb, and rowan trees, the blackberry bushes, the cherry, wild cherry, plum, hazel, and chestnut trees as well as oaks and beeches. All were considered fruit-bearing trees.

The forest's natural plant production could feed only a very small population. Even with the resources added by hunting and fishing, it is estimated that under western European climate the maximum density of population that could live on it was no greater than one inhabitant per square kilometer (0.3861 square mile) except in particular cases where a given population benefited from the production of an ecosystem extending far beyond the limits of its territory; for example, people living along a river or a coastline where they could fish.

By contrast, agriculture allowed, with the techniques of the Middle Ages, one inhabitant on average to feed on two hectares of cultivated land (about 5 acres). This comes out to about 1,450 hectares for five hundred inhabitants, taking into account the surfaces occupied by forests, streams, marshes, roads, and houses. This was—according to Le Roy-Ladurie—the average population of the "standard" village in those times (eleventh–thirteenth century)[4]. I have shown elsewhere[5] that this figure is equal, precisely, to the average surface of the 37,962 French "communes" today (the smallest administrative unit in France, i.e., village or township). It is an extraordinary case of permanence during thousands of years of economically balanced territorial structures inherited from the past, sometimes even based on the big Gallo–Roman estates. This represents an approximate average population density of thirty inhabitants per square kilometer (forty-eight inhabitants per square mile), which corresponds to the estimated French population in the early fourteenth century; it is based on the 1328 inventory of Philippe VI de Valois.

Although the forest could not ensure the livelihood of the entire population, it assumed a few specific functions that were important in the economy of the time: it was the place where honey was found; it was the main source of feeding for animals (especially pigs, the main source of animal protein); the wild produce was used as complementary and extra in ordinary times and as the last resort in case of shortages.

It's everyday role might have been even more important. It was in the forest that people gathered many wild plants and fruits that did not constitute the bulk of alimentation, but completed it and, in particular, brought by their variety the oligo-elements and vitamins that were lacking in the basic food—bread and meat. The reduction of the forests and the increase of cereal culture to feed a growing population occurred before a greater variety of food products—new fruits and vegetables from the Orient and later from America—had developed in western Europe. This might have resulted in deficiencies in the human diet, creating a favorable condition for the Great Plague which occurred in the middle of the fourteenth century. Indeed, most pandemic outbreaks occur under the cover of a weakening resulting from insufficient or deficient food and from overpopulation. Further research could perhaps confirm this hypothesis of a relation, until now unsuspected, between the reduction of forests and the extraordinary development of the bubonic plague. In particular, this might explain the greater or lesser extension of the plague in different regions.

Honey

Honey, a transformation product based on vegetal raw material, must be included in the forest's food resources of plant origin. At a time when neither cane sugar nor beet sugar were known, honey was of great importance. It is often mentioned in ancient texts, as it was already in Virgil's *Georgics*. Furthermore, it was also used to make hydromel, a drink commonly consumed throughout Europe. As organized apiculture was not yet practiced, honey was found mostly in the forest. The search for bee swarms and nests was stimulated by the fact that wax was as much in demand as honey. In Germany, a corps of special foresters, the *Zeidler*, were in charge of harvesting honey and wax. In France, the *bigrii* or *bigres* were in charge of capturing hives.*

Hives were assimilated to *épaves*, "unclaimed objects," and thus belonged to the lord who exercised the right of dispensing justice in the forest. In some cases, the right was granted to a village, a town or a monastery. The thirteenth century charter of Bains-les-Bains (Vosges) stipulates that if a hive is hanging from a branch, the finder can keep it for a fee, but if the hive is on a tree trunk, he keeps only half and the other half goes to the lord. A text of 1328 about the abbey of Senones, in the Vosges, prescribes that if someone finds a hive, he must advise the abbey's cellerar who will

♦ ♦ ♦

*The word is attributed to Germanic origin: *bi-keri* in Francique meant guardian of bees, from which is derived the Anglo–Saxon word *bee gard* or *beeward*.

have the tree cut down; the finder will then be entitled to half of the bees.[6]

In principle, a tree could not be cut down to take the hive, unless the wood was of no value. However, since it was extremely difficult to capture the swarm on site, the rule was increasingly stretched. Trees with hives were often put up for sale.

Incidentally, these trees were sold under the denomination of "swarms." Formulas such as the following can be found in the sales contracts dated 1325: "for the delivery of 25 swarms . . . that were in the guard of Chaumontois." In 1425: "for the delivery of 12 oaks, that is 8 swarms and 4 fallen by natural cause. . . ." In 1456, for the sale of "3 swarms and one broken, near the oak of Colletorse. . . ."[7]

Stealing swarms was severely punished. In 1404, the inhabitants of Bray, Bonnée and of the Bordes in the Orléanais were fined 60 sous parisis for such a theft; later, in 1445, a fine of 32 sous is mentioned for having felled an oak with hive; in 1451, for having pulled out an oak "where there were flies" and brought it home. The offender was fined only 15 sous.

The Salt of the Forest

All animals need to absorb salt for their digestion; that is why sheep, goats, and even chamois and ibexes in their natural environment are given blocs of salt (called by the French shepherds, *"pierres à lécher"*) that provide them with what their physiology requires.

Recent Swedish studies show that salt particules, carried from the waves and the ocean spray by the wind and the clouds, settle all over Europe in decreasing density, of course, from West to East. The digestive system of the different species that eat plants must adapt itself to varying doses of salt, and their meat and milk yield is affected. Thus sheep from salt meadows are famous for the quality of their meat and western European cows for their milk production.

The salt settled on the ground and the plants is soluble and is slowly washed away by the water. In the forest, part of the salt settles on the leaves and the branches that represent a large surface. That salt takes longer to be entirely washed away and taken into the ground than salt on a vegetal carpet of grasses or cereals of slight height and small reception surface, compared to the enormous developed surface represented by the leaves of a tree. Furthermore, while the roots of meadow plants are superficial, tree roots go very deep: they retain the salt at different levels and bring it back up with the sap.

As a result, on an equal ground area, the forest contains a much greater amount of salt than the meadows. Animals that graze in the forest or are fed leaves taken from the forest trees, find naturally in the leaves they eat, the bark they lick, and the twigs they nibble on the salt that today, in the meadows or the mountain pastures, must be given to them as a supplement. This advantage of the forest pasture practiced in the Middle Ages appears to have remained unrecognized. Salt is so useful to man that at all times it has had a symbolic value. Yet, to find it, man must go through a whole series of operations. The forest, however, draws it free of charge from the depths of the earth. Man himself can benefit from it through the meat of the forest's wild and domestic animals and through the trees' fruits or leaves with which he prepares drinks.

Forest Animals and Game

Hunting doesn't affect only the forest; it has multiple purposes. Many animals normally live in open spaces—moors, humid zones, mountains, etc. However, during the Middle Ages, the open spaces in the plains were taken over by agriculture and grazing and in the zones dedicated to these activities man was almost always present. As a result, most wild animals had been relegated to the woods from which they came out only occasionally, either to look for food or because they were being pursued.

There have always been many books about hunting and poaching, its illegal form. Hunting has unleashed passions and still does. My purpose here is only to define the relations between hunting and men's agricultural, silvicultural and pastoral activities, and the impact of this activity on the forest.

For man, as for all carnivores, the first motivation for hunting was to find food. This motivation remained important for the peasant of the Middle Ages who had few occasions to eat meat, while the privileged people ate plenty of it and wasted much of it. The forest was a "standing meat reserve." At the time of the Crusades, wild boars were slaughtered en masse in the forests of Auvergne to make provisions of salted meat. In certain regions, Vercors and Pyrénées for instance, bears (which peasants were allowed to kill because they were considered harmful) represented an occasional but not negligible source of meat.

The distinction between domestic animals and wild animals wasn't always very clear. Certain animals, classified as domestic, had to be actually hunted with battues and nets to be caught: this was the case of the horses that were let loose in the forest stud farms and almost returned to a wild state. Pigs—which sometimes crossbred with wild boars—were running almost free and, according to Jehan de Brie, were very difficult to handle. By contrast, animals like deer, introduced in England by the Scandinavians, lived in parks like the stud-farm horses and didn't have all the characteristics of wild animals but were nonetheless hunted for entertainment. Deer represented a considerable source of meat and its population had to be limited, if it wasn't to ruin the woods. Certain wild animals such as falcons, hawks, and ferrets were man's auxiliaries.

During the Middle Ages, animals also provided many useful products: furs, leather, skins, bladders, sinews, guts, teeth, bones, horns, blood, rennet, etc. As with pigs on today's farms, nothing went to waste.

Moreover, certain wild animals attacked man or his domestic animals, or destroyed the crops; so man had to defend himself and attempt to eliminate them. This was one of the first functions of hunting as soon as man started cultivating the soil and began the offensive to dominate Nature. Some animals were also a nuisance because they ate the farmers' crops as well as the forest's wild produce—tubers, berries, honey, leaves, etc.—which man gathered to feed himself and his domestic animals.

Hunting and trapping—one of the traditional forms of hunting— have multiple and useful functions for human populations. Nonetheless, by his intervention, man upsets the natural balance and it is difficult to foresee what the consequences might be. On the one hand, the overly complete elimination of the carnivores leads to a proliferation of small game, particularly harmful to crops; the systematic destruction of wolves, foxes, martens, and weasles has often allowed other species, such as rabbits, to develop to the point of jeopardizing the forest's new growth and the food crops. On the other hand, the proliferation of the big herbivores like deer—as a result of the elimination of their predators—can prevent the reconstitution of woods. Certain species progressively destroy the forest when their population isn't controlled or limited; for instance, on five hectares of forest with an average soil fertility, just one roe deer prevents the natural regeneration of the woods; it can be guaranteed only by protecting the plantings. Only a few species, such as limetree because of the bitterness of its bark or certain thorny bushes, are spared by the animals.

During the Middle Ages all the utilitarian purposes of hunting —defense of cultivated areas, protection of men, preservation of the forest, various productions of animal origin, food proteins, etc.— were partly neglected or diverted for the benefit of certain privileged categories of the population. Hunting became an end in itself and a game instead of being an activity serving the entire population; it became a sport and a passion for the kings and the lords.

In ancient times, for Xenophon, Plato and Lycurgus, legislator of Sparta, hunting was first of all a character builder that involved deprivations, got hunters used to dangers, and constituted a physical as well as a moral education for the men and training for the horses. For Xenophon it was "indispensable to the maintenance of empires because it formed warriors."[8]

These ideas are not far from those of the writers in the Middle Ages who wrote about hunting, particularly Gaston Phébus in the fourteenth century. Dogs played a major role in the hunting described by Xenophon, and hunters were not reluctant to use nets and traps. But the ancient authors disdained to talk about the alimentary aspect of hunting. For Socrates, who represents a popular point of view, hunting was a pastime for aristocrats who indulged in it, especially in Sparta, to the detriment of the country people. In France this idea was prevalent among the people until the Revolution of 1789.

Under the Roman Empire, and still in the early Middle Ages, everyone was allowed to hunt. But progressively, from the thirteenth to the sixteenth century, in almost every region non-nobles were forbidden to hunt most of the wild animals.

• • •

During the Middle Ages the forest sheltered a very wide variety of animals that were hunted and trapped because they were a danger to the population, their meat was appreciated, their skin, fur or horns were sought, or because they were believed to be detrimental to the crops.

There were big carnivorous mammals such as the wolf and the lynx and big herbivorous or granivorous mammals such as the wild boar, the bear, the deer, and the auroch (which disappeared in France around the twelfth century but remained in central Europe for several centuries more). The little mammals included carnivores such as the genet, the wild cat, the marten, the fox, the otter, and the badger (the last three less specifically from the forest) and rodents such as the hare, the rabbit, and the squirrel. Among the harmful, or supposedly so, insectivores and rodents that were trapped, several small species were important to the game because they constituted the carnivores' food, such as field mice, field voles, moles, and shrew mice. The birds included woodcocks, ducks on the ponds, pheasants and—not exclusively from the forest—partridges, wood grouses, thrushes, quails, pigeons, etc.

Some birds of prey, like the falcon and the hawk, were used for hunting. These birds were so highly valued that people did not hesitate to cut down a tree—even an oak—to obtain a nest and then take the young birds to train them for hunting (just as trees were sometimes cut down to obtain the wax and the honey from the hives). "If they cannot be obtained otherwise without danger." Accounts mention oaks cut down to obtain hives or capture birds of prey. In 1455 a man was condemned for having felled an oak and taken the birds.[9]

The method seems surprising. However, as explained in an act of 1453, perhaps it wasn't the tree with the nest that was cut down but a neighboring tree that was leaned against the other to facilitate its access. "Jehan Rousseau, sergeant of the Gomez guard, made him cut down an oak in the above mentioned guard, next to another oak in which there were birds of prey and after he felled that oak, at the request of the said Rousseau, he went up to take the birds. . . ."[10]

The method appears brutal. It shows indeed, on the one hand, how much the forest appeared to be inexhaustible during the first part of the Middle Ages whence the customs were adopted and, on the other hand, the high value given to certain of its natural productions.

Certain animals were harmful to the cultivated land, while others attacked men and sometimes made life in the villages very difficult.

The feudal system entrusted the lords with the function of protectors and armed defenders; the workers in return gave them their means of subsistence and did all the manual labor. In regard to ferocious beasts and wild animals, the lords thus had the duty to protect the men who depended on them—as well as their cultures. Their hunting also provided meat for everyone. When King Dagobert organized battues against the aurochs or when Charlemagne led hunting expeditions, it was to protect cultivated areas threatened by wild animals. A few centuries later, Louis XI organized hunts against the wolves that were threatening the villagers.

In the Middle Ages, and particularly in war periods when there were other things to do than organize battues, wolves were a real plague, against which, in France, a special corps was created, the *Louveterie*. As wolves were eliminated, new hordes of them arrived from central and eastern Europe. In England, which was separated from the Continent by the English Channel—where there were fewer forests than in France and which was spared some of the wars of the Middle Ages—few wolves remained by the thirteenth century. However, in the early twelfth century, the duke of Richmond took his officers to task for allowing wolf packs near the abbey of Byland in Yorkshire to scare the population.[11] A reward was granted to whoever killed a wolf. In 1210, King John gave 15 shillings to two hunters who had killed wolves. This high amount seems to indicate that it rarely happened. The total elimination of wolves in England has been attributed to a special disposition by which exiled lords could return to their province and take over their rights if they could prove that they had killed a certain number of wolves. The number varied in each case, and could reach a hundred; the proof was given by the presentation of the heads of the animals.

In France, wolves were not rare as evidenced by the toponymy. At the time of Charles VI, packs of wolves roamed the countryside in the winter.[11] They remained long after the Middle Ages. Attacks by wolves are mentioned in 1438, 1439 and 1440 in the *Journal d'un bourgeois de Paris*, as well as several times in chronicles of the sixteenth century.

By assuming this role of protectors of the peasants and defenders of the cultivated lands against wild animals, the kings and the lords took a fancy to hunting, in which they also saw, as the writers of ancient times did, a useful training in the handling of arms, in horse maneuvers, and in terrain orientation. Hunting dangerous animals was a school for self-control, skill and courage. As the lords would rather not have non-nobles acquire this knowledge of handling weapons, they did their best to prevent the commoners from hunting, at least in the paramilitary way they did themselves. The commoners were restricted to using methods such as traps, lassos, nets, and battues in light enclosures and without any weapons other than clubs and spears. The fear of seeing the villein bear arms was so great that even the monastery forest guards were sometimes authorized to carry bows only by a special privilege granted by the lord of that forest.

In their hunting, the lords did not disdain using traps and enclosures and the peasants were often used as beaters. In the wonderfully illustrated books on hunting, the *Livre du roi Modus* and the *Traité de la chasse* by Gaston Phébus, traps and nets are depicted. The enclosures into which the small game was driven were generally made of those wattle panels used to build fences around the pastures and the forest zones requiring protection. Traps are also mentioned in the romances. Tristan, forced to live as an outlaw in the forest, invents the bow *qui ne faut*, a trap that from its description is very much like a device figuring in one of the miniatures of the *Livre du roi Modus*; its principle is still used today for mousetraps. Soon, however, Tristan obtains a bow and arrows and assures himself of a regular supply of meat.

After the conquest of England, the Norman kings, as early as the end of the eleventh century, adopted very restrictive measures concerning hunting activity. They appropriated, to reserve them for game, vast territories in the less-populated areas or where, as in the New Forest, they wanted, for political reasons, to get rid of a hostile population.

The areas under the law of the forest were not necessarily wooded; generally, they also included pastureland. In these territories, henceforth, game had priority over farming. It was an extension on behalf of the king of the *droit de garenne*, which had long existed in France and in Normandy.

The forest was defined as: "A certain area of woods and productive grazing land reserved for the wild animals and the beings of the forest, the hunting ground and the *garenne*, so they will remain there in the safe protection of the King for his delight and princely pleasure."[12] The animals protected by the forest law were the red deer, the fallow deer, the roe deer, and the wild boar.

Commoners were allowed to hunt only animals considered harmful to the game: fox, wildcat, badger, and also squirrel and hare; sometimes, the list also included rabbit (*coney* in English, *connin* in French) and wolf. Enclosures marked off more specialized areas. For example, Windsor Park was originally an enclosed space to prevent deer from invading the rest of the forest. Punishments for offenses committed in royal forests were severe: for hunting a deer, a free man had to pay 10 shillings, a non-free man twice as much, and a serf for the same offense "lost his skin," and if he killed a stag was sentenced to death.

Forest law was applicable to large areas but in many different ways, depending on the region. In some counties, such as Essex, almost all of the territory was classified as forest; on the other hand, in very populated counties like Norfolk and Suffolk, the forest law was not applied. In Kent, when Odon de Bayeux created a wild animal park in Wickambreux, he had to give pig grazing lands to the archbishop in exchange for the areas fenced off. From the Thames to the region of Southampton where the New Forest had been created, one could circulate without getting out of the king's forests. This state of things was favorable not only to the king's hunting and pleasures, but also allowed groups of Saxon resistants, such as the famous Robin Hood, to elude for a long time the authority of the Norman lords. The area under forest law continued to grow under the first Norman kings. This had the positive result for the future of maintaining many territories as forests in a country which—at the time of the Norman conquest—had a proportion of wooded surface much inferior to France during the same period.

In France, in the Middle Ages, the legislation concerning the royal forests was never as strict for hunting offenses as it was in England. However, it became progressively stricter while, in England, it tended to become more lenient. In France, there are quite a few examples of harsh punishments ordered by certain lords. One example often cited is the lord of Coucy who ordered foreign students of noble families hanged because, unaware of the local customs, they had hunted rabbits on his lands. This savage repression created a scandal and Enguerrand de Coucy had to pay a hefty indemnity and enlist to go for three years to the Crusade. Faced with the feudal lords, the king of France tried to present himself as the protector of the population by relying on the developing towns as well as on the *villeneuves* and the *bastides*—the creation of which he favored— granting franchises to the inhabitants and imposing his arbitration in their conflicts with lay and ecclesiastic lords.

In France, until the middle of the fourteenth century, peasants generally had the right to hunt except for the "big beasts." Commoners were authorized to hunt only "with dogs and clubs," since they were not allowed to own weapons. However, the dogs were so well trained and so strong that, even without arms, the peasants (and even more so the poachers) managed not only to hunt deer by driving them with their dogs—but even did the same with wolf and wild boar.

In the *villeneuves* that tried to attract farmers, hunting rights were generally granted. For example, the inhabitants of the villeneuve of Bois-Ruffin (Eure-et-Loir), created between 1113 and 1129, had the right to capture everything they found in the woods under the one condition that they had to give half of their catch to the officer who maintained law and order for the lord in the woods.[13] Of course, the hunters were reluctant to give away so much of their game and often tried to hide it; this fifty-fifty condition was the origin of the countless lawsuits involving hunters, of which traces have been found in the archives.

In the early fourteenth century, the commoners' hunting right was not yet disputed even when it wasn't, as in the villeneuves, specified in writing. *L'instruction sur le faict des chasses* (from 1322 or 1328) mentioned: "Non-noble people can hunt with dogs everywhere, out of the *garennes*; they can hunt hare and rabbit with greyhounds, running dogs or dogs, and birds, with a club."[14]

The nobles, however, tried by all means to restrict the commoners' hunting rights. As long as they had to admit those rights in the forests of which non-nobles had the use, the lords worked at reducing the surfaces on which the latter could exercise them by developing *garennes* (hunting preserves) and *défens* (forbidden zones) in their territories. The king did the same in his domains.

The zones in which the nobles reserved certain uses to themselves, "*haies, défens, garennes*" (and also forests, since this term originally meant a place out of public use), were often fenced off and even surrounded by walls (as the wood of Vincennes was by King Saint Louis) or else they were marked by ditches or heaps of felled trees called *plessis*.

The *haies* (hedges), were at once borders, buffer spaces, and reservations for restocking game. They were often completed by almost impassable *plessis*. However, when they covered only small territories their main role was rather to set, by a sort of no-man's-land, a limit.

The *garennes*, on the other hand, were sectors reserved by priority to hunting and where it was absolutely forbidden to hunt or set traps for other than the beneficiaries. Theoretically, pastoral and even agricultural activities were authorized, but as a practical matter it was very difficult to maintain them. The violation of a hunting preserve was severely punished; according to an ancient custom from the tenth century, a vassal could lose his fief if he hunted in his lord's *garenne* or fished in his ponds without authorization. This offense was considered as serious as if he had laid hands on his lord without legitimate and serious motive, or had carried out an armed rebellion: "The vassal loses his fief when he strikes his lord, bears arms against him, fishes in his ponds without his authorization or hunts in his *garenne*." Later this harsh punishment was replaced by a fine. [15]

The *garennes* were detrimental to agriculture and were the cause of many lawsuits since the lords extended them excessively on all categories of land and sometimes forbid access to them. The existence of these hunting preserves led to an increase in the game that damaged neighboring fields. Damage caused by wild animals, deer, wild boars, etc., are frequently mentioned. As the size and number of hunting preserves continued to grow and more of them were enclosed, Jean le Bon, to put an end to these excesses, ordered in 1355 the suppression of all *garennes* created in the previous forty years. [16] However, he was made prisoner the following year and was not able to have his decision implemented.

Charles VI renewed the prohibition, that had had little effect, and wrote in his ordinance: "The crops and the vines of the poor people were so damaged that these unfortunates didn't have enough left to live on and were forced to abandon their houses." [17]

During the second part of the fourteenth century, the commoners' hunting rights were considerably reduced. One might wonder if these measures, going back to the second part of the reign of Charles VI, were not the result of the progressive madness of the king who, starting in 1392, gave more and more free rein to the appetites of the nobles. In 1393, the duke of Burgundy, uncle of the king, received full power and authority in the royal forests on matters of hunting; also, the king recalled the interdiction to hunt in his domain without a written authorization from the duke. An ordinance of January 1397 issued, at least in name, by Charles VI, reserved the right to hunt to kings, princes, and noblemen because "this exercise is, in times of peace, the one that is the closest to the use of weapons, for which it seems it was made." The only hunting still allowed to commoners was hunting harmful animals, such as wolves, or passing birds.

As the farmers could no longer hunt, they could not protect their crops. In 1366 and 1412, the inhabitants of several towns and villages near Orléans complained about the damage done by the nearby forest game: "The wild animals which have been or are in covert . . . damage the cultivated lands." As soon as the wheat comes up, it is "eaten and destroyed by the great multitude of animals," and the fields have to be guarded night and day.[18]

Charles VII, who wasn't a hunter, allowed the nobles to hunt as they wished, but Louis XI who wanted to reserve hunting for himself tried to reduce everyone's rights, nobles and commoners alike.

By privilege or custom, the inhabitants of certain towns or regions kept their hunting rights longer. This was the case of the inhabitants of the Hainaut (perhaps, because at the time when this province belonged to the French crown, it was a border march), those of the Dauphiné, the peasants of the Vosges, the inhabitants of Béarn as well as those of the regions near the Pyrénées on the Spanish border. In these last cases, the privilege was justified by the fact that these subjects of the king were inhabitants of a frontier zone, who had the right to bear arms at all times. In the Languedoc, in October 1501, King Louis XII, acknowledging the inhabitants' right to hunt and fish outside of the *garennes*, recalled that they had always had this custom and privilege with the exception of the big "red and black" beasts, the hares, partridges, and pheasants and there, too, only with dogs and clubs.[19] In the forest of Blois, the holders, by virtue of a thirteenth century privilege, had the right to hunt not only by day, but also by night, except in the *garennes*. Charles d'Orléans, in the early fifteenth century, confirmed this privilege, that was abolished by François I in the sixteenth century.

The clergy was not forbidden to hunt, but their right to do so was attached to their establishment—not to their person. The greatest variety prevailed in ecclesiastical hunting rights: some, such as the occupant of the diocese of Orléans, had the right to hunt as a high lord, but this was exceptional. The abbey of Chaalis had the right to hunt except the big beast. The abbey of Saint-Benoît-de-Fleury owned *garennes*. In the thirteenth century the abbey of Saint-Germain-des-Prés repurchased from Gautier le Cornu forest and *garenne* rights at Arrabloy. In 1479, the abbey of Ferrières received hunting rights from Louis XI on the *garenne* of Montargis with the exception of the "red and black beasts." The bishop of Orléans owned a *garenne* at Pithiviers. The commandery of Boigy also owned one. In general, however, when a lord yielded certain rights to religious establishments, he kept the right to hunt for himself.

One of the justifications that is given in the preambles of the texts forbidding non-nobles to hunt and trap is that it is an activity that is too enthralling, a *métier trop coquin*, that might divert the commoners from the function assigned to them in the society of the Middle Ages: work with their hands and, essentially, farm the land. One should also add that, although hunting could allow commoners to obtain food with less hardship than farming or stock breeding, it made it difficult for the lords to collect a portion as dues in kind or as taxes. For that matter, wherever hunting was—or had been —allowed to commoners, it wasn't a tenth or an eighth of the production that was levied—as for the crops or the animals—but generally half of the game; probably it had been taken into account that hunters often did not publicize the extent of their catch.

François I, who was a passionate hunter, adopted a certain number of measures from 1515 on that concerned not only the forest but also game. For instance, he tried to prevent the underground trading of game so as to discourage poaching.

From the fifteenth century on the forests were planned according to the functions devolved to them by the king and the lords who owned them. The latter were more concerned with the maintenance and development of wild animal populations than with forestry or pastoral exploitation, and the organization and the style of the hunts led to a multiplication of trails through the forest for the hunters.

For fox hunting, in particular, large, straight roads were built with star-shaped crossroads where one could see far and gather the hunters. They also needed underwoods where one could gallop but where there were still enough bushes and undergrowth for the animals. Water points, too, were necessary for the survival of the forest fauna.

The coppice with standards, a compromise between the needs for firewood and carbonization and the needs for lumber, was a formula that appeared to be compatible with the organization of the royal hunts. This planning of the forests, especially of the royal ones, became apparent mainly after the reign of François I, a famous hunter who gave the regulations concerning the forest an impulse that would assert itself in the next century.

The plans are still apparent, not only in the forests but in many French towns. Around Paris the peripheric neighborhoods and the suburbs inherited their layouts and the network of avenues, round-abouts, and star crossroads from the forests organized for hunting, all of which preceded the nineteenth century urbanization of the city. Cartography also progressed, thanks to hunting, because at different periods the king had maps drawn to delimit the forests, establish the traffic pattern for the hunts, and help the hunters find their way. These maps have remained extremely useful for the analysis of the utilization of the ground and, in particular, the analysis of the forests since the end of the Middle Ages. The initial objectives of hunting—protecting the cultivated land—were increasingly forgotten and flouted by the lords and—above all—by the king. On the contrary, the peasants, who little by little lost the more extensive hunting rights that they used to have, couldn't even efficiently protect their cultivated fields. Their only solution was poaching, *braconnage* in French—called *bricolage* in Normandy—which was severely punished. Furthermore, on the occasion of royal hunts, not only were the peasants enrolled as beaters but their fields were sacked, their fences broken, and their crops devastated by the passage of the riders and the dogs.

The ecological role of limitation of the animal populations that has today devolved to hunting was totally ignored. While carnivorous predators most often attack the weaker, older, sick or slower animals that are easier to capture—thus contributing to a certain selection—hunters, on the contrary, sought the most beautiful specimens, often the most desirable breeders.

Fish

Water and forest have always been linked so closely that special corps were created to manage both areas: waters are, in fact, often associated with wooded areas. Many rivers were for a long time bordered by forests. The bottoms of the valleys, which were sometimes flooded, could not be used for cereal crops. Even if they were not in a flood area, they were generally constituted of lime soil, heavy and deep, that the plows of the time were unable to till until harnesses and the necessary tooling were improved—and after civil uses of iron were developed. Furthermore, many ponds, lakes, and rivers have wooded shores; and forests where there are no ponds are rare. As long as the Norman incursions prompted the inhabitants to set their housing far from the rivers on which the Viking ships arrived, the shores of the main rivers were often voluntarily left to the forest. Later, these forests were sometimes protected to a certain depth on the riverbank to facilitate lumbering by the proximity of a watercourse. Along the Seine River, it was forbidden to clear the forest up to six leagues (2.4 to 4.6 statute miles) on each side.

Fish played an important role in the gathering economy long before the Middle Ages. Already in Paleolithic art, salmon is often represented; on the engraved reindeer antlers dated from 10,000 to 15,000 years B.C. that were found in the southwest of the Massif central and in the Pyrénées, salmon appear most frequently after horses, reindeer, and bison. Even though the cohabitation of man and salmon was at the latter's expense, there still were quite a few of these fish in the rivers during the Middle Ages; and quite a few other species were eaten as well.

Fishing was of particular importance in the Middle Ages. On one hand, it was not as restricted as hunting. Most inhabitants, whatever their status, had the right to fish; the clergy that didn't have the right to hunt could fish. On the other hand, religious who led to the consumption of fish many days of the year.

Lay lords, and especially monasteries, often organized river bays, ponds, and back waters to raise fish. Furthermore, the building of dams and diversions to install water-powered mills favored the creation of stretches of water upstream and the installation of fish preserves or various devices to catch fish. Open pits from which clay was extracted for the making of tiles or pots were particularly well suited because of the clay's impermeability and were sometimes transformed into ponds when the vein of clay was exhausted. Fisheries are often mentioned in the acts involving monasteries since many of them dug out or arranged ponds in order to have a permanent supply of fish. For instance, monks created numerous ponds in Bresse where the traditional building techniques used clay, which mixed with straw forms the cob.

Fisheries were a source of considerable revenue for their owners because the ponds were often leased. The renters were generally under the obligation to restock the ponds with fish at a given time before the end of the lease. Thus, in 1496, the ponds of Châteauneuf, near Orléans, were leased for 140 livres per year. In 1417, the pond of Baratte in the same area was rented for 60 sous per year. In 1450, fishing in the ponds of Voves was awarded for 60 livres tournois.[20] The leases were generally for six or seven years and the obligation to restock with young fish had to be executed two years before the end of the lease. The restocking was confirmed by an official report.

The abbey of Saint-Benoît-sur-Loire which had owned, since the eleventh century, a fishing right on the Loire River's shores, derived important revenues from it; it also had fishing rights in the Loiret. According to a cartulary of 1250, the abbey's sergeant, Hughes Béraud, who was in charge of working the traps and nets, not only received half of the catches made with these devices and a quarter of those made in other places by other fishermen under his supervision, but also was remunerated with two deniers every time he pulled out the traps of the cellarer father, which contained the fish for the monks' table.[21] This report shows that in this case the amount of fish produced was far greater than the convent's needs and that most of it was traded.

Fishing had such an important role in alimentation that fishing instruments are cited among the peasants' usual tools in the treatise on tools by Alexandre Neckham (end of the twelfth century). In some regions in England and in France, for instance along the Saône River, the inhabitants lived essentially from fishing. Generally, fishing was allowed only on weekdays and, sometimes, only to professional fishermen.

Pollution of the waterways already existed, particularly because of the tanneries and the slaughterhouses and, of course, downstream from the cities. However, as it derived from organic or biological refuse and not from chemical products, and as it was much less generalized, it did not have such a disastrous effect as it does today on the aquatic fauna; and the rivers had much more fish. In certain regions where, today, salmon is relatively rare and is being reimplanted with great difficulty, in the Middle Ages, contracts specified that farm laborers could not be forced to eat salmon more than three times a week.

Little by little, rules, generally inspired by customs, were promulgated to avoid the depopulation of rivers due to anarchic and abusive practices. The aim was to prevent damaging methods such as night fishing, the use of forbidden devices, fishing in the spawning season, and the capture of young fish.

> ♦ *It is also forbidden to fish by night with any kind of device for two months from mid-March to mid-May. Because the fish spawn at that time and leave their spawn and the night fishermen hunt them and destroy all their spawn. And no one should try to catch the spawn of dace nor roaches nor daces during this period. And everyone will be allowed to fish with approved devices except during the previously mentioned period. And any new devices made will have to be made on the king's model. That is each stich the size of a* gros tournois *from Easter to Saint Remy and larger to catch bigger fish. And from Saint Remy to Easter the size of a* parisis. *So that the sizes mentioned will easily be able to pass through the nets as is illustrated below.*[22] ♦

Some forest guards were specialized in the supervision of waters. Thus, in the forest of Orléans, there were two pond guards, one in Lorris and one in Chateauneuf. Judging by the number of condemnations they obtained in the thirteenth century, they must have been very active. Officially, they kept for their own use one-fifth of the value of their catch by day and one-third at night.

In general, professional fishermen had to set aside part of their catch for the lord or his agents. The sharing of the fish caught was specified in the acts: for example in the polyptych of the *viel rentier* of Audenarde (Belgium) (1275) it is specified that the eels caught in the pots were divided between the lord and the Church, five for the sire and four for the other party.[23]

Fish were certainly an important commodity and were actively traded. In a tariff of the Salbris toll in 1448,[24] a period when, after the Hundred Years War, trade was once again active, the toll amount for horse and donkey charges of fish is mentioned. The text enumerates: salmon, lamprey, aloses, cuttlefish, herrings, etc., which proves that many fish came from the sea. This document mentions cartloads of freshwater fish in which the fish were counted by fives. This indicates a production that went far beyond the limits of local consumption. But, of course, this toll was in Sologne—a region particularly well stocked in fish.[25]

Forest Pharmacopoeia

Many of the animal and plant products of the forest served in the pharmacopoeia, either as remedy or as poison. A few are still used occasionally for healing in the French countryside; oak bark for burns and chapped skin; honeysuckle—the bark for the treatment of gout, the leaves for sore throats, the flowers for headaches and eye aches. Lichens are used for their fibrifuge, purgative, and tonic action. Black bryony berries are an emetic. Ivy is used for digestion, expectoration, and for cuts and bumps; periwinkle for the brain, bilberry for the intestines and the eyes; juniper as a hemostatic; black elder as laxative, sudorific and diuretic; dwarf elder as antirheumatic; *scoparius* broom as heart regulator. Some buds were also used: beech buds as diuretic and against obesity; elm buds against eczema; pine against what is today called decalcification; alder and birch buds were considered to be beneficial for the brain and the nervous system.

Other qualities were attributed to some plants in the Middle Ages. Crescence says of the *chaste aignel* or *agnus castus*: "It is called the *chaste aignel* because it restrains lust and makes whoever carries it chaste as a lamb. . . ." Following with some extremely specific details on the effects of this plant on men, Crescence ends by saying: "When women are too anxious for the company of men, when they have too much ardor to make love, a fumigation is done from below and they are immediately healed." Some plants like the *satirie*, also called *genitilles de chien*, allegedly permitted having a boy or a girl. Others, such as the seed of *érenque sauvage*, the pine cone and coriander had aphrodisiac effects. According to Crescence, bistort served "to limit women's superfluous time: they will be steamed from below and bathed in water in which the root will have been cooked."

The *creteau* or *rismarin* was used for nephretic colics and to prevent urinary retention; the *barberon* or *pied de veau* for scrofula; lettuce against insomnia; borage against faintness. As for pines of which "the growth is happier in moist and windy places," Crescence mentions that the pine cones "grow the blood of people with consumption." Diplan was said to push arrows out of the body and dissolve venom.

Some remedies could also be used as poison: black bryony berries, emetic up to a certain dosage; or digitalis, called in the past *"Gant de Notre Dame"* (Our Lady's Glove) that slows down and can paralyze the cardiac muscles. Coriander dissolved in wine "sets people in furor and engenders lust" but was also said to kill dogs.

There was no lack of poisons and the names given to them are sometimes colorful: *crève-chien* [lit. dog-killer], deadly or black nightshade; *vigne du diable* [lit. the devil's vine], bryony; *tire-loups* [lit. wolf puller], *aconitum lycoctonium; raisin de renard* [lit. fox's grape], black fruit of the herb paris or true love; *bois-gentil* [lit. pretty wood], spurge olive or red fruit of the daphne; *bonnet-carré* [lit. square bonnet], spindel-tree; Solomon's seal, *polygonatum vulgare; herbe à pain* [lit. bread herb], whose red fruits are toxic for lords and ladies. Many other trees or bushes could provide dangerous products: the yew's (*taxus baccata*) wood and leaves are toxic but the fruit can be eaten if one doesn't crack the seeds. Caesar writes that Catuvolcos, one of the Eburon's chiefs, committed suicide with yew, "a very common tree in Gaul and Germany, after his army was defeated."[26] Nowadays, careless cows are sometimes tempted by the leaves of this beautiful tree and this leads to complex lawsuits between neighbors.

There are still other poisons: buckthorn has fruit looking like little black plums (*rhamus cathartica*), which are purgative in small doses; the *viorne obiée (viburnus opulus)*; from climbing ivy (*hedera*) is extracted an emetic resin called hederin; from the tubers of cyclamen an irritating powder is extracted; ruscus or small holly has very decorative but toxic red berries; mistletoe, red sorrel, and male cornel are poisonous; lily of the valley contains a substance that slows down the heartbeat.

But, of course, it was all a question of dosage and preparation.

And without waiting for "new age" medicines, modern allopathic
or homeopathic medicine has also used as medication most of these
toxins, of which the witches and sorcerers of the Middle Ages as
well as the kings' doctors made use and which were sought in the
forests, observing detailed protocols to guarantee their efficacy.[27]

Pleasures and "Diversions" of the Forest

In a book published in 1560 and titled *Quatre traictés utiles et delectables
de l'agriculture*, an anonymous author, who honestly quotes the ancients as his authority and adds his personal experience, explains in
his preamble what he believes to be essential for an estate. His point
of view is that of an estate owner who considers both what is useful
and what is pleasant and seeks, as was the rule in the Middle Ages,
maximum self-sufficiency for his estate.

Woods, under their various aspects of provider of fuel and timber,
source of game, and dispenser of wild fruits occupy the most important place. Of the nine points considered essential, three are
concerned with forestry:

> ♦ *Cathon, in his book on agriculture, says that one needs nine
> main things. The first is a vineyard producing great quantities
> of wine; the second, a garden full of little streams; the third, a
> willow grove and an osier bed; the fourth, a main river; the
> fifth, a meadow; the sixth, a big field of wheat; the seventh, a
> coppice; the eighth, bushes and a hunting preserve; and the
> ninth, a forest producing acorns. From all these items it is clear
> that water and wood are the most important. If you have water,
> meadows, gardens, osier beds, and willow groves can be set along
> the water and the rivers. If you have woods, you can have
> coppice, hunting preserves, bushes and a forest of full-grown
> trees, because any coppice well kept becomes a forest of full-grown
> trees if only it is pruned and the undergrowth cleaned to make
> it grow. ♦*

The author enumerates the main elements that make up the agro/
sylvo/pastoral balance of a harmonious rural estate in the Middle
Ages: the vine is mentioned first; the intensively cultivated and
well-irrigated garden is mentioned second. Then he stresses the

importance of the trees that produce wood for tools, containers, wickerwork, furniture, fences, and enclosures, that is essentially willow and osier. In the fourth place, he mentions the river (which produces both fish and the energy for the water-powered mills and also allows irrigation and provides the water indispensable to life). The fifth point is the meadow, which, in the sixteenth century, was finally considered essential by any stock breeder: it is amazing to see that this item is set before the wheat field, which only comes next. Seventh is the coppice, which provides firewood; and eighth the strong bushes and the hunting preserve, that is, thick woods, difficult to penetrate where game seeks refuge and the places reserved for that game. Ninth is the forest of full-grown trees with its main production, acorns that feed the pigs. It is probable that if these points are classified by their importance, the order would have been slightly different in the thirteenth century.

The author then enumerates all the advantages of woodlands:

♦ *The main pleasure and diversion provided by a wild wood is that when it is very close to the country house—as it should be —it is nice to look at, has different shades of green, is quite delightful and pleasantly limits the view.*

The second diversion is that the wood close to the home is always full of little birds that sing all summer and spring everyday and most nights, like the nightingales and others sorts of birds, whose song is nice to hear and one has this diversion and music indeed inside the house if it is near the wood.

The other pleasure is that in the wood are many pigeons, woodpeckers, starlings, thrushes and other kinds of birds and it is a diversion to see them fly about; you can also have the diversion and the profit of capturing them with small devices, snarings, and nets.

The fourth pleasure is that there might be in those woods rabbits, hares, deer, wild boars, squirrels, wolves, foxes, and other small beasts pleasant to look at and very useful for food and subsistence.

The fifth pleasure is that when it is hot, you can stay outside in the shade of the wood that protects you from the sun; you remain cool, protected from the heat. The wood remains nice and green on the branches as well as on the ground that maintains its green grass thanks to the freshness and the shade of the trees.

*The sixth is that in winter—when you are in your home—
the woods protect you from the harshness of strong winds and of
the cold, which are diverted and lessened. You are in a retired
place where you can read, write and think about your business
without being distracted by the view of a distant landscape since
you cannot see through the woods or the bushes.*

*In addition to the pleasure provided by the forest, there is a
lot of profit to be made out of the grazing of animals in the
shade, out of the acorns, chestnuts, beechnuts, and other fruits
from the trees that are given to the pigs and other useful
animals, out of the coppice that can be cut every year to provide
firewood, for gardens and fences, hoops, sticks and stakes for the
vine. And if there are chestnut or hazel groves, one can also
make hoops for the wine casks. So woods will provide not just
pleasure but also great profit if one wants to exploit them.* ◆

3 · the farmer in the forest ·

Agricultural Evolution and the Forest

AT THE BEGINNING OF AGRICULTURE, amidst the vast expanses of a new territory, man first took advantage of naturally cleared sectors, then started moving the arable clearing about. Forests or moors were cleared by fire creating the surfaces necessary to feed the population, by taking into account the anticipated crop yield. The fields, fertilized by the ashes, were cultivated then abandoned after a year or two to the wild vegetation. When all the areas easiest to farm in a given sector had been exploited, the whole tribe moved and established its camp elsewhere. There was no lack of space; human population was scattered. Later because of competition from other human communities—and unless there was a conflict and one group was eliminated—the territories belonging to each group had to be delimited. The territories were generally separated by forest zones constituting a border, a sort of no-man's-land with imprecise limits, often an object of dispute and conflicts between neighboring communities. It was within the more confined limits of these territories that the cultivated areas moved. The community was then able to benefit from a fixed location at a site most favorable for living or for defense against ferocious animals or unfriendly men.

To avoid returning too quickly to the same place at the risk of finding a soil that would not yet have recovered its natural fertility, the rotation of these fields had to be methodically organized. Gaston Roupnel, that marginal pluridisciplinarian, in his magisterial and poetic *Histoire de la campagne française*—inspired by Tacitus famous text about the agricultural customs of the Germans in the first century—described in the 1930s the medieval villages of the north and northeast of France as applying this system based on an indispensable collective organization: "The agrarian territory was thus a sector of renewed soil that traveled along the horizon around the village. After about twenty years the terrain on the horizon was finished. A new rotation was then started that gave back to the crops, successively and in their immutable order, all the abandoned old sectors, which the forest had time to take over and of which it had reconstituted the fertile humus."[1]

The similarities between this process and the mode of exploitation of the soil still in use today in several West African countries have been underlined by Gilles Sautter.[2] The persistence of similar systems in other countries such as Sardinia[3] and Portugal has also been noted.

Nonetheless, Roupnel's description of the mode of exploitation which, according to him, existed in the early Middle Ages in all of northern and eastern France, is on some points rather idealistic and rigid. The system presupposes not only a collective organization, very systematic and rigorously organized, and thus a very solid social structure, but also a particularly fertile soil where the mere return of the forest for twenty years and the effect of fire at the end of that period would be enough to reconstitute an identical fecundity of the soil.

Although that might happen in intertropical regions with a luxuriant vegetation and on some particularly fertile European soils, it is not common. Furthermore, in most cases, it is rare not to have cyclical factors that disturb the process: rapid population increase following a lucky and peaceful period or decrease due to repeated poor crops, exceptional climatic circumstances, epidemics, invasions, troubles or brigandage, or simply following the establishment of a more abusive authority, requiring increased obligations and forcing the farmer to obtain more from the land.

As for the reconstitution of fertility, rare are the soils for which twenty years are sufficient for the return of the forest to spontaneously reconstitute the superficial fertility. Furthermore, even on the mere surface of a more-or-less large clearing, the disappearance of the forest cover for a year or two, and its slow reconstitution, can allow erosion to occur and to modify at each return of this phase the conditions of the new growth. Even in the absence of erosion, the species replacing the ones that were pulled out or simply cut or burned are generally different; this is due to the effect of openness, as the shade species are eliminated in favor of the light species, but also to the action of man and his herds who favor the new growth of certain species (oak or beech, for example) because of their fruits (acorns and beechnuts eaten by both men and animals) or because of their wood production (for construction, tools, wickerwork, fences, etc.). Thus, following different processes in each context, the composition of the forest and of the soil changed little by little. There were as many possible evolutions as there were territories, and different geographical, historical, climatic or ecological circumstances. Very rare must have been the cases where, without any thoughtful intervention of man based on long experience, the fertility could reconstitute itself identically and intact, following a cycle in which the afforestation would have represented, so to speak, one of the breaks of a longer duration than that of a crop rotation alternating wooded fallow land, possibly broken by intermediate cuts of firewood, with a short crop phase.

Thus, each generation was faced with a different situation and even within a single generation, everything could change. Little by little, however, it became apparent that the farmer tried to guarantee his security, increase his stability, let his children benefit directly from the result of his work on the soil, and tried to acquire a certain autonomy in his activity and in the organization of his chores.

Facing him, the lord realized that there might be an advantage in improving the condition and means of his dependents, in commuting the payments in kind and in labor—the tithe and the *corvée* (labor service)—into taxes in money, in *cens*, in fixed rents, perhaps more moderate, but guaranteed by contracts and on which he could count with fewer hazards. From the eleventh to the thirteenth century outside circumstances lent themselves to the change. First of all, the climatic conditions seem to have been more favorable, as Le Roy Ladurie[4] indicates when he evokes the mild period of the years 1000–1300 (ninth to twelfth century). The peasant's condition, according to Georges Duby[5], had improved and the peasant, less overwhelmed, didn't have the impression any more that he was working for the sole benefit of the lord. The invasions, which until the ninth century had produced great insecurity in the countryside, stopped when the Normans settled in Normandy in 911; when the Hungarians, whose incursions threatened the east of France, were definitely driven back—from the year 955 on—toward central Europe; and when the Saracens were finally expelled in 972 from their last bases of forays in Provence. Furthermore, from the end of the eleventh century, the departures for the Crusades induced many lords to sell some of their properties to obtain cash to pay for equipment for themselves and their soldiers. It also pushed them to negotiate with their dependents the commutation of diverse obligations, to sell them charters, franchises, to substitute taxes in cash for obligations in kind in order to guarantee to their families a regular income during their absence, and for the cases where they would not return from their distant expeditions. Faith and allegiance to their suzerain certainly prevailed on nobles most attached to their families and their domain to join the Crusades, such as Joinville at the side of Saint Louis. But it can be argued that it often was the lords who were the most adventurous, the least interested in the prosaic management of their domains and, at the same time, the least inclined to protect the farmer and the land, who were the most numerous to throw themselves into this fascinating adventure. So the consequences for the peasants were on the whole favorable and contributed to a progressive improvement in their condition.

Little by little, the farmer, who (in spite of the harsh punishments and the active solidarity between the lords to capture and bring back to their point of departure the runaway serfs and peasants) was often tempted to flee in order to find more tolerable living conditions by clearing some remote place in peace or by joining the enterprise of a *villeneuve*, tended to become more sedentary. Less taxed, less exposed to arbitrary requisitions, he settled down, a little more assured that he could harvest what he sowed; that he could keep a sufficient part of the fruit of his labor; that he could benefit from the improvements he brought to the soil he cultivated; and that he could increase and improve his tools, and develop his livestock.

The territory took shape, in the form of a combination of dwellings and collective and private spaces.

Houses were generally grouped in hamlets, sometimes in villages, to allow for a measure of collective defense against marauders and brigands, if not against organized troops. Closest to the houses were the carefully cultivated individual gardens and orchards, protected by permanent fences against trespassing beasts. Because of their location they could be maintained and permanently supervised by the women as well as by the men and benefited from human fertilizer.

Further out was the zone of permanent crops, which should rather be called the permanent zone of crops, since to maintain their fertility, these fields had to lay fallow, sometimes a year out of two, or, at the least, one year out of three where the three-field system —of which the first traces appeared under Charlemagne—had spread. Ten centuries later, this practice still governs the legislation and rules the existence of millions of Frenchmen, since the "three-six-nine" residential lease is certainly nothing other than a relic of that agricultural cycle whose periodicity thrusts itself upon the leases of rural exploitations; we still observe Carolingian customs!

In some regions it was the custom to cultivate for several years in a row then lay the land fallow several years in a row: thus in Sologne, the land was cultivated for three years after which broom was planted, which was harvested five years later as firewood.[6] This intermediate system between the one of the cultivated fields and the other of temporary clearings is similar to systems still used in certain African countries.

Cultivated fields were, in most areas, cut up by temporary or permanent systems of fences to prevent the cattle from wandering into them during the periods when they were not allowed there. Little by little, these collective fields became privately owned and were surrounded by ditches, embankments and sometimes by hedges that marked the limits. This, however, did not prevent the community practice of having common land; it allowed everyone's herds, even the animals of the poorest, to remain in the fields for some time after the harvest to graze on the stubble, and, at the same time, brought a little manure to the soil.

As one got closer to the outlying ring of forest (if one can call by that name the zone generally the farthest from the dwellings but which, due to particularities of the topography and the nature of the soil, could in some places be very close to the village and in others much farther away), one first reached half-forest, half-farm zones. There could be found the temporary clearings most often cleared by fire and that frequently, because of the fertilizing effect of the ashes, gave a higher yield than the permanent fields poorly fertilized by the temporary passage of the animals. The most precious cereals were sometimes planted in these temporary fields that were cultivated for a year or two and then returned to a coppice of short ten to fifteen years revolution or sometimes to the forest for a longer time. Thus, in the region of the Grande Chartreuse, wheat was cultivated on the farthest clearings, on the wooded slopes.[7]

The wooded areas formed a last zone, often peripheral but including also all the grounds too hilly or not fertile enough for farming. With the population increase due to the long period of relative peace and the improvement in the peasants' living conditions from the end of the tenth century to the middle of the thirteenth century, the surfaces of the cultivated lands and the temporary clearings became insufficient to produce, with the low crop yield of the period, the necessary subsistence. In the eleventh century, numerous famines occurred and a great effort to increase cultivated areas was undertaken by countless modest and sometimes clandestine initiatives, many of which have remained unknown, as well as by a number of large-scale enterprises, of which the written contracts have left us the evidence. Humid zones were drained and dried; flood areas were suppressed by building dikes in some parts of France and England; and, as in Holland, cropland was sometimes created by pushing away the sea or draining areas situated below sea level. In France, it is especially at the expense of wooded areas that most permanent clearings were multiplied.

Everywhere, the forest receded before the logger's axe and the settler's plow. Not satisfied with temporarily clearing the land, and then letting the forest restore itself, big enterprises and countless small farmers attacked and reduced the forest. To attract workers, the clearing contractors and ecclesiastic or lay lords, offered them particular benefits: it was the period of the *villeneuves* and the *ville-franches* that sprouted all over the country and left numerous traces in the toponymy as did the temporary clearings (*essarts*) of the previous period.

The lord, who owned the woods of which the ordinary men had the use (following rules and with specific restrictions), took care that his woods would not gradually melt away through the proliferation of clearings. But quite often it was difficult to totally prevent the illicit clearings, and sometimes he had to endorse after-the-fact operations that he had not been able to prevent, and retaliated by merely taxing the offenders.

In the whole country, the forest receded as cropland spread and, gradually, it lost its nutritious role not only because it became smaller but also because in an increasing number of sectors, the lords opposed its free usage and reserved it for hunting. Furthermore, the consequences of the agricultural/pastoral exploitation of the forests were also felt by the indispensable production of wood, particularly lumber construction, as soon as the forests no longer offered inexhaustible new spaces to the settlers.

As the spaces available for clearing and extending cropland were not infinite, the farmers in the twelfth and thirteenth centuries had to improve the yield of the permanent crops. They managed to do so to a certain extent by perfecting their tools and farming practices and by developing in some regions the three-field system, which increased by 50 percent the crop possibilities of a given field compared to the biannual system of fallow land alternating with crops. The *essartage*, temporary cultivation of a clearing—then left to the new growth of wood (indispensable production of which could not be indefinitely reduced by permanent clearings)—became a secondary factor in the production of subsistences, the main part of which was now produced by the permanent fields.

Because of the diminishing forested surfaces, the wild produce of the forest became increasingly secondary in the production of food. It was the beginning of a total agricultural revolution: the agricultural mutation of the period which witnessed the building of the Gothic cathedrals can be considered an extremely important event for all of Europe. It was accompanied in several countries by the development of enclosures that transformed agriculture from a mainly collective organization to a private enterprise, collective arrangements remaining only for certain stations linked to breeding; and then, mostly in mountain areas.

In the plains, the development of privately owned fields did not suppress all the collective practices, but they moved toward the sharing, at certain periods, of the means that a farmer could not easily possess on his own, such as a harness hooked up with several horses—which made it possible to use the newly perfected plow that one sees in the miniatures and that allowed the cultivation of deep heavy soils. But this development of permanently cultivated fields went hand in hand with the beginning of the specialization of meadows that allowed stock breeding to dispense with the forest which, until then, had been essential.

During this period, the monks were about the only ones who devoted permanent spaces to the production of animal feed, especially in flood zones but, little by little, even in other places. Indeed, as circumspect managers and great stock breeders, they understood the importance of a balance between crops, stock breeding, and the forest. Because they had the financial resources and owned vast estates, they could, in contrast to the simple peasant, allow themselves an organization less-strictly centered on cereal production; they greatly increased their breeding animal stock, by using the forest and rejected crops. Meanwhile, the forest started to become the specialized domain of tree culture. This evolution resulted, in the long run, in an increasing specialization of agriculture, animal husbandry, and forestry.

At the beginning of this transitional period that was essential for the organization of French rural space, from the tenth to the fourteenth century, the forest still played an important and polyvalent role in the rural economy. At the end, apart from cyclical and local mishaps, the forest was only an economic factor, indispensable in the agricultural/forestry/breeding balance, more and more sought for its main production—wood—but less and less for its many secondary productions, even if its role in the pastoral economy remained unchanged for a long time in certain regions.

Several periods can be distinguished in this transformation, which does not develop at an equal pace in the different regions.

First, the temporary clearings gradually modify the structure of the forests where they are made. Then comes the period when, as the population increases, the surfaces that have been permanently cultivated must be increased: the villages split up and some of the inhabitants settle in remote spots to cultivate newly cleared zones. In a third phase, or concurrently with these private initiatives, the big clearing enterprises are organized, often through a collaboration between ecclesiastic and lay lords, with the participants contributing land, capital or men.

Clearing and Deforestation

It is by a misuse of language that the French term *défrichement*, "clearing of land," is often used in the more narrow sense of deforestation in order to farm. Originally, the word *friche* meant "fresh, new"; it simply meant land that had not yet been cultivated, but was not necessarily a wooded area. Fallow land is often confused with the *friche*: in fact, this term describes the preparation of the fields that precedes sowing. Fallow land succeeded the stubble period during which animals were admitted to the cultivated fields, where they grazed on the remaining cereal stalks. Normally, it lasted five to eight months. First, the field was plowed to destroy the weeds. Then it was hoed to complete this work and dry out the roots. Then the field was plowed, sowed, and harrowed to bury the seeds.

All new land (*terres en friche*) is not covered by forests. However, in moderate climates, most of them tend toward one form or another of this plant formation. Clearings (in French, *défrichements*) thus include not only those made in wooded areas, but also the conversion into farmland of waste covered by wild vegetation of any kind. We will examine here only forest clearings.[8]

Clearing a wooded space appears a priori to be a simple operation: one takes away the trees and the bushes, clears away the brambles and the shrubs; and an open space is thus created; it is cultivated. The reality is quite different and more complex, and the result depends not only on the existing environment but also on the methods used for this operation. In sum, an open space is created in the forest by eliminating the wooded cover—the complex ecosystem, varied and often rich in living matter—to substitute for it successive food crops, generally monocultures. However, transforming a wooded piece of ground into a cultivated field, whether temporarily (as was often the case in the Middle Ages where the forest was expected to give back to the soil its fertility after a year or two of culture) or indefinitely (to create permanent fields) raises a number of difficulties. It is necessary to know them in order to examine the different clearing techniques and their consequences.

We saw that the forest includes a whole series of levels, superposed "strata," maintaining rich and complex interrelations. In a cultivated field, on the contrary, there is only one visible stratum, to which must be added, of course, the underground stratum, which, it so happens, acquires in this case a considerable importance. The soil is much more exposed to the elements since in the fields it is protected only (and imperfectly and seasonally) by a thin, often scattered, layer of vegetation. As a first consequence of this situation, the cultivated soil is much more fragile than the forest's soil and easily modified in its consistency and composition by the action of the elements, by the sun, wind, water, frost, and also by animals and man. Thus, the farmer must compose and preserve the cropland himself by reasoned exploitation, by carefully measuring what he is adding to the soil and what he is retrieving from it. If farming is interrupted for a few years, everything changes. If a farmer neglects his land for a while, the soil will be considerably modified. If erosion takes hold on open land, it might mean, in few years, the disappearance of all farming accessibility. On the contrary, if the farmer spares no trouble and has a way with it, the soil can improve, lose its sterile components such as stones and rocks, be mixed with products that change it or enrich it—lime, chalk, marl, manure, etc.—be mellowed, acquire a texture or a relief more favorable to farming, become more fertile.

In open country the wind is also a harmful factor: so, in most cases, it will be desirable to break up the clearings in the forest, in order to avoid over-large open spaces. Trees could be maintained— and it has been done—to form wooded strips or hedges (in the modern sense of this term). But the trees that grow in hedges are not the same as the ones that grow in the woods: exposure to sun and rain, drying up by the wind, proximity of other plants, the nature of the soil and humus, exploitation conditions—everything differs. Few forest species succeed in hedges because the ecological conditions are different. Thus, the "linear forest" of *bocage* (mixed woodland and pastureland) regions does not have the same composition as the "massive" forest, even if, in many respects, it can answer the same needs. Hedges in bocage regions are not, as one could believe, remains of the forest, even when the land formerly was wooded.

In a forest of large trees, the stumps constitute an obstacle to farming and are difficult to extract in order to obtain homogeneous, light, and deep soil, cleared of all its obstacles. But in a forest already degraded, where the trees have not yet had time to grow, the farmer will have few difficulties in eliminating the stumps. This will induce the farmer who operates temporary clearings to prefer the degraded forest to the primary or reconstituted forest.

Plants and Fire

Today, motorization has considerably multiplied man's means to fell trees, convert wood, discharge lumber, remove stumps, plow and harrow. Until then, because of limited resources and the scarcity of iron tools, the ancestral methods that spared men's labor through the use of fire, were widely used for forest clearing, particularly during the Middle Ages.

However, on one hand, they were not sufficient to totally clear an area where there were trees of a certain size: felling these remained a prerequisite, and removing the stumps an additional operation. On the other hand, a second objective was often sought: the aim was not only to clear the ground of the forest's secondary vegetation and of the smaller trees in this expeditious way, but also to increase the soil's fertility thanks to the combustion residues. This second objective was not specific to the forest. It gave way to particular techniques that a thousand years of experience had perfected to ensure in the most efficient way the fertilization of the soil by the combustion products. The third result, obtained by burning, was the sterilization of undesirable plants' seeds. Indeed, to the present time, the stubble is burned after the harvest for this purpose, thus avoiding the use of weed killers.

Several phenomena linked to the use of fire are favorable to farming: the burning can help eliminate, in addition to undesirable seeds and parasites, some of those residual substances, previously mentioned, that slow down or inhibit vegetation; furthermore, when well controlled and following certain techniques, fire can allow plants

to have access to useful elements that otherwise would remain unassimilable and unused.

The chemical effect of fire is very important: it makes part of the
soil's excessive acidity disappear since the ashes of the humus and
plants burned are basic and neutralize this acidity, that is characteristic of the humid temperate climate of western Europe. Also,
this acidity is unfavorable to vegetation, especially to cultivated
plants; only plants of almost no economic value (heather, carex, and
peat moss) prosper in an acid environment. Furthermore, humus
that has been heated maintains for several months a mineralization
speed superior to that of nonheated humus; this provokes a liberation
of nitrogen that would have otherwise remained unassimilable. The
effect of the sun heating a forest humus after a clear felling has
similar consequences. This phenomenon is put to use in Scandinavia
but it needs time and continuous good weather, which is rarely the
case in western Europe. Fire, then, is the most rapid and surest
solution.[9]

In addition, certain forest plants—such as ferns—do not liberate
their fertilizing elements by fermentation; they decay poorly, which
makes them good litter matter but does not give a good compost.
Their ashes, however, contain phosphate, nitrogen, and potash, and
constitute an excellent fertilizer.

It is noticed nowadays, after accidental fires, that some forest
regenerations and retimberings are favored by the fire; they are a
few more justifications for the fire techniques that have been used
for thousands of years by farmers in many countries. These techniques are applied not only in primitive countries, but also in very
advanced countries where the results obtained by fire have been
studied scientifically and the techniques brought back into use.
Fundamental element of the ecology of most North American forests,
the "let burn" technique used in natural parks, has helped to prevent
the catastrophic fires that used to destroy the forests when considerable quantities of inflammable litter accumulated and thus has
favored the growth of species less sensitive to fire.[10]

The peasants of the old days had noticed the effects of fire as well
as the properties of plants: the collective memory had slowly registered them and the techniques that were used derived from those
observations. They followed specific rules that guaranteed their effectiveness and permitted the creation of temporary arable clearings,

without provoking permanent degradations; in short, men established a reproducible cycle whose periodicity, empirically determined on a given soil, was traditionally repeated. Among the agricultural techniques that use fire, the two main ones—sometimes confused—are *essartage* (clearing of the ground) and *écobuage* (burn-beating).

Clearing of the Ground (Essartage)

Contrary to *écobuage, essartage* designates an operation that is specific to the forest. During the Middle Ages, the term *essart* is often used simply to designate an area from which the trees have been eliminated, extracted, uprooted, whatever the means used, whether it was *exarare* (with a plow), or *exardere* (with fire). If one retains, as the origin of this word, *sarrire* (which could justify the fact that, for instance, in Belgium, *essart* is said *sart* and that friars who make clearings are called *frères sartaires*), *exsarrire* would evoke only an operation common to all cropland, whether or not of forest origin: namely, weeding. Yet, *essartage* designates a specific global operation, including several phases and executed in the Middle Ages more or less entirely with the help of fire, which would justify my hypothesis that this word derives from the Latin *exarsus* meaning burned (found in the Justinian Code). Indeed, the term *exarsia* was used in certain acts to designate in Latin the *essarts* and the spelling *exsart* is also found in several texts.

The *essart* could be either a clearing to create permanent fields—the meaning it rapidly took and has maintained in the toponymy—or (this seems to be the original meaning) a temporary clearing, cultivated for a year or two and later returned to the forest and exploited in coppice, said of short "revolution." This last term means that a cut was made every six to twelve years, depending on the soil. A few trees were sometimes left to give shade, which was favorable to the new growth of some coppice species, to act as seed bearers, and to provide small timber. Those trees were then cut every twenty-five or thirty years, when places were made for the crops.

This process really constituted a crop rotation spread over many years. It included, for example, two years of food crops (of several kinds, in a succession dictated by experience; and different, depending on the regions and the local customs), and then two or three periods (of six to twelve years), during which the coppice grew until the next cut, at which time a few tall standard trees were left in place, to be cut only when the land was cleared entirely, in order to farm it after thirty years, or less.

Indeed, the authorities made sure that temporary clearings did not become permanent fields to the detriment of the forest capital, which represented a sizable source of income for the nobles and the king. Thus, in 1116, King Louis VI, who had had to endorse, after the fact, unauthorized clearings made in the region of Corbreuse, on the southern edge of the forest of Dourdan, specified, on this occasion, that the farmers who cleared the land would limit themselves to two harvests and then would have to leave and operate elsewhere.[11]

It is, of course, evident that the process left little chance for the trees to develop to a point that would allow them to be used as rafters or construction posts. The only trees that could be kept for a long time were the ones that were on the edges of the lots or the ones that could possibly be spared on the inside by maintaining the fires far enough away so as not to jeopardize their survival. These trees, however, limited the crops' productivity in their immediate vicinity, and hindered plowing and harrowing.

The herbaceous vegetation that developed annually under the trees can be considered an "associated crop." Almost everywhere, it served as feed for the animals, except during the first few years of each new growth of coppice and during certain seasons of the year during which one avoided exposing it to the teeth of the domestic herbivores. The temporary fences—forest protections—as well as the ditches and the embankments played a major role in limiting their trespassing.

The successive clearing operations, which must not have changed much from the Middle Ages to the end of the Old Regime, included first of all, and preferably in winter, the felling of trees: on one hand, those that could be used as lumber or as wood for carpentry, and on the other hand, the trees of lesser quality or of smaller diameter that, together with the branches of the bigger trees, became logs or firewood for cooking, heating, making charcoal, and industry. The barks of certain trees, such as oak, lime, and birch were also removed.

After the felling and the seasoning (which could last a year), the fire was lit on the side under the wind so that the smoke wouldn't bother the workers and the fire wouldn't spread too quickly. The workers burned the branches, twigs, miscellaneous plant debris, and the low vegetation, supervising the fire to prevent its extension to the neighboring forest ranges. The inflammable matter was spread on the whole surface of the ground to fertilize each part equally, but also to prevent overly hot fires that would have been difficult to control. The fire was guided with long gaffs with which the workers spread out the ashes or, on the contrary, reassembled the combustible matter to revive the fire.

In the Ardennes forest, people cleared every eighteen or twenty years, cutting the deal in the winter and the oak in the spring, after the rising of the sap, to facilitate pulling off the bark. According to several authors, it seems that it was desirable for the fertility that not only branches and plant debris be burned, but also that a certain quantity of dirt be carbonized at the same time. It helped eliminate parasites and undesirable plants.

This clearing technique was applicable only as long as the forest space had sufficient reserves to allow for a rotation of the cultivated lands since it required, for two years of culture, up to ten times more surface (2/30) than the one cultivated under the three-field system (20/30). It must be noted that from the point of view of the farmer, a "secondary" forest, degraded and composed of small trees, is much less difficult to clear than a "primary" forest where the big tree trunks resist fire and force him to make a preliminary cut. Subjected, on the one hand, to frequent coppice cuts for firewood and, on the other hand, to clear fellings every twenty or thirty years to allow for cropland, the forest never matured. Thus, the farmer limited his labor to the detriment of the forest's development.

Bernard Palissy, the famous ceramist, described around 1580 the particular method of clearing by "covered fire" (in French, *essartage à feu couvert*)—the usual clearing was by "running fire" (*feu courant*). In this process, the cut wood was covered by turf, with air passing below, and the branches were burned to reduce the whole thing to ashes that were then spread out on the ground. Then the ground was plowed and rye was sowed. The periodicity indicated by Palissy was sixteen years, sometimes less. According to him, wood production during that period was as important as if the forest had not been clear felled. Actually, all the authors insist on the fact that the clearing by fire, well conducted, was not harmful to the forest, but that, on the contrary, an improvement of the environment occurred, especially favorable to oak, of which the new stump growth or the fructification were stimulated.

Burn-beating (Écobuage)

Écobuage (burn-beating) was a technique that was different from the *essartage* (clearing) and was not restricted to the forest. Its objective was more the fertilization than the clearing, but it could be one of the latter's complementary operations, using a more elaborate method of burning reminiscent of the technique described by Bernard Palissy. Jacques Le Goff believes that:

> • The clearings, especially the burn-beating, consumer of *terre gaste* exhausted the soils and especially destroyed this apparently unlimited wealth in the medieval world: wood. [12] •

This pessimistic statement should perhaps be modified; the destruction might have been due less to the process itself (which can be deliberately used without abuse), than to the fact that the pressure on the forest was too considerable because of the enormous need for cropland, the consequence of very low-yield food production and the increase in population from the eleventh to the thirteenth century.

The French term *écobuage* (burn-beating) refers to a very specific technique described by several ancient writers. It would correspond to a revolution more rapid than the itinerant clearing. It is, in fact, a form of crop rotation with a fallow lasting several years. These different periodicities must have been adopted depending on the regions and the soils. *Écobuage*, writes Duhamel du Monceau in 1762, applies to "lands that are plowed only every eight or ten years." They are thus soils on which, in the meantime, the natural vegetation—generally coppice—is allowed to grow. Burn-beating was applied to periodic clearings very close to each other. It was a technique of clearings alternating with coppice of short revolution: between two burn-beatings, firewood, as well as grass around the young trees, was allowed to grow.

Burn-beating consists first of all of removing, by more-or-less important strips, the superficial layer of the ground with the grass and its roots. In the seventeenth and eighteenth centuries, this operation was done with specialized tools: *taille-pré* (in English, meadow-cutter), *hache à gazon* (a sort of axe for cutting lumps of earth and grass), *croissant* (crescent; a sort of heavy sickle) and *bêche* (a special form of spade).

Sometimes, several men, working in line, picked up very long strips of grass; this allowed the workers, with the same manpower, to treat an equal surface much quicker than it could be done by an individual worker. In several regions of France and in England, special plows were used to cut and detach the turf. In the Middle Ages, however, iron was scarce; people had to make do with all-purpose tools, less specialized and less efficient; on the other hand, with the hoe or the mattock one could more easily operate around the stumps that one wanted to keep to favor the new growth of shoots.

After drying the turf, "furnaces" were built by setting lumps of grass one against the other so as to constitute little truncated stacks. An opening was left on the side of the dominant wind and, in the center of the stack, a cavity that was filled with dry wood, straw, and brushwood. Then, the fire was lit. The combustion had to be constantly supervised so it would not be too hot or die out; and wherever flames came out too strongly the outside shell had to be covered again with turf. The fire was maintained for at least twenty-four hours, until all the turf was reduced to powder.

The ashes were spread uniformly on the whole surface of the ground, and a little later the land was plowed. Millet, radishes or turnips were sowed if it was early enough in the season (June); in the fall, after plowing again, more deeply, a cereal was sowed. Depending on the regions, the whole operation was done in the spring or early summer. Normally, in this process, the ashes were spread on the ground from which the turf was taken, which maintained on site the soil's fertilizing elements. But sometimes, the ashes were used to fertilize other soils. In that case, this method of exploitation led to a progressive deterioration of the soil.

The farmers in the Middle Ages went on using fire techniques in agriculture for very valid reasons. They had noticed—which recent findings confirm—a high increase in the crops' yield—the quantity of seeds harvested from the same quantity of seeds sowed—during the first years after the treatment by fire (to the extent that there was no export of fertilizing matter). In conditions quite similar to those of France in the Middle Ages, nineteenth century Russia had seed yields of two to five for one in permanent fields and up to ten or twelve at the most. Forty to fifty for one are mentioned for a year or two, in fields that were burn-beaten, then returned to the forest. These figures seem exaggerated. It appears, nonetheless, that for a piece of ground cultivated temporarily for a year or two, and using fertilization by fire, the yield is considerably superior to that of a permanent field. If one uses average figures, let us say, three for one for the yield of the permanent fields, and thirty for one for a plot cultivated for two years out of twenty, the return would thus be the same, that is including a production of wood for fuel and other small uses.

It must also be added that labor was helped considerably by the fact that the farmers plowed in the depth of the ashes or in the ground loosened by the fire; this was very important, considering the weakness of the plowing equipment that the Middle Age farmer used.

From Clearing to Harvest

The use of fire did not solve the problem of felling the big trees when the clearing was in a primary or reconstituted forest and not in a forest degraded because it was periodically cultivated. For those big trees, a technique, still in use in developing countries with few resources, consists of killing them by cutting off the sap's circulation. Two principal methods are used: either lighting a sufficiently hot fire around the foot of the tree or making a peripheral cut. Both methods aim at stopping the circulation of the sap, which moves mostly in the superficial layers near the bark. These techniques, however, result only in making the tree fall much later and, if the trunks are very large, are not sufficient. So if one wants to clear rapidly, one has to cut down the tree.

The main tool, which goes back to the earliest times, is the axe or hatchet (in French, *cognée*). Handled by one man, it cuts deeply into the tree, causing splinters resulting from two successive blows at a slight angle and, step by step, makes it fall.

Another way to fell a tree—but especially easy to convert it—is to saw it, generally with a tool operated by two men, the "crosscut saw" (in French, *passe-partout*). The period that we are interested in is the one in which the use of the saw was developed and although the saw was used more for wood conversion than for forest work, it nonetheless had consequences "upstream" on the forest itself.

The billhook, of which many different forms exist, one- or two-edged, was a tool adapted to clearing and used mainly to cut away the branches. It was also used to cut trees of small diameter. Of general use, but not useful as a weapon—contrary to the axe—it was even part of the official panoply of certain clearing monastic orders. The billhook was sufficient in the coppice and could be used to shape stakes and vineprops that were very important products for farming in the Middle Ages.

However, neither fire nor axe eliminated the tree stumps which were deeply rooted in the ground; they hindered cultivation. This nuisance was, however, acceptable if only temporary farming was planned. In this case one of the products expected during the interval between the crops was firewood and the trees came back more rapidly if the stumps remained (even stumps that have been exposed to fire produce shoots). On the other hand, to create permanent fields, it was worthwhile to clear the ground of the stumps. To do so, either the farmer had to use oxen or horses to pull the stumps out; or he had to dig very deep all around the stumps in order to remove them.

The operation that followed was to plow the clearing, sometimes simply by hand with wooden hoes, iron-strengthened spades or mattocks, and sometimes with a plow. The plows suited to this work were generally sowing plows without wheels, or else equipped with a small single axial wheel; indeed, this type of sowing equipment allows the farmer to plow between the stumps more easily than with the two-wheeled plow and to move on uneven ground. It has been noticed that where clearing remained a constant practice, as in Canada, the use of the plow with wheels developed slowly.

However, one of the advantages of clearing by fire was that, quite often, it wasn't necessary to plow. The seeds started directly in the layer of ashes and drove their roots into the ground below, cracked and loosened by the effect of the heat.[13] Thus it was an extremely economical process at a time when manpower was overworked and poorly fed and the tools rare and not very effective. In the United States, in New Hampshire in the early nineteenth century, thirteen to nineteen hundredweights (*quintaux*) of wheat to the hectare were obtained that way without any plowing. But that was in a primary or reconstituted forest or in places where the coppice, particularly dense, produced abundant ashes.

Next, cereals were sowed, of a species corresponding to the soil and the climate; it was often started with rye. The seeds were covered by dragging branches on the ground or with a harrow, an instrument that appeared in the eleventh century and that is represented on an embroidered tapestry called *Tapisserie de Bayeux*, which relates the history of the conquest of England in 1066. Originally, the harrow didn't include any metal parts. In certain regions of France, such as Brittany, it was only at the end of the nineteenth century that harrows with metal teeth appeared. Until then, the harrow was made entirely of wood; some of them can still be seen in France.

The harvesting tool of Middle Ages—as with most ancient people—was the sickle, often a serrated sickle with which one "sawed" the stalks; a model of one is displayed in the Abbeydale Industrial Museum in England. Cereals were cut just below the heads leaving the stalks. Indeed, on the temporary clearings where the stumps were left, only the sickle was easy to use. The scythe, that is represented in certain miniatures, appeared in the thirteenth century, but in certain parts of Brittany, it began to be used only in the twentieth century. Anyway, it was an instrument to harvest hay, not cereal. The animals brought to the fields after the harvest ate the stubble that remained, thus preparing the ground for plowing. Their droppings fertilized the soil, a very logical process.

Temporary crops allowed the farmer, by alternation, to also obtain wood on the same piece of land. Certain authors estimate that the wood production was identical to that of the permanent forest: the two years of crops were thus "stolen" from the forest without reducing its production. This might have been true for firewood; however, for lumber that requires much bigger trees, the consequences of the system—added to the suppression of forests by conversion into permanent fields—were disastrous.

From the point of view of subsistence requirements, the substitution of temporary cultivation for permanent cultivation (for which the yield was low due to lack of fertilizer, plowing, efficient harrowing, and rational crop rotation) was a solution that, while certainly requiring less work, was well suited to the agricultural tools and farming means that were available. It went along with, a collective land tenure, but that corresponded to the ways and means of the period's stock breeding, essentially based on the use of the forests and the right to use common land. One should not forget, however, that the process of temporary fields required a surface ten to twenty times more important than that of permanent fields. If the greater part of the land had been maintained in rationally organized permanent forests it would have provided more ligneous matter, while the fraction of land permanently farmed would have also given, with rational crop rotation and fertilization methods, a higher yield and thus higher production; but such methods of intensive agriculture did not correspond to the possibilities, knowledge, and organization of the society of the period.

Under normal and cautious operating conditions, clearing by fire and burn-beating did not exhaust or deplete the soil, but such was not the case with the other farming methods, in which what was taken from the forest was transferred elsewhere without compensation; *effeuillage, ébranchage, émondage, soutrage, étrépage* were the French names referring to the different techniques of taking forest products for the benefit of cultivation or breeding and that included thinning out the leaves, stripping, pruning, and clearing the undergrowth. We will examine them in another chapter.

The Threatened Forest

The farmers of the Middle Ages endeavored above all to obtain cereal crops, the traditional basis of food. The rest, except for meat— seldom present at the peasant's table—was only *companagium*, garnish for the bread. When new lands were cleared, whether temporarily or permanently, it was almost inevitable that cereals would be planted and, generally, two years in a row when it was in temporary clearings, which were later returned to the forest. Yet, cereals are less qualified than legumes to be planted first on soils reclaimed from the forest, particularly if these have been cleared by fire.

Recent research has shown that on burned forest grounds, especially of pines or firs, it is advisable to plant legumes such as beans, peas, broad beans, or lentils, to reconstitute the soil's nitrogen that these species fix due to the bacteria that live in their roots' nodules.[14] As early as Charlemagne's reign, there are traces of the use of a three-field system including, successively, cultivation of plants such as beans, cultivation of a winter cereal, and fallow land. It can be noted that the farmers had observed the advantages of planting leguminous species first on the soil of burn-beaten land.

However, the agricultural progress that started during the Carolingian period was able to bear fruit and continue two centuries later only after the end of the invasions of the ninth-eleventh centuries. At the same time the weather had become more favorable. Thus, from the eleventh century onward, it became possible once again to improve the methods, the techniques, and the material used, and to apply the peasants' empirical knowledge.

The effectiveness of fertilization by fire had been so well recognized that there now existed a trade in ashes as fertilizer. However, at a time when soap did not exist, ashes were also sold as detergent. This double outlet created an additional risk everywhere of depleting the forests' soils. The authorities worried about it. Later, in the seventeenth century, they tried to forbid clearing by fire, a technique that was the fruit of centuries of experience but had become impracticable in general. The population growth from the eleventh to the thirteenth century entailed an increasing need for cropland. The cleared grounds were more and more often converted into permanent fields in which fertility had to be maintained by new methods—rotation of the crops, fertilizer, ameliorators—and so the forest dwindled.

Clearing by fire and burn-beating, practiced at sufficiently long intervals and to the extent that the fertilizing residues were not exported and used elsewhere, maintained a degraded forest but did not necessarily deplete the soil. Furthermore, a measure of fertilizing matter was brought by the droppings of the animals that were introduced into the fields after the harvest; in the meantime, almost everywhere, the animals found their food in the forest itself. To the extent that this grazing was limited, organized, and controlled, it did not prevent the forest's regeneration. However, the balance between forest and clearing, as well as the balance between forest and grazing was fragile.

Then again, the periodic revolution of the forest, corresponding to the temporary clearings, favored certain species, such as alder and birch, since these "pioneering" species can develop in open space. This process also favored oak that was exploited for its bark, which was used for tanning. It was especially to obtain more oak coppice that clearing by fire was used until quite recently in certain areas.

In all places where the demand for firewood and charcoal increased, especially near the towns and in the vicinity of industries using wood—mills, forges, glassmaking, pottery, lime and plaster kilns, mines and salt works—the coppices were inevitably overexploited. From then on (and it was due more to the coppice exploitation than to the process of clearing or the practice of forest pasture) the forest deteriorated because the exports were not compensated for by imports. Clearings became permanent. Acidophilic species multiplied. The moor gained little by little. If the exploitation was not interrupted, the soil's degradation increased, particularly in poorly irrigated regions and on slopes.

On such lands, the brutal denudation provoked by uncontrolled fire can have catastrophic consequences. In the United States, after the fire of pine forests, the quantity of sediments removed in a very short time by erosion has been estimated at forty tons per hectare (one hectare = 2.47 acres)—that is, a uniform depth of three to four centimeters (1¼″ to 1½″). In the southeast of France, the evolution, although slower in general, has had similar results: the gullied lands of the Dévoluy, the Hautes-Alpes, the haut Languedoc and the haute Provence are evidence of it. But there, during all of the Middle Ages, overgrazing more than fire contributed to the soil erosion.

However, with the population increase from the eleventh to the thirteenth century, the forest was no longer the inexhaustible and forever available reserve of cropland that it had been until then. Temporary cultivation gave way to permanent fields and the crop yield suffered from it. The progress of agricultural techniques allowed yet only modest yield increases, mainly due to crop-rotation methods avoiding long fallow periods. It was the beginning of a slow and very progressive improvement that was marked by the work of the sixteenth century agronomists, the eighteenth century physiocrats, and ended with twentieth century high-yield agriculture, mechanized, industrialized, specialized, and artificialized with all the new environmental problems it creates.

The period corresponding to the bloom of Gothic architecture is particularly important for the study of the forest: it is a turning point when the forest faced with an increasing population revealed its limits, when agriculture started to change, and when sylviculture started to be conceived of as a specialization of the land, the cultivation of trees. The forest progressively ceased to be that area intimately linked to the agricultural and pastoral cycles, producer of food for men and animals, provider of animal proteins as well as source of wood, fuel, and miscellaneous materials that it had been.

Forest Tools

The evolution of tools is an important factor in the history of the forest in the Middle Ages, especially for the felling and converting of trees. The tools and the different means used for clearing the ground are really part of agriculture, and are examined in the corresponding chapter.

In this transitional period—the centuries following the year 1000—the development of the use of saws considerably increased man's impact on the forest and the consumption of wood; in particular, the use of mechanical saws, driven by hydraulic force, transformed the conversion and, especially, lengthwise sawing. It can be noticed, for example, in the evolution of frameworks from the twelfth to the sixteenth century.

One must examine at which phases of the woodwork, and how and for what reasons this introduction and diffusion of the saw occurred and what the causes were.

> • *The introduction of the saw in forest work was a revolutionary innovation. For over six thousand years, man had used a single tool: the axe. His resistance to the use of a new tool is thus understandable.*[15] •

It is difficult to agree entirely with Killian's statement, especially when one has used—and sharpened—a crosscut saw, at a time when there was not even a thought of motorizing anything—let alone chain saws. The very late adoption of the saw for forest work, differing sometimes by several centuries in certain regions, appears to have more complex and subtle reasons. An innovation that solves multiple existing problems by giving a clear advantage over what has preceded always imposes itself. However, all the conditions and constraints of the time must be considered.

The saw's principle—a thin serrated blade, attacking the material to be cut by the impact of successive sharp ridges in a movement to and fro—is perhaps as ancient as that of the axe. As early as the Neolithic Age, man used serrated knives functioning like saws.

Applying a totally different principle, the axe is a bludgeon, armed with a heavy and cutting edge.

The saw—like the file, its child—has always been a pacific instrument, though sometimes used as an instrument of torture. The axe, by contrast—like the knife, head of a entirely different line, that works by slashing but also by thrusting—owes its success, mainly, to its versatility. It was used as both a weapon and a tool, and was perfected because of its military uses. In a thousand years its shape has changed little. The axe's effectiveness is due to the use of centrifugal force that augments man's effort; the instrument is thus certainly related to the hammer, the hoe, and the pickaxe but also to the sling. The axe is an imprisoned sling: it does not get away from the hand of the thrower who can repeat his blow.

The saw is the tool of patience, of detailed and precise work. Among primitive people, it is often the women's tool. It is with the saw that the hardest materials are finally conquered. It is the tool that allows one to "trick" the material. Indeed, the sickle was for thousands of years a bent saw, related to the one still used, concurrently with the billhook, by pruners and which the Germans call a "fox tail." The sickle of the Middle Ages illustrated in some miniatures was most often serrated as a saw. "The peasant," writes Marc Bloch,[16] "assembling the cereal heads in the other hand, saws the wheat." He adds: "It is only by a comparison of the act of the wood sawer with that of the sickle handler that the [French] verb *scier*, which comes from the Latin "secare" (to cut), has taken its present meaning."

The oldest reproductions of saws are Egyptian. The Bible mentions the use of saws in the construction of the temple of Solomon. The Romans' frame saws were identical to those represented in some of the manuscripts from the Middle Ages. They were carpenters', not foresters', tools. It is interesting to note that one of the oldest reproductions of a saw in a Middle Ages document—where they are relatively rare—shows the cutting of a stone. This miniature, from an eleventh century manuscript, comes from the library of Mount Cassin and shows two workmen cutting a slab of marble with a tenon saw very similar to today's saws.[17]

Different kinds of saws are illustrated in the miniatures. In the "Biblica pauperum" (thirteenth century), a saw is used to cut a tree; it is a representation of the martyrdom of Isaac who, according to the legend, was sawed while he was inside the hollow tree in which he had found shelter. This seems to indicate that in the thirteenth century saws were sometimes used to fell—or at least to convert—trees. In the psalm book of the duke of Berry, for the martyrdom of the apostle Simon Zelote, it's a crosscut saw that is represented. On the other hand, it is a saw shaped like a strung bow, similar to modern metal saws, that is represented in the scene of the martyrdom of Ysias in the Lambeth Bible.

Looking for saw reproductions in Middle Ages documents, one finds mostly scenes of martyrdoms (Isaac, Simon Zelote, Julie of Tarse). In scenes of work yards or forests, it is unusual to see any illustrations of saws before a very late period. On a fifteenth century miniature, two carpenters are shown using a tenon saw; the scene represents the construction of a war machine at the time of the siege of Jerusalem by the Crusaders.[18] However, because it was painted three centuries later, this miniature might contain anachronisms.

For forest work, it is certain that the adoption of the saw was slow throughout Europe, with differences depending on the regions. In certain countries, saws became known only at the end of the seventeenth century: thus, in Russia, it is only in 1691 that the czar, Peter the Great, authorized German experts to establish the first mechanical sawmills on the Dvina River. "Until then," writes Ljubomirov,[19] "the word saw itself didn't exist in that country."

In western Europe, the development of saws was made possible by the development of metallurgy—initiated by the armaments industry. The alloys and the methods of hardening metal and manufacturing weapons had already been perfected through exchanges with the Moslem world. That is how the recipe of the famous "Damas steel"—which, in reality, originated from Indian techniques—reached the West. During the twelfth century, iron mills dragging "trip-hammers" became common in Europe. The first known examples are in Catalonia—at the limits of the Moslem world—in 1104,[20] then in 1116, at Issoudun, in the center of France,[21] and finally in Sweden—on the other side of Europe—in 1192.[22]

Thanks to the development of metallurgy, the coats of mail, the helmets, and the heavy breast plates were replaced by lighter and more resistant armor made of large, articulated steel shells. It also became easier to make ribbons of sheet steel which was thin, supple, and strong, with strictly parallel sides, and suited to the manufacturing of saws, which were difficult to make by hand. Before the end of the Middle Ages rolling mills appeared, the first of which are mentioned during the second part of the fifteenth century.

The art of forging for a very long time remained without important modifications: "The smith's tools of fifty years ago," wrote Albert Hugues in 1935, "were not very different from what is described in an inventory of 1442." Indeed, the inventory of village forges, started in 1935—and of which Lucien Febvre rendered an account in the *Annales*—includes no saws, while all the other usual tools are included. Also in the list of what was made or repaired by a village smith in the middle of the twentieth century in Catalonia, there are plowshares, horseshoes, wedges, pickaxes, spades, billhooks, hooks, rings and chains, pliers and hammers as well as axe heads,[23] but no saws.

The saw not only requires a particular quality of steel—it needs to be at once supple and resistant—but it also requires a method of cutting and sharpening the teeth. For tools, in general, it is by a stone sharpening that one obtains a sharp and lasting edge without weakening the metal; that is how knives, axes, billhooks, scissors, scythes, and sickles are sharpened—but the saw must be cut and maintained with a file. Furthermore, one must also be able to set it, which consists of slightly and alternately bending to one side and the other the successive teeth in relation to the blade's plane to avoid getting the saw stuck in the wood and to facilitate the removal of the sawdust during its use. Thus the saw's teeth must, in addition to the various qualities required, be able to sustain this torsion without damage.

A saw is also fragile: a broken tooth is difficult to repair, even by a smith, while a good axe head cannot break and any logger knows how to repair—with a sharpening stone—a small jaggedness in the cutting edge. Thus, in the Middle Ages, the saw appeared as an instrument that was not very rustic, required delicate maintenance, and was better suited to the skills of the cabinetmaker, the surgeon or the carpenter than to the work of the logger.

In addition, the saw required for its manufacture three layers of metal, including a center layer which used a different quality of steel than that used for the two faces. It was produced on a small scale and, notwithstanding the development of metallurgy, was much more costly than the axe. It remained so until the twentieth century. In 1820, a saw still cost six times more than an axe.[24]

The saw is almost irreplaceable for sawing lengthwise; it is work very different from that of the logger and it is convenient for cutting tree trunks sideways without wasting wood. But, generally, lumber wasn't sawed or converted on its original site; it was dispatched in big pieces, either floated or drawn by horses. Thus, in the forest, the saw lost one of its main advantages.

However, the saw was indispensable for the mechanization made possible by the use of hydraulic power, as soon as it was discovered how to change the circular movement of the water-powered wheels into a reciprocating movement. In the thirteenth century, in his sketch book, Villard de Honnecourt designed a saw for cutting wooden piles under water; on another page, he shows a mechanical saw for cutting lengthwise, with a device that automatically advances the wood.

Mechanical saws, propelled by water power, developed rapidly. But such sawmill equipment required the investment of large amounts of capital and thus belonged to rich people. Peasants and woodsmen could use them only against payment; and when they were working for themselves, they had no reason to bring their wood there. Individuals needed either firewood or, from time to time, lumber for construction. Firewood usually is of small diameter and thus easy to cut with an axe. Lumber generally did not need to be resplit or resawed lengthwise, because one simply chose trees with a trunk size corresponding to what was needed.

Once hydraulic saws had been developed, their owners were sometimes accused of being responsible for the deforestation of certain regions, because they produced a much higher yield than work done by hand. In some situations, their use was even forbidden. Thus, in the southern Alps, at the end of the thirteenth century, the consuls of Colmars (south of the Allos Pass) ordered that the hydraulic saws be destroyed; the order was carried out. But the chronicle mentions that, following this action, the poor people, armed with handsaws, invaded the woods and caused much more damage than had been done earlier.

Handsaws were sought because they were tools that could be used in relative silence, and thus were very useful for smugglers and clandestine woodcutters who could not work with an axe without being heard from very far away. This particularity also interested the military: for the sappers who dug and buttressed the mining tunnels with wooden posts and crossbars, silence was essential; so not surprisingly it is in the hands of military carpenters that saws are represented. However, it is one of the reasons why in the forest, the use of a saw was in many places considered an aggravating circumstance in case of offense or as presumption of bad intentions. Thus, the *Eschiquier des Eaux et Forêts* held in Rouen on October 8, 1402 specified concerning the use of the saw in the forest: "Although the use of the saw is generally forbidden to all free users who take delivery of wood marked by the forester, they will be allowed, after delivery, to cut their wood with a saw as long as it was first cut with an axe."[25]

It must also be noted that farmers and foresters consider that cutting branches with a saw compromises the new growth; and that, for hardwoods, which grow back from the stump, cutting the trunk with a saw prevents the shoots from developing and may sometimes provoke the rotting and death of the remaining tree. With an axe, one can "round off" the cut and "smooth" it to protect the stump against water infiltration and rot. Furthermore, forest operators, who employed workmen, thought that there was nothing to gain by using a saw to cut down trees. The crosscut saw was operated by two men who didn't do more work in one day than a single logger using an axe. And, with wet wood, the axe worked much faster than the saw, because sawdust sticks to the saw's teeth and "stuffs it."

Thus everything converged to limit the use of the saw in the forest: the force of habit, the difficulties of manufacturing, maintaining, and repairing saws, their fragility and cost, the fear of smugglers, the preoccupation with the conservation of good trees and also, rightly or wrongly, the manpower economy.

Of Words And Things: Essartage, Écobuage, Rotures, Novales

Etymologists generally attribute the origin of the French word *essart* to the Latin verb *sarrire*. For other authors, *essart* and *sart* (term used in the Ardennes and in Belgium) would derive from *serere* (to plant). But the supine from which derived nouns are formed would be in the first case *sarritum* and in the second *satum* (irregular verb). One could also have thought about the verb *exarare*, which means to dig out while plowing and could evoke the uprooting of stumps, but the supine is *exaratum* just as distant from *essart* as *sarritum* and *satum*. So these hypotheses appear unreliable.

However, in certain acts the spelling *exarsia* is used to designate the *essarts* and elsewhere there is the spelling *exsart*. And indeed, the word *exarsus*, past participle meaning "burned" (from the verb *exardescere*) is noted by Gaffiot in the Justinian Code.

So we think that the most probable etymology, which the words *exarsia* or *exsarts* appear to confirm, would signify land cleared by fire. Indeed, the French people of the Middle Ages used the verb *ardre* (in modern French, *ardeur*) and the past participle *ars* meaning "burned" (Joan of Arc was *arse*). At a time when the feeble existing resources made fire the efficient auxiliary used everywhere, it seems logical that to clear the ground men thought of fire. And the word *artigue*, which in the southwest refers to an *essart* and which is as usual in the toponymy of the Bordelais as the *essarts* are in the Parisian basin, also evokes fire. Indeed, Higounet mentions among the names of the oldest *artigues*, Chartigat, specifying that the original name was Exartigas. Furthermore, in Wallonie, a similar word has been noted, *artiwe*, an old Walloon word that gave *arti* (*artu* in the Ardennes, near Liège).[26]

As for the *sarts* of the northeast that gave the qualifier for the *frères sartaires* (clearing friars), the word might be an alteration of the word *sors* (plural: *sortes*) that referred to a parcel of land given to a farmer by lot (in French, *par tirage au sort*) when the forest was cleared, particularly in cases of temporary clearings. There might have been some confusion in the popular language between *sart* and *sort* and perhaps also a little confusion with the Latin word *saltus*, which described a degraded forest where sometimes fields were cultivated and at other times cattle grazed.

Etymologists do not seem to have given much thought to the origin of the word *écobuer* which, however, intrigued Littré (and which in certain regions is said *égobuer*). In old French, *buer* meant "washing clothes" (of which the French word *buanderie*) and, in the sixteenth century, *buée* meant vapor. There is thus an idea of fire and of vapor—such as that released by the humid turf burning. The beginning of the word might come from *écot* meaning twig or shoot—it's a rather frequent word in place names—and that served to form the construction word, still used today: *écoperche*, referring to a scaffolding pole. But it would be more natural to think of *écope*, a word still used by sailors, that comes from the Dutch word *schope* referring to a wooden shovel and parent of *chope* designating a measure of liquid or, as per Littré, to *escoube* (meaning a broom). John Sinclair in the early nineteenth century[27] translated into English the French term *écobue*, designating the tool used to peel the ground, by "cobbing hoe." There is, however, no trace of a verb "to cob" in English, but the word "cob" refers to the mixture of hacked dirt and straw called *pisé* in French and is reminiscent of several French words such as *gobetis* (rough coating), *engober* (to cover pottery with a layer of clay), *gobelet* (little clay vase), etc. *Ecobuer* or *égobuer* would thus link the sense of working the ground, of shoveling, of picking up dirt as with an *écope*, and evoke the vapor or smoke that would have impregnated the end of the word: considering how easily popular language is influenced by consonance analogies, this hypothesis has nothing that could be deemed unlikely.

Other terms that seem, specifically, to designate certain operations can be found in the texts relative to land clearing. *Ruptitia* is a plural noun derived from the Latin verb *rumpere*: to make a breach in the forest in order to create a road (*rupta*) or to build a house or establish a cultivated area. The French words *route, routier, routine, roture,* and *roturier* have the same root. *Roturier* originally meant the person to whom had been granted (for rent) a lot to clear (*ruptura* in Latin from which *roture* in French); and, finally, any man subjected to dues to the lord, thus any non-noble. It is also a word that came out of the forest.

Extirpare, which is often found in ancient texts, means to pull from the ground, to extirpate, to take out the stumps and also seems to apply to permanent clearings (or planned as such), which included rooting out the stumps.

Novale (plural: *novalia*), a noun already used by Virgil, refers to a piece of land recently cultivated on a clearing (from the forest or not); taxes by the same name were applied to the *novalia* and they were generally not as high as similar taxes on older cultivated lands, so as to encourage continuation of the clearings.

4 · actors and phases of the clearing of the ground ·

Flux and Reflux of the Forest

ALL AGRICULTURE ORIGINATES FROM a clearing. At the end of the Roman Empire and following the great invasions that consummated its breaking up, wasteland and forest overtook the cultivated areas and once again the land had to be cleared. It would, however, be a simplistic and mistaken view to imagine, at the start, a romanized Gaul covered mainly by cultivated fields, brutally devastated by the barbarian invasions and returning to wasteland, then to forest. Quite the contrary, there was no lack of wasteland from the Late Empire on.

The vast Roman Empire, with its decreasing population, was a tempting prey, an available space. In particular, facing the demographic pressure of the people of Germania—themselves driven by invaders, such as the Huns, coming from central Asia—Gaul appeared as a rich land, relatively devoid of men, a land to be taken.

It has been noted that certain Merovingian sites, for example, between the Seine and the Oise rivers, were five to six times more populated than the Gallo-Roman hamlets that they had replaced.

Then again, it has been established that many of the clearings made during the Early Empire, which had favored the constitution of huge estates of two thousand to four thousand hectares (one hectare = 2.47 acres), were reoccupied by the forest as early as the third century, long before the invasions, while the inhabitants were concentrated in urban centers. In other places, it was during the fifth century that the estates were abandoned and returned to wasteland. Such was the case of the estate of Fontaine-Valmont that was once again cultivated in the sixth century after clearing; all the Roman buildings were destroyed and their sites planted. Whether it preceded or followed the invasions of the fifth century, it is to this "return to the earth" of many Gallo-Roman buildings, that we owe startling aerial photographs. As the ruins were covered by fields, meadows or forests, the plants grew differently on the different parts of the area and reconstitute today the detailed plan of buildings and agglomerations that disappeared fifteen centuries ago.

The new occupants had to develop new cropland in order to feed the population. Between the Merovingian and the Carolingian period, many clearings occurred and the forests were substantially reduced. Thus, the region of Palaiseau, for the most part covered by the huge Yveline forest in the sixth century, included by the time of the Carolingians—as it is described in the polyptych of the abbot Irminon—only about thirty hectares of woods.

To the extent of their needs in cropland, the Carolingians worked hard at making the cultivated clearings permanent and at redeveloping the ancient Gallo-Roman estates. The forest had an important place in the economy of an estate and the king made sure it wasn't reduced. In the capitulary *De Villis* it is prescribed to the prince's agents that "if there are spaces to clear, they are to have them cleared but they are not to allow the fields to increase to the detriment of the forest," which seems to indicate that these instructions concerned temporary and itinerant clearings that did not reduce the surface of the woods if they were cleared only at long intervals of time and for a few years.

In the ninth and tenth centuries the population appears to have remained stationary and the clearings became rare. It is only in the second part of the tenth century, when the invasions stopped—

particularly the repeated Norman incursions—that the agricultural clearings started anew, induced by the population increase.

Monks have been credited with a leading role in the clearings; it is mostly due to the fact that ancient writings bear testimony to it, which is not the case with the modest, but certainly countless peasant clearings, that most history does not mention.

Squatters, Hermits, Friars, and Saracens

Many conversions from waste or woods to cropland are known to us by documents. But it is evident that everywhere most peasants who tried to increase the surface that they cultivated to improve their living conditions did so secretly or irregularly, either by cultivating a clearing located deep in the woods where the peasant hoped he would not be noticed and would thus avoid the *champart, dîme or cens,** or by nibbling away at the edge of the forest, a feat which could remain unnoticed.

By contrast to the repression in matters of hunting offenses that was often ferocious, in most cases for this type of violation, the offender was merely liable to a fine and then had to pay the usual taxes. The lord, having avoided the cost of settling colonists, was content with the benefit of the increase in value created—or at least expected. The profit from the dues that he levied on the forests' products was not negligible, but it was certainly easier to supervise and collect taxes on agricultural products in open areas, where the harvest comes at more-or-less fixed periods, than to control what was happening deep in the forest. The archives mention countless reports, lawsuits, and miscellaneous conflicts regarding the use of the forests: the forest guards had much to do to track down and fine all the offenders and the charters included many clauses specifying the rights and sanctions in this matter.

Documents allude to the irregular clearings—what today would be called squatters' actions (which corresponds exactly to the original meaning of the English word). For the Early Middle Ages, S. Lefèvre,

◆ ◆ ◆

Champart, dîme: dues in kind, fixed or proportionate to the harvest; *cens*: tax paid either on a personal basis or for a piece of land farmed by a commoner.

who studied the archives of the Ile-de-France, notes that there are few references: "The clearings already made are tacitly acknowledged and the authorities just try to limit them for the future."[1]

During the tenth century, King Hughes Capet, who had built the castle of Saint-Léger in Yveline, assembled in the village of Essarts-le-Roi all the clearers dispersed in the Yveline forest. He probably wished to bring some order to their disjointed initiatives and also facilitate the tax collectors' task. References to irregular clearings became increasingly numerous later on; a few significant examples can be cited.

Often the lords didn't even know if their woods had been cleared or not. In the foundation charter of the town of Givry in Argonne (thirteenth century), the following formula is included: *Si forte alia nemora mea eis jam concessa extirparentur*, that is, "if it so happens that my other woods already granted to them, have been cleared. . . ."[2]

As it was impossible to control or to stop the movement, the authorities were realistic. In a 1025 ruling at Rozay-en-Brie, the collection of the *cens* was authorized if the forest was cleared with the consent of the canons of Notre-Dame de Paris, who owned the forest, or fines in the contrary case; thus the offense was foreseen and the fine established in advance. One is led to believe that the case was not unusual. We mentioned in the description of the clearing techniques that, in 1116, Louis VI endorsed—after the fact —clearings made south of the Dourdan forest. Likewise, in 1171, the count of Champagne recognized—to the abbey of Cheminon— the ownership of a field that had been cleared by the inhabitants of Maurupt, who apparently had no right to it.[3] Accused of having cleared without paying the taxes, the inhabitants of Sainte-Mene-hould gave the excuse that it was only "mean coppice and ugly bushes" that they had thus developed.[4]

The peasants were not the only ones to clear irregularly. The chapter of Notre-Dame-de-Paris having made clearings without the authorization of Gaucher de Chatillon on lands situated between les Noues and Montjay, Gaucher, in 1204, endorsed the offense. As for the nobles, they did not hesitate to encroach on lands that did not belong to them.

In addition to the farmers' often secret initiatives on the fringes of the cultivated territories or in remote places—and of which the

Early Middle Ages history has maintained almost no traces in the documents—the first clearings mentioned by local tradition and by a few texts are the work of the hermits, "the only men of God," according to Duby, "who, with their own hands, participated efficiently in attacking the wasteland, and who cut down trees and opened up new fields."

Clearings are frequently mentioned in the lives of saints and hermits: Saint Fiacre is given credit for the clearing of a forest in the Brie, Saint Diel of a canton of the Lure forest, in the Vosges. The hermit Raoul said "de la Futaye" settled in the forest of Saint-Sulpice near Rennes in the canton of Nid-de-Merle, which is today mostly deforested. Another hermit, Salomon, settled in the forest of Nid d'Oiseau near the Oudon River; Renaud chose the forest of Mélinais south of La Flèche; André took, as a retreat, the forest of Chaussière, at the edge of Anjou and Brittany, and Engelger chose the forest of Fougères. Meanwhile, other disciples of Robert d'Arbrissel took "as theater of their ascetism"[5] the Concise forest, northeast of the one of Fougères. But as many of these hermits acquired a following, they stopped living alone and created small abbeys. Robert d'Arbrissel, who had retired to the forest of Craon, found himself surrounded by so many disciples that he had to send them into other forests, after which they gathered in colonies and founded new abbeys. Vital de Mortain, disciple of Robert d'Arbrissel, dispersed his companions in the forest of Fougères, until the lord who owned the forest, Raoul de Fougères, wishing finally to recover it for hunting, settled the question by giving another forest to the hermits, the forest of Savigny, where they founded an abbey by the same name.

The romances of the period mention the presence of these loners in the forests. Thus in Tristan: "One day they chanced upon a little house set on the side of a dale; there lived brother Ogrin, the hermit." It is this friar, whom life in Nature appears to have made more indulgent to sin who will advise Tristan to lie to the king, so that he will take back his queen by saying that he did not make love to her.

While the hermits didn't fear handling the axe or the spade, the monks of the great orders, in particular the Benedictines and—except at their beginning—the Cistercians, did not particularly make it a rule to work with their hands; according to Duby, they gladly accepted lands with men donated to farm them. Nonetheless, whatever the hands working the soil, the monasteries certainly played a role in the clearings. The Order of Cluny alone included 1,184 monasteries in France in the early twelfth century and the Cistercian Order founded 694 abbeys. So, by their mere number and even though they sometimes favored breeding—since they still had to have some fields around their establishments—the monasteries certainly had an important impact on the forests.

The Order of Cîteaux was founded at the end of the eleventh century (1098) by Robert de Molesmes. With Saint Bernard, he tried to revive manual labor, which was considered a penance, a consequence of original sin. More preoccupied with asceticism than the Clunisians, the Cistercians made it a duty to perform manual labor, at least for half a century, or as long as Saint Bernard lived. Quickly, however, they returned to their primary mission of prayer and study, leaving the hard labor to others more suited to working with their hands.

Generally, monastic orders initiated the development of wastelands or forests by building an isolated farm or a small group of dwellings, including everything necessary for exploitation of the land. It was called the *granche* or *grange*. Hospites (in French, *hôtes*) settled there and their first mission was the clearing of the land. Sometimes there were loggers, pruners, rooters, and specialized clearers who went from place to place as their services were required. However, the term *hôtes* is used rather to designate those who became sedentary once the clearing was accomplished and settled down to farm in the *hostise*.

The status of the hospites must have varied widely depending on the cases and the periods: serfs, free men, farm hands, farmers, holders, enjoying more-or-less freedom, subjected to more-or-less taxes. On their own estates, the nobles used the same methods to develop wasteland and forests.

The monks started a system that appeared to be more interesting for them, a system of direct valorization by men specializing in manual labor, but who were subject to the monastic discipline and rule: the lay brothers (in French, *frères convers*). The institution of the lay brothers allowed the altar monks to devote themselves more fully to prayer and study, once again forsaking manual labor. The lay brothers, second-class monks who had much less religious education and fewer obligations, constituted the manpower for heavy labor and had the advantage over the hospites of not having a family to feed. All the trades were represented among the lay brothers: in addition to farmers, there were masons, fishermen, weavers, cobblers, tanners, bakers, fullers, and smiths.

Thus, in search of greater efficiency and higher profits, the monks, good managers, left to professionals the manual, arduous or specialized work. Altar monks brought their contribution, if necessary, only during extremely busy periods—grape and cereal harvests—when all the available labor had to be recruited to accomplish the work as quickly as possible and when it must not have been a bad thing for the friars to mix with the laborers in order to supervise them and maintain the rhythm, while mortifying themselves by performing manual labor.

Apparently this system of direct valorization by lay brothers—which appeared at first to present many advantages—was not always profitable, and, sometimes, monasteries returned to the leasing system. In an act of 1324, it appears that the provost responsible for the administration of a monastery, who, until then, had had a farm cultivated by his lay brothers—"since the method was very disadvantageous and since, as a faithful administrator, he wanted prosperity and the greatest profit for his monastery"—decided to lease the farm to two peasants against the payment of fixed rent and a portion of the fruits and animals.

Even if monastic orders often protected wooded areas because they wanted the isolation provided by the screen of forests, the fact that many abbeys were located in places from which the forest has partially or completely disappeared, shows that they were responsible, directly or indirectly, for important deforestations in the surrounding areas.

"You will find more in the forests than in the books," wrote Saint Bernard, "the trees and the rocks will teach you things that no master will tell you." Cistercians, Premonstrants and Carthusians chose to settle in the forests.

For a long time, history textbooks maintained and spread the stereotyped image of the monks as destroyers of the forest in the name of civilization and agriculture; it was recalled that the panoply of the companions of Saint Colomban included a billhook, that the Teutonic Knights were called the "monks with the axe," that the Cistercians had purposefully created brothers responsible for the clearings called *"frères sartaires."* Then the tendency was to try to reduce the importance of the monks' role in the clearings by recalling that for centuries they were about the only ones who left written traces of acts and that, in fact, the role of the small peasants had been much more important.

To give a balanced view, one must admit that the monks understood the essential place and function of the forests in the economy of that period and, for that reason, effectively contributed to maintaining some of them.

But one should not go to the other extreme and neglect their role in the reduction of wooded areas. First, it is probable that when nobles transferred certain land to a monastery, they granted or bequeathed more readily forests that still needed to be developed and cleared rather than lands already cultivated, developed, and maintained. In all the provinces, religious establishments, abbeys, priories, monasteries, and convents settled in wooded sectors contributed to thinning the timberland, whether by clearing certain parts, by the simple result of the grazing practice—one of the main uses of the forest—or by the development of villages in the vicinity of their abbeys.

All through western Europe, many abbeys attracted around them agglomerations, which sometimes became important towns. In England, where urbanization came later, many of the cathedrals are ancient abbeys; while, in France, it is already existing towns that became the episcopal dioceses. In particular, when those monasteries, which often were depositories of relics, became centers of pilgrimages, it led to a commercial movement and the settlement of a permanent population. The necessities of providing for that population and its visitors, induced the development of a cultivated ring, perforce taken from the forests where the monks had originally settled. Many towns named after saints had such an origin.

Almost everywhere, one can notice the disappearance of forests near religious establishments, even if in many cases they prevented their total destruction.

In the southeast of France, writes Higounet, that region's specialist, the abbeys encouraged the clearings. The abbey of Moissac had the forest of Agre cleared. North of the Bordelais, the woods of Petit Angoumois were thinned out by the monks of Baignes and of Barbézieux. Some abbeys preferred to acquire lands already cleared, such as the abbey of Sauve Majeure in the Entre-Deux-Mers,

which nonetheless organized clearing operations in the Bagadais.
The settlement in the twelfth century of the Cistercians, the Premonstrants, and the Orders of Saint Jean de Jerusalem and of the
Temple brought about attacks on the forest, among other places near
the Cadouin, in the Bergeracois, near Faize, north of Libourne,
near Bonnefont more in the south, near Lescaledieu in the Bigorre,
near Berdoues and Gimont in the Gers.

In the Île-de-France, too, many clearings were initiated by abbeys.
For example, the abbey of the Premonstrants of Lieu-Restauré near
Crépy-en-Valois cleared a little forest granted by Saint-Médard-de-
Soissons. During the same period, the Coucy forest was cut in two
by the clearings of the Premonstrants. It was the canons of the abbey
of Chambrefontaine near Mongé who cleared the woods of Fontaine-
Doon near Dammartin-en-Goële and settled there in 1210. The
abbey of Chaalis made important clearings around the *grange* of
Vaulerent.

In the forests of the Orléanais, many religious establishments
were built in the woods, sometimes simple village churches such as
Saint-Germain, Saint-Vincent and Saint-Médard-de-Vitry, sometimes convents such as the priory of Ambert, the convent of Bucy
Saint-Liphard, the monastery of Flotin founded in 1169 and the
Benedictine house of Chappes-en-Bois founded in 1167 and confirmed in 1172 by donations from the king. The priories of Gué de
l'Orme and of la Coudre and the abbey of Viveret show evidence of
breaches and clearings in the forest. In 1140, Louis VII in a charter
in favor of the friars of la Coudre specifies that they may settle in
the forest, that they freely own the said territory and that they may
extirpare (clear) and *excolere* (cultivate) the cited grounds, to plant
cereals, vines or anything else. It is only later that, worried by the
extent of the forests' disappearances, the lords specified more frequently in their donations of forests that temporary or permanent
clearings were excluded from the rights granted to the monasteries.

All through France, the names of many abbeys evoke the old
forests that those establishments frequently contributed to reduce if
not to eliminate. Such abbeys can be found in all the provinces.
But often the qualifier *"Bois"* (wood) has disappeared from the toponymy at the same time as the forest. Thus, Sainte-Marie-du-Bois
(Ruisseauville), Silvamajor (Saint-Nicolas), Saint-André-au-Bois
(Saint-André-sur-la-Canche). Elsewhere, the original meaning of the
word has been forgotten. Thus the words *silva* and *salva* are confused

and the French term *sauve* doesn't evoke the original forest anymore. All the more since the existence of many *sauvetés* makes one associate more readily *sauve* to *salva* than to *silva*. But the names of Sauvelade, Sauvemajor, Sauvebone, Sauvestre, Sauvebénite, etc., refer to *silvalata, salvamajor, silvabona, silvestris, silvabenedicta*, etc.

Other names evoke dominant tree species, such as Belfail, Beaufay, Belfays, La Bussière, Haut Faget, etc. Some clearly recall their forest past, such as Forêt-Moutier, Marienwald, Sault (saltus), Bellebranche, Maubuisson, Silvanes, Boscodon, Grandselve, and Silvacane. Around most of these ancient abbeys, the only woods left are generally isolated spinneys, but stories sometimes bring back reminders of the ancient forests. It is the case, for example, of the "great forest," the "Saulve Majour" (sylva major) south of Bordeaux: completely cleared since it was granted to Saint Gérand by the duke of Aquitaine, Guillaume VI, it is said that it was so dense that "no one could get close to the church without cutting his way with a sword or an iron tool."[6]

The popes granted special privileges to monastic orders, specifying that they could not be tithed for their lands—even for the cleared parts. At the end of the twelfth century, the pope specified, for the order of Cîteaux, that no one should dare "exact or extort" tithes from the monks, even on the "novales," (that is, the fields created from clearings) "that they cultivated themselves, at their cost, and on which their animals grazed." In 1182 and in 1187, the same advantage was granted to the Benedictines.[7]

The case of the secular Church, which also encouraged the clearings, is often forgotten. Tithing all the cultivated land, including the recently cleared *novalia*, it was bound to encourage the farmers to clear the land and, sometimes, helped them settle. The case of the chapter of Notre-Dame-de-Paris, an important land owner and forest promoter in the Île-de-France, is only one example among numerous others. Furthermore, reducing the forests was the occasion to cut down or to "christianize" a few of those numerous sacred trees around which were maintained superstitions inherited from paganism that the Church had a hard time covering with a Christian varnish.

Some of the actors involved in the clearings have been, perhaps, too much forgotten: the Saracens who, stopped in 732 in Poitiers in their advance toward the northwest of France, went all the way to Burgundy by the Rhône Valley and remained in certain parts of southern France until 972. They are said to have cleared the forest on the left bank of the Saône, between Burgundy and Franche-Comté, which became very productive lands.[8] It is likely that in the more southern territories, where they remained for a long time, they not only introduced new species (in particular, saracen corn—buckwheat), irrigation methods, construction techniques (Saracen tiles and Saracen stairways), and stock breeding habits, but also developed lands taken from the forests.

Protected Zones and Clearings

The French words *défens, garennes, forêts, haies*, and *banbois* were terms used to designate zones, generally covered by woods, that were forbidden, either totally or for certain uses, and either permanently or at certain times of the year. Sometimes, these areas were fenced off; sometimes, the limits were just marked in one way or another, as what is called "brandonner" in Brittany to indicate to herd drivers the places that they may not cross.

Certain parts of the forest were closed (*en défens*) at certain seasons, to forbid access to animals, to prevent people from hunting or taking construction timber, or to allow the coppice to grow back. Certain zones were, by the lord's will, permanently forbidden. The *garennes* were little hunting areas—sometimes walled in—that the nobles reserved for themselves.

The forests were also areas (originally not necessarily wooded) that were set outside (*foris*) of the regular usage and were reserved for the lord or the king; little by little, the term was used to designate all important wooded areas. We have followed here today's usage and often use in this book the word "forest" to refer to a large wooded area as opposed to a "wood," designating a zone of smaller dimensions.

The French term *haie* (hedge) has several meanings. On one hand, in the Middle Ages this word referred to a wooded area constituting a border on the limits of an estate, a territory or a province; on the other hand—and it is the meaning it has nowadays—this word designated a sort of plant "fence" of bushes, brambles, and thorns sometimes mixed with a row of taller trees, limiting a piece of land and also constituting a windbreaker.

In bocage countries, the linear hedges divide the country; their suppression, to create large fields of one piece, has shown their usefulness as windbreakers, and also as a reserve for small game. They are also sources of production of certain fruits and of wood used for wicker and firewood. The *haies* of the Middle Ages were sometimes reinforced and strengthened, in their defense function, by woven felled trees called *plessis* that prevented access except in places meant for passage.

These wooded areas that functioned less as a wood than as a deep vegetation barrier, and that incidentally constituted a game reserve, were for a long time protected against clearing and pasture so that they could go on playing their border role. This denomination (*haie*) ended up referring to any wooded area of elongated form situated on the edge of an estate or a territory, but where the inhabitants could not exercise their usual rights. The grants often specified that the *haies* were "reserved" or excluded from the transaction.[9]

For example, in 1160, the monks of Saint-Benoît, granting usage rights at Clairefontaine to the enclosed nuns of Saint-Rémy-des-Landes, indicated that these rights applied to "all the wooded area with the exception of the hedges and the forest." The last term is used here in its original meaning, as opposed to the word *nemus* (signifying wooded areas in general), to refer to the reserved part of that area. In 1160, Louis VII, granting land for farming near Fouilleuse to the abbey of Vaux-de-Cernay, specified that the limit was the hedge of Neauphle (where there is still a state forest called *"la haie de Neauphle"*).

Sometimes, even during the period when there were many clearings, new "hedges" were created to constitute limits, which did not mean that the area was reforested but that a wooded area was given a specific function. Thus Jean de Montfort in 1248, and Robert de Dreux in 1274, allowed the monks of Vaux-de-Cernay to create hedges. In 1211, in an agreement between Blanche de Navarre, countess of Champagne, and Milon de Nanteuil, it was specified that a hedge of one hundred arpents situated near the wood, object of the agreement, was reserved, thus excluded from all clearing. In 1223, it was prescribed to a certain Pierre Tristan, an inhabitant of Passy-en-Valois, to maintain on a wooded surface of seventy arpents, a hedge that separated his house from the Ferté-Milon.

However, because of the demand for arable land and the greater profit derived from fields for the lords, hedges and even sometimes *défens* began to also be cleared. In 1210 the settlement of Villeneuve-sur-Auvers was created on a *défens*, probably by settlers sent by the chapter of Notre-Dame-de-Chartres. In 1230, it was decided to clear part of the hedges of Nangis at the place called "Queue levée." Other texts show that in the same region hedges had already been cleared among other places at Croix-en-Brie. In the Beauce, "hedges" cleared or to be cleared are mentioned: in 1241, at Outarville; in 1243, at the Chapelle-aux-Planches; and, in 1253, at Saint-Nicolas-de-Courville.

Nowadays, many names of places that contain the word *haie* attest by their environment bereft of woods that, finally, many hedges were deforested, entirely or partly, and converted to cropland. On the contrary, wooded areas devoted to hunting were seldom cleared, although when it appeared interesting to do so, nobles sometimes sacrificed their hunting grounds. Thus, the count of Chalon accepted destruction of his deer parks and hedges in exchange for material compensation at the request of the friars of Cluny who wanted to settle their peasants there.[10] It was also the case when lords participated in big clearing operations, generally in association with ecclesiastic communities.

Vineyards and Forest

The forests' retreat is often imagined as linked only to the need for food, but many of the clearings are the consequence of the propensity to drink. In the Middle Ages the production of wine was one of the principle objectives of agriculture in France.

The cost and the difficulty of transportation, the reduced level of exchanges in the peasant economy bereft of cash as well as economic and political insecurity encouraged autarky and self-sufficiency. Furthermore, the consumption of fermented liquor was a hygienic measure. Spring water wasn't found everywhere and, with the development of stock breeding, was not always free of pollutants of animal origin. Drinking water often came from wells, cisterns or rivers whose quality was not controlled. In addition to the inurement, the oenophilist tradition, and the prestige attached to intoxicating drinks, the consumption of fermented liquor—wine, beer, hydromel and cider—corresponded, thus, to a necessity.

The regions where the vine was cultivated in the Middle Ages did not extend farther north than they do today. They did, however, include regions where it is no longer cultivated because other territories lend themselves better to it and because today the diminishing cost and greater facility of transportation contribute to eliminate viniculture in places where it is not sufficiently profitable. Therefore, important surfaces, taken from the forest, were devoted to vineyards. Thus, the Parisian region had one of the largest vineyards of the Occident, since its surface was linked to the importance of the population (which, in 1328, had a density of fifty to seventy inhabitants per square kilometer [one square kilometer = 0.3861 square miles], almost twice as much as in the whole kingdom). The Gâtinais, the region whose name recalls its earlier afforestation (*gastine* = waste = area left uncultivated, i.e., to the woods), and which has remained throughout the centuries a center of honey production, produced wines that were very much appreciated by the king of France. In 1285, it appears in the king's accounts that a certain Hubert Brun, a cupbearer, purchased wine in that region on behalf of the court. In 1311, Thomas Hasle, sent to buy wine by the king, was condemned to life imprisonment for having derived a personal advantage from his position. The fact that the kings of France encouraged the installation of *villeneuves* (new settlements, new villages) on the road to Orléans had strategic and commercial purposes. But, the kings also thought to guarantee the security and continuity of their wine supply from the Gâtinais as well as cereals from the Beauce.

In the early twelfth century, Abbe Suger, regent of King Louis VI, had a certain number of clearings made, among others in Vaucresson, and invested twenty pounds for the creation of a vineyard in Saint-Lucien, so he could produce wine on his own estates. His purpose was to reduce his abbey's expenses for wine purchases, in order to devote the maximum of the revenues to the construction of a basilica. Every rural estate at the time included a vineyard, unless the soil absolutely did not lend itself to it; and it was very profitable.

At Châteaudun, the Templars had their headquarters in the borough of la Boissière. In that sector, whose name indicates the earlier presence of an area covered with woods (*buxeria*), they accumulated donations for over a century and made purchases of vineyards. In 1181, they had received from Geoffroy de Lille the vineyards that he owned at Châteaudun and in 1190 they bought from the abbot of Bonneval his vineyards at la Boissière. It was the starting point of the important vineyard that they constituted in that previously afforested area: acquisitions of vineyards by the Templars are mentioned in 1204, 1219, 1224, 1226, 1234, 1249, 1255, 1258, and 1292. The interest in vineyards as illustrated here must not have escaped the notice of the common people and the reputation of those military friars as wine lovers, having become proverbial, survived the dramatic suppression of their order, judging by Rabelais who evokes the "three or four bumpkins" that Panurge made "drink as templars in the evening."[11]

Clearings are often mentioned that have as their exclusive purpose the planting of grapevines. Indeed, the lords favored the extension of vineyards in all places where the soils were favorable. They made more profit on the taxes from the vineyards than on those from the crops, and fermented liquors, in barrels, were easier to export than grain, which was difficult to preserve and which had to be protected against heat, ergot, mold, weevils, rats, and mice. It seems that forest soils were particularly suited for plant vines. Maulde writes, "The oldest documents describe the vines growing in close proximity and on good terms with the woods."[12]

The lord, whether lay or ecclesiastical, benefited from the right to sell his wine first. The farmers could put theirs on sale only a certain number of days later since, at a time when wine didn't keep well, the new wine—which is making a comeback today—was particularly appreciated. Old popular songs attest to it.

> • *Il nous faut du vin*
> *Et du vin nouveau, ho!*
> *Et du vin nouveau!* •

"From the eleventh century onward, on all sides, vineyards lie in the shade of the forest's edge"[12] and others are even taken from the forests themselves. There is no lack of examples of clearings made to create vineyards.

In the thirteenth century, count Thibaut de Champagne, who had had a hillside cleared near Sainte-Menehould to plant grapevine, gave to a few inhabitants other hillsides to clear on the condition that they would also plant vine. Not far away, the prior of Chaud-fontaine did the same with regard to his vassals of Neuville-au-Pont and of Passavant. In a few years, a considerable vineyard developed in that region.[13] In the thirteenth century, Saint-Ladre-du-Puiset owned wine presses on the edge of the forest. In the Orléanais, Chanteau, le Hallier, and la Cour Dieu, all of them monasteries located in the forest, owned vineyards. Around the fortifications of Boiscommun the vineyard took over the military bank all the way to the other side of the ditches.[14] In Burgundy, woods and wasteland receded, writes Fourquin, to the benefit of the vineyards and not of the fields. The names of certain vineyards in Volnay, for example, such as *"En essart"* attest to the expansion of vineyards on lands recently cleared. The word "chablis," better known to the public by the wine bearing that name, designated—and still does—to the forest rangers trees that were felled by natural causes. In the Bordelais, certain vineyards also came from clearings.

Of this marriage of the vineyard and the forest, one must also see the resulting conveniences. Wood was indispensable during all phases of the grape harvest and the making of the wine. First of all, the cultivation of the vine required a lot of props. The vineyard also had to be protected from the herds at all times. The forest provided the fences. It also provided the material for the barrels and the tanks, for the wine presses, and for the vine growers' tools. The proximity of the vineyard–forest was at the same time advantageous and rational but it didn't exist without risks for the forests.

The exploitation of the forests' wood for the tools, instruments, and other accessories necessary for the vineyard's operation entailed the consumption of important items—especially of oak trees, chestnut trees, and wild cherry trees for the props. Sainct Yon indicated that forty- to sixty-year-old oaks, which in a few dozen years would have provided frame wood, were cut down to make *eschallats de quartier*; that is, props made of wood split into four sections as is still done today for fence posts made of wood from chestnut trees.

To give an example, the town of Auxerre was a very important center of production of a highly rated wine, not only because of its vineyards, but also because of the possibilities offered by its geographical location—it was favored by waterways and forests. For the cultivation of the vineyard as well as for the conditioning of the wine and its transportation, the important resources in wood situated upstream brought all that was necessary. Furthermore, with the wood, barges and boats were built, with which (thanks to the position of Auxerre upstream of important consumers such as the Parisian region, Normandy and England) wines were exported with the greatest ease. "The people of this country," wrote an Italian

Franciscan in 1245, "do not sow, do not harvest, do not stock the granaries. All they need to do is to send their wine to Paris by the nearby river that flows directly there. The sale of the wine in that town provides them with good profits that pay entirely for their food and clothes."[15] In the region of Bordeaux the forests and waterways also played an essential role in the development of the vineyards.

The interest in vineyards in the Middle Ages was not without disadvantages from the point of view of subsistence. The vine was a culture that was so favored that one of the reasons for the insufficient productivity of the seeds (which in the Middle Ages, at the most, were multiplied by five or six; while today, one can obtain sixty seeds for one) might derive, according to Fourquin, from the fact that the fertilizers were reserved for the vineyards. Marling of the soil was done, especially in the forest after clearing (since it reduced the soil's acidity) and this practice is attested to by many written documents, but marling did not replace manuring.

In fact, even on the best soils, cereal culture was extensive; the vine, by contrast, was intensively cultivated, and the object of a lot of care. In addition, the vineyards were among the few zones in which mostly everywhere it was forbidden at all times to allow animals to graze, even after the harvest. In a very few cases, certain animals—the ones least susceptible to damaging the vine plants and that could, by grazing between the plants, contribute to manure the soil—were admitted under supervision (and in return for substantial indemnities in case of damage caused by them).

The Promoters

Irregular clearings were not the only ones. Once it became necessary to increase the cultivated land to feed the growing population, numerous clearings were certainly authorized by the lords, and even encouraged by them, or organized at their initiative. Sometimes it was a joint initiative of several lords, lay or ecclesiastical, who shared the profits from the operation.

In other cases, the lay lords simply granted to an abbey the right to clear a wooded area but reserved other uses for themselves. Sometimes the abbey paid rent for the right to clear the land. It was almost always the lay lord who relinquished part of his estate for the profit of a religious organization, which slowly increased the Church's forest estates. In particular, the lands pledged by the knights leaving for the Crusades, as guarantees for the loans that allowed them to fit themselves out, were rarely recovered since the Crusader, if he came back, was often incapable of repaying the loan. These donations, sales, and grants were numerous and not only during the period of the Crusades.

Certain noble families appear to have been particularly favorable to clearings—the family of Châtillon, for example, in the twelfth and thirteenth centuries.[16] It was almost always religious communities that were granted the right to clear certain wooded areas, either by donation, or by payment of rents. For the family of Châtillon, the first written document found that is concerned with clearings, is the one by which in 1160, Guy, lord of Montjay, granted to the abbey of Saint-Maur-des-Fossés, to cultivate clearings made around Neuilly-sur-Marne (and which, in this deed are called *ruptitia, novalia,* and *exarsia*), which seems to designate different categories that might have been clearings obtained by felling trees, those conquered from wasteland, and those resulting in clearing by fire.*

In 1167, Guy de Montjay granted to the priory of Gournay-sur-Marne the tithe on the clearings "made or to be made" in the territories of Montjay and of Ozoir-la-Ferrière. In 1168, he left to the hospites of Saint-Martin-des-Champs, in Bondy and in Sevran, cleared lands for ten livres parisis. (The livre parisis was money minted in Paris. It was worth 25% more than money minted in Tours.) It might have been an endorsement after the fact. His son, Gaucher III, nephew of Louis VII on his mother's side, abandoned his rights of *"gruerie"*** on the woods of Serris in 1193 and authorized the abbey of Saint-Denis to start building an unfortified village, Villeneuve-Saint-Denis. In 1196, he authorized the clearing of the woods of Jossigny. In the deed, he seems to indicate that part of it had already been cleared: "the part, popularly called the *Essart"* (*extirpatum est quod vulgo dicitur Exsart*); it might also mean that the area previously meant to be temporarily cleared, had been "extir-

◆ ◆ ◆

*On the subject of the term *exarsia* used in this *act* for the clearings, and on the subject of the term *extirpatum*, see chapter three.
*On the subject of the words *gruerie, gruyer*, see chapter 10.

pated"; that is, the stumps had been removed (thus, with the intention of establishing permanent crops). In 1213, Jean de Beaugency abandoned to Saint-Mesmin-de-Micy the right to cut, sell, clear, and convert to cropland all the neighboring woods. In 1205, Gaucher de Chatillon relinquished—to the abbey of Saint-Denis for four hundred livres parisis—his rights on the wood of Tremblay, with the authorization to clear it. In 1206, he granted to the abbey of Saint-Germain-des-Prés part of the wood of Lilandry at Saint-Germain-sur-Morin, in order to clear it. In 1218, Blanche de Navarre transferred to Gaucher for his chaplain sixty arpents (one arpent = 0.85 acre) to clear. Hughes, Count of Saint-Pol, son of Gaucher, authorized in 1225 the abbey of Sainte-Geneviève to convert woods into fields and meadows, specifying that the beneficiaries could convert the land to cropland or, if they so wished, convert them to "grazing land without wood" (*sine nemore ad usum pratorum*), which proves that woods were considered a normal grazing place.

In several French regions, particularly around populated consumer centers, the toponymy attests to the creation of hamlets in places where there used to be woods. In northern France, there are myriads of *essarts*, but there are even more names of places designating a wood, a tree specie or a special wooded sector that served to name a hamlet or a village. It doesn't necessarily mean that it was a clearing of the same period.

Marc Bloch estimates that although the movement of land colonization in the southwest of France was slowed down for several centuries—by the emigration toward the virgin land of the Iberian Peninsula slowly reconquered from the Moslems—the clearings in this region were not less numerous from the tenth to the thirteenth century. A great many names of places with *artigues*, or derived from that word, confirm it.

These *artigues*, according to Higounet, come for the most part from peasant conquests—clearings or increases of existing territories. Written traces appear in later contributions to abbeys, such as the donation of several *artigals* made in 1136 to the abbey of Bonnefont-en-Comminges. The land surface cultivated around certain villages sometimes doubled between the eleventh and the thirteenth century, as in the plain of Nay in Béarn. The abbeys participated in these clearings. However, there is no trace in that region of the big enterprises of a regional character, of promoter operations, as were done in the Parisian basin, in Normandy, and in Brie.

The Big Enterprises

Since the foundation of new territories in the middle of wasteland or forests was prepared by written documents—some of which have remained in the archives—we know more about these large operations than about the multitude of dispersed clearings that were made around the existing villages.

To make such operations possible, the lords had to accept reductions of their areas, forests, wastelands, and *gâtines* where they indulged in their favorite pastime. Despite their love of hunting in the twelfth and thirteenth centuries, they preferred to reduce their hunting grounds and fill up their money chests and granaries. The acceleration of clearings in the twelfth century appears to have corresponded to this new state of mind of the landowners. It might also have been a consequence of the Crusades during which the nobles' needs for cash increased as well as their taste for luxury. It was, in any event, necessary because of the growth in population. The settlement of groups of several dozen families constituting totally new villages created problems other than the simple clearing of a few fields or the construction of an isolated farm or a *grange* on the limits of the cultivated area or in a clearing.

For any operation—even if it wasn't very big—that went beyond the limits of a single estate, the association between the different landowners was indispensable. The land was often poorly divided, haphazardly broken up: the Templars, for example, for years patiently followed in certain regions a concerted policy of regrouping land to constitute viable exploitation units that replaced the multiple lots resulting from the hazards of donations or acquisitions through the centuries.

The nobles were thus led to associate. Given the number of parcels of land that throughout the country belonged to the secular Church or to monastic communities or of which they had the tenure, their participation was most often indispensable. In addition, they often had more financial resources than the small or middle lay lords.

The neighboring abbey generally had more money than the lordling and could more easily make the cash advance necessary to buy the tools and the livestock needed by the clearers to start their work. It was an association, a *pariage*, between the noble and the monastic community; it aimed at developing the land by establishing, to the detriment of the forests, new agricultural operations, with the help of the excess population from the villages, the monastic or the lord's estates.

The lay partner contributed by relinquishing part of his manorial rights. The division—generally by half—of the other estate revenues and of the revenues derived from dispensing justice, supposed to bring him later on, without any difficulty, increasing profits. The abbey generally put up the capital and sometimes contributed a human capital, taken from its domain. Traces of these operations are found in the ancient contracts.

For the implementing process, the promoters who were going to reap the benefits often made an agreement with a contractor or a foreman who organized the operation and benefited from part of the new territory or its revenues. This could be one-third of the profits of dispensing justice, a certain number of buildings in hold, or a fraction of the rents. Sometimes the son of a noble family managed the operation and became the local squire; in other cases, it was an ecclesiastic, sometimes even a commoner.

A few examples will illustrate the diverse forms of these contracts.[17]

In 1113, the monks of Saint-Père-de-Chartres and the lord, Urson, agreed to clear new land and to divide the tithing and tax revenues. In 1117 the dean of the chapter of Notre-Dame-de-Paris signed with Baudoin de Dourdan an association contract: at his own cost he had to settle colonists on the land of Erainville and divide the revenues with the chapter. In 1160, in the Orléanais, Bouchard de Meung entered into a partnership with the Hospitalers of Saint-Jean-de-Jerusalem to whom he brought a piece of land. A village was built: Bonneville-les-Montpipeau. The revenues and charges from the gristmills, common bakehouses, etc., were divided in two.[18] In 1206, Eudes, abbot of Saint-Rémy-de-Troyes, entered into a partnership with Blanche, countess of Champagne, to build a *villeneuve* in the woods of Saint-Rémy. In 1210, Blanche made an agreement with the lords of the region of Reims to operate a clearing.

Sometimes ecclesiastics became contractors, managing the clearing and the development and paying fixed rents to the community. Thus, in 1225, near Vernon, the canons Aubri Cornu and Guillaume Poulet received from the chapter of Notre-Dame-de-Paris woods to clear as well as land already cleared (*essarts*)—previously granted to Gautier Cornu who had become archbishop of Sens—on which they could build one or more villages.

Some of these operations failed or did not reach the overly ambitious objectives set at the start; it could have been due to a poor evaluation of the possibilities, the profitability, and sometimes even the promoters' right to use the land.

In 1169, Rahier de Montigny and the canons of Notre-Dame-de-Chartres had planned to clear land between Gault-du-Perche and Arville, where a church was built; no crops followed. In 1175, the lord of Courtalain had decided with the canons to develop about two hundred and fifty hectares (one hectare = 2.47 acres) in the forest of Gault-du-Perche; but in 1300, only a few dispersed lots were still being cultivated.

The *villeneuve* of Froideville—established in 1175 on lands belonging to the chapter of Notre-Dame-de-Paris—was destroyed in 1224 following a lawsuit. In 1185, David de la Forest was commissioned by the chapter of Notre-Dame-de-Paris to clear three hundred arpents (one arpent = 0.85 acre) of woods on the south edge of the Dourdan forest. He must have given up; only a *grange* was built that finally remained with the chapter.

The big reclamation operations required resources that went beyond those of the local lordlings, even in association with others or with ecclesiastics. The big pioneering operations were started by the most important lords, who owned large areas of wasteland. As they wanted to increase the number of their subjects and soldiers as well as their revenues from taxes and their profits from dispensing justice, they found the necessary financial means for their operations, even if it meant in some cases associating themselves with religious communities who controlled large cash reserves. When they chose to clear a distant site, not only did they have to find and transfer the workers and their families, but they also had to install them, build their houses or give them the means to do so, relieve them of their duties for a while, and provide them with tools and seeds.

Men were the most important element in these operations that sometimes involved population transfers over long distances, whether they aimed at conquering the sea on the lowlands, converting flood zones or, more commonly, clearing wooded areas. To start cultivating new lands in a profitable manner, it was necessary to attract volunteers (you couldn't just export workers). First some "advertising" had to be done, particularly where there was overpopulation, where the charges were the heaviest, where the soil did not provide enough to feed the farmers and their families. The religious establishments with their numerous "branches" were particularly well placed to disseminate this advertising; this was another advantage of their participation in such operations.

The collective operations extending the cultivated area throughout the country could be done only if the men found appreciable advantages in these operations—not only material advantages, but also the possibility of exercising more initiative, of enjoying a certain stability, of bequeathing their tenure to their children, and of freely chosing their wife. They no longer wanted to be serfs *corvéable à merci* (bound to do any forced labor) or peasants who—whatever their status—remained subject to the lords' arbitrariness. They wanted to become men who had not only obligations but also defined rights.

Within the framework of these organized clearings, the hospites (French, *hôtes*) who executed the operation were each entitled to a house, generally built in wood or cob, with a garden where they could cultivate "roots," that is, vegetables. Sometimes they also had an orchard. They paid dues in kind or rents (*cens*) in cash to the lord or the abbey. They had cropland that they cultivated individually or collectively and places where the livestock could graze, particularly in the woods. For certain taxes, such as the tithe on produce (in French, *terrage*), the hospite had to leave the sheaves in the field after the harvest until the amount had been recorded by the lord's agent who levied a certain proportion of the sheaves. Since it was impossible for the controller (*terrageur*) to check everything at once, important losses sometimes resulted from bad weather or stealing. Often, the peasant, who didn't want to see his harvest destroyed by the weather, didn't wait for the visit of the tax collector and this provoked lawsuits. For the right to pasture the pigs or other animals in the woods, the peasants had to pay the *pasnage* or the *paisson*. Their usage rights to dead woods, forest weeds, construction lumber, and miscellaneous resources of the forest were specified.

The authority that judged the small offenses was the monastery or the lord; the latter always kept to himself the right to dispense "high justice" for important offenses. The fines and the profits derived from dispensing justice were divided among the associated lords. A "mayor" was designated, generally by the lord, to act as an intermediary between himself and the inhabitants. Sometimes the lords maintained full ownership of a within the farming area;

they exploited it directly with agricultural workers or sometimes paid neighboring hospites to do so.

In the old villages, rights and obligations were regulated, often in detail, by the customs that were transferred from generation to generation, with a certain evolution. But soon, people became dissatisfied with the orally transmitted customs that were too easily diverted or broken by the strongest: written documents, acts, and charters gave permanence and the force of law to the conventions.

The legal and practical mind of the Normans combined with the resurgence of Roman law, started under the Carolingians, contributed to the progressive substitution of the written document for the oral tradition. Little by little the old Germanic customs disappeared, such as the ordeal by fire or by boiling water and the judicial duel, which was still accepted as proof of one's rights in the Early Middle Ages—not only in the romances of chivalry but also in everyday life. They were replaced by new provisions such as witnesses, confessions, and oaths on the gospels.

This tendency to substitute law for arbitrariness certainly had an influence on the necessity of offering status and advantages to the pioneers who were enlarging the cultivated areas. But the workers' pressure was not negligible as they were the indispensable providers of consumer goods; thanks to them, those individuals who didn't perform any manual labor could live in more-or-less leisure and luxury.

To attract clearers, the lords had to grant them a certain number of privileges—and guarantee them in writing. Promoters tried to outbid each other in the advantages granted to those who settled in the new centers—all to the benefit of these settlers. And to avoid depopulation and the flight of labor from the old villages, the lords were slowly pressured to grant similar rights to their inhabitants. Thus, the great offensive of agriculture against the forests was present at the origin of a general improvement in the condition of the peasants in France.

Villeneuves and Villefranches

As long as it didn't affect their interests and didn't encroach upon the reserved areas (*défens, haies,* and *garennes*), the lords had no advantage in making the peasants too miserable or in completely discouraging their initiatives. They gradually came to realize that this desire for autonomy—this tendency of the farmer to work harder when he didn't have the perception of doing it for the sole benefit of a master—could be used profitably to develop their estates.

The first step toward this autonomy to which the farmers aspired—a deep-rooted tendency that even today provokes the productivity failure of most modern attempts at agricultural collectivization—was the progressive transformation of payments in labor and arbitrary levies into taxes that took into account the land granted or were based on agricultural and breeding production.

Since the peasants who settled in the clearing areas were no longer in the vicinity of the castle and of the lands exploited directly by the lord, payments in labor, which could then only be unusual, had to be replaced by payments in money—"bought back"—or by dues in kind. If the peasants had enough to live on and were encouraged to produce, this system could be more profitable for the lord.

Agricultural surpluses were essential for the general improvement of the conditions of life and the development of trade and cities— as well as allowing the upper class to lead a more luxurious existence. But surpluses could exist only under certain conditions: the farmer had to be able to live and equip himself, he and his animals had to be robust, he had to have enough land to exploit, and finally he had to be motivated. Thus the creation, within the framework of the clearing operations, of the new villages or hamlets, the *"ville-neuves"* (of *villa*; in Latin: rural estate) in which the inhabitants benefited from a certain number of advantages and privileges that attracted them. At first these privileges were all material—allocation of lots, lands, tools, livestock, and exemption or reduction of dues for a certain number of years.

Certain dues, payments in labor, obligations or prohibitions were not enforced, especially when they were particularly vexatious for the peasants without being of much profit to the lord. The hospites were considered "free" and were excused from: the rights of *chevage* (a yearly head tax); *formariage* (the prohibition of exogamy); *taille seigneuriale* (tallage); and the *corvée* (payments in labor).

Although clearing to enlarge the cultivated areas and feed an increasing population was the first reason for creating those *ville-neuves*, other preoccupations existed: to push back the forest, to enlarge the *"plain pays"* also meant an increase in safety, a reduction of the areas where brigands, soldiers having broken bounds, outlaws, opponents, and enemies could hide.

Sometimes the political intentions were apparent: to be able to count on faithful subjects, the landowners—and especially the king—granted to some *villeneuves* freedoms and franchises that went as far as the granting of a certain autonomy, along with political privileges. The town was under the authority of a mayor, designated by the lord and an intermediary between the latter and the rural community; a measure of self-management was given to an elected council, composed of magistrates and *jurés*. The *villeneuve* became what is called today a "legal entity" and its inhabitants were burghers.

Frequently the *villeneuves* that had such a council (sometimes called "commune") also exercised a political or strategic function. Sometimes, they were fortified to allow them to have a certain protection against lightly armed troops, if not against regular armies. They constituted strong points and supply bases for military or simple police operations and held resources in men who could bear arms in case of need or serve as auxiliaries for transport and military operations. Such was the case of the strongholds (*bastides*) built by the king of England as well as by the king of France on the border that separated their states in the southeast of France. It also was the function of several *villeneuves* built at the initiative of the king of France, in particular those along the road from Paris to Orléans, on the roads to Chartres and Troyes, and aimed at making them safer.

Sometimes the more important lords also built fortified *villeneuves* on the edge of their estates or to assure the safety of an important road. Such was, for example, Villeneuve-le-Comte, founded in 1230 by Gaucher de Chatillon, which was granted a charter, a mayor, and twelve magistrates.

The place names of Villeneuve, Neuville, Neufbourg, La Ville-neuve, Bourgneuf, Neufmarché, Neuvy, Neuilly, etc., often followed by a qualifier referring to the neighboring town, to the founder—the king, bishop, duke or count—or to the saint whose name the founding abbey church bore—Saint-Denis, Saint-Pierre, etc.—did not necessarily belong to agglomerations with communal franchises. It could be merely a new village or a hamlet recently created to enlarge the cultivated area or welcome a population overflow. But when the names evoke franchises or freedoms, they are generally *villeneuves* that were granted a franchise charter; it is the case of towns with names such as Sauveté, Sauveterre, Francheville, Franchebourg, Villefranche, etc.

The charters included several clauses: they gave woods to clear or authorized the clearing of certain woods; they confirmed the ownership of a forest or constituted that forest; they reduced the dues and abolished the tallage; they suppressed the prohibition of exogamy (*formariage*), the right of *main-morte* exercised by the lord (confiscation of the inheritance) and the right of "*forfuyance*," that allowed the lord to search for and bring back runaway peasants; they created a council composed of elected members charged, under the direction of a mayor designated by the lord, with administering the town and levying the fines for all minor offenses. In particular, the charters of the free towns explained in detail the rights on the woods and on the fines imposed in case of infractions.

In 1182, Philippe-Auguste created at Chevrières near the forest of Cuise a *villeneuve* in which the colonists were exempted from most taxes; they were subjected to considerably reduced fines in case of an offense: some fines were fixed at one-twelfth the usual amount. The act specifies: "In case of offense the fines will be: for the offenses liable to 60 sous: 5 sous; for the offenses liable to 5 sous: 12 deniers."[19]

Perhaps Philippe Auguste lowered the fines so would-be offenders would not be dissuaded and he would retain the income from the fines. However, the price that had to be paid to profit from the advantages of that *villeneuve* was not negligible: according to Duby, the fixed taxes (*cens*) were relatively high.

"Economically speaking," writes Perroy and Devèze after him, "the settler's condition may be less favorable than that of the peasants on the ancient estates: at the time of his installation he is forced to do the hard work of clearing and then to endure years of uncertain yields; most of his holdings are on 'cold' soils of lesser value than the rich territories of the older clearing. But for the twelfth-century peasant, the attraction of freedom is the strongest. The *villeneuves* attract not only the overflow of the population that seems to grow at a rapid pace but also the poorest and the more heavily taxed of the holders on the ancient estates, particularly those whose legal conditions are low and despised, the *hommes de corps*, the serfs."[20]

The freedoms of the colonists of the *villeneuves* were seriously limited by the presence of the lord's civil servants: on one hand, often a mayor (who could become a small village tyrant if he abused his position); on the other hand, collecting sergeants who collected the money taxes and *terrageurs* who gathered the payments in kind.

Nonetheless, the benefits granted to the peasants who settled in the *villeneuves* incited the inhabitants of the ancient villages in the same region to emigrate and settle there. In a way it was the purpose of these operations since the amount of cropland available was becoming insufficient for the increasing population. But it could end up depriving labor in the existing territories, that still had to be farmed as well.

So the lords, whenever possible, exercised their right of *forfuyance* and had the runaway peasants captured; agreements were made among the neighboring lords to capture the runaways and return them to their masters: for example, in 1212, near Clermont-en-Argonne, peasants who had taken shelter with other lords were exchanged.

The nobles wanted to prevent the flight of their own labor, but readily tried to entice the others' labor away. In the *sauvetés*—inside of a perimeter marked by crosses—peasants who had left a territory where life was too hard found shelter under certain conditions. In the inquiry ordered in 1243 by the bishop of Macon on the subject of the custom of Prissé, a village with franchises, it was said: "If someone, coming from elsewhere, remains in the village for one year without being claimed by a lord, he will be considered a burgher of that village and defended as a freeman by the lords."[21] So, just like the lost object today (which after one year and one day belongs to whoever has found it, if in the meantime it hasn't been claimed), the runaway peasant at the end of that same lapse of time belonged to the community that had welcomed him.

That is why the lords were often careful to specify in the charters they granted that their own subjects could not settle in a new village. Sometimes mutual agreements between neighboring lords prohibited men coming from certain other villages in the area to settle in the *villeneuve*. In 1229, in the charter of Givry-en-Argonne, the lord specified: "In the town above-mentioned all can come and live with the exception of those who come from my towns or from my fief or from Chaudfontaine, Parois and Rahéricourt." In 1230, in the charter granted to Vitry, the count of Champagne indicated: "If it so happens that any of my men, holders or guards, come to live in the community of Vitry, the burghers will only be able to keep them with my consent or by my will."

But the coercive or repressive measures taken could not stop the movement that attracted the peasants toward those clearing communities where life was freer and the outcome of labor better shared. Many lords had to grant franchises to existing villages to prevent or slow down the depopulation of their estates. The reason is sometimes artlessly spelled out, as in this 1331 charter: "So that my friends and subjects, the inhabitants of my town of Binarville, stay more willingly there."[22]

When Philippe le Bel gave franchises to certain villages on the border of Champagne, the countess Blanche de Champagne asked him to promise not to do it in a whole neighboring sector. Nonetheless, she herself enfranchised many villages on the very wooded border of Argonne, where she wanted to attract colonists to operate clearings while, at the same time, she did not want to see the inhabitants of southern Champagne emigrate. Maas enumerates that just in the county of Champagne more than eighty-five villages were enfranchised in less than a century and cites yet another example in 1420.

The abbeys appear to have been less inclined to grant franchises than the lords. Sometimes the men from the abbeys were granted certain freedoms in two steps: in a first step, the abbeys received the right to dispense justice to their men, a right previously exercised by the lord, and the cancellation of the debts these men had previously owed to the lord; in a second step, the abbeys exempted their men from paying miscellaneous dues.

Of course, if the lords were so generous in the conditions they offered to the inhabitants of the *villeneuves*, it was because they found it to be advantageous for them. The lords of the *villeneuves* lived on their income. All they needed to do was to designate a mayor and a tax collector and they received more substantial dues than they used to. Their holders were more interested in the land's yield, of which they kept an important part, than the overtaxed peasants who cultivated—mainly for the lord's benefit—cropland that was hardly sufficient to feed their families. Furthermore, the lords remained administrators of justice and the exercise of the right to dispense justice was a source of sizable profits. Small conflicts, breaches of rules, and offenses were multiplied by the customs' complexities, the often approximate delimitations, the greater freedom enjoyed by the inhabitants, and the many temptations that occur when one is in the shelter of the woods. And on each arbitration, each judgment, each fine, the lord took his share.

There was no relationship between the building plans of the *villeneuves* and their possession of franchise charters. Certain *villeneuves* were built by following regular plans and sometimes were linked to the rural parceling. Some were closed units, often encircled by walls, inside of which were regularly set-out lots each with a house and its garden area; the roads, which at first had been the clearing axes, diverged from the entrance gates of the village. Other *villeneuves*, built from a road originally cut through the forest, included on each side of the way lots set like the teeth of a comb: the houses and the gardens were set close to the road, then came the cultivated fields and, at a progressively increasing distance, the forest. There is a striking resemblance between these village streets—of which examples are found in Normandy (forest of Aliermont), in the Île-de-France (Darvault), and in Thiérarche (Bois Saint-Denis)—and the Canadian colonization lots set in the same way along a waterway. It must be remembered that the French word *rue* originally meant a breach in a forest (*rupta*). A number of villages in the Val-d'Oise, the Côte-d'Or, the Somme, the Meuse, the Vosges and the Haute-Saône are called Rue or Rupt.*

Other *villeneuves*, on the contrary, were built from an existing nucleus—*grange*, hamlet, group of farms—and had a less systematic layout, dependent on the preexisting agricultural lots, with sectors where the clearing zones are recognizable by their more regular geometrical forms. Sometimes, a new *villeneuve* was built next to the first one, because of the population increase: Suger created La Courneuve, near Saint-Denis, next to La Cour Saint-Lucien. Le Perray on the road to Chartres doubled up the *villeneuve* of Coignières, established at the end of the twelfth century. Grand-puits, on the road to Troyes, was doubled in 1186 by a priory and a hospites' village. It must be noted that these three creations were near important highways and contributed to the safety of these roads.

◆ ◆ ◆

*Among others: Rue (Somme), La Rue (Côte-d'Or), La Rue Dorée (Val-d'Oise), Rupt-aux-Nonnains (Meuse), Rupt-sur-Saône (Haute-Saône), Rupt-en-Woëvre (Meuse), Rupt-sur-Moselle (Vosges).

The Villages Split Up

The permanent clearings had started several centuries earlier by isolated and sometimes secret little strokes, while at the same time the system of itinerant clearing was practiced in a more organized and collective way. During the twelfth and thirteenth centuries, individual and isolated land clearings were continued, concurrently with the collective "colonization" operations: the new villages and hamlets, the *villeneuves* of land reclamation, the large operations on the wastelands, marshes, forests, and the sea. While the individual operations were necessarily smaller than the big ones, they still had an important impact on the forest zones, that were sometimes partially transformed into bocage by the multiplication within the forest of permanent cultivated lands, which in some places ended up filling the entire area.

Duby estimates that the operations that developed in this forest and pastoral environment were less deliberately geared toward cereal farming: "There were more trees, more meadows, fewer wheat fields: this corresponded to the new consumer tendencies of a more developed economy; from the end of the twelfth century onward, people wanted more meat, less bread, more wool, leather, and wood. The exploitation of the forest by stock breeders and by the entrepreneurs of forest products was becoming more systematic. This appeared in the form of many small enterprises as well as in the creation of brand-new territories."

While new territories were being created around the existing villages, farming became more intensive under the pressure of the steady population increase and thanks to the increase in livestock —made possible by the extension of meadows (rare at the beginning of the Middle Ages) and the consequent increase in the production of manure. Agricultural techniques, in particular crop rotation, were perfected. The improved balance, thanks to the areas conquered in the forest and the wastelands, allowed for an increase of subsistence that made famines almost disappear in the twelfth century.

But as the clearing movement continued it slowly destroyed the delicate balance between intensive farming near the housing, areas cultivated with cereals and with a part (sometimes authoritatively limited) for legumes, and areas devoted to breeding, among which the wooded areas were of prime importance. When breeding was reduced by lack of pastureland, it meant the loss of an essential resource that had contributed to maintain—by the manure—the fertility of the cultivated fields.

From the end of the twelfth century onward, the relative peace that reigned in the countryside (the "first one-hundred-year war" started in 1152 and ended with the Treaty of Paris, signed by Saint Louis in 1259, temporarily disturbed only a few regions) brought about almost demographic expansion and mostly everywhere split up the villages: in places that were too distant from the main village to be easily developed, dependencies were created; these dependencies were constituted to the detriment of the forests, or simply of clearings that were too far away to be, until then, regularly cultivated. These isolated dwellings seem to have multiplied in the thirteenth century[23] and intensified the deforestation process. Frequently, they were near the edge of the forests in which they made permanent clearings wherever the soil lent itself to it.

The lordlings themselves followed the movement and built their fortified houses, their modest castles circled by a fenced orchard and ditches, near their holders' recent clearings, near their men so they could supervise more closely. Duby suggests that the donations made by many nobles during the previous centuries to religious establishments, abbeys or churches (such as those of which we gave examples) might have led those who didn't have enough cropland left in the middle of their territory to re-settle in the middle of fields that had been developed more recently. This movement not only contributed to extending the clearings, but especially made them permanent. At the same time, around the towns, wealthy burghers bought recently cleared lands and created areas to be exploited by grouping neighboring lots in order to form an estate apart from the existing villages. Traces of this scattering of the dwellings can be found as early as the twelfth century; a few examples illustrate it.

In 1224, the documents in a case between the people of Corbreuse and the inhabitants of Brétencourt show that two isolated houses had been built, one in 1175 and another in 1195. In 1275, three knights owning in common the Marizy wood in the Morvan attracted land clearers, but instead of creating a *villeneuve*, they planned to have dispersed dwellings.[24] In Brie, in the Massif Central, in Bresse, and in Beaujolais there are traces of the creation of many such dependencies during the last two-thirds of the thirteenth century.[25] The same type of situation occurred in England and in Bavaria.

Sometimes they were not residences but craft or preindustrial installations that were built near the woods in order to reduce the time and cost of transporting fuel. Later on, the authorities worried about seeing people, whatever their activity (and not only those who were professionally important consumers of firewood for their industries such as forges, glassworks, tile works, pottery, lime kilns, etc.), settle too close to the forests. Measures were also taken concerning individuals, even simple farmers: most forest rules forbade building houses within the forest without authorization and also prohibited individuals from making their own charcoal at home. Still later, with the forests' devastation, it was forbidden to build in their vicinity.

But in the twelfth and thirteenth century, this breaking up of the villages did not yet appear to be a danger. All around, the villages spread by forming dependencies, while the movement to create new villages, *"villeneuves,"* slowed down.

The Land Clearings Slow Down

As early as the twelfth century people began to realize that forests would not always be available. Thus in 1113 the lord Urson gave to the monks of Saint-Père-de-Chartres the land of Bois-Ruffin to use as they wished, it was mentioned in the document that pig grazing was to be shared "as long as there were woods."[26] It seems that people worried when they saw so many woods slowly disappear. The lords kept some forests for themselves by putting large areas in *défens*: either pasturing was forbidden or when it was allowed, all clearings or *novales* were forbidden.

It was in the early thirteenth century that documents began to contain rules aimed at conserving the wooded areas. Examples can be found all through that century.[27]

As early as 1200, the king of France, Philippe Auguste, arbitrating a conflict between Saint-Médard-de-Soissons and the lord Jean de Thourotte, concerning a wood, prohibited all clearings. In 1207, he allowed the monks of Fontaine-Jehan, to whom he was granting a wood, to cultivate it (*excolere*), but not to build or to bring in any hospites; thus, he limited their rights to a mere extension of cropland and avoided the establishment of a new hamlet and new inhabitants which, inevitably, would have required other clearings.

In 1212, when granting eighty arpents of woods in the forest of Crécy to the abbey of Farmoutiers, Gaucher de Chatillon specified that he not only reserved the right to hunt but also the right to clear and that he would guard the woods and exploit them by selling their production every year, a quarter of which would go to the abbey. In 1214, Mathieu de Montmorency forbade the priory of Bouffémont to clear the neighboring woods in which, in addition, he reserved the apple, pear, and medlar trees. In 1215, Philip Augustus forbade the monks of Longpont to clear woods in the Retz forest. Seeing how important the damage was in the forest du Mans near Meaux (Seine-et-Marne), Thibaut IV, in 1226, set 1,800 arpents in *défens* to protect them. In 1264, an agreement between Thiébaut, count of Bar, and the abbey of la Chalade specified that the monks would no longer be allowed to clear, as they had been doing. The monks had the usage right "except that in those woods they were not allowed to clear." The wording indicates that it was a periodic clearing that the count wished to stop, but that the woods still existed.[28]

The evolution in the Île-de-France from the middle of the twelfth century to the middle of the thirteenth century reflects the increase, followed by progressive slowing down of the clearings, prior to the troubles of the fourteenth century. It might have been the beginning of a fear that this precious resource—wood—should not be reduced too much. It might also have resulted, as several historians have noted, from the disappointment created by the low crop yield of many forest soils when they were no longer cultivated temporarily but permanently.

One might wonder if the ancestral methods—temporary crops on burn-beaten land, long fallow periods, extensive culture, exploitation of the forests' natural resources—did not correspond better to the technical means and to the possibilities of agriculture in the period. But in all the areas that suffered from population pressure, it was impossible to return to the methods of temporary clearing. At the end of the thirteenth century the forest was, everywhere, largely penetrated and reduced. It was now, on one hand, up to the agronomists who, inspired by the farmers' experience and the teachings from ancient times, tried to perfect the agronomical techniques and to spread them; and on the other hand, it was up to the forest specialists who slowly, in a few centuries of effort, tried to eliminate from the wooded areas all agriculture and grazing. But before they obtained that result, the abuses of pasturing, especially in southern France, transformed large areas into virtual deserts—partly because of the populations' and local authorities' lack of prospective views.

In northern France the forest was partly preserved. One of the reasons was the process of appropriation by the upper classes—particularly its use for hunting—and their effort to reduce the rights of commoners to the traditional uses of the forest. In the long run, abuse by the nobles was so great that it can be considered as one of the causes of the Revolution of 1789. Then again, as early as the fourteenth century, the perturbations of the Hundred Years War and the "black plague" provoked the desertion of many villages and—except certain *villeneuves* that had a more solid collective structure and sometimes fortifications—many of those that had been created to colonize the forest areas. By the middle of the fourteenth century, the population of France was only about two-thirds of what it had been at the end of the thirteenth century and the pressure on the wooded areas was reduced by that much.

5 · stock
BREEDING and
the forest ·

Livestock Mobility

IN TODAY'S FORESTS, where there are few big carnivores left to maintain the ecological balance by eating herbivores, young plants are often threatened by the proliferation of certain wild animals such as deer, which not only eat grass but also graze on little trees, causing their disappearance. In the Middle Ages, those carnivores—wolves, lynxes, foxes, wildcats, martens, genets, and sometimes bears—that attacked domestic animals and even men— were hunted, but they still represented an element of natural regulation that had to be taken into account.

Wild herbivore populations were limited by the carnivores and by hunting and poaching, but did not do much damage to the forests, which still covered large areas. The main risk came from the herds of domestic animals that, during most of the year, found

their food in the forest. These herds would have progressively provoked the disappearance of the forest if there had not been good
organization and strict supervision. There were systems of parti-
tioning and fencing; the forest was sufficiently light to allow the
animals to find enough grasses and low plants to feed on without
attacking the trees; and the number of animals was limited, to allow
for the maintenance and the renewal of the vegetation. Overgrazing
also involves the packing of the soil by trampling and the disappearance of the underwood plant species and of the herbaceous level,
which induces the erosion of tender or sloped grounds when the
climate is not sufficiently humid. This is what happened in the
Mediterranean zones where the pastoral overload destroyed the forest.

In the temperate and humid climate of western Europe, the forest
must have appeared to the Middle Ages man as a border, broken
by a few openings and more or less porous in its mass. But it
constituted an essential resource of this agro-sylvo-pastoral economy
in which grazing moved from the field to the forest and within each,
following the rhythm of the seasons and the crops.

The plant capital—it seems commonplace to repeat it—is attached to the ground, rooted in the soil for more or less time—
depending on whether it is a tree, a perennial plant or a cultivated
annual plant.

The animal capital, the livestock, was a polyvalent resource: it
was necessary for human nutrition through the milk, eggs, and
meat; irreplaceable for certain nonfood products of great utility such
as leather, horn, rennet, parchment, fur, bones, gut, etc.; and, at
the same time, important as an energy reserve for agriculture, transport, construction and the early transformation industry. It also
offered an advantage particularly useful at the time: it was mobile.
It is by using this evident but precious characteristic of the livestock,
mobility, that the Middle Ages man tried to ensure at best the "full
employment" of the soil. According to the time of the year and to
the characteristics of the different animals and their effect on the
plants, he moved his herds in the fields, in the meadows and in the
forests, trying to draw the maximum from the land but to stop
the grazing before deductions would have adversely influenced the
renewal of the exploited resource.

The animals were used in different ways—sometimes contradictory
—instead of being, as today, specialized and selected for a specific

purpose. They were insufficiently fed with surpluses that couldn't be used by man or with products he didn't want, either for physiological or for cultural reasons. As a result, the animals' energetic performances as well as their alimentary production was extremely mediocre.

Moving in search of food is the life-style of certain hunting populations and of the nomadic stock breeders; it is also the basis of the more systematic principle (and whose periodicity is annual) of transhumance. It is the same way in itinerant farming: the farmer follows the fertility of the soil from place to place. But in the Middle Ages, this process was not limited to the animals. Just as the roving herds, the courts of the Merovingian and Carolingian kings moved with bag and baggage from one royal estate to another, exhausting in a few weeks the resources accumulated during the year by the patient labor of the peasants attached to the land. Then the entire gang moved to another estate, on which it descended like a swarm of locusts.

This process was not very different from the raids sometimes systematically carried out by tribes of nomadic warriors against their sedentary neighbors. The only difference was that slightly more regular obligations existed: a pressure without violence and an organization that anticipated the masters' requirements, while allowing for the reconstitution of the resources. The lords used the same method on their territories where each of their vassals owed them hospitality.

Right of Common, Common Land and Meadows

Pasturing occupies a considerable place in the "customs" written down from the end of the fifteenth century. These customs codified the customary rights that, until then, had been verbally transmitted or resulted from numerous contracts, conventions, charters or edicts established throughout the years. "Almost all lands," writes Michel Devèze, "whether cropland, meadows, wasteland or forests were used as pasture."[1] And elsewhere, he notes that "the forest is only a huge grazing area in addition to the moors, marshes and wasteland and makes up for the lack of meadows."[2]

Part of the grazing was done in open spaces. The periods when grazing was authorized in the fields, the country roads or the meadows, by virtue of the right of common, were strictly limited where this system was in force—that is, especially in the north, center, and east of France.

The customs, written down in the sixteenth century, but reproducing the previous customs, specify on which zones the right of common was to be exercised. Thus, the custom of the Nivernais indicates: "The right of common is exercised on the roads, meadows—*en prairies dépouillées*—lands, woods, and other properties, neither fenced nor closed, except when these properties are forbidden by custom."

In other customs (Boulonnais, Châlon, Troyes, Vitry, Blois, etc.) the following are mentioned more specifically: "The timber forests and coppices after the fourth bud" (fifth bud in some customs).

Thus, the right of common covered all the woodland with the exception of what was forbidden (*en défens*) either permanently or temporarily. Furthermore, it wasn't limited to the lands of the parish, but generally extended to the neighboring areas of the adjacent parishes without going beyond the chief town of those parishes which, of course, created conflicts. Herds were generally grouped and entrusted to common shepherds. The periods and the locations where the right of common was admitted were strictly defined: any violation was penalized by a fine, which was increased if the guilty animals belonged to "strangers."

Apart from the forests where the authorized periods were very numerous, there was only the wasteland and the paths where grazing was allowed at all times. On cereal fields, it was generally the custom to wait three days after the harvest to bring in the animals so that, during that interval, the poorest of the community could glean from what was left. Sometimes this period was a little shorter, as in the Loire River region. The herds found edible fodder in the fields because the harvest was generally done with a sickle just below the cereals' heads. The chickens, let loose in the fields after the poor people's gleaning, pecked the lost grains as well as wild plant seeds; in this way, they did the work of partially eliminating parasitical species, work that today must be done by hand or—double-edged weapon—with herbicides; they also found worms, snails, and insects, thus enriching their food. This exceedingly short passage of the animals in the fields had only a limited fertilizing effect. As soon as the period of tilling and sowing started, grazing was, of course, forbidden. If the land was fallow, there was no time limitation. Indeed, in many places the primitive alternation fallow/crop was still practiced; so there were, in this case, areas where grazing could be done during the whole year.

In the vineyards, more numerous in northern France than today, grazing was generally forbidden at all times and penalized by fines, the amount of which depended on the period when the offense occurred. If the animals were pigs or sheep, they were confiscated. For the other animals, between the harvest and the month of March, the fine was small; it was much more important from that date on, and was increased after the feast of Saint Laurent (early August) until the time of the harvest.

Despite the fact that most cropland was reserved for the production of cereals and, at times, of a few legumes, there were some meadows. But they made up a small percentage of the territories, only about 2 percent of the cultivated area in the ninth century, in the examples studied and no more than 6 percent at the end of the Middle Ages.[3]

These meadows were essentially natural grasslands corresponding to areas unsuitable for cereal farming: either wet or flooding meadows, sometimes called "river meadows" or dry meadows (called *champaux* in the West and *sécherons* in some other regions). Nonetheless, there were also artificial meadows that were defined in the seventeenth century as "those where grass is grown by man with the help of brooks."[4]

The Cistercians, great stockbreeders who practiced irrigation and the selection of species, wanted to maintain large areas of forest around their abbeys, because the forest was the basis of their domain's wealth: it was the necessary pastureland. "The Cistercians," states Roupnel, "only cleared the areas where the meadow was an advantageous substitute for the forest."[5]

Indeed, they had realized that it was impossible to feed regularly and sufficiently, year-round, the horned beasts, the horses, and the sheep solely on the forest runs, the fallows, and the stubble. So they strived to develop meadows in all the places that didn't lend themselves well to cereal cultivation either because of their soil or because of their location, such as wet low grounds and flood areas; they became draining specialists and as such, they were called upon to manage important development operations in different parts of Europe.

The Templars, resourceful managers and soldier-monks, who did not farm their estates themselves, also saw the advantage of developing meadows. They even cleared land to create some. Thus an 1165 Templars' charter, concerning the wood of Souhel, states: "that they clear in the forest up to 200 *jougs* for their own needs, either to make fields or to make meadows as they wish."[6] In the thirteenth century, the population displacements on the Templars' estates in the region of Chartres evoke a qualitative development with the help of labor; regarding animal husbandry, the acts and the accounts attest to the multiplication of meadows, among other places around the mills, the culture of vetch (of which they might have noticed the function of green fertilizer) and, finally, the organization and alternation of mowing and grazing in the forest.[7]

The Cistercians and the Templars were not the only ones interested in meadows. Several abbeys created meadows to the detriment of the woods. In 1123, Jean, bishop of Orléans, granted woods to the abbey of la Cour-Dieu to make meadows (*extirpando eis ad usum pratorum*); this was confirmed by his successor, Bishop Manasses de Garlande who, in 1171, gave to the abbey a house at Pré Cottant.[8] In 1181, the abbey of Cheminon received from Gaucher d'Etrepy "as many woods as necessary to have one hundred cuts of meadow" against payment of rent.[9] In 1183, the abbey of Moutier-en-Argonne received, from Warin de Busseil, woods on the territory of Suizy "to make meadows."[10] In 1237, Saint Louis gave to the convent for unfortunates of Saint-Loup-des-Vignes, 168 arpents (one arpent = 0.85 acre) to clear for crops or to make pastureland.[11]

The majority of the rural population didn't have the large estates and financial means of the monastic orders and, as they had to face more pressing needs, they would have found it extremely foolish to create permanent meadows—just to let the animals graze year-round. But meadows were certainly not unusual because the hay harvest is often mentioned in establishing the amount of payment of certain taxes. Nonetheless, the fodder came most often from grass and forest leaves.

These meadows, whatever their nature, were considered not as pastureland but exclusively as fodder crops to provide feed for the animals during the cold season. The animals were admitted to the meadows only several days after the hay harvest. They finished the reapers' work, while bringing a little manure by their droppings. From the month of March, the meadows were closed so that the grass could grow back. Sheep (as well as goats and sometimes also geese, as in Normandy) were forbidden at all times to enter the meadows and so were pigs, according to most customs.

Only in mountain regions were larger areas reserved for the production of fodder because of the length of the cold season which, because of the altitude, requires the garnering of large amounts of feed for the animals. But slowly the deeds started listing meadows and mentioning the hay harvest. The hay harvest also appears in the miniatures: in these illustrations, the sickle, the harvesters' tool, was often replaced by the scythe which allows the worker to cut close to the ground.

The meadows then acquired a more important place in the agro-sylvo-pastoral balance. But, at the time of the great demographic push of the twelfth century, in most territories it was essentially on the wasteland and in the woods that animals found their feed, except for the periods when the right of common was authorized.

Although grazing allows, by the droppings, a certain restitution of the vegetation eaten, the manure produced is irregularly spread out and washed away by the rains, so it does not help the soil much; in addition, in the cultivated fields, little time was spent by the animals. This insufficiency of manure was detrimental and weighed heavily on the crops' yield. The methods of improvement that ameliorated the chemical composition of the soils could not make up for these insufficiencies in organic and fermentable cover.

The agronomical works of the Middle Ages, which were widely disseminated after the end of the thirteenth century, were inspired in part by the writings of ancient times; the documents insisted with much reason, on the importance of manures and contained various prescriptions concerning them. However, for the farmers to be able to apply them, it would have been necessary to ensure a better balance everywhere between animal husbandry and agriculture and reserve larger areas for fodder; with the population increase and the greater pressure on the woodlands, forest grazing could not suffice and deprived the fields of priceless wealth: manure. That is what the Cistercians had understood, and the main reason why they had considerably developed animal husbandry on their estates.

Forest Runs

"Foresters and agronomists now seem to agree," wrote the agronomist Kuhnholtz-Lordat in 1939 (but today this agreement is still far from being unanimous), "on the possibility of having at the same time livestock and forest. The creation of forbidden areas and the parceling out can be understood in such a way that grazing would no more be the tree's enemy."[12] And he wrote elsewhere: "The sylvo-cultural-pastoral balance could have been achieved for a long time if the notion of recuperation had been applied to the forest and if the livestock and the space reserved for crops had been limited concurrently, principles perfectly well known in the Middle Ages by the Cistercians, who had realized with the means of their time the balance between fields, stockbreeding and forests."[13]

With all the difficulties in defining and applying a rigorous organization, it was what men tried to do all through the Middle Ages almost everywhere, more-or-less successfully, in spite of the often adverse external circumstances and the incidence of social and political contingencies.

A large part of the woodlands were thus subject to the "right of common." It must, however, be understood that the grazed forest of the Middle Ages must have rarely been the dense and shaded forest that we are used to: in general, the tall trees were scattered, sometimes even scarce, in the oak groves where the pigs fed, as well as in the coppices where, because of the periodic felling for firewood, the trees, except for a few seed-bearers, were not very tall and let the light through, thus favoring the growth of grass.

The stockbreeders of the Middle Ages were not in favor of allowing the animals to graze in their meadows. Today, it is often recommended, to replace grazing on site, that the animals be fed with cut grass. But it has been recognized that, on one hand, the trampling (which, however, on very wet grounds, as was often the case for the natural meadows of the Middle Ages, can have drawbacks), and, on the other hand, the animal's teeth are two factors often favorable to grass: it "tiles" more, it thickens at the base, it leaves a larger place for the legumes, which makes it more nourishing. Consequently, grazing is favorable for permanent meadows if they are not too wet, and for temporary meadows with complex flora whose duration one wants to increase.[14]

These reflections by a modern agronomist, following experimental findings and comparative tests, show the merits of the use that the people of the Middle Ages made of meadows (which were generally natural meadows on wet, low grounds), on which they did not allow the animals to graze. They also justify and explain their method of forest runs where it was rare to mow—a difficult task anyhow because of the trees, stumps, and shoots—but where they strived by the controlled movement of the herds to avoid overgrazing and the exhaustion of the herbaceous cover.

Today, "staggered grazing" is recommended and practiced by dividing the meadows in fenced lots to improve the use of the grass and facilitate its new growth. This system avoids the disadvantages of free grazing on large areas. When the entire grazing field is thrown open all at once to the animals, they waste grass—especially in springtime. They squash part of it—which makes the hardiest species multiply—and, finally, they choose the tender grass—which ends up in overgrazing. The practice of the run, to the extent that it was well organized and well applied by the herdsmen—and this function wasn't entrusted to just anyone—corresponded to the modern system of staggered grazing. It was an "itinerant" grazing, during which the animals successively covered the different forest ranges and, if it was well managed, allowed the herds to feed without degrading the plant cover. To avoid this degradation, the number of animals admitted to graze in the forests had to be limited. Each household could send a certain number of animals, sometimes strictly fixed.

The recycling of fertilizing matter was ensured by the animal droppings that fell on the ground on which they grazed, thus closing in a very simple way the fertility cycle without deterioration by depletion. The division of the forest into ranges—separated by ditches or fences that prohibited access to some of them when it was necessary to let the trees grow back—facilitated confining the herds to successive sites. The advantage of this system of direct manuring was already known in ancient times. Pliny, in the first century A.D., wrote: "Some think that the lands are well fattened by keeping the herds outside in an enclosed area."

The places where the animals were allowed to graze in the forest were periodically defined. The areas forbidden for grazing were mainly those where it was necessary, after a cut, to let the trees grow until they had reached a sufficient size so that the animals couldn't damage them. Heavy fines were levied in the cases where the animals penetrated into the forest outside of the authorized places, or before the protected sectors were fenced off. After the creation of the administration of the *Eaux et Forêts* its officers had, among their missions, to make sure that the following rules were respected: "No beast will go in the coppice until the wood can defend itself against the beasts, because an animal who isn't worth more than 60 sols or 40 livres can cause damage of 100 livres or more in a year. It is expressly forbidden to all the officers of the *Eaux et Forêts*, to let any animal graze in the forest if the coppice is not protected and declared such by the officers."[15] To reach those sectors the herds had to follow well-defined roads. The animals' access was also regulated by time, taking into account the local environment and the way in which different animals feed. The trees' new growth depended, first of all, on the nature of the soil, whether it was more-or-less irrigated and drained, on its exposure, etc. One had to have a long experience of an area to know when the animals could be re-admitted after the cut, all the more since the period between the cuts of coppice could vary from simple to double. Chauffourt recalls the variety of rules: "They are different customs and uses practiced in this Kingdom: in some places the coppices are open for grazing three years after the cut, in other places four years, five years and so on."

Actions were taken against the herdsmen whose animals wandered out of the sectors that were reserved for them. However, the agent had to take things like accidents into account as well as circumstances outside of the herdsmen's control, such as attacks by wolves', wasp stings, panic, etc. The rules provided that "if by chance the animals flee because of wasps, deadly terror, wolves pursuit or other inconvenience, and if the herdsman rushes to follow them, there should be no fine."

Elsewhere, it is mentioned: "All through the year if an animal gets in the forest by running away and if the shepherd can clear himself from having knowingly directed it toward the forest he will pay no fine for that. . . ."[16] On the contrary, if there was a fraudulent intent, the penalties were increased; for example, the agent could impose a fine of 60 sous per animal if a person caused damage with his animals in someone's field at night, but only 12 sous if it was by day.[17]

In the charter of Lorris, according to an 1155 text confirming an older one, it is stated: "If an animal from the Lorris parish penetrates into the forest while fleeing from a bull or followed by bees, the person who owns the animal will not have to pay a fine to the agent if he can swear that that animal entered in spite of his supervision. But if he knew about it, he will pay 12 deniers for that animal and if there were several he will pay that amount for each."[18]

Grass grows back more-or-less quickly on the same soil, depending on the seasons. Nowadays, stockbreeders allow the grazed grass to grow back by giving it "rest periods" that depend on the season. Thus 25 to 30 days are necessary in April, 15 to 18 days in May, 20 to 25 in June-July, 30 to 35 days from end of July to early September; but, in the fall, grass needs 40 to 60 days to grow and, in winter, 100 to 150 days."[19] With the system of runs, a good shepherd could also keep track of those variable times of the growth of grass and move his herds accordingly. So, because it takes longer for the vegetation to grow in the fall and in the winter, where the climate allows the herdsman to leave the animals outside, the herds had to move more often to find pastureland, which compromised the future growth of the vegetation.

To prevent the herds from penetrating where they were not permitted to go, the boundary limits to watch were marked by stakes equipped with straw wisps, constituting visible marks, with branches placed across the passageways, bundles of thorns, picket fences or supple branches woven as hurdle (a method used especially for enclosing land or live-stock). These palings, or wattle fencings, were sometimes made of mobile elements that were moved to follow the rotation of the crops or the phases of the trees' new growth. Certain areas were permanently enclosed, such as the gardens, and often the vineyards. A previous fragmentation of the territory facilitated the installation of gates or extra fences. It is one of the advantages of the system of bocage and its meshwork of hedges, ditches, embankments, and sometimes low walls, that were frequently used in several French regions. This organization is more compatible with the methods of animal husbandry than with those of farming. Today, farming requires considerable space for the maneuvering of the enormous agricultural machines. In the twelfth-thirteenth centuries, with the improvement of the harness equipment and the use of horses in single file, it already required much more space than when plowing was done with a hoe or with primitive plows drawn by oxen.

The forests were not open to all of the population, only to the beneficiaries—inhabitants and border residents of the forest—and excluded all "strangers." That is why no domain, estate or territory, whatever its size, was considered viable if it did not include enough hectares of woodlands. In the west of France, in Normandy, and in Anjou one had to own forestland to exercise the right to dispense justice. And when, by the Treaty of Verdun in 843, Louis, Charles, and Lothaire divided Charlemagne's empire among themselves, they came to an understanding, as Pirenne showed, so that each part included an approximately equal amount of arable land, vineyards, important cities, and also forests.

To prevent animals from other territories from using the pastures and overtaxing the woodlands, the inhabitants who were the beneficiaries of the usage rights were entitled to catch the foreign animals—pigs, sheep, goats, horses, etc.—that they found in the forests, as well as the shepherds or herdsmen of those animals, and turn them over to the officer in charge of the forest.[20] So that the owners could be determined, animals were branded, as is still done today for transhumant animals or for those that are left in semi-freedom in the steppes or the pampas.

The customs of Embrun provided that if foreign herds penetrated their territory, the inhabitants had the right to seize one sheep out of each flock and, after five days, if it had not been repurchased, to slaughter it and divide it with the consuls and the nobles.

In wet regions such as the northern half of France and in cold regions such as the Jura or the Massif Central, the animals are required to spend part of the winter in a shelter and be fed there. The forest already provided a shelter much superior to the one they would have had in the meadows; shelter against the wind and also (less completely than in a cowshed, of course) against rain. Indeed, it has been noticed nowadays that animals in "free stalling" spend much more time outside without harm, even when the weather is very cold; they adapt: their fur is much thicker and they are more robust than the animals crammed into the stables, where the hygienic conditions are not as good as outdoors.

In regions with a temperate climate, the animals could thus go without cowsheds, stables or sheepfolds. However, when food was scarce or when they were sheltered for the winter, they had to be given fodder. Due to the light development of the hay meadows, an important proportion of this fodder was taken from the forest, by taking leaves off the trees. These plant deductions without equivalent counterparts contributed to impoverishing the forest.

But the method of the runs per se could have been maintained without degrading the forest. Unfortunately, the wise measures imposed by the customs, that had permitted a happy cohabitation of animals and trees, gave way everywhere under the pressure of the increasing population that required more cropland and grazing land. Added to the pressures and deductions that were made in the forests, this state of things—especially in the hot, sunny, and less irrigated regions of the southern half of France—led to the degradation of the woods. In certain areas where the interests of the sheep breeders led to the conversion of forests into pastureland—in spite of the risks of erosion—an often irreversible degradation of the soil was provoked.

Deductions in the Forest

For want of meadows to harvest in sufficient quantity, the stockbreeders had to find additional fodder somewhere, so that, in the cold season, the animals were assured of enough to eat or at least to survive. Naturally, they turned toward the forest. All woodlands or "hedges" of any size were used. These deductions, under certain forms, have remained traditional until today in certain regions of the Pyrénées, the Alps, and south of the Massif Central.

The agronomist Olivier de Serres, author of *Le Mesnage des Champs*, depository of an old agricultural and pastoral tradition, recommended this practice in the following terms: "In addition to the grass, the second quality fruits and the leaves of the trees will greatly help feed your livestock."[21] Then again, as the hay from the cultivated meadows was reserved for the animals' feed, the materials necessary for the litters also had to be found in the forest or the wasteland. The forest was thus the main place where fodder and litter for domestic animals were extracted by hand.

These deductions of leaves were called *ébranchage* or *effeuillage*; sometimes the word *émondage* was also used to designate the cutting of branches and green leaves for the animals, but the word more often meant cleaning the tree, taking away the dead parts, the undesirable branches, lichens, mosses, and ivy.

The leaves of different trees—ash, elm, and poplar—were used to feed the animals. For the litter, in addition to the trees' small branches, several smaller plants were used, especially fern, heather, and broom. This last plant was particularly appreciated because it decomposes very slowly and provided the animals with an elastic, insulating, and dry carpet.[22] Elsewhere, boxwood was used, especially since this bush with bitter leaves is little appreciated by the herds.

Apart from its use to make brooms, broom had a particular importance in the economy of certain regions. In the Ardennes, it had been noticed that broom thickets protected the young oak shoots against the bad weather and favored their development while, at the same time, the young plants provided litter and after a few years, firewood.[23]

In that region, broom also provided a fertilizer: fresh broom was spread on the roads where the passage of herds and wagons shredded it; then, piled up, it decomposed and provided good fertilizer. Elsewhere, broom was grown for several years, then the twigs and leaves were cut for litter and the branches for firewood; in Sologne, broom was left to grow for five years, after which the ground was cultivated for three years; then the same cycle was repeated.[24] Broom was a coppice of rapid periodicity, providing excellent firewood, alternating with temporary clearing.

The twigs, branchlets, broom bundles—all the plants that served as litter—were used as manure after they decayed. The plants that decomposed poorly were burned and the ashes used as fertilizer. Sometimes, small branches were also used to facilitate traffic through the mud or to fill up holes—the "pot-holes"—in the courtyards of the farms or on the roads.

The *soutrage*, which is still practiced in the southwest of France, consisted of cutting the leaves, the little branches, and the low plants to make, first of all, litter for the animals. Once mixed with the animals' droppings these leaves and twigs, piled up, were transformed into manure that was spread on the fields to fertilize the soil. This method was particularly recommended for clearings located in the forest or on the edge of it. In the cases where the plants used for the litter didn't rot, they were burned on the fields. This is what was done with ferns, often used as litter, in Brittany for example, precisely because they don't decompose easily; they must be burned so that they can free the fertilizing elements (nitrate-, potassium-, and phosphate fertilizers) that they contain. The farming people of the Middle Ages didn't know any chemistry but they had noticed the results of the method. Another process, the *étrépage*, consisted of taking the plants from the moors or the inferior layers of the underwood with part of their roots and a few centimeters of humus, as in the case of *écobuage*, but using these deductions to make manure without burning it.

These different kinds of deductions, just as the extraction of humus that was practiced in certain forests—and even the gathering of dead wood—slowly impoverished them. In particular, the *effeuillage* provoked considerable damage when, to make things go faster, big branches or even whole trees were cut down instead of just leaves and twigs. Such abuses were mentioned as having taken place in the southern Alps, but the rules were made only in the sixteenth century, when people started to worry about the consequences of such methods. While, in the long run, taking off the leaves—and even more so, branches and trees—impoverished the forest, the pasturing on site of the animals that left their droppings—and thus closed the cycle—did not necessarily prevent the reconstitution of the soil's fertility if it was controlled, if the number of animals was limited, and if they didn't remain there in all seasons. However, as the population increased and the forest diminished, these conditions could no longer be fulfilled.

Cattle

During the Early Middle Ages, animal husbandry occupied the largest place in the rural economy of northern France; we know from the estates' records—that exist for the northern part of Carolingian Europe—that it was essentially an outdoor stockbreeding, where pigs held the main place. But oxen, which at the time were the common draft animals, were also important. The French name given in the Middle Ages to the bovines, *almailles* or *aumailles*, from the Latin *almalia* (of *alere*, to feed), indicates that they were animals that provided food, by their milk or meat, or by their work. While pigs, half-wild, were raised essentially for their meat, cattle was polyvalent. They provided the indispensable towing force for the plow, the harrow, the cart or the bar wheels, provided milk (easily preserved as cheese), meat (mainly veal) and, finally, miscellaneous by-products such as leather, horn, sinew, etc.

The use of the cows' milk and the towing function of the oxen required keeping them near the crops; they could not be left to roam loose as the pigs did—or as do cattle nowadays in countries of extensive breeding, where they are raised for meat—or kept in semifreedom as the sheep were, far from the center of work activity. Thus, although cattle were allowed in the forest, they remained mainly on the edge of it. They were not subjected to the same restrictions as sheep or goats, which are much more destructive. In all of the northern half of France, goats and sometimes sheep were generally forbidden to go into the forest. For example, in the woods of Trappes (Yvelines) the following were authorized: "horses, oxen and cows, and other animals, except goats and sheep that in no case are allowed to enter in the woods."

Sometimes the worth of a forest was estimated by the number of pigs or oxen that it could feed. Thus, a 1250 inventory of the manor of Kinkenholt near Gloucester noted: "Pasture in wood, plain and grazing ground for twenty-four oxen, which is worth twelve sous. And pasture for six cows, which is worth six sous." Then, an item which indicates that different sectors were used for different kinds of animals, a pasture for five hundred sheep is mentioned and another "in the woods and elsewhere" for twenty pigs.[25] Indeed, the underwood suitable for pigs, in the oak and beech groves, producers of acorns and beechnuts, was not the same as the light woods or aerated coppices where grass suitable for cattle could grow. Nor was it the same as the one on a poorer soil, hilly and rocky, with less grass, that could be sufficient for sheep or goats. In addition, it was thought that acorns could be harmful to animals other than pigs; according to Aristotle,[26] whose opinions were respected in the Middle Ages, the acorn makes ewes miscarry and the cows' milk dry up.

The periods when the animals were in the fields (after the harvest), in the meadows (after the hay was cut), and in the forests (after the passage of the pigs) were strictly defined. Cattle were not admitted into the forests all year-round. The grazing of the commoners' cattle was limited by the periods reserved for the pigs' pasturing, by the zones set "in defense" either for several years to allow for the new growth or to reserve them for hunting, or temporarily, and also by grazing periods reserved for the nobles. For example, in the English royal forest, the king reserved four weeks for his herds, two before and two after Saint-Michael. It was only afterward that the owners of woods included in the royal forests, or even just bordering them, could let their animals into their own woods.[27]

It was only on the wasteland and the paths that grazing was allowed year-round. Harsh winters created particularly difficult problems in dealing with cattle: they had to be sheltered. If snow covered the ground, they couldn't graze and, during that season, there were no more edible leaves on the trees. Fodder stocks were often insufficient due to the lack of hay meadows. In those cases, some animals did not survive or had become living skeletons by the end of the winter. And when the oxen had to be hitched to the plow for the spring sowing, their towing power was much reduced, while the cows provided very little milk, and that was reserved for the calves.

Pigs

Pigs fit much better than cattle in the agricultural-forest-breeding system in which the forest was the main pastureland. Indeed, Nature provides them with their most substantial food—acorns and beechnuts—precisely in the winter when vegetation is reduced and when, for the other animals, food starts to create the most problems. And pigs are just ready for human alimentation in the middle of winter, when the supplies start to dwindle if the harvest has not been very abundant. Furthermore, everything from the pigs is used and, for centuries, man has known how to preserve the meat in different ways. In addition, they are omnivorous animals that eat everything they find, leftovers from human food as well as very diverse plants; when they don't find anything on the ground, they look for their food below the surface and feed on tubers and roots.

This explains the considerable development of pig breeding and its relationships with the changes in the forests. In England, it was noticed that during the period which followed the Norman Conquest, in the eleventh century, the number of pigs diminished; this was linked to the fact that the king and the Norman lords appropriated many forests and forbade their use. The interdict on pork in certain religions has been linked to the differences in the conservation of forests within a given country; thus, in Albania, the plant cover would have been maintained better in the Christian cantons, where pigs were raised, than in the Moslem sectors, where sheep and goats were raised.[28] Sheep, and especially goats, are certainly more dangerous to the vegetation than pigs. Pigs feed mainly on acorns, beechnuts, fallen fruits, seeds but also tubers; but, when they do not find enough food on the surface of the ground, they dig and in so doing they bare the roots, which causes the trees to perish, unearths the buried seeds, and compromises the new growth of grass.

People tried not to allow pigs into the meadows and the fields. In the woods, when they were allowed to eat the fallen acorns and beechnuts, they had to be moved to another area as the fruits were consumed; of course, they could not be admitted to the areas where the forest had to grow back; herbivores, on the contrary, could be admitted before the shoots came out of the ground because they eat only the superficial vegetation and their trampling can help sink the big seeds into the ground, such as acorns and beechnuts, thus favoring their rooting. These prohibitions became more rigorous through the centuries.

"In the sixteenth century," writes Marc Bloch, "the time restriction on allowing pigs to feed in the forest or on gathering acorns was general while in the Middle Ages individuals and communities often had the possibility of letting the pigs graze in all seasons." But already, in the written rules of the thirteenth century, restrictions on this subject appear, thus reflecting previous customary regulations.

The forests suitable for pig grazing—the *pasnage*—are essentially forests of oaks sufficiently tall to bear acorns, forests of full-grown trees. But oaks and beeches must be forty years old or more to bear fruit in significant quantities and give a "full" harvest only every two or three years; production can thus be very irregular from one year to another and the trees must have reached the minimum age. Thus, pigs cannot graze in coppices cut every ten years. In certain countries, such as Spain and Tunisia, one can still find woods developed for pig breeding; it has been calculated that one hectare (2.47 acres) of such oak groves produces a nutrition production equal to a hectare cultivated in cereals with the very low-yield crop obtained in the Middle Ages.

Those "oak orchards" organized for pig breeding give an idea of what could have been the woodlands used for that purpose in the Middle Ages. Indeed, it was in the *"hauts bois,"* to use an expression of that period in the forests of full-grown trees that the king and the lords reserved for the largest part of the acorn and beechnut production for their own herds or to sell to a *paisonnier*.

In the forest sectors where the pigs pastured, other animals were generally excluded from the end of September to the end of November—at the time when the acorns and beechnuts fall. Pigs were admitted until spring if there were enough acorns in the regions of the center and the north, but only until Christmas in the southwest.

When other animals were found in the woods, during the periods reserved for the pigs, their owners were fined. The number of pigs that could be admitted in the oak or beech groves was sometimes limited annually—for example, in Normandy—in proportion to the abundance of acorns that was estimated to be on the trees before the opening of the wood to *pasnage*. Each user was then told the maximum number of pigs that he could bring into the woods. This wise precaution avoided the deterioration of the woods and might have contributed to the fact that the forests of Normandy remained for a long time among the best preserved of the kingdom.

Generally, the user had the right to let the pigs eat the acorns fallen naturally; this allowed the user to spread the pasturing over several months and to always have ripe fruit. Some miniature paintings, however, show peasants beating the branches to feed the pigs who were searching for their pittance at the bases of the trees; generally, it was specially authorized to cause the fruits to fall when snow was on the ground.

In certain cases the users had the right only to the *pasnage*: the pigs ate on site. In other cases, they were also entitled to gather the fallen acorns and feed their pigs in the shed.

In this matter, too, there were privileges. The common users had to wait for the lord's animals to go through before bringing their animals to the forest; they were entitled only to what was left: such instructions are frequently mentioned in the ancient documents. Thus, in a cartulary cited by Duby, it appears that the canons of Saint-Vincent-de-Mâcon entrusted a man named Landry to guard the woods in order to prevent anyone from gathering the acorns before the canons' pigs had been brought in. Landry also had to check that only beneficiaries brought their animals on the runs. The rules also mention meadows that are harvested and then open for a certain time to the animals—with the exception of pigs.

In some regions, September was called the "month of the woods" because it was the time when the acorns were ripe and the pigs were admitted into the forest. The pig was an essential element of the peasant economy; it was one of the rare sources of animal proteins.

The pig was slaughtered toward the end of the year, after having taken full advantage of the acorn season. As long as there were still bears in the Vercors—an animal sometimes dangerous for the herds and the herdsmen—when a peasant killed one, he cured it. His family then ate bear meat instead of pork and the pig was sold to make a little money.

As long as the forest remained almost limitless, which was the case until the twelfth century, it wasn't necessary to worry too much about restrictions on the pigs' runs. It was the domestic animal characteristic of the forests where it roamed in hordes, as it does today in Corsica. A forest was even estimated not by its ground surface but by indicating its perimeter and calculating the number of pigs that it could feed; thus, the polyptych of Saint-Germain-des-Prés in the tenth century mentions "a wood estimated at one league in circumference where fifty pigs can be fed." That would mean, if the wood were more or less square, less than 100 hectares. In that same estate, according to Longnon,[29] the ratio between the number of pigs and the surface of the woods was: 100 pigs for 153 hectares. In Flanders, for the domain of Poperingue, it was 100 pigs for 85 hectares,[30] but in that region the soil is said to be particularly fertile. Higounet estimates that this ratio, variable of course depending on the forest environment and the productivity of the oaks that grew there, must have been approximately one animal per hectare.[31]

Since a wood of full-grown trees was generally kept deep in the forest to limit the risks of stolen timber, the pig keepers couldn't go home every night. Some users, however, had the right to build cabins; these were called *loges*, in French. The same name was sometimes used for the charcoal burners' cabins. The word has left traces in many place names, such as the Camp des Loges in the forest of Saint-Germain (which became a military camp), the Loges-en-Josas in the valley of the Bièvre, and Fay-les-Loges.

Horses in the Forest

The horse had a special place among the domestic animals. Symbol of nobility, of which the first degree was the knight [T.N.: The French word for knight is *chevalier*, from *cheval*, "horse"], the horse was essential and indispensable in the feudal world for the lord and for his men. Royal ordinances forced every nobleman to raise a certain number of horses. Some provinces were famous for their horse breeding: Poitou, Brittany (among others, the regions of Loudéac, Redon, Paimpont, Lanouée, Quénécan, Branguily, Guingamp, and Léon). In Normandy, in the Valois, and in the Île-de-France (where the king maintained a stud at Saint-Léger-en-Yvelines) there were organized breeding farms.

For centuries, studs were mostly set in the forest; they consisted of herds of horses that were let loose to pasture in semifreedom. This custom is evoked in literature. Chrétien de Troyes, in the thirteenth century, describes Perceval: "He enters into the forest . . . takes the bit from his horse and lets him graze the fresh greening grass."[32] In the sixteenth century, Rabelais relates that, grateful to Gargantua who had returned the bells of Notre Dame, "the citizens of Paris . . . offered to maintain and feed his mare for as long as he would like . . . and sent her to live in the forest of Bière."[33]

Thus, the forest was the normal pasture for horses. But it wasn't feasible to let them wander in the whole forest and to also hunt at the same time. A certain segregation was necessary. The right of studs (*haras*) mentioned in the ancient documents means the right to use the forest to pasture the horses, but the French word *haras* was often used to designate a particular sector of the forest. Certain zones of the forest that were more suited to be horse pastures became specialized; the cover could not be too thick, so that the grass could grow and the soil had to be of such quality that the vegetation was sufficiently abundant and nutritious for the horses. Monasteries as well as lay lords tried to obtain pastures for their horses. In many cases, when lords granted woods, they kept for themselves the right of horse-breeding or the use of certain localized studs. Often, too, they acquired additional studs so they could keep the rest of their forests for hunting and still fulfill their obligations to supply horses to their suzerain. In 1223, Amaury de Montfort while granting to the abbey of Joyenval 200 arpents (one arpent = 0.85 acre) to clear reserved the right to have a stud. In 1238, he gave to the abbey of

Vaux-de-Cernay 1060 arpents, half of which was to be cleared in exchange for usage rights in the forest and particularly the right to horse-breeding. Jean de Montfort ceded, in 1248, forty arpents to the leper hospital of Grand Beaulieu in exchange for a stud.[34]

Horses began to be used in agriculture in the eleventh century. On the embroidered linen called the "tapestry of the queen Matilda," which relates the conquest of England, one can see a horse harnessed to a harrow. In the Parisian basin, Fourquin believes that at the end of the eleventh century when Suger was building the abbey of Saint-Denis, the plows were still pulled by oxen while, at the time of Philippe le Bel, less than two hundred years later, all the important estates used horses.

This development was made possible by the progress achieved in the making of harnesses. It became efficient to use draft horses when the shoulder collar and the harness of horses linked in single file were perfected. The latter increases the traction force applied to the plow without trampling over the part of the fields already plowed. These progressive changes made it possible to cultivate heavier and deeper soils and also facilitated the rooting out of tree stumps; thus, transforming forest grounds into permanent fields.

Horses are more fragile and require more care than oxen; however, they are also quicker, which is particularly important in rainy areas where one must take advantage of the good weather to perform the agricultural operations that require draft animals. Harrowing, as illustrated in the "tapestry of Bayeux," is an operation that is done with a horse because it is important to cover the sowed grains very quickly before they are eaten by birds; the use of the harrow and horse thus made it possible for less seed to be wasted on the birds.

Both the particular climatic conditions of northern and western France and of England, as well as the military needs, contributed to the increased use of horses in the countryside. It then became necessary to increase the ground surfaces suitable to feed them. These were light forests or half-wooded zones, similar to the savannas or the steppes in which horses are still raised today in freedom in new countries, and natural pasture meadows that were formerly found only in sectors not suitable for cereals. However, a horse's balanced diet must also include oats, that the English in the old days, before adopting porridge, defined as the "food of horses and Scotsmen"— which might explain the hardiness of these mountain people, with whom the English were in conflict for such a long time.

Thus, in addition to the forest pastures, sometimes complemented by meadows that assured the winter feed, oats were cultivated for horses. As a spring cereal, oats could fit in the system of temporary clearings limited to two years, by allowing full use of the cultivated soil, where, successively, winter cereals, legumes, and spring cereals grew. Oats could be cultivated in the forest's natural or in man-made clearings. Chrétien de Troyes describes, in the romance of Perceval, the sowing of oats in the spring in the heart of the forest: "It was at the time when trees flower, groves and meadows turn green, and the birds in their Latin sing gently in the morning and everything is consumed with happiness. The son of the widowed Lady got up alone, in the forest, quickly saddled his hunting horse and taking three javelins, left his mother's manor. He thought that he would go see the harrowers who were sowing oats with twelve oxen and six harrows."[35]

The cultivation of oats also fit into the three-field system of permanent fields, of which the first examples go back to the Car-olingian period. The three-field system developed in the thirteenth century; it replaced the traditional alternating fallow and crop and allowed agricultural production to increase considerably. This sys-tem spread so much that it became the standard operating procedure to settle farming leases and agricultural land leases for three years or a multiple of three; the 3-6-9 lease is still used today for all sorts of rural or urban leases.

Small Livestock

Breeding sheep and ewes in the forest created special problems; sheep mow shorter than the other domestic herbivores and, espe-cially, destroy young shoots and small trees. It was recommended —and, whenever possible, done—to let the sheep graze on moors, fallow land, and wasteland, what is called in the Ardennes the "*savarts*," a word used in other provinces for poor chalky soils.

In the Orléanais, sheep could graze all year-round in the woods but only in view of the flat country, near the edges; in other words, they were allowed to nibble only at the edge of the forest, starting from the common land or the fields after the harvest, but they could not penetrate the forest. At the same time, it was a safety measure for the animals because supervision of sheep within a wood, if there is any coppice, is almost impossible—and the wolves were a very real danger at the time. Furthermore, this rule contributed to avoiding what was called the extensions of the forest, the spaces recovered by natural seeding on cultivated land, that often were subjected to disputes and lawsuits; the sheep by attacking the young shoots, reduced or eliminated these extensions.

The little flocks of sheep belonging to simple villagers and led by a common shepherd did not constitute a real danger to the forests, especially in the northern half of France that is well irrigated and has no shortage of open wasteland suitable for the sheep. Dispersed around each village—under the responsibility of a shepherd who was punished if he allowed his flock to encroach on the forbidden areas or neglected to supervise it—these little flocks were led to graze alongside the roads or at the edges of the forests and thus caused no harm to the woodlands.

Goats were much more dreaded: they were less docile, individualists, had plenty of initiative, loved young shoots and even little branches and bark, were able to climb onto trees to feed and, even in forests of high trees without low branches, they could damage the tall trees by gnawing on their bark if they didn't find anything more tempting. Only a few species of trees, such as lime trees on which the bark is bitter, were safe. In the Middle Ages, in northern France, goats were considered to be evil-minded creatures; it is the term used by Sainct Yon. He-goats reeked of the devil. Even the she-goats, those "cows of the poor," had a bad reputation and witches were often accused of having some kind of relationship with these so-called diabolical animals. Goat herds were found only in Mediterranean countries, where dry and scarce vegetation grew on the arid soil. They were subject to many precautions, restrictions, and penalties—even in southern France.

In the customs of Navarre, written in 1552 on the basis of a document dated 1288, itself reproducing a text from a hundred years earlier, it is written that whoever finds a goat in his young coppice can kill it; and, furthermore, that the owner of the animal owes him an indemnity for the damage caused, based on the estimate of two sworn experts. In Brittany, a goat found in a young wood was fined the same as cattle; while for a sheep it was one-quarter the amount. In the east, as in Normandy, goats were excluded from the woods at all times. In Poitou, Saintonge, Provence, and Vaucluse goats were generally admitted into the forests but their number was limited for each household. In the southern Alps, several measures were taken: in 1311, at Moustiers, certain sectors were allocated to the goats; if any went beyond those limits they were confiscated. In 1484, at Baume-sur-Verdon, the number of goats authorized to graze in the area reserved for oxen was three per family. At Saint-Paul-sur-Ubaye, a family was forbidden to own more than five goats, ninety sheep, and six heads of cattle and, in the middle of the sixteenth century, the inhabitants themselves asked to have these numbers continued.

For sheep, the normal pasture was the open wasteland, the moor, the *causse* but in many regions they also grazed in the forest or at least on the edge. Flocks were entrusted to qualified shepherds; the treatise by Jehan de Brie, *Le bon Berger* (the good shepherd), which had a large distribution in the Middle Ages, after describing the author's career, first shows him as a child in charge of the geese and the goslings, then the pigs—who were more difficult to lead. While leading horses, he was wounded and so was put in charge of the milking cows, but again he was wounded by one of them. Having again recovered, but perhaps not being very strong, he was given eighty lambs to keep and to protect against wolves and other predators.

In this sheepfold treatise, he describes the shepherd's tool, the crook, which has nothing to do with the ribboned accessory of some eighteenth century paintings; it is both a weapon to defend oneself against the wolves and a tool allowing the shepherd, thanks to a sort of spoon or crook at one extremity, to pick up, without bending down, gravel and grass lumps to throw at the animals that separate from the flock, as shepherds still do today to call in the stray sheep. This instrument, well operated, must have been used to throw stones at wolves. It might have been at the origin of the game of golf ("g" and "w" are interchangeable), that was born on the vast pasturelands of Scotland and Great Britain.

The Gold of the Fleece

As long as the animals belonged to the owners of the same territory and used in common the possible spaces on their lands—meadows if they existed, fields at certain periods, and forest runs at others—a certain control was exercised on each other to avoid the deterioration of the common property. With the development of the wool industry, the rise of international trade, and the realization by the big sheep owners of the profits that they could make, another frame of mind developed.

Walter Map, a humorous ecclesiastic, noted in 1184, in the margin of a Benedictine manuscript that, when these monks didn't find deserts to settle in, they "created them."[36] In the same way, when the big sheep owners didn't find open spaces, grassy moors that constituted the pastureland for these animals, they destroyed forests by allowing too many animals to graze—with all the resulting ecological consequences.

But when the practice of transhumance (rational use of the contrasted seasonal possibilities of the lowlands and of the mountains, thanks to the herds' mobility) developed and when large herds, belonging to privileged men who sought not just to live from them but to make profits, also developed, the use of the soil changed. The owner of the flocks didn't care about the future of the mountain pastures where he sent his sheep against rent payment and which he didn't own; he searched only for immediate profit. As for the local communities that were often conscious of the danger (at least to a certain extent, because it was only in the sixteenth century that ecological catastrophes, brought about by the deforestation of the mountains, showed the consequences of overgrazing), they were torn between the important profits that they could make and the concern for the long-term consequences of an evolution of which they saw only the premises. The pressure of the interests at stake, the drawing up of agreements—protected in high places—to develop sheep breeding or the wool production that supplied an expanding industry and was the object of an increased demand did the rest, and in many countries won over the forest.

Clearings are often perceived as being the main cause of the rapid decrease of the forests in France and in the rest of Europe. But from the thirteenth century on, the development of areas devoted to sheep grazing, where the density of animals was much greater than what would have allowed the conservation of the forest, was also one of the main causes of receding woodlands. It was induced by the wool interests, stimulated by the achievement of higher living standards, and by the population increase between the eleventh and the thirteenth century that created a huge market.

The perfecting of weaving techniques also played a role. From the middle of the eleventh century, the horizontal loom, with pedals allowing the production of pieces of finished material 20 meters long, transformed this craft into an industry and considerably increased the demand for wool. The by-products of sheep breeding also had their importance: meat, parchment, and wool skins. All this production, in an environment of improved living standards, had outlets. Soon, the huge wool market was controlled by groups of men who had little concern for the conservation of forests and the self-sufficiency of the local agricultural production of subsistences was threatened by the extension of pastures. The merchant class also had an interest in the specialization of the products of the different regions because it led to a movement of international exchanges.

To meet the growth of the textile market, the Italians, Flemish, and French looked for other sources of wool. In Spain, grazing lands slowly gained on the forest, which had already been considerably diminished by the Reconquista's military tactic of eliminating the forests since the eighth century. In the fifteenth and sixteenth centuries, the considerable use of timber required for the needs of the Spanish navy further contributed to the deforestation: wood was sacrificed for America's gold.

The brotherhood of the Mesta, of which the principal shareholders were the monasteries and the high lords (the treasurer was the great master of the order of Saint-Jacques de Compostelle), controlled both the sheep breeders and the wool market.[37] The order of the Golden Fleece, founded in 1429 by the duke of Burgundy, is a symbol of the considerable importance of sheep in the economy of that period, particularly in Spain. It is estimated that, from the middle of the fourteenth century to the middle of the fifteenth century, the total number of sheep in Spain grew from 1.5 million to close to double (2.7 million in 1467).

Consequently, Spain slowly became dependent on Sicily, Sardinia, France, and the Baltic countries for its cereal supplies.

A similar development took place in Italy: in the northeast of Apulia where in the thirteenth century between the Apennines and Monte Gargano there were wheat fields, many villages disappeared. The same phenomenon occurred in Latium, Campagna, the Roman countryside and the kingdom of Naples.

In England, the increase of the sheep flocks was first attested to by the increase in wool exports, which had already reached about 7,000 tons in 1353. Cultivated lands gave way to pastureland in the east of the country, from where wool was exported to Flanders through Hull and Ipswich. In these regions the population decreased as the wool industry developed and grew larger.

The Great Plague has been made responsible for most of the abandoned villages of which numerous traces can be found in Great Britain, but it seems that the considerable development of sheep-rearing also contributed. In the fourteenth century, changes in the crops due to the necessity of producing fodder for the animals, increased England's dependency for food production, principally cereals, on imports that came especially, by way of the Hanseatic League towns, from the vast cereal regions south and east of the Baltic countries.

In Provence, the *terre gaste* of the southern Alps, a half-pastoral half-forest area where the local communities let their sheep flocks graze, presented no serious problems until the end of the thirteenth century, when it was transformed by the organization of transhumance between the southern low valleys and the mountains. Early in the fourteenth century the lords claimed the right to allow their sheep herds to graze freely wherever they shared the rights with the local communities. Tens of thousands of animals invaded the pastures and many conflicts arose between the local communities and the lords. The *nourriguiers* (capitalist stockbreeders) of the lowlands sent their flocks of sheep to the mountains, which were leased by the local communities and the lords. The privileged class derived important profits from this expansion, as for example, King René, count of Provence who in the fifteenth century owned big herds of sheep. The local communities also benefited: in some sections, there were on average one hundred sheep per household. Stockbreeding brought wealth all the way to the valleys of the Briançonnais, Queyras, Trièves, Valbonnais, and Champsaur. This prosperity is attested to by the fact that in 1343 the trustees of the mountain townships didn't hesitate to buy back their privileges from the Dauphin for the large sum of 12,000 gold florins, plus an annual rent of 4,000 florins.[38]

However, stimulated by the profits derived from this breeding, the overly large grazing load most everywhere in the southern Alps slowly provoked the recession of the already light forest cover of the *terre gaste* and of the adjacent dense forests. Whole regions of the high Alps and the Alps of Haute-Provence were transformed by erosion into totally bare mountains and, for the most part, would no longer be able to serve as pastureland. The invasion of the sheep flocks also affected the Massif Central and the Pyrénées with, as consequences, not only the recession of the forests but also a partial desertion of the countryside, which was cultivated only around the villages because of the need of space for sheep and goats.

When it became feasible to transport merchandise without too many risks—with an escort, if necessary—the monastic orders, thanks to their multiple settlements, were able to specialize their estates in various ways, proceed to exchanges among the abbeys, and buy what they did not produce. By becoming stockbreeders on a large scale they might have provoked more deforestation than by the clearings, of which such a large part is attributed to them.

In the Landes, the Rouergue, and the Quercy, and especially in the Causses, the Cistercians maintained large herds of sheep around their commanderies of Bastet (Causse de Gramat), Lacapelle-Livron (Causse de Caylus), and Sainte-Eulalie (Causse de Larzac). In Gascogne and at the foot of the Pyrénées, the abbeys of Bonnefont, Gimont, Grandselve, Lescaledieu, and Sauvelade benefited from the right of run for their herds that they sent in transhumance into the mountain pastures of the Pyrénées.

During the following centuries the consequences on the cropland—and even on the pastureland—of the erosion provoked by this exaggerated exploitation became apparent. But in most cases it was too late to bring any remedy.

6 · fuel ·

Domestic Consumption of Wood

THE FORESTS WERE, ABOVE ALL, the essential fuel sites for individual and collective domestic uses: home cooking and heating, bread baking in the communal bakery, distilling, etc. They also provided fuel for early industrial uses such as pottery, tile, and brickworks, lime and plaster kilns, glassmaking, saltworks, ironworks, distilleries and casting foundries.

A considerable amount of wood was used in the home. Fireplaces were inefficient and the houses, with no windowpanes and no insulation, were extremely difficult to heat. "A whole tree," writes Maury, "was often needed to light a cottage for just a few evenings." For lighting, some people used torches made of long splinters of resinous wood or of rolled bark. Such torches were used as late as the nineteenth century in a few places in Germany, in Slovakia, and in Switzerland in the Tessin. In other places, torches were made from split logs of pine or fir, as well as from woodbine, birchbark or pinecones. The torches were mounted in special supports or receptacles that can still be seen, sealed in the walls of a few castles.

Throughout most of France, heating and cooking were done with open fires, which meant a huge consumption of wood just to keep warm during the cold season. And indeed, little by little, people were developing a taste for greater comfort as witnessed by the progressive use of window glass for domestic use first by the kings and the lords, and later by the townspeople. Due to the inefficiency of the systems used, great quantities of wood were also consumed by the peasants who considered the forest an inexhaustible source and who, by customary rights, were guaranteed a free supply of wood under the condition that they gather it themselves and respect certain rules in the process. In the north and east as well as in the mountain regions, where people burned resinous wood that consumed itself very quickly in an open fire, stoves were used to slow down the combustion and retain some of the heat. However, in the plains, the system most often used was the big, open fireplace where the logs, as they burn, are pushed toward the center under a suspended pot. This type of fire requires hard woods such as oak or hornbeam which burn slowly and produce many embers.

Charcoal was also used for cooking, but mostly in southern France, where wood had to be brought from far away and heating was not much of a problem. Charcoal was burned in a nook under the mantelpiece, called the *potager*, or in movable appliances made of clay or metal, like the ones that are still used in the Mediterranean countries and in Africa.

Because of the heating and cooking systems, the wood supply was a major problem for any individual or community. No village or castle could exist without its life-supporting wood reserve. Towns as well had to have a reliable supply. As a result, the possession of, or at least the customary rights to, sufficient woodlands were among the objectives of urban communities. Each city had its belt of forests in which it tried to protect and increase its rights. Monasteries, too, acquired forested properties as extensive as possible, not only for the wood, but also for the various forest products and for their value in feeding the animals. Towns needed forests first for firewood and second for construction timber.

Since many forests around Paris were reserved for hunting by the king and the lords, townsmen had to find their wood further away;

however, during certain particularly severe winters, the king was forced by parliamentary decree to accept wood cutting in his reserved area. This happened during the winter of 1418 in the forest of Laye and, in 1446, in the forests of Senart and Bondy. Soon, however, as the forests of the Parisian region became insufficient, wood had to be brought from still farther away. Paris went as far west as Vernon for its wood and also in the Andelys. The Andelle River was used to transport wood from the forest of Lyon, and the Ourcq River for wood from the forest of Retz. However, the huge reserve of wood in the Morvan would be exploited only in the sixteenth century, when a single political authority, the king, was able to guarantee the free circulation of wood and thus organize its floating all the way to Paris.

All towns, large and small, had their wood site and their firewood rights (*droits d'affouage*). Gaillac had a right (called *"gaudence"*) on the forests of Grésigne. Besançon exploited the woods upstream along the Doubs River. The people living alongside the forest of Orléans obtained from Philippe Auguste rights on those woods. In the charters awarded to the towns, especially in the ones inspired by the famous "Lorris law," many rules dealt with customary rights to wood. The Lorris law specifically stated that the men from the town of Lorris could take from the forest as much dead wood as they needed for their own use.

Today in France, gathering dead wood, whether *"estant,"* that is, not yet detached from the tree; or *"sec et gisant,"* that is, fallen to the ground by natural causes, is not—contrary to what is often believed—authorized. Indeed, collecting dead wood, either by detaching it from the trees or by simply picking it up, interrupts the recycling of certain organic matter and impoverishes the soil. As this element cannot be neglected in the forest's ecosystem, wood collecting is subject to the authorization of the landlord or his representative. The situation was the same in the Middle Ages: collecting dead wood had to be specifically approved. Generally, the users also had the right to take what was called the *morts-bois* or *morbois*, meaning wood of species considered unsuitable for any other purpose or that did not bear fruit; almost always, the right included (customs varied with the regions) bramble, dogwood, elder, broom, willow, juniper, and alder. However, most of these species were used not only as firewood, but also to make tools, baskets, fences, canes, etc.

Various rules applied to firewood: in some places people could collect wood only on certain days, while in other places the quantity was limited to individuals or families. The charter of Minorville (1263) in Meurthe-et-Moselle states that all the wood on the territory belongs to the town, and that what is left after the inhabitants take their firewood, is placed in common. The charter of Deuxnouds (1298) specifies that all the wood of Deuxnouds belongs in common to the inhabitants of the town, except for a certain number of arpents that each person has for his own use and cannot sell.

In Lunéville, each family could collect one cart of wood or as many loads as they could manage to carry on their shoulders on every Friday and Saturday from Saint-Martin's day (November 11) to Christmas. At Andolsheim, an estate that belonged to the abbey of Saint-Denis, a text of 1300 specifies that the beneficiaries could enter a certain forest on only one day per year—the day before Christmas—to gather dead firewood. But whoever loaded his cart to the point of breaking it or getting it stuck in the mud, had to pay a fine of thirty deniers. Thus, the legislator wanted to prevent abuse, but it was also an incitement to build solid carts—repression bred technical progress.

In the "Fors" of Béarn (at the end of the eleventh century), the cutting of firewood was free for the minor species of trees, while the mutilation of oaks, beeches, and chestnut trees was punished by a fine of twelve deniers per animal-load or four deniers per man-load. It was increased if the offense occurred in a *bédat* (from the Latin *vetatum*, forbidden) which corresponded to the *défens* or forbidden area in the north. In this case, the fine was proportional to the number of branches on the felled tree.

Strange customs allowed a delinquent to avoid the fine if he wasn't apprehended immediately in the forbidden area: for example, the charter of Gourchelles (lower Seine; 1202) specifies that if the delinquent manages to get out of the forest far enough to "turn over his load between himself and the woods," he will not be pursued any further. This rule made it difficult to carry away a big tree, but not to take a few small bundles of wood. In Lunéville, the poor inhabitants had the right to carry wood out of the forest on their backs; however, if they had a billhook and could not run away, the guard had the right to take the tool. This, however, was at the guard's own risk since the text specified that if he received a blow while doing so, he could not complain.

In the east of France, very old customs required that a man shout three times before cutting wood in a forbidden part of the forest. If, after loading the wood on his back, he managed to get out of the forest without being caught by the guard, or even if, when he saw the guard, he managed to throw his axe beyond the ditch marking the boundary of the area, the man was not liable to a fine nor to the seizure of his tool (custom of Grendelbruch, near Obernai). Cutting green wood was sometimes severely punished. Thus in Ribeauvillé, according to a record of the fourteenth century, a charcoal burner caught by the forest guards while cutting green wood either had to pay a heavy fine or have his thumb cut off, (after binding it with a strap the law specified, to prevent loss of blood).

Providing wood for baking bread—the basic nourishment at the time—was a constant need. Originally to save fuel, village communities used a common oven where each family could, successively, bake their bread. In places where each family had their own oven, the latter was used only occasionally to bake bread that lasted several weeks. So, having a common oven was both an economy of investment, as only one oven was built for several families, and a saving of fuel as the oven functioned more-or-less continuously. But, of course, it was generally a privileged person, lay or ecclesiastical, who had the bake house built and later charged a fee for its use. And often, just as mere peasants were forbidden to own millstones—so that they would have to bring their grain to the communal mill and pay a fee—they were also forbidden to have their own baking oven and were compelled to use the communal bake house (*four banal**).

When, from the eleventh century on, the population started to grow, the everyday consumption of wood resulted in deductions greater than the natural renewal of the forest and therefore contributed,

♦ ♦ ♦

* *Banal*: for the use of all, by obligation, and entailing a fee to the lord. Derived from the Frankish word *ban* meaning a proclamation, an edict. Many derivatives of this word are still used in French such as: *banlieue, bannir, bannière, forban, abandon*, etc.

particularly around the towns, to increased deforestation. In many places customary rights started to be more strictly regulated.

The transportation of fuel, whether for industrial or domestic use, was an acute problem. Finding the fuel was one thing, but transporting fuel to the place where it was used was another. In the Middle Ages, transportation was a deciding factor in technological choices. For instance, in construction, this problem was solved by certain technical solutions that were a determining influence on the architecture itself.

To facilitate the transportation of firewood, it was converted on the spot and, whenever possible, streams and rivers were used to float the rough timber and the biggest logs downstream. Nevertheless, this required not only favorable geographical conditions, but also an understanding among the riverside residents alongside the whole length of the waterway used, or the intervention of a collective or superior authority. An important part of firewood and, in particular, the wood used in the bread ovens consisted of bundles made up of small pieces that had to be transported on the backs of men or animals or in carts. To reduce the weight to be transported one must use a fuel of higher caloric power for an identical weight: that is why, especially in the towns, charcoal was widely used for cooking as it still is today in many regions.

The domestic use of charcoal, however, resulted also in abuses that were detrimental to the forests and had to be repressed. Some nearby residents of the forests made charcoal in their garden which, since the wood was processed in a pit, was easy to conceal. Consequently, a decree prohibited the making of "charcoal pits" in houses or gardens "within or along the forests."[1] The penalty was the tearing down of the houses belonging to the inhabitants who were committing the offense. Yet, records show that in spite of the severe penalties the offenses continued. To give an example: a judgment of the *"Réformation des Forêts de Normandie,"* on December 7, 1534, condemned a certain Roger Bénart for having made "charcoal pits" in his garden near the forest of Breteuil, to a fine of one hundred livres and to prison and, furthermore, to be evicted from his house situated "along the said forest" and to "find a house elsewhere far from the forests." The heavy penalty imposed shows the importance given—just after the Middle Ages—to the reconstitution and preservation of the forest that had been dangerously depleted. The risk taken by the offender indicates that the sale of charcoal must have been exceptionally profitable. The "law of Beaumont" established a fine of ten sols for those who made charcoal or ashes with the intent of selling the product and the penalty was, of course, much increased if the offense was committed in a forbidden area or if trees of fresh growth had been damaged.[2]

Early Industrial Consumption of Wood

Early industrial uses, such as the transformation and the processing of metals, the manufacturing of fired goods, including ceramics, pottery, sheet glass, leaded glass, tiles, bricks, the cooking of binding agents for construction such as lime and plaster, the treatment of brines used to dissolve the rock salt extracted from the mines, etc., involved a considerable consumption of wood. The problem of transportation was solved in several ways. Sometimes there was no problem, as when the original raw material to be transformed as well as the fuel to be used were found at the same place; for example, when a deposit of siliceous sand, suitable for the manufacturing of glass, was found next to a beech grove, or a quarry of brick clay or limestone near woodland, or when iron ore was found right in the ground of the forest, as in the Périgord where this led to a proliferation of forges in the valleys. In the Puisaye, the potters' kilns were built near both the forest and the clay site. In the Argonne, the extractions of clay for pottery and tile clay resulted in the creation of ponds, notably around monasteries that owned tile works such as the abbeys of Rupt-aux-Nonnains, of Beaulieu-en-Argonne and of Cheminon. Since monks were required to eat fish during certain periods, they converted the abandoned quarries into fish ponds.

Still, in most cases, a choice had to be made: transport the fuel or transport the raw material. This choice depended, first of all, on the respective weights to be transported and on the transportation facilities available at the site. For example, if it was possible to float the wood, a manufacturing site could be installed downstream, sometimes quite far from the forest that provided the fuel. In this case, however, political and real estate conditions played a role. Indeed, as noted before, Paris could not be supplied with wood from the Morvan until the king of France controlled the productive region as well as the course of the Yonne and Seine rivers.

The higher the value of the ore used, the less reason there was to transport fuel that, at equal value, would have represented a weight and volume infinitely larger to transport. It was then rational to set up the industry near the forest. This happened mostly in the type of manufacturing where the added value was important (glass-making, forges, etc.) and the weight of the raw material much less than the weight of the wood needed to process it, or when the manufacturing process required very large quantities of fuel.

In certain cases, too, special devices were necessary to bring the raw material to the forest. When the forests of the area of Salins-du-Jura were no longer adequate for the processing of salt extracted from the mines, a very long aqueduct was built that brought the salt—previously dissolved in water at the bottom of the mine and brought to the surface—to the forest of Chaux where the brine was evaporated to recover the salt.

The wood consumption was often greater than the forest's natural regeneration. So sometimes, when it was possible, the processing facilities were moved to remain near the fuel.

For many early industrial uses, any wood was suitable as fuel. For some industries, however, particular species were needed. As a result, the manufacturers placed their factories near the forests that contained the corresponding species and favored, by all means, the planting and the development of these species. Thus, for the glass-works, beech was systematically used in the Middle Ages because the ash of this wood contains not only potash but also lime—which is not the case with oak ash. This ash replaced the aluminum oxide, lime, and potash that today are part of the composition of leaded glass that includes a little over 50 percent of siliceous sand, 22 percent of lime and 17 percent of potash, iron oxide, and aluminum oxide. It has, however, been impossible to determine the exact composition of the leaded glass windows of the Middle Ages. Due to these particularities, glassworks settled, whenever possible, where they could find both very fine sand and beech groves, such as in the Forez or at Crépy-en-Valois. It is quite possible that one of the reasons for the progressive replacement of beeches by resinous trees in the Forez was due to the glassworkers, who moved their instal-lations as soon as they consumed the woods.

The Argonne was a wood-supply center for glassmakers. In 1448, the duke of Lorraine confirmed their rights in the woods; during that period, they made bottles and cups for the viticulturists of nearby Champagne. The later development of the glassworks of Baccarat, Cirey, and Saint-Gobain was linked to the vast forests in the regions where they operated. Glassmakers sometimes bought forests or made sure they could use the wood. It was the case of the glassworks of Assas, north of Montpellier, that were abandoned in the fifteenth century because of the lack of wood in the area; in 1432, the owner had acquired the usufruct of lands located in the very wooded area of pic Saint-Loup to obtain fuel. In Provence, because of the wood shortage, the glassworks used charcoal and continued to use it even when coal became available; the charcoal came from Burgundy by the Saône and the Rhône rivers.

Lime and plaster kilns, tile works and potteries were among the largest consumers of wood. However, these vast masonry installations could not be moved and if the wood supply became too expensive they had to be abandoned. In particular, the pottery kilns used huge amounts of wood; in spite of the perfecting of kiln techniques since the Middle Ages, those of the "Korean" type—still used in the early twentieth century—consumed one hundred to two hundred cubic meters of wood for each firing. In Saint-Amand in the Puisaye, for thirty potters there were as many loggers working on a full-time basis. The wood was also used to construct the barges that exported the products via the Loire River to Nantes and Brittany.

The Flemish brickworks, which made possible the enormous development of the towns in that region that was bereft of stone, existed thanks to the wealth of wood in the Lowlands. The Houtland, which means the woodland—Holland—became a country particularly poor in forests and in which it became necessary in modern times to re-create some despite the density of the population. It was the forest that allowed the blossoming of cities in northern France, Flanders, and Holland: all were built with bricks. Later, mineral coal took over from the exhausted wood supply and permitted the activity of the brickworks to be maintained; it also extended the area of construction with bricks to regions poor in wood, such as Picardy. As early as 1200, the city of Bruges bought mineral coal from England. The use of coal as an energy fuel was discovered in 1198 in Liège and slowly mined coal became an important element in the development of that town. The first traces of imports of English coal to the Île-de-France go back only to the fourteenth century; in 1325, a boat loaded with wheat from Pontoise came back with coal from Newcastle.

Bell foundries—most certainly quite busy at the time of the widespread development of religious buildings from the twelfth to the fourteenth century—needed, in order to melt down the alloy of pewter and copper that was used, a fuel composed of a mixture of hornbeam (in the birch family) and oak logs and were not satisfied with the less-noble species that generally were used for heating or for the firing kilns.

Ore mines and the forges that extracted the metal from the ore also required large quantities of wood or charcoal, because the ore was treated at the factory site to avoid heavy transportation costs. Between 1310 and 1340 the region of France that extends from the Ardennes to Lorraine passing though Barrois and Champagne became an important producer of iron. A Parisian burgher, Gentien Cocatrix, paid the debts of Saint-Remy of Reims, which amounted to thirty five hundred livres in exchange for the right to exploit the iron mines in the forest of Othe for fifteen years. The count of Bar loaned money to the burghers of Pont-à-Mousson to build a new forge and an installation driven by hydraulic power in Briey. The count of Savoie, the Dauphin, and the king of Navarre were personally involved in the exploitation of the mines on their estates.[3]

In the Alps, the mines of Allevard were particularly active, and in everyplace where the wooded back country was not adequate to feed, by its sole production, the workshops that treated the metal on site, the forest diminished. It is what happened in the dry climate of the southern Alps, to the Queyras, where the deforestation, that provoked several catastrophic floods, was due to the exploitation of the iron ore of Château-Dauphin and the silver ore of Largentière-la-Bessée. The high Alpine valleys were, writes Bautier, covered with mines and forges that supplied the famous weapon factories of Milan and Brescia.

Monks were not the last to be interested by industry and as they often owned large forests, they owned many kilns and forges. The abbey of Montier-en-Der acquired, in 1179, the wood of Grigny near Saint-Dizier for the fuel necessary for the kilns of Saint-Dizier. In 1188, the abbey of Ecurey received the woods of Froillet to clear them, but also "to make bricks, and install iron forges with the right to extract ore on all the territory of Morley."[4]

Many place names throughout France evoke these exploitations of iron or silver, which are today exhausted, as well as the lime and plaster kilns, the forges, the tile-, brick-, pottery- and glassworks that the forests' wood supplied. Traces are found in the form of piles of scoria called *ferriers, laitiers*, etc., depending on the region. Names like Largentière, Laferrière, Argentière, Ferrière, and Ferrette are common and are sometimes found in regions where the forest has taken over and all traces of the installations have disappeared.

In the fifteenth century, there appeared to be a recession in the metal industry; this was due to the disappearance of many little forges, of forges in regions where there wasn't enough wood left or where the ore was becoming exhausted, or of forges that were in areas without rivers or even roads that permitted easy export. In England, the decline of the forges of the famous forest of Dean appears to be due to the overexploitation of the woods. Other centers of iron production developed around Sheffield and Durham as well as in Lancashire. During that period, England had to import iron from Spain, Sweden, and Westphalia.

The users of iron bullion, in turn, needed fuel to forge weapons and tools. These iron-smiths, wheelwrights and farriers preferred to use charcoal, which burns at a higher temperature than wood and has the advantage of a higher caloric power for the same weight. To save iron in the manufacturing of horseshoes, old ones were remelted and the resultant product was mixed with new iron.

In their efforts to protect the forests, the authorities sometimes attempted to prevent large consumers of wood from settling close to the woods: "Forges, kilns, brickworks, glassmakers, and other shops" were "forbidden in or around the king's forests without explicit permission of that lord."[5] It was hoped that the transportation difficulties and cost would be dissuasive. But the profits were sufficient to allow the industrialists to overcome these difficulties and make up the extra expenses.

The use of hydraulic power to hammer the iron with tilt-hammers (heavy hammers, hoisted by cames turning around the mill's shaft, that fell down on the metal), produced genuine small-scale industrialization. Forges of higher yield than the hand forges were developed along the rivers, instead of continuing to look for the proximity of fuel and ore; this entailed an increase in transportation.

As these higher-yield forges worked much quicker than the hand forges, they consumed much more fuel. The authorities sometimes ordered their destruction not only to protect the forests, but because they were noisy and polluted the air. In the middle of the fourteenth century, the Dauphin, Humbert II, ordered all forges to be destroyed in an area of three miles around the town of Grenoble.[6]

Tilt-hammers existed for a long time because the energy was free. The weapons factory of Klingenthal in the Vosges, founded in the eighteenth century, still used these machines after the Second World War; its last tilt-hammer was decommissioned in 1964.

Charcoal

Obtaining fuel by "burning" wood may appear surprising at first. In fact, only part of the wood is burned in order to eliminate certain components and obtain a purer product that is richer in carbon. The wood, protected from the air, is very strongly heated, which allows it to eliminate certain organic components: bark, sap, tars, and humidity. Nature, through a similar process, converted fossilized forests into mineral coal.

Charcoal has the advantage of being easier to use and more efficient than wood for metalwork, because it releases more heat with a smaller volume. Furthermore, charcoal is more practical to transport than logs or faggots as it can easily be put into bags or baskets. Because of the difficulty of transportation in the mountain, the friars of the Grande Chartreuse sold their wood as charcoal and supplied their own forges in the valley with this fuel—which they transported by mule.

Charcoal developed enormously during the Middle Ages and this industry remained very important until mineral coal progressively replaced it during the nineteenth century. In France, coal consumption surpassed charcoal consumption only by 1860. For a long time, as indicated by a survey of 1829, consumers distrusted iron made with coal and preferred metal that had been melted down with charcoal.[7] Charcoal's gentler and more regular heat produces tools of better quality—among others, woodworking tools: axes, billhooks, planishers, scissors—with better cutting edges. In addition, iron melted down with charcoal acquires a high carbon content and resists rust better. The extraordinary durability of certain wrought-iron products of the Middle Age that have lasted for centuries and have remarkably resisted corrosion has been remarked upon. It is the case of certain gates, and of the clamps retaining the shafts of the little columns, in the cathedral of Chartres, built in the thirteenth century.[8]

Masters of the fire, smiths, ironworkers, and locksmiths inspired fear; they were suspected of maintaining relationships with the powers of Hell; they were consulted to cast spells or untie them, and sometimes to heal diseases or repair broken or dislocated limbs. In many countries today, notably in Africa, smiths still have a magic function.

This reputation was not without disadvantages. The ironsmith Biscornet, who created the remarkable ornaments of the Sainte-Anne portal of the cathedral of Notre-Dame in Paris, was burned as a sorcerer on the place de Grève; it was said that he had made a pact with the devil in order to produce that work—today's *compagnons* still don't know how it was done. Biscornet's trade secrets disappeared with him; and perhaps they owed more to his ability, experience and lucky combinations of ore and fuel, than to the help of the devil.

Bell foundries used a combination of wood and charcoal. In the eighteenth century, in order to cast four bells for the monks of Sainte-Corneille, the founder required eight bags of charcoal and nine cords of dry wood, in addition to boards. Making charcoal requires know-how, qualified labor, and constant supervision. To obtain a good yield in relation to the quantity of wood treated and good-quality charcoal as well, it is necessary to constantly supervise the carbonization for seventy to eighty hours. The best places are the old bases of charcoal pits, because the ground already burned is waterproof and withstands the heat better. Two methods are used: either holes are dug in the ground or stacks are built with branches around a central chimney for the draft. The stack or the woodpile underground is carefully covered with dirt, turf, and leaves; it is then made airtight with coal ashes so that the combustion can be regulated through the reserved air intakes. Throughout the combustion, the charcoal burner opens or closes the air intakes in order to guarantee slow, constant, and complete combustion.

In the Middle Ages and until the nineteenth century, a whole population of charcoal-burners lived in the forests. This marginal population was very independent; these nomadic men, with their face blackened by the charcoal, lived with their families in wooden cabins and moved from time to time to new exploitation sites (in forty days a single charcoal pit can use up one hundred hectares of forest). They inspired fear in the townspeople and even in the sedentary peasants, as shown in the literature of the period.

Charcoal was the object of long-distance trade, especially in Mediterranean countries that were poor in wood, where fuel had to come from very distant places, and thus any economy in weight was welcome. Charcoal, for the same weight of fuel, produces much more calories than wood (30 against 18). But if one considers the forest, making charcoal, by combustion of part of the wood makes the other part a "purer" product that is richer in carbon, and ends up using almost three times more wood to obtain the same amount of calories.

With the techniques of the Middle Ages, eight to ten kilograms of wood were necessary to obtain one kilogram of charcoal that provided as many calories as 1.67 kilograms of wood. Modern techniques have increased the yield and almost two times less wood is needed; but in the Middle Ages, using wood in the form of charcoal led to consuming five times more wood than if it had been burned directly. To make one ton of refined iron, over 65 cubic meters of wood were needed. A good coppice produced on one hectare about 84 cubic meters every sixteen years. One can thus understand the impact on the forests of all human activities consuming this fuel, activities which were in addition to all those that consumed wood without any transformation.

To have enough fuel in an area close enough so that transportation would not make the forges economically unprofitable, forge masters were led in certain cases, as in the east of France and in England, to acquire forests. In Sweden, forges were allowed to function only if they owned sufficient woods, of which they had to organize the renewal, and which they had to exploit rationally. But this was not often the case in France, where the forges and other miscellaneous consumers frequently instigated the disappearance of the neighboring forests and subsisted thanks only to wood imports and, later, to coal. During the Middle Ages, the authorities often took measures to prevent these activities from eventually causing the disappearance of the forests.

Because of the importance of forges for armaments they always benefited from particular privileges. English iron and mine masters had great influence for the acquisition of wood. Thus, in 1486, the commissaries of the king's mines were entitled to take all kinds of woods, coppice, and charcoal necessary for the metal works. They were also allowed to commandeer means of transportation by water or land at "reasonable prices"; they even had the right to commandeer labor among the peasantry under the condition that they pay them a "reasonable" salary.[9] However, to manufacture the indispensable charcoal more than coppice was cut; even timbers, which by their species or their sections would have been useful for construction or for the navy, were cut. In 1558, in England, a royal ordinance forbade felling oaks, beeches or ash trees of over a foot in diameter at the base—which already represented big trees—that grew less than fourteen miles from the sea or from a river navigable from the sea. But, ten years later, derogations were granted. It has been said that in England, the charcoal industry, making the exploitation of the forest profitable for the peasants, contributed to preventing the forest from being cleared for culture. Following similar reasoning, A. Maury wrote, in 1856, in France: "The increasing consumption of coal that gradually diminishes the revenue of forest owners is a new danger for our woods, as it tends to paralyze the attempts of reforesting that can only remedy the devastations our trees have been subjected to for the last sixty years."[10] But in England it has been noticed that the area of the forests fell from 15 percent of the total area in 1086, to 10 percent in 1350; and after 400 years of stability, went down to 5 percent in the nineteenth century. The forest—or what was left of it—was saved only by coal, a fuel more suitable for industry than charcoal.

Ashes

As a by-product of wood combustion, ashes were carefully collected for different uses. Ashes contain active products, among them potash, phosphates, and various alkaline substances. Ashes of homogeneous qualities without scoria or other impurities were needed for certain uses. For these, wood was burned with the sole purpose of obtaining ashes. These ashes were used as soap or detergent. Laundry was washed by mixing ashes in water that was boiled in caldrons. They were also used to scrape surfaces that were going to be painted and to remove mold. Ashes were thus the object of a very active trade, and the nobles did not disdain the profit they could make from it. At the end of the thirteenth century, among four servants that the lady of Valois maintained in her woods at Viry, there was a clearer, a trapper, an archer, and the fourth was an ash-maker.[11] The ashes sold in Paris were used by the laundries as well as by individual households.

In glassmaking, beech ash played an important role because the lime it contains played the indispensable role of catalyst. That is why glassworks always settled near beech groves or encouraged the growth of that specie. Certain cinders were used in agriculture; they were sold as fertilizers and were used instead of the potassic or phosphatic fertilizers that are used nowadays. But frequently the ashes were spread directly after burning the bushes and the branches of the felled trees, an operation done prior to transforming the land into field or meadowland. The most-appreciated grass grew on burn-beaten land and the shepherds were often accused of burning forests in order to spread the grazing lands. Today, pastoral fire is still practiced in certains regions such as the Pyrénées. But if burn-baiting, without exports of ashes, whatever the system used—running fire, *écobuage*, etc.—preserved the fertility by maintaining on site the chemical elements resulting from the combustion and closed the cycle, the systematic manufacturing and trade of ashes contributed to progressively impoverish the forest soil.

To protect the forests, measures against ash-makers had to be taken, but for the king's forests these measures were promulgated only in the sixteenth century. Sanctions had to be taken, even against individuals, to prevent ash-making—that was tolerated by custom for private use—from becoming a trade; the "law of Beaumont," which served as the model for many other charters, portended a fine of ten sols for whomever made ashes for trade.

7 · LUMBER ·

The Wood Empire

THE WESTERN EUROPEAN TRAVELER who today flies over Scandinavia is impressed to see the forest spreading as far as the eye can reach, barely broken by clearings. And, if he visits forest exploitation sites in Sweden, which today includes 23 million hectares of forests, he encounters a scale of exploitation that cannot be compared to what he might have seen in his own country: huge composite machines move on a very wide front, felling the trees and converting them at once, advancing without respite as reaping machines leave behind them billets, lopped, barked, regularly set, cut lengthwise and ready to be dispatched by road or by water. This huge site for the processing of a material that is perhaps the most precious for man, as well as the easiest to work, and that today still constitutes the wealth of the Nordic countries, was the premise of the extraordinary expansion of what has been called the Norman Empire.

Of course, the Normans were successful because of their qualities of courage and organization and their technical and military capabilities. But none of that would have been possible if they hadn't had at their disposal, at the outset, a supply of inexhaustible wealth—wood—that allowed them to build those fleets whose countless ships decorated their bows with a dragon's head—hence their name: "drakkars." In these shallow-draft vessels the Normans found their way all through Europe, all the way to the Black Sea, and all the way to Africa and America, sailing across the seas, rowing up the rivers, and if necessary carrying their boats over land from one river to another as they did in Russia.

That is how the Normans and their descendants were able to plunder, devastate, and exploit so many countries. And it also allowed them to conquer several, which eventually prospered under their rule. They assimilated and adapted with exceptional flexibility and rapidity the customs and the religion of the conquered lands, without losing their original qualities. Carried by wood, by iron, and by fire, the Normans, woodsmen and men of the wood, for a long time had as their main weapon the axe, with which they slew their enemies with as much dexterity as the loggers cut down trees. On the famous tapestry, which relates the conquest of England by William the Conqueror, most of the riders have lance and sword, but many of the foot soldiers are armed with the big Norman axe.

In many countries where they landed, the Normans didn't find woods of the same quality as the northern ones. The slow growth of woods in a cold country gives them a finer texture, a greater hardness, a stronger resistance, and a minimum of knots. Furthermore, because of the very rigorous climate, these trees are cut down during a period of total interruption of the sap's rising. Finally, floating the trees before they are converted eliminates the sap and provides them with excellent conservation characteristics. According to modern tests, Swedish pines have resistance to rupture 30 to 40 percent greater than American pines, and their resistance to flexion is about twice that of the resin trees of temperate regions. That is why the Normans could have lances and axes that, for an equal resistance, which were lighter and handier than those of the Franks, Germans or Saxons, made of heavier woods from deciduous trees or when made of resin wood from their own countries, had to be much larger and heavier.

Wherever they were, the Normans made sure that they could find enough wood. Once they settled in Normandy and peace returned, with the improvement of the climate in the tenth-eleventh centuries, they extended the fields and made clearings, but always managed to keep enough wooded areas. The Normans later took the first pretext to invade England, which was sparsely populated, still forested, and had a jagged coastline offering many port sites—tempting prey for a sailor-people. Later, the maritime development of England would be based on its wood resources, reinforced very early by Scandinavian imports. These imports have become traditional. Today the United Kingdom still imports three times more wood from the northern countries than France does.

The Normans were always particularly interested in the forests: "In Normandy," writes Maury, "the forests were the object of much more attention than elsewhere." He notes that even before Normandy came under the control of the king of France, "the ducal power had carefully taken care of preventing encroachments." The situation was identical in Anjou, domain of the Plantagenet, where "as early as the eleventh century the lords forbade the removal of oak wood, principal and most important specie of the forest."[1] Of course, this solicitude for the forests was exercised mainly for the benefit of the dukes of Normandy and the lay and ecclesiastical lords. Indeed, in Normandy and in Anjou, one had to own a forest to exercise the right to dispense justice.

In the fourteenth century, as a result of this policy of annexing and reserving the forests for the nobles, the duchy of Normandy was, according to an ordinance of Charles V, "covered with forests and bushes more than any other part of the kingdom," and that, in spite of the numerous clearings made in the time of Saint Louis. The interest of the Norman kings in the forest was such that they didn't hesitate, as soon as they conquered England, to appropriate most of the woods under a variety of pretexts and, in certain cases, such as that of the New Forest in Hampshire, to evict peasant populations and destroy villages and churches in order to extend the forest. In the eyes of William the Conqueror's contemporaries, this brutal operation appears to have brought misfortune to the family. His son, William the Red, died there, killed by an arrow, then his grandson Richard, and finally his grandnephew Henry, who remained suspended from a tree by his hair, like Absalon.

Later on, the kings of England were pressured into modifying the laws that regulated the forests and reducing their exorbitant privileges. But they kept an important part of the forest estate. Indeed, it was frequently due to donations of lumber from the royal forests that English abbeys, cathedrals, and castles were built, all of which required huge quantities of wood.

Before the Norman Conquest, the Saxons built their structures almost exclusively with wood. The church of Greensted, northeast of London, built in 845 of assembled split tree trunks and formerly covered with a thatched roof, is perhaps the oldest wooden church in the world that is still standing. The Normans introduced into England the techniques of building with stone and prospected the quarries. Nonetheless, wood remained for a long time a dominant element in English construction and Viollet-le-Duc noted that the framework of monuments of the Middle Ages in England were distinguished by their richness and the large size of the lumber used. England has also preserved a great many wooden houses; this resulted not only from a conservative spirit and from the insularity that protected the country since the eleventh century from invasions, fires, and destruction caused by war, but also from the lesser scarcity of wood up to a certain period. Although England at the time of the Norman Conquest included a percentage of forested land that was much less than France (it has been estimated that it was no more than 15 percent, while it was about 25 percent during the same period in France), its population was only two-fifths of the French population.

The fact that the cathedrals and great abbeys of the English Middle Ages often have their main naves and side aisles lined with wood is not because the English (who used French architects) did not know how to or didn't dare build stone vaults. As determined as the French were to build monuments as prestigious as their means allowed, they appear to have given their preference to width over height, which might have encouraged them to use wood. But there are many examples of stone vaults for which they even developed original forms. The use of wood techniques, in which they achieved great results, as well as the quality of their Middle Ages frameworks that had impressed Viollet-le-Duc have left numerous marks on their greatest buildings. Even when the Gothic style asserted itself in England, in some of the great religious edifices, stone vaults were sometimes imitated in wood in such detail that the visitor who is not forewarned can be mistaken. The structure and the appearance of ribbed vaults, of which the English developed original forms with "fan-vaults," often has something in common with wooden constructions made of narrow strips bearing on main frames, in the manner of the ship sheathing that bears on main frames. This technique was inherited from the Northmen with whom, for centuries before the conquest of William the Bastard, the English had maintained close links in peacetime.

The Vikings' vessels, a few of which were found in Scandinavia —in peat bogs or in mud—attest to the extraordinary perfection of the work of their marine carpenters and their remarkable mastery of naval architecture. The Normans transferred this knowledge to the construction of buildings: the Gothic framework owes a lot to the techniques of the shipbuilders. The relationship is apparent between the main frames that formed the skeleton of the Northmen's ships, and which were maintained in the construction techniques of the wooden navy for centuries, and rafter-trusses which were used for timber-framed roofs during the twelfth-thirteenth centuries— first in Normandy and also in the Ile-de-France—above the naves of the churches.

Construction and Civil Engineering

Any builder must solve the problem of erecting a shelter: a hollow volume in which the inhabitant is protected from the elements, not only laterally by partitions, walls, and closings that permit access and light, but also above, by a roof. The easiest way to defy gravity by an element overstepping the void between two supports is to have monolithic elements able to cross the span. A wooden cross is an important span without adding a huge weight. By its composition it can withstand compression, traction, and flexion; in addition, it is light and of a density less than that of water. Finally, the tallest lumber in our temperate zone generally has the largest diameter, as the trees naturally have a circumference proportional to their height. Wood is thus a material that is particularly well suited for making lintels, joists, floors, horizontal elements bearing on two supports, and supporting charges.

In our climate, even in masonry construction, the simplest and most common solution for floors (and often even for lintels) was to use wood, which was abundant all through the Middle Ages in western and southern Europe. It was a material that was particularly easy to extract, work with, and use; and, in addition, it was in most cases accessible free of charge for everyone's needs.

As a result, wood wasn't economized and the greatest part of all construction, from cottages to fortified castles, was in wood. It is necessary to examine the diverse construction techniques—and the context in which they were used—to realize how considerable wood consumption was.

Several elements combined to gradually develop the use of masonry in construction: the disadvantages of wood, mainly its combustibility and putrescibility, the pressure of constraints such as the shortage of certain categories of timber; and also the perfecting of extraction and cutting tools for stone. The frequent fires, particularly in the towns, encouraged development of the different uses of masonry, without ending the use of wood; this was seen by the appearance of fire walls, facades, vaults in the lower stories, and arches to replace lintels.

Relations between the forest and building operations were numerous, but sometimes quite subtle. It is easy to perceive the relationship between the method of construction and the supply of wood. In countries poor in wood, houses were built with dirt, cob, turf, dried or fired bricks, rough or cut stones set dry and masonry linked with mortar. Elsewhere, timber framings were limited to a strict minimum: a skeleton filled with cob. Where wood was very abundant, houses could be made entirely of wood, either in piled-up trunks or in so-called "palisade-walls." But the availability of the material and its abundance were not the only criteria. For example, wood, an excellent insulation material, is best suited to cold countries, while stone or agglomerated dirt are better for hot climates as their thermal inertia allows the nocturnal coolness to moderate the heat during the day. But in the old days, builders seldom had a choice. Nonetheless, in the lines, the volume, and the appearance of a house in a given environment, many factors apply other than the availability and the relative abundance of one material or another.

Social, economic or cultural factors can also play a role and can lead to a more-or-less important expenditure for wood.

The massive shape of the farms in the Jura has sometimes been attributed to the harshness of the climate and to certain traditions. But one of the main reasons for their low and squashed appearance comes from the fact that in those regions where the forests belonged to the communes, the quantity of wood allocated to each household was proportional to the area occupied by each house. Thus, it would have been disadvantageous for the inhabitant to build high, with several stories, since it was not the floor surfaces but the hold on the ground that was taken into account. The choice made for construction was influenced by this consideration, essential in a region with cold winters. In such regions, where wood was abundant, the houses were built entirely with this material. Thus in the Jura, it has been calculated that a farm and its outlying buildings, of which the surface on the ground was five hundred to six hundred square meters, required three hundred to four hundred cubic meters of pine and spruce rough timber; one-half was squared by axe in the forest, one-quarter was sawed in the village to make boards, and one-quarter, in spruce, split to make shingles that covered the roof.[2]

Most rural houses were covered with thatch or wood. Certain woods, not very putrescible, were split and used to make wooden tiles. Oak and sometimes pine were used in the plains, and in the mountains, spruce or larch. The houses, built entirely with wood, were constituted either by horizontal woods, such as the *mazots* of the Valais, the Russian isbas, the Scandinavian houses, the cabins of the Canadian trappers or by vertically joined woods often joined by grooves (palisade-walls). Originally, the latter types of walls were made up of juxtaposed pieces of wood that were simply driven into the ground like the stakes of a fence; archaeologists have found traces of those Early Middle Ages constructions in several countries. Those walls were very similar to stockades on which a roof would have been set. In the more elaborate forms of that type of wall—which belong to the carpenter's technique—the elements are assembled at their base with a horizontal sill bearing on a low wall and, at their top, with a superior crosshead supporting the roof rafters.

In most houses, even when they were not entirely in wood, but included walls in masonry or cob, a considerable amount of wood was used—particularly, for the lintels, the doors and windows, the paneling, the ceilings, the framings, and the floors. Rustic vaults were used to cover the basements and sometimes even the ground floor, as wood keeps poorly when in direct contact with the ground. But floors were usually made of wood. They were often constituted by juxtaposed, joined beams, sometimes interlocked by dowels, on which was spread sand or a rough work of lime or plaster mortar with pieces of tile, bricks or crushed stone. On that reasonably horizontal surface tiling was sealed. Such floors used a considerable amount of wood, about one-fifth of a cubic meter of wood by square meter of finished floor. Some, a little less costly, were made of nonjoined beams; they are called "French" floors.

As for the walls, much construction, especially in houses, was mixed: wood and masonry was used. They included a wood skeleton, the timber framing, composed of pieces of about fifteen to twenty centimeters per section, rectangular or square, of which the vertical elements of the height of the story were capped by horizontal cross-beams and maintained by slanted braces. The spaces between the timbers were filled with dirt, bricks or stones, apparent or drowned in mortar. This technique of half-timbering is called *colombage* in French, a word that has nothing to do with the birds [T.N.: *colombe* is dove] but derives from *colonne*, the columns designating the vertical pieces. On the ground floor, the timber framing generally rested on a low masonry wall that insulated it from the ground and inhibited the rising of humidity.

That is the way most town houses and many rural houses were built in northern and western Europe in the Middle Ages. Countless examples remain in different French provinces, especially in Alsace and Normandy. Even more can be found in England as well as other wooded countries of Europe; each region has its own traditional style of timber framing, recognizable by the arrangement of the "columns" and the horizontal beams, by their spacing, by the designs formed by the angled pieces, slanted or crossed, sometimes curved, by the color of the fillings that were sometimes in bricks but were generally coated. This technique allowed the front of the house to have very few walled-up fillings and, when the use of glass developed, the builders created real "architectures of light." In the towns, particularly, the narrowness of the lots, generally inherited from the strips that made up the fields, and the great depth of the buildings (which permitted a less-dense street network), made largely opened facades, genuine walls of glass divided by the timber framing, an indispensable feature to obtain sufficient light inside.

In addition to the consumption of fuel entailed by the manufacturing of glass when the frontages were largely lighted, the construction in timber framing required large quantities of timber, mainly of medium diameters. For secondary constructions, outlying buildings, fences, and palisades, smaller timbers were used, or when it wasn't necessary to have absolutely straight timbers, ripped timber. Nowadays split timber—often chestnut—is still used for fences, palisades, and stakes because it is less sensitive to humidity and rot than sawed wood.

These supplementary uses also entailed great consumption of wood. But the lavish use of wood was solidly in place—and anchored.

The production of stakes was a very important economic activity: many fortifications were still made of wood, in the form of palisades of pointed stakes; in many places, the development of vineyards required props; and the method of collective pastoral and agricultural exploitation as well as protection from wild animals required large quantities of fences to park the animals, protect the crops and also, in the forest, to protect the young plants from the grazing of domestic animals and wild herbivores. So, it is not surprising that certain forests were called *sylvae palariae*; in other words, forests intended for the purpose of producing stakes. But to obtain sufficiently thick timber, this production required a longer revolution than the coppice used for firewood. These timbers were used not only for stakes, but also for the framework of structures and supplied rafters, posts, beams, etc., for small buildings such as rural houses. As the distance between the walls of those houses was no more than six or seven meters (about eighteen to twenty-one feet), the framing could be made of little trusses spaced every 0.60 to 0.90 meter, instead of the traditional, massive trusses—that supported horizontal purlins—placed every four or five meters (about twelve to fifteen feet). This system required only wood of small sizes. Under a rustic and primitive form, it was already the principle of the rafter-trusses that would have a spectacular development in the twelfth and thirteenth centuries in Gothic architecture and especially in cathedrals.

Timbers of large diameters were rare and reserved for noblemen and military uses. To obtain such pieces, one had to allow the trees to grow for much more than thirty years: one had either to manage to keep enough seed-bearers or to reserve certain parts of the forest to permit trees to grow for eighty, one hundred or even two hundred years. But the demand for all the smaller diameters, and the pressure on the forests from the twelfth century on were so strong that such large trees became increasingly rare.

The building of foundations was another Middle Ages construction technique that was costly in terms of wood use. In marshy ground, or just on bad ground, entire towns like Amsterdam in Holland were founded on stakes driven into the ground. Such stakes kept quite well if they were entirely and permanently submerged. Some cathedrals, too, had foundations using that system. Sometimes, too, inside the thick walls of the monuments of that period, big pieces of wood have been found—they served for clamping; later, because of the poor preservation of the timbers enclosed in the masonry and because iron was becoming more common for civil uses, this system was abandoned in favor of tie-irons, but was still used to bond the foundations.

Pierre de Crescence, in his treatise (thirteenth century) which describes the uses of wood, alludes to this use for which he recommends oak: "Oak is strong and durable and has a lot of strength both under ground as over ground with masonry of mortar and stone."

There were also temporary works: scaffolding, planking, access ramps, palisades, casings, templates, molds, forms, etc. For these, masons and carpenters used wood with minimum trimming and many of these finished elements could be reused only as firewood. The Gothic builders tried to economize by reusing certain elements—thanks to their efforts for standardization—by facilitating the dismantling and the reuse of templates.

Civil engineering works, especially bridges, also consumed a lot of wood and—until the early tenth century—were often destroyed by the Normans during their incursions. It is only from the twelfth century on that the main bridges were built or rebuilt with stone, such as the one in Avignon that remained famous in children's songs:

• *Sur le pont d'Avignon*
On y danse, on y danse
Sur le pont d'Avignon
On y danse tout en rond •

Such bridges were less sensitive to vibrations than wooden ones thanks to their greater inertia, so people could even dance on them without risk. Following a technique already used by the Romans and of which traces were found under some of their highways—for example in the Hautes Fagnes—certain roads, built on unstable or marshy grounds, also had their foundation of stakes driven into the ground.

Among the great timber consumers, one must also include water mills and windmills, which required pieces of large diameter and considerable length. Water-mill shafts, according to the *Encyclopédie Française*, were made of big pieces of oak six to eight meters (about eighteen to twenty-four feet) long. As for the wings of the windmills, they reached a span of twenty-five meters (about seventy-five feet), which corresponds to the cross formed by pieces of wood over twelve meters (about thirty-six feet) long. The mechanisms of these mills —the tail that served to orient the turning windmills, the levers and the hammers of the bank-, iron-, or fulling-mills, the mechanisms of the hydraulic saw, etc.—all used big pieces of wood, some of which wore down quickly and had to be replaced from time to time. The presses, which existed in each village, also used very big pieces of lumber.

Shipbuilding used great quantities of wood and required big pieces among others for the keelson, the mast, the keel, the midship frames, and the bow as well as great quantities of boards for the sheathing of the ships' hulls. Certain vessels, such as the barges on which wood or pottery were brought down on the Loire or Seine rivers to supply the cities, made only one trip and were then converted into firewood at their destination. We will describe more about naval ship construction when we discuss the uses of wood by the military.

War and Navy

Military uses were also important causes of wood consumption and, of course, they had top priority.

The Romans had been great builders of temporary wooden fortifications; wherever their legions stopped, however briefly, and there were woods nearby (which was the case everywhere in western and central Europe as well as in Great Britain), they built fortified wooden camps. The permanent stone fortifications that they erected elsewhere, such as along the *limes*, followed plans inspired by their wooden constructions: square towers and straight walls. Arab fortifications in North Africa followed the same model.

The wooden fortifications of the Middle Ages differed little from the ancient Roman constructions. In a few hours, an entrenchment could be built and, in a few days, a fortress. Their technique was well perfected: the military men, eventually with the help of commandeered loggers or peasants, could complete this type of construction very rapidly. A few particularly spectacular examples are related in the old chronicles.

It is said that the lord of Bourbourg, in the north of France, in conflict with the lord of Guines, in one night built a castle prepared by carpenters, on an ancient mound near Audruicq. At daybreak, his enemies were faced with a real fortress that they were able to overcome only by a regular siege. It was because his castle was a wooden one that the lord of Puiset was able to rebuild it rapidly three times between the years 1111 and 1118, on each occasion when it was destroyed by the troops of Louis VI. The Normans, who traditionally were carpenters, built wooden castles that, on flat land, were erected on mounds of made ground. After the Norman Conquest of England, many wooden castles on mounds were erected by the conquerers to control the country. Some are illustrated in the embroidered linen attributed to Queen Matilda. The chronicle relates that the fortified castle of York was built in eight days!

However, wooden fortifications and wooden bridges were often destroyed or burned by the enemy. There were incessant incursions of Normans in northern France until the treaty of Saint-Clair-sur-Epte, by which Normandy was given to them in 911—while, in the west, Nantes remained in the hands of another Norman gang until 919. During the tenth century, the Hungarian raids went on in the east. In the south the Saracens were evicted from Provence only by 972. There were many other occasions of wanton destruction during the local feudal fights and the wars waged by the king of France against his various neighbors. Furthermore, siege devices were becoming more powerful and the accuracy of incendiary projectiles was improving. Finally, in the eleventh and twelfth centuries, it became increasingly difficult to obtain frame timber, especially in the large diameters. Meanwhile stone-cutting techniques improved with the progress of metallurgy.

So, more and more often, stone masonry replaced wood in the

construction of fortified castles and town fortifications. Stone towers could be round or even almond-shaped; their shape deflected the projectiles and considerably attenuated their impact, as long as the hit wasn't directly on the tower. The donjons and the fortified towers built by Philippe Auguste in the early twelfth century were round. For the superstructures, wood remained in use for a long time; in particular, the hoardings, those overhanging galleries—which allowed the defenders to send projectiles or pour pitch, melted lead or some other unpleasant matter on the besiegers who had reached the bottom of the walls—were for a long time built with wood. When a siege was expected, the hoardings were put in place on beams set in special holes in the wall under the crenels. The users were protected from the projectiles by wooden palisades or fences of woven branches; the French word *hourd*, as well as the English word "hoarding," are indeed close to the English word "hurdle" that designated such a palisade of woven branches.

Caesar, during the first century B.C., already had mentioned the use of hurdles for footbridges between towers of campaign fortifications and for the crenelated defense palisades.[3] Later the wooden protectors were set on stone bases that were permanent; finally, the cantilevered constructions became completely permanent and were built in stone. They were called bratices—overhanging constructions placed, for example, over a postern—or machicolations, a construction along the towers and ramparts.

Apart from the actual constructions, military operations also consumed a lot of timber for a wide variety of applications, both offensive and defensive: turning towers, bastilles (small fortresses), removable bridges, battering rams, assault ladders, sapping, roll ways. Devices such as trebuchets, catapults, and balistas also used timbers of different diameters and often very big elements. These devices do not appear to have been modified following the growing shortage of pieces of big sections, the consequences of which were felt more in civilian constructions, which were less favored.

Furthermore, in addition to the boats, hoppers, and barges which served for commercial transportation, the war navy started to develop during this period and required large-sized pieces. The tonnage of the ships increased with the progress of naval construction. Already, the ships that transported the Crusaders to the Holy Land had nothing in common with the Norman drakkars, nor with the vessels that had permitted the conquest of England in the eleventh century.

Saint Louis left for the Crusades in 1247 on a boat 31 meters (about 190 feet) long, a 550-tonner that carried five hundred soldiers; he returned on an even bigger ship that carried eight hundred men. In the fifteenth century, twenty cubic meters of the best timber, half oak and half pine, were needed for each ton. Some ships were of one thousand tons burden. In the sixteenth century, the Spanish Armada represented a total of three hundred thousand tons. One can estimate from these figures the wood consumption required to construct these ships, which were exposed not only to the dangers of the sea, but to destruction and burning in combat.

The kings of France were fully aware of this. To guarantee the wood supply for the Rouen naval shipyards, Charles V organized the exploitation of the Roumare forest by the ordinance of September 3, 1376, which constitutes one of the first French texts that provided guidelines about the management of forests. In the following year, thirty-five galleys came out of the Rouen shipyards; under the leadership of Jean de Vienne, with the participation of Portuguese and Spanish ships, they attacked England where, successively, the ports of Rye, Portsmouth, and Dartmouth were burned down, after which the island of Wight, Winchelsea, and Hastings were sacked. A few years later, Charles VI built a huge wooden fortification in Rouen; it was capable of being dismantled piece by piece, included towers every twenty meters, and enclosed four hundred hectares (almost one thousand acres). This huge movable prefabricated fortification was meant to be used for the siege of London; seventy-two ships were necessary to transport it from the shipyard to l'Ecluse in Zeeland. It is off l'Ecluse—which is situated east of London, across from the mouth of the Thames River—that the French fleet had been beaten and destroyed by the English forty years earlier. But the planned siege of London never made history.

Wood and Tools

Any building technique depends first of all on the characteristics and the forms of the materials used. Wood, a natural material, goes through successive stages: it develops more-or-less rapidly depending on the soil, the climate, the altitude, and the humidity; the shapes under which the usable wood presents itself, depends also on the exploitation methods used in the forests, from which were derived the available types of lumber—as well as on the conditions under which the different users can obtain it. Finally, during the Middle Ages, as in any period and in any context, the technical means and especially the tools with which lumber was cut down, converted and prepared, and the transportation problems were primordial factors, not only for the exploitation methods of the productive forests but also for construction itself, as closely linked to the characteristics of the available timbers as to the building techniques.

An axe is all that is needed to fell a tree, trim it, and square it. Several types of axes existed: squarer's axe, pruner's axe, carpenter's axe, felling axe, trimming axe, weapon axe, boarding axe, axe with two symmetrical edges or with an edge on one side and a pick on the other, splinting axe, hatchet, etc. To prepare the wood, two kinds of axes were used: the broad axe, an asymmetrical axe suitable for the squaring and dressing of the wood's faces; and the adze, an axe with a bent head, of which the edge is perpendicular to the handle. It is often illustrated in miniatures. Axes are simple and rustic tools, are long lasting, not fragile, and can also be used as weapons. In this capacity, they were traditional in peoples originating in wooded countries, such as the Normans. Joinville, who, in his history of Saint Louis, cites the "Danish axe" several times as being among the weapons used by the Saracens, specifies that it is with a "carpenter's Danish axe" that he almost got his head chopped off when he was a prisoner in Egypt.[4]

The axe's head is massive and relatively easy to melt down, forge, and sharpen. The saw, by contrast, requires a delicate touch to manufacture, is relatively fragile, and requires frequent sharpening and swaging. It wasn't a rustic tool: it required care and maintenance and, furthermore, was costly to buy. In the inventories of village forges that were carried out in France during the first part of the twentieth century, at the instigation of the historian, Lucien Febvre, all kinds of tools are listed but almost no saws, which proves that the smiths didn't manufacture any; it was custom-made industrial production.

So, in the Middle Ages, whenever possible, people used timbers that were simply roughed down and squared with an axe. Timbers were split only for specific uses that did not require rectilinear and flat faces, such as fence posts or vine props. In the twelfth century, the use of the saw had just started to spread, and even when a peasant owned one, sawing lengthwise by hand was a delicate and difficult operation requiring the skill of an expert. However, during the same period sawmills started to be used—mechanical saws operated by water power. Villard de Honnecourt illustrates such a sawmill in his sketches.

But the scope of these tools implied important investments; only rich people, lay or ecclesiastic, or communities could afford them and they charged high prices for their use. However, the hydraulic saw could not be as easily imposed on the peasant as the bake house or the flour mill, which were necessary for everyday life. Besides, to get the benefit of the saw, the peasant had to transport his rough timber to the sawmill, often quite distant from the place where he planned to build, and then carry home the sawed pieces of timber. It was much simpler—and more rational—to transport the timber directly from the forest to the construction site.

Under these conditions, the peasants were led to use, as much as possible, timbers of small diameters, that were easier to cut down and transport. As for the nobles, even when they searched for them, they found it increasingly difficult to find large-diameter timber. Anyway, during that period, all users (except for when they needed thin boards for floors, paneling or furniture, which required the intervention of lengthwise sawyers or of the hydraulic sawmill), looked for trees of which the dimensions corresponded to the pieces of wood needed; then, all they needed to do after cutting them down to size was to square them. One did not fell bigger trees in order to cut them into several pieces. Nonetheless, the regulations attempted to limit the wastefulness that applied to the old saying: "Too strong never failed." Charles V's ordinance of 1376 recommended "not to cut trees thicker or higher than was necessary."

Sawed boards became common in France only at the end of the thirteenth century, with the development of the sawmills. In some countries rich in wood, such as Canada, boards started being used only in the 18th century. In Russia, sawmills appeared only by the time of Peter the Great, who tried authoritatively to impose them. In central Europe, such as in Austria, it was only by the mid-nineteenth century that saws regularly came into use in the forests.[5]

Carpenters—as opposed to cabinetmakers or joiners—took a long time to adopt the saw. Until the end of the thirteenth century all the frameworks were cut with axes. Saws were kept for work that required meticulous care, such as joinery, window-making, cabi-network (in French, *menuiserie, ébénisterie*), and for those tasks for which the tool was almost indispensable: for example, lengthwise sawing. Boards were manufactured at the sawmill; saws were used to cut pieces with very wide sections or to make connections that required great precision, such as tenons for mortises, dovetail joints, *traits de Jupiter* and other ingenious devices that are the pride of carpenters.

Leport, a *compagnon du Devoir* and skilled carpenter, who studied the framings of many ancient monuments in France, reports that, upon examining the joints of the frames made during the eleventh and twelfth centuries, he noticed that they were made with very great precision, work which required the use of chisels to make the mortises, of drills to pierce the holes for the dowels, and often the use of saws. Workmen with drills are depicted quite often in the miniatures of the fourteenth and fifteenth centuries. Leport found the proof of their use in the twelfth-thirteenth centuries: the mortises are finished with a chisel, but in the bottom, one can see the depression made by the point of the drill. The faces of the timbers show mostly axe marks; it was only from the fifteenth century on that the saw was used. This use developed further during the six-teenth century: the frames of that period included as much sawed timber as timber squared with an axe.

Nevertheless, for a long time carpenters must have been reluctant to use the saw, the tool that rapes and weakens the wood by cutting its fibers. Thus, in the castle of Langeais, built in 1470, the frame doesn't include any sawed timber while, in the same region, the framing in the castle of Azay-le-Rideau—built fifty years later—includes sawed timbers. But only the faces, almost invisible, turned toward the roof were sawed: all the visible faces are squared with an axe. As for the rafters that bear on these main timbers, they are sawed, but the surface has been planed to cause the marks of sawing to disappear. This method can be found in several buildings, such as the Saint-Laurent Church and the Saint-Médard Church.

In relation to the sawing of the unseen parts of the fifteenth century frameworks, it must be mentioned that since they had rafters that are also sawed, this peculiarity is rational since sawing allows the carpenter to obtain a better planimetric result, which is partic-ularly useful for the surface on which the rafters bear. The regularity and flatness were not of great importance for the Early Middle Ages roofs, most of them in thatch. But with regular elements, such as tiles made with molds and even standardized like the famous "tiles of Henry the count of Champagne," or slates cut at precise and constant measures and as flat as possible, regular planimetric support and the setting of the slates ensured a better tightness of the roof and prevented or reduced wind damage.

As long as carpenters had available, at will, trees with diameters corresponding to the sections they needed without having to saw them, the technique of squaring by axe remained logical and competitive. In addition, one obtained symmetrical timbers, thus much less apt to "round" or "to be stressed." Indeed, since pieces of sawed or splintered wood are taken on the side of a tree trunk with a large diameter, they often have a tendency to get out of shape; it is said that the wood "pulls toward the heart."

This method of choosing trees for construction purposes had a negative impact on the exploitation of the forest because it prevented the trees from reaching their full maturity. For best profitability, trees should be cut when they are one hundred to two hundred years old—depending on the species—that is, when the tree's annual production in volume slows down or stops.

This exploitation technique would appear aberrant and anarchistic today when the production of a tree is estimated by the cubage it can supply, converted into pieces of standardized sections. But the system, in effect in the Middle Ages, was not without advantages. By squaring the tree with an axe, taking away only the outside part—the sapwood, which does not keep as well—there are fewer risks of rot, but also of distortion of the timbers, used in their plenitude, in all their force. Such timber resisted time much better as long as it was protected from water and was aerated. Therefore, Gothic and even Romanesque frames have remained intact for eight to ten centuries, and, in roofings, dating from the sixteenth, seventeenth, and eighteenth centuries, older pieces of wood that had been reused can be found to be perfectly preserved. This method of wood exploitation remained in use for a long time. The idea of taking one element in each trunk according to the latter's size, was so well established in the mind of builders that during the eighteenth century, the size of trees was still designated by the caliber of frame timber that it produced.

If one considers only the theoretical profitability of the wood capital, if one seeks the maximum utilization of a volume of standing timber, one might conclude that there was wastefulness in these methods. In fact, to the extent that nature was generous and that the forest still had sufficient resources, this way of using trees according to their size was technically sound. But as the pressure on the forests and the agricultural-sylvicultural-pastoral techniques led to a general rejuvenation of the trees available for construction, the builders of the time had to conceive of new techniques corresponding to the timbers of smaller sections—with which they had to be satisfied. In Gothic architecture, this state of things had consequences not only on the framing but also on the techniques and even the shape of construction, from the simplest to the most prestigious—the cathedrals.[6]

Nature's Store

For the builder of the Middle Ages, the forest was a huge store, abundantly stocked, in which, God willing, he would find, in addition to firewood, exactly what he needed in each case. Of course, one needed to "rummage" and spare no trouble, especially if one was looking for timber of exceptional size or shape, because the filing, the arrangement of this huge living warehouse was not systematic. To a certain extent, it would become so later on with the rational exploitation of the forests, a long and exacting task to which the foresters would apply themselves throughout the centuries, all the way from the Middle Ages to our days.

Nonetheless, there were people who, by profession, knew the forest and whose statements and knowledge were precious for researchers: hunters, foresters, peasants who poached a little, users who picked mushrooms and berries, people who gathered dead wood, etc.

Searching for timber of ordinary size—to make rafters, small beams or poles—normally did not create any great difficulties because it didn't require trees that had reached their full maturity; in thirty or forty years, in a good soil, a specie suitable for construction would produce a trunk that, trimmed, would correspond to what was needed. And from one rafter to another the size could vary slightly without any drawbacks; the safety margins specified by the builders were sufficient.

But if several main girders were needed, each of which could be taken only in a tree over one hundred years old, it was more difficult to find in this "store of nature," especially when (as was the case in the eleventh to the thirteenth century) it was requested more and more often and trees frequently had not been allowed to reach their full maturity.

Indeed, around the villages, the system of itinerant farming was often used: a forest lot was cleared each year and cultivated; then it returned to fallow and natural reforestation for the next twenty or thirty years. When the system had been in effect for several decades, it became impossible to find trees over thirty years old, except in forest ranges that were well protected by owners who kept the production for their own needs and for military uses.

Sometimes appropriate trees could be found in very large forests deep into the woods and far away from the regularly exploited areas. Sometimes one had to look even farther and organize a real expedition to distant forests, far from the towns; but this was within the reach only of people with considerable means.

As clearings became permanent more and more often, and as fields in many areas replaced the destroyed forest, woodlands became increasingly smaller. And under the pressure of the continuing demand for firewood, for construction lumber, and for all other uses, all of the different categories of wood grew more rare. As the principal demand was for timber of medium diameters—from which were made palisades, props, joists, rafters, and the timber framings for house construction—few trees lived to be old enough to produce the timber of large size, that became the most difficult to find.

At the "time of growth" from the eleventh to the end of the thirteenth century, there was a shortage of all wood, except firewood or timber of small diameter. "Nature's department store" no longer had in stock all that was necessary.

For example, the abbot Suger, regent of King Louis VI, had to go himself on an expedition to try and find a few beams—only twelve beams—that were missing for the Saint-Denis basilica, his life's work. What an adventure! Prior information, investigations, explorations, searches: nothing was left out. And if "Jesus and his Martyrs" had not themselves guided the poor man deep into the woods, through the brambles and the thorns, to the trees which corresponded exactly to his needs, he would have had to search much longer, mount an expedition to the Morvan or farther, or try to negotiate what he was looking for out of the territories in which the king of France could freely get his supplies. The passage in which Suger relates his expedition is well known, but it must be recalled here in its freshness:

> • *In order to find beams, we had consulted wood workers in our area as well as in Paris; they had answered that they didn't think that we could find them in these regions because of the lack of forests and that we would have to send for them in the region of Auxerre. They all agreed. We were crushed by the thought of so much work and of the long delay that it would entail for the construction. One night, upon returning from Matins, I started thinking in my bed that I ought to scour the neighboring woods myself, look everywhere and shorten these delays and labors. I believed that I could find these beams. At once, leaving aside all other preoccupations, I left early in the morning with the carpenters and the dimensions of the beams and went rapidly toward the forest of Rambouillet. Going through our land in the valley of the Chevreuse, I summoned our sergeants, those who guarded our land and all those who knew the forests well and, entreating them under oath, I asked them if, in this area, we had any chance of finding beams of these dimensions. They smiled, and indeed they would have laughed out loud, astonished that we did not know that in all this estate there was nothing of the kind to be found. Milon, the lord of Chevreuse, who was our man and owned half of the forest, had fought for a long time against the king and Amaury de Montfort; he had built defense towers three stories high and hadn't left anything intact or in good condition. As for us, we rejected everything that those people told us and, with bold confidence, we started walking through the forest. Around the first hour, we found a beam of sufficient dimension. What more did we need? By the ninth hour or a little earlier, going through the forest, the coppice and the thorn bushes, to the astonishment of all those who were there and surrounded us, we had designated twelve beams: it was the number we needed. With joy, we had them carried to the saint basilica and placed on the roof of the new construction to the praise and glory of the Lord Jesus who had reserved them for*

> *himself and his Martyrs and wanted to protect them from thieves.* [7] ◆

Fifty or sixty years later, Suger would certainly have had much more difficulty. That is why the builders—constantly confronted everywhere with this problem—had to imagine ways to make up for the increasing difficulty in finding timber of a certain size.

By small and successive touches and by the constant search for ways to economize on a material that had become rare, this constant preoccupation of the builders eventually led in all types of construction—religious, civilian, and military—to deep modifications; the evolution of the forests contributed to the transformation of architecture and sent it in new directions.

The Use of Lumber

A piece of wood is really a cluster of fibers, glued to each other; to ensure its solidity it is best to avoid, as much as possible, cutting or tearing them. To rough down pieces of timber, the Middle Ages workman attacked the material by hand, with tools shaped to suit different uses: the broadaxe with an asymmetrical blade; the adze, of which the blade perpendicular to the handle had a shape and curve that varied depending on the work to be done; the plane, held with two hands; the chisel, that was used with a mallet, etc. The workman progressively planed the faces of the piece; he respected the fibers and, when he tried to obtain a piece of maximum size, he removed the superficial parts, younger and softer, and took only the harder parts to obtain the needed section, to dress the piece.

Thus the pieces used in the Middle Ages framings were not elements with regular and parallel faces, but personalized elements, taking advantage of the particular shapes and characteristics of each piece of timber. Often, in Gothic frames, the rafters set in the direction of the greatest incline were, as were the trees from which they were taken, of a bigger size at the bottom than on top. Since they were set based on a very steep incline, it was perfectly logical, because the increased size of the section toward the bottom made for stronger resistance.

Often, pieces of wood that, because of their position in the building, needed to be planed on only one or two surfaces, were dressed only on those faces, thus avoiding a waste of manpower and unnecessary wear and tear of the precious iron tools.

Such details surprise us, since we are accustomed to timber cut to standardized sizes by industrial sawmills. On the part of the builders of the Middle Ages, it was proof of the existence of a practical mind and a mark of their ingenuity in taking advantage of the shapes provided by nature, logically, without doing any additional work, unnecessary for the planned use.

The different wood species had different assignments. Besides, the carpenters of the *"grande cognée,"* as Etienne Boileau calls them in his book on trades (at the end of the seventeenth century), there were other specialties: the hutch-makers (*huchiers*) and the trunk-makers (*bahutiers*) who made furniture, the joiners (*huissiers*) who made doors and door frames, the wet coopers, the wheelwrights, the roofers and the *cochetiers* who built the river boats or passenger barges, called in French, *coches d'eau* (water coaches), the turners, and the panelers.

We saw that the big pieces of timber were obtained by trimming and squaring by hand. When smaller pieces were needed, they were obtained as often as possible by splitting rather than by sawing, using wedges in iron, or even, sometimes, in hardwood, such as the pear tree. It's only for elements of wall or ground covering, such as framing strips, panels, and parquets, which do not require the very great mechanical qualities of resistance in length or of flexion necessary for the framing pieces, that saws were used to obtain elements with parallel faces. Even then, the pit sawyers tried to follow—as closely as possible—the wood grain, which is easier to do with a crosscut saw handled by two men, than with the mechanical saw that requires very straight logs.

Some people tried to make trees grow as straight and high as possible, not only for uses such as ship masts, which used the trunks with their decreasing diameter, but also for other uses such as lumber for construction, civil engineering, and military uses. This objective led to a forestry that privileged certain species, proceeding by selection and ending up sometimes in monoculture. The period of the year during which a tree was felled was very important because its future preservation depended in great part on the condition of the tree when it was cut down. Here is what Pierre de Crescence recommended for stave wood:

> • *The month of November when the moon is decreasing is a good*
> *time to cut down stave wood because the past fall weather, the*
> *age of the moon, and the present coldness of the air provoke the*
> *sap to go away with the tree's natural heat through the roots*
> *and into the ground that remains warm at that time. For the*
> *trees that one wants to cut down, it is good to cut them to the*
> *marrow and then to leave them there for a while so if there still*
> *is any sap, it leaves by the cut.* •

And he adds further on: "All the trees cut on the south side are useful. But those cut on the north side, although they are tall and good-looking, spoil easily."[8]

As early as the Middle Ages the preference for oak and beech— because of their double function of providing fruit for pigs and men and material for construction, fire and charcoal making—had led to an important modification of the forests' composition. But there were no species without some kind of use and the forest was not the object, as it is today, of the systematic elimination of clearings, organized with a unique and dominant purpose. There was still a great variety in the forests during the Middle Ages and different species, depending on the nature of the soil, grew side by side.

It wasn't always easy to find nice straight boles, although they tried to obtain them in the royal forests with methods similar to those used today. But some people took advantage of the natural characteristics of what was available, of the morphology of each tree. Even certain trees bent or twisted, or presenting particular shapes, found a use corresponding to their shapes. Joints are the weak point of any framing or any tool or wooden machine; today they are reinforced with metal parts. In the Middle Ages, metal was scarce and precious; whenever possible people preferred to find the piece already "joined" in nature. Thus, a pitchfork was made of two or three pieces of wood, diverging from a handle; and, as is still done today—generally with nettle trees—wooden pitchforks were made from different species of trees, that were especially pruned. Plows were made of one piece of wood including a central part cut in a trunk with stilts formed by two symmetrical branches; they can still be found in some countries.

Benches, stools, even spiral staircase stringers are sometimes made today from massive pieces of wood, by using the setting of the branches. What has become research in certain "ecological" con-

structions was a natural step in the Middle Ages. The method was
then much more developed and systematic; the navy, in particular,
used pieces of wood of special shapes that had to be looked for or
for which development was encouraged. These pieces had specific
names, which corresponded to the different shapes and thus permitted their classification: stem, futtock, fork, floor timber, forefoot,
and stanchion. In the forests, trees were shaped from their earliest
age, thanks to cables secured to the ground. Fifty or sixty years
later, a big piece of timber that had the needed curve was obtained,
while maintaining maximum resistance, since the fibers had not
been bent artificially (which, even with the use of steam, can provoke
tears or defects in its solidity). For less sophisticated uses, the natural
shapes of the wood were also much used.

One can see in the miniatures how the beginnings of the branches
were used on scaffolding poles to rest the horizontal pieces without
any need for joints, which always weakened the resistance of the
wood and constituted the weak points of a frame, or for rope tying.
Generally, by avoiding unnecessary labor when pieces of regular
shapes weren't needed, workmen used tree trunks without taking
off the beginnings of the branches—which could eventually serve
as notches—with the advantage of being stronger. Several sketches
by Villard de Honnecourt illustrate this idea; on others he shows
how one could take advantage of the particular shape of certain trees.
For example, he illustrates a war machine of which some parts,
much like children's slings today, are made of forked trunks. Elsewhere, he draws an automatic hydraulic saw, which makes use of
the elasticity of certain trees as well as their special shape.

From Wood to Stone

Whatever the technique used—walls of solid wood or timber framing with fillings—one of the consequences of the great amount of
wood used to build houses was that fires, whether accidental or due
to war, most often resulted in the destruction of whole neighborhoods or entire towns.

In the towns, particularly, in which the only fuel for cooking,
heating, and crafts was wood and where the houses—surrounded
by the ramparts—touched each other, the fires, frequent because of
the systems of heating and lighting used, were devastating. From

1200 to 1225, Rouen was burned six times. Among the best known of the towns that suffered fires, which reached the cathedral and thus were noted in the archives, are: between 989 and 1210, Chartres, three times; during the same period, Bayeux, Noyon, and Reims, twice; and only once, Orléans, Sens, Périgueux, and Nevers. Between 1293 and 1333, Laval and again, Sens and Nevers are mentioned among the burned towns.

It was only with the urban development of the twelfth century that the seemingly endless fires led the town authorities to recommend and sometimes even to regulate building in stone and to encourage roofs made with tiles, slate or roofing stone. In 1189 and 1212, the "Assizes of construction" were held in London; the document published on the first occasion, in 1189, indicates that, at the time of the great fire of London in 1136, the buildings in the city were constructed with wood and the roofs thatched or covered with straw or other similar material and that, following that fire, "many citizens, to reduce as much as possible those risks, built on their lots stone houses covered with thick tiles."[9] The great fire of London had been preceded by—and was followed by—many other catastrophes of the same kind. For example, in York, successive fires destroyed, in addition to the cathedral: the abbey of Sainte-Marie, the main hospital, thirty-nine smaller churches, and the Holy Trinity priory—plus all the individual homes.

It has been suggested that the evolution from the Romanesque style to the Gothic style was accelerated in England by these series of catastrophes that led to entirely rebuilding most monuments; this factor must also have intervened in France for the cathedrals. Because during this period when builders had no doubt about their abilities and always tried to do better, it would have been unthinkable to rebuild identical structures. On the contrary, they used the latest construction techniques and tried to do better than their predecessors.

Where the Romans had built previously, especially in the towns, the stones were often reused and, sometimes, as in Verulamium, in England, the tiles of their monuments as well. In the cities, there were a few more stone constructions, mostly public buildings. But all the private houses were built with wood. The contemporaries paid tribute to Charles d'Orléans, count of Blois, father of Louis XII who, as he was not a great hunter, during the twelfth century had a large part of the forest of Blois cut down in order to build houses in the town for the burghers and the officers, "preferring," says the chronicle, "to house men rather than beasts." Even when builders started to construct facades in stone or brick and—in compliance with the safety ordinances—dividing walls in masonry (influenced by the picturesque movement of gables, so frequent in the Middle Ages), the back facades on the courtyards and the gardens were still made, generally, with timber framing. They remained so until the twentieth century in many common urban buildings and can still be found in several French towns.

In England, the number of buildings that remain with timber framing is greater still because the country was less devastated by wars over the centuries and because there were less resources available in stone. The lack of stone was such that for a long time the quarries in Normandy supplied the sites of many English castles and churches with stone for their construction—all the more, since the English lords had maintained for a long time their interests in Normandy. This is why, when parts of several prestigious English monuments, demolished by the German bombings of 1939–1945, had to be rebuilt, the stone came from Normandy. The general use of wood, and the fact that in England the use of stone remained unusual for a long time, had consequences for the organization of the building trades. Salzman writes:

> ◆ *Since almost every building included a certain quantity of wood in its roofing and its floors there was, in each town, enough work for a good number of sedentary carpenters, who quite naturally associated to form a guild, as did the other craftsmen. However, stone constructions were so rare that many small towns didn't have any apart from the church and in the larger towns stone houses remained exceptional. Consequently, the mason who wasn't lucky enough to have found work among the personnel of a cathedral or an abbey, had to work intermittently and spend a great deal of his time traveling from one place to another in search of work.*[10] ◆

As the masons were itinerant, they were led in England, in order to defend their professional interests, not to form local corporations or guilds but to create an organization covering the whole country and having places to stay in the main towns: the lodges. Secret signs of recognition allowed the members to introduce themselves and to be admitted. Such "passports" weren't necessary when, as in a local corporation, everyone knew each other. That is how Freemasonry started.

Outside England, the situation was different and there was less division between the masons and other craftsmen. In France, where the lack of capital led to only occasional new building sites, the masons were not the only ones to move frequently. This led to the organization of the *compagnonnage*, divided into separate professional organizations that permitted their members to go from town to town in search of work. It is only recently during the nineteenth and twentieth centuries, that the *compagnonnage* started grouping workmen from different trades into the same organization and in the same *"auberges"* or *"cayennes."* It still distinguishes, however, in their esoteric appellations the men who work in the workshops: the *"pays,"* and the building-site men who work on the scaffoldings, the *"coteries."*

Thus, in England, it was due to the relative abundance of wood and the long lack of development of their quarrying activity, that led to different organizations for the trades using these different materials. Let us recall that stone was so rare in England that it was considered a miracle, when exploitable stone was found on the site chosen by William the Conqueror to build an abbey, in thanks for his victory at Hastings.

From the Forest to the Cathedrals

The need to save wood and the shape of the timber extracted from the forests had consequences at all levels of the building process. They influenced the choice of certain techniques and, consequently, the forms that characterize the Gothic style.

For the frameworks themselves, still visible today in many Gothic buildings, the characteristics of the available materials forced the builders to invent new devices. Gothic builders forced themselves to bring back—on a small number of pinpoint stays—the weights and the thrusts of their arches, which rose to heights until then inconceivable, and replaced the walls, until then broken only by narrow openings, with immense stained-glass windows. Art historians, archaeologists and architects have been surprised that these same builders devised a framing system that led to the opposite, since the roofs and the frames weigh down on the whole length of the frontages and charge the arches above the windows.

Indeed, it was a system of trusses very close to each other (0.60 to 0.90 meters) composed of rafters used as trusses and called rafter-trusses (apparently initiated, in 1147, at Saint-Pierre-de-Montmartre) that was used for over three centuries in the Ile-de-France, in Normandy, and almost everywhere in the northern half of France, instead of the classical system used until then which included spaced trusses made of timber of large diameter bearing the roof rafters via horizontal pieces—the purlins—that went from truss to truss.

With this system, inherited from ancient times—that had been used by the Roman builders and would reappear only in the late fifteenth century—it would have been possible to link the bearings of the trusses with the bearing points of the stone construction that supported the arches. But this rational layout would have required for the purlins, as well as for the trusses, timbers of very large diameters, while the new system—composed of lighter, very close trusses—used pieces of much smaller diameters. This was exactly what it was still possible to find in the forests where, as the chronicles and the legends show, trees of large diameters were increasingly rare. Writes Viollet-le-Duc.

> ◆ *The cleared forests of the continent no longer provided those twice secular trees in quantities such that the builders would not have been forced to replace the volume of the timbers by a judicious use of their quality.*[11] ◆

In the sketchbook of the thirteenth century architect, Villard de Honnecourt, this constant preoccupation with economizing on the builders' timber was revealed: in one sketch, he illustrates a bridge using only twenty-foot poles; in another, he shows how to build a floor when the available pieces of timber are too short; elsewhere, he draws a "good light truss" and shows, by several examples, how the craft of carpentry applied itself, again, in the words of Viollet-le-Duc (who noted elsewhere that the classical system of trusses was maintained in regions where wood was still abundant), "to the search for combinations making up for the small size of the timbers used."[12]

The use of this type of framing had several consequences: on one hand, the use of pieces of smaller scantling led—so that they would not bend under the weight of the roofing—to giving them a stronger slant, a characteristic of the roofs of Gothic churches. On the other hand, timbers of smaller diameters for the roof were lighter and considerably facilitated the hoisting and the placing of the frames. Viollet-le-Duc, without questioning the reason for this practice, which can be due to transportation difficulties from the forest, the convenience of hoisting at considerable height, and the availability of timber, notes that. "The Middle Ages carpenters appear to have feared to use even in the largest frames, timbers of big scantling. If they needed a big piece, such as a spire crown post, they tied together four stems."[13] On that point, one might think that it was also a wise precaution, since a big piece—consisting of four "stems" solidly assembled in an adequate way—is less likely to warp, to "corkscrew," than if it is made out of one piece.

Enlart, for his part, indicates that, "In the fifteenth and sixteenth century, the rafters, beams and crown posts of very large dimensions were systematically made of several pieces because of the shortage of large trees and especially of the hoisting difficulties,"[14] and he describes the construction system taking into account these constraints which was used for the cathedral of Reims in the fifteenth century.

The urban environment in which the houses, surrounded by the town walls, crowded the cathedral, caused the builders to change their plans: to raise the lighting bays of the naves above the neighboring roofs to allow light to enter the cathedral. In this search for height, towns tried to outdo each other, but not without risks, as shown by the example of the nave of Beauvais which, being too high, fell down. The lightness of the Gothic frames was an essential element that allowed the builders to erect their structures to reach the giddy heights that still surprise us. This characteristic of the frames also helped to set them into place before the building of the arches, thus allowing them to cover the building site with an "umbrella" during the construction of these delicate parts, which could not be exposed to the rain since the lime mortar used was slow to harden.[15]

For temporary works—the templates and the casings among others—the necessity of saving wood and of using timber with small diameters also incited the builders to create designs that responded to these constraints; the system of ribs, characteristic of Gothic arches, satisfies these imperatives. It is not that the ribs constituted, as has often been thought, a bearing skeleton; but, in the process of Gothic construction, they were the only elements of the arches that required genuine templates—which furthermore did not need to be able to bear the entire weight of the span thanks to the progressive loading allowed by the groined vaults. As for the compartments of the vaults, situated between the ribs, they could be built on partial and summary casings bearing the principal templates of the ribs. In addition, the standardization of the curves (in particular of the ribs) represented a factor of simplification and economy in the stone cutting and allowed the reuse, without loss and waste, of wooden templates that served as support for the ribs during the construction of the church.

The Gothic builders also tried to avoid the use of scaffolding set on the ground, which would have required great quantities of wood, because of the height of the cathedrals; they rested them on the construction itself, just below the level of the arches. Eventually, they built in the masonry of the cathedrals galleries and stairways, allowing circulation and access to the upper parts of the building during the construction, which also saved on the timber that would have been required for floors, footbridges, staircases, and temporary ramps. The spiral staircases and galleries also avoided or reduced the amount of scaffolding needed for maintenance work on the facades, the walls or the higher parts of the edifices.

Thus, during all phases of the construction—in many details of the technique used and even in the forms taken by the cathedrals (whose amazing blossoming from the twelfth to the fourteenth century transformed the appearance of France)—one finds the mark of the forest, of the modalities of its planning, and of its management during those centuries, as well as the methods by which timber was felled, exploited, and prepared for use.

This impression is also exemplified in the ornamentation, which during that period took a realistic and naturalistic turn and borrowed much from local plants and, particularly, from trees; leaves, intersections of branches, fruits, real or mythical forest animals, provided the sculptors with countless models. Even the ribs in the arches, in the first part of the Gothic period, imitated the intersection of simple flexible tree trunks. Later, these clusters of round stems were replaced by elements with sharper groins. First inspired by Roman models, the column capitals rapidly evolved toward original forms, the leaf-works borrowing their designs from the local species, from which the sculptors, with great freedom, drew inspiration. Leaves from trees of different species (or from ivy, as in Reims), bouquets, buds, fruits, volutes or intersections of boughs and leaves took over the capitals; more-or-less stylized, it was always the tree leaf that dominated.

Thus the forest, after stamping its constraints on the techniques and the shapes of construction, contributed largely to the renewal of decorative art during this period.

Of Words and Things: Le Merrain

The classic Latin word *lignum* was used for a long time to designate wood material. Derivatives in French, such as *ligneux* and *lignite* are still in use but tend to get confused with the word *ligne* and its parents, which come from the Latin *linea*. Of course, in the Middle Ages, lineage, which was so important for the nobles (of *linea*, line), must not have been confused with the *lignerage* (of *lignum*) that designated the right to take wood for fire and other small everyday uses.

The right to take construction lumber was called the right of *marronage* or *marnage*; those terms were still in use a few years ago in the Vosges Mountains to designate that category of wood. Construction timber, stave wood, was called in the Middle Ages *merrain* (*merrien, mesrien,* or *mairien,* depending on the spellings). The word derives from the classic Latin word *materiamen*, that designated the big logs meant for construction or naval use.

The word *materiamen* comes directly from *materia* (material) of the Greek-Latin root *mater*, mother. *Materiamen* is the mother stem of the tree that gives shoots; it is the stem, the principal trunk, the one that provides beams and balks (*madriers*, as they are called in French—a word from the same root) at a time when the tree was selected, according to the size of the framing element needed, then just felled and squared with an axe.

The words *materiamen* and *lignum* appear in very old documents such as the *Capitulaire de 789*, the *Loi des Francs Ripuaires* and the famous *Capitulaire "de villis"* that goes back to the time of Charlemagne. The word *merrain* has remained in use by professionals to designate more precisely the wood used to make barrels, a technique that hasn't evolved much through the years.

8 · miscellaneous products and uses ·

The Forest Site

IN ADDITION TO THE EDIBLE PRODUCTS and the wood, the forest provided many products of plant or animal origin.

The forest supplied the resin with which torches were coated, and from which pitch was made. Pitch was used to manufacture war products—such as the incendiary materials, the formula for which the Byzantines had transmitted to the Francs—that were called "feu grégeois." Birdlime was made from certain saps and barks or the fruits of plants such as mistletoe or holly. Tar was extracted from the resin trees and used to seal containers and the hulls of vessels.

Barks had many uses. Birchbark was used to make shoes, straps, containers, and paper or to cover roofs; ropes and baskets were made with lime bark. In the thirteenth century *chantefable* "Aucassin et Nicolette," the author describes an atrocious villain whose leggings are fixed by straps of *"tille"* (lime bark). Tannin, indispensable for the treatment of leather, was extracted from the bark of several trees, mostly birch and oak. The best came from oaks (*quercus robur* and *quercus pedunculata*) twenty to thirty years old; the dried bark was pulverized. From the twelfth century on it became a true industry, thanks to the hydraulic "tan mills" which manufactured the powder. However, the oaks had to be protected from the barkers, who not only took the bark of the felled trees, but debarked them while they were standing—which killed them if too much bark was removed. "It is allowed to take a third of the tree's bark to make tan," says the custom of Soule in the Béarn. With chestnut and oak bark, decoctions that strengthened hemp were made.

The leaves and the small branches of certain trees served as fodder and litter for the animals. Brooms were made with broom and birch. Mattresses were made with beech leaves (the "wood feather") as well as with arex (vegetal horsehair).

Several dyes were extracted from forest plants—black was made from the nut gall; vermilion was gathered from the kermes oak; from buckthorn berries, a yellow colorant was extracted; and madder (the French name *garance* comes from Frankish) has tubers that provide the well-known dye. Dyer's greenweed (or dyer's broom) furnished a yellow colorant. Bilberries were used to stain objects.

Wax, a very important product in the Middle Ages, was harvested from the swarms. Besides its use for ropes, which were coated with wax to prevent them from fraying, it served for candles, which were in great demand. The period's piety and the symbolism of the flame—anterior by far to Christianity—led people to buy and burn candles frequently. It was also in the interest of the clergy, who profited from the sale. Wax was also used for the seals that the nobles, lay or ecclesiastic, and later the burghers, appended to their statutes to authenticate them.

The idea of printing, which does not use anything other than little seals—each of them representing a letter in relief that are aligned to form words—might have been suggested to Gutenberg by the use of this very common accessory, sometimes even set in a ring, with which people printed their personal mark, initials or coat of arms in the soft, heated wax.

The "wax workers" prepared the wax by mixing it with water, kneading it, then exposing the mixture to the sun. It was recommended that this be done during the April moon, which allegedly resulted in a better product; the wax could then be used. For lighting, however, wax candles were a luxury; peasants used torches made of resin wood split into thin tongs. There must have been at that period more bee swarms than today, because large-scale wax production was certainly necessary to supply the religious and civil needs of the population; pesticides—today the main factor that prevents the overdevelopment of the bee population and even their keeping, and that almost caused the disappearance of butterflies—did not yet prevail.

Both truly wild animals and the more-or-less domestic ones that often roamed in semifreedom in the forest provided many useful products in addition to meat. These were the raw material of a traditional industry that went back to Paleolithic times: horns, guts, sinews, bladders, bones, and especially leather, of which considerable and varied use was made. One can mention: saddles, straps, reins, whips, thongs, leashes, boots, laces, shoes, belts, coats, bonnets, blankets, in leather or in fur, etc.; and for martial uses: shields, sword scabbards and trimmings, helmets and breastplates which were originally made of leather as their French name *cuirasse*, from *cuir*, indicates.

With the horns and the bones, miscellaneous small objects or common accessories were made: knife handles, buttons, netting needles, needles, hooks, etc. Hollow horns traditionally served to make calling or musical instruments—that are still called horns—such as the oliphants (in principle, cut from elephant ivory). The word "horn" indicates, of course, that it was made originally from animal horn; later on, several shapes were executed in copper, such as the hunting horn.

An *arc de cor* was a bow made of two horns assembled symmetrically on a yew handle. The strings of bows and crossbows made of gut were stronger than those made of braided hemp. Before the introduction of window glass, animal bladders were used to cover casement windows in the houses of rich people.

Parchment and vellum, made of the skins of the wild or domestic animals found in the forest, were indispensable for official documents and manuscripts until—at the end of the Middle Ages—the invention of paper (which, made at first with rags, would later become one of the great outlets for wood) furthered the development of printing and the dissemination of books. The need for parchment led to the selection of the lamb species in order to obtain sheets as large as possible with the parts of the skin that could be used.

Many craftsmen, whose trade was linked to wood or to other forest products, either as fuel or as raw material, lived in the forest or on the outskirts. Often, they moved when they had exhausted the resources of raw material in a certain area. Indeed, many of these activities required only relatively light and movable equipment. But even installations such as the hydraulic sawmills in the Vosges Mountains, for example, were moved from place to place when the local resources were exhausted.

These artisans, caring little about the future and the management of the forest estate, caused serious damage when they were not strictly controlled. Some, such as the charcoal-burners, lived deep in the woods and were difficult to supervise. The authorities tried many times to enforce conservation measures. Finally, Colbert, Minister of Finance to Louis XIV, forbade all the owners of these workshops to settle less than half a mile from any forest—counting on transport difficulties to slow down the consumption of wood. He also forbade them to make ashes in the forest.

Craftsmen from other trades, who often had rights to the wood, came from the towns to get their raw materials: turners, wheelwrights, jug-makers, smiths, wet coopers, hutch-makers, carpenters, and cabinetmakers helped themselves. Each trade took what it needed: butchers, hooks for the meat; bakers, the wood for the shovels used to put the bread in the oven; weavers, timbers to build their looms; smiths, tool handles or anvil bases; cabinetmakers, wheelwrights, and carpenters, took timber. Tanners debarked the felled trees and sometimes even standing trees. Resin tappers bled the resin trees on site. Peasants with usage rights took whatever they needed to maintain their houses, their fences, and their tools.

From the Weapon to the Tool

Besides construction, wood had countless uses. Based on experience, advantage was taken of the qualities of the different species of wood in the forest. To make bows, a weapon with prehistoric origins, commonly used for hunting and for war, flexible woods were used; species such as yew and ash are still used today in regions where archery has remained a traditional popular sport. The complex shapes, with curves and countercurves of certain bows used in ancient times—and in countries poor in wood—correspond to the use of animal horn, not wood; it is the traditional shape of Cupid's bow. For the bowstring, either plant fibers such as hemp were used and coated with wax to prevent fraying, or material of animal origin, such as catgut, made from the intestines of wild or domestic animals. The process of manufacturing crossbows necessitated the use of several kinds of wood, as well as metal for the bracing system. Arrows were always made of wood; metal was used only for the head and the barbs, and the fletching was made of tied bird feathers. Javelins—light, pointed projectiles—were made of wood and used for hunting; Perceval, on his way to hunt in the *gaste forêt*, takes javelins.

The bows and, later on, the crossbows were the main portable offensive weapons for shooting long distances, until the arrival of portable firearms. Charlemagne had prescribed that each soldier be equipped with a bow, an extra bowstring, and twelve arrows. In England, archery was a national sport, encouraged by the public authorities; that was how the English army was able to have units of well-trained archers who, at the beginning of the Hundred Years War, played an important role in defeats of the French. Because the strings and catguts of the bows had to be greased to function properly, they attracted rats and mice; the English army had warrant officers in charge of taking care of the cats that protected the armories against the rodents. It is said that one of the reasons for the French defeat at Azincourt is that the French archers, who were not as well organized, found their bowstrings gnawed and unusable, while the weapons of the more farsighted English were in good condition.

Ash is a useful species for several reasons: while ash wood, flexible and resistant, provided bows, lances, javelins, and arrows, the leaves of the tree were commonly used to feed animals and the small branches were used for their litter. That the last foothold of the Moslems in southern France at the end of the tenth century was Fraxinetum—now called La Garde Freinet (fraxinus = ash)—is perhaps related to the problems of the forests. In addition to the fact that they found wood for their ships, their buildings, and their fortifications in the forests of the Maures around them, they had with the ash (still abundant today in that valley), at the foot of their main haunt, both a material useful for their armament and to feed their animals as well. Among the different woods found to be useful for the manufacturing of lances and javelins, but also of bookshelves, Crescence mentions beech.

Another use of wood was in the manufacturing of musical instruments, particularly string instruments of which there existed a great variety—viol, vielle, cither, lute, rebec, monochord—made with different kinds of wood. For this use, Crescence recommended cypress as:

> ◆ *very beautiful and sweet-smelling {wood} of which one can make very beautiful planks for musical instruments such as the guitar and lute, and used also for delicate works.* ◆

Sculpture, in full bloom in the twelfth-thirteenth centuries used, besides stone, several species of wood among which Crescence cites poplar as "good to form and carve images." But many other woods, in particular, harder and more durable woods, were used for these artworks, of which a certain number have survived. Near certain pilgrimage centers, a cottage industry of wooden sculptures developed: thus, around the abbey of Saint-Claude in the Jura, texts mention as early as the fourteenth century that there were artisans making devotional figurines carved in beech, hornbeam, hazel, boxwood, and walnut tree. A few centuries later, this cottage industry would find a new outlet—in the manufacturing of pipes. Beech was also used to make weavers' looms.

Some of these woods—the hardest—provided the wedges with which other woods were split; others provided axles, machines, vehicles, and the mills' cams; pear tree, hornbeam, and elm were used. Of the latter, Crescence notes that it is "very good to make beams and also wheel hubs for carts and mills as well as ladders, shafts for waggons and carts and wedges to split . . . because the wood is strong and hard to cut." Yokes for oxen were also made with hardwood, such as maple, of which Crescence says: "So it makes very good yokes for the oxen, cutting boards and bowls." A lot of turned wood was used for furniture: feet, bats, slats, etc. The style of Brittany's furniture and beds gives an idea of the decorative variety that was obtained by wood turning, where the wood turner used tender wood of fine grain as well as hardwood, depending on the requirements of the job.

Wooden clogs, very common as early as the fourteenth century, must be mentioned among the wooden objects. This industry—which used poplar, alder, birch and, for the better quality clogs, walnut—was a traditional activity in the forest. But no one knows for sure when, in the different French regions, clogs began to be used. Clogs were widely used in cool and humid regions. In the northern regions, the Lowlands, and the Scandinavian countries, soft light woods were used to make big enveloping clogs; in France, lighter clogs in hardwood such as beech or walnut, were more common. They were sometimes made more comfortable by the insertion of leather uppers (and thereby avoided having to put on—to protect the feet—those slippers in felt or sheepskin that one wears today in wooden clogs). This type of clog is also called in French, *"galoches,"* what Baïf, learned scholar, father of the poet of the Pléiade, defined as being the "sort of shoes that the Gauls wore when it rained." The orator, Cicero, mentioned the *gallicae* as being shoes that were specifically for the Gauls.[1]

As Edmond Pognon indicates, there are no clogs in Middle Ages iconography, even in the latest.[2] In the fifteenth century, Villon alludes to clogs in a ballad,[3] and Rabelais talks about them in the Tiers Livre of *Pantagruel*.[4] In the sixteenth century, they are included among the trades mentioned in the ordinances, a little after the death of Anne de Bretagne, wife of two successive French kings, who was named in songs the "duchess in clogs." At that time "clog-makers, bushel-makers, bowl-makers and other craftsmen of the wood trades" were forbidden to settle in and around the forest, as Charles V in 1376 had already forbidden the "navy carpenters" and the workmen making "wine casks, frameworks, barrels and others working with wood."[5]

It might be that the increased prohibitions on hunting in the forest made the commoners go from leather to wood for their shoes, when they did not go barefoot (which was probably quite common in the countryside) and contributed to the development of clogs—for those who could afford them.

Considering how, still in the early twentieth century, children in Brittany were admonished to take care of their clogs and to go barefoot as often as possible in order not to wear them down, it is easy to imagine what a luxury wooden clogs must have been for the peasants of the Middle Ages.

Trees provided the greater part of everyday tools as most of them in the Middle Ages were entirely made with wood, the only material available to the peasants. Pitchforks and rakes were made with timbers chosen to avoid joints, as much as possible. Still today in some regions, certain species of trees are specially grown to make pitchforks; certain branches are cut and curved while still on the tree, so that they will grow to the desired shape, thus providing a fork with two or three branches, both flexible and solid.

Shovels, spades, hoes, and weeding hoes were also made entirely of wood, simply reinforced with a layer of metal on the edge exposed to wear. But some kinds of tools, especially shovels, could not be made just with branches cut in the coppice; the "blade" had to be cut in timbers of larger sections and of different species as people couldn't afford, because of the high cost of iron, mixed tools with a wooden handle and a metal blade, like today's shovels and spades.

For each tool, usage gradually improved them to the most suitable shape. The characteristics of the wood were taken advantage of in the best possible way; branches were chosen, cut, and divided according to their shape to make handles for shovels, hoes, and pickaxes, etc.; or even scythe handles in one piece if a branch of the right shape was found. Even the plows' stilts—the simplest ones have a single stilt—were made of a natural fork, of which the common part formed what is called in French, the *"aage."* The name that is used for the swing-plow in certain regions of France, *fourcat*, evokes very well the forked (*fourchue*) shape of the instrument.

Thus, in the tools, one found again the branch, the tree, the forest. And even when they were manufactured in series by the craftsmen, each handle had its own shape, very slightly different from any other. Today, the buyer carefully weighs the hammer or the billhook that he covets, estimating its balance and swing. In the old days, the artisan or the peasant had tools even more personalized; sometimes he supervised for several years the development of a branch that he had recognized on the tree as suitable to supply the tool that he would need. In this, too, there was a subtle complicity between the tree and man.

Wickerwork and Fences

Among the techniques using wood, those that use interlacing systems, similar to weaving, were used as far back as can be remembered for wickerwork; the technique had multiple applications.

Most containers which were not meant to hold liquids used these techniques: baskets, sieves, trays, hurdles, and mats for cheeses. The flexible branches of several bushes or trees were used—willow, rush, hair-grass, hazel, and especially osier, of which Pierre de Crescence enumerates the uses:

> ♦ *It is a little tree that grows in the gravel of the rivers and has several very nice looking small canes. It is cut in April when the sap rises. The canes are pulled from the bark and are used to make baskets, props, bird cages and to dry cheese.* ♦

Furthermore, the techniques of wickerwork with the same raw materials were often applied to other areas. An important application was the light fence, fixed or movable, that was indispensable to mark off the parks in which the grazing animals were enclosed or that prevented them from entering into the zones where trees were growing back. What is made today with industrial metal latticework or with barbed wire was made of wattle fencing of interlaced branches and split wood. Rustic fences of this type can still be seen in several regions of Europe, in Switzerland, Austria, and Yugoslavia; they are often made by shepherds during their spare time. The frames of the fences as well as the stakes, the props, and the tall props (*hautains*) for the vines were made of split wood or poles.

The chestnut tree, which also had the advantage of providing fruit, was a particularly appreciated variety; at the age of three, it provided hoops for baskets or barrels; at six, props for vines or climbing vegetables; at twelve, poles, stakes, and fence posts; at fifteen to eighteen, it could already be sawed to provide floorboards. The chestnut tree, not very putrescible, was often used to constitute the frame of the fences or hurdles, in which more flexible branches, interlaced perpendicularly, constituted the web. Stronger elements were used to create palisades against wild animals around the villages or even for light fortifications or the lateral protection of mobile siege devices. Those military uses of hurdles remained for a long time; the "gabions" that were filled with dirt were still used in the static warfare in 1914–1918. Even shields were sometimes made of a frame of wattle on which animal skins were stretched: Caesar already mentions the system in the first century B.C.[6] and different primitive populations still use it today.

Hurdles were also used as planking on building sites. In the miniatures one can see these elements that were used to constitute ramps or work floors on the scaffoldings. They played the role that today are played by those all-purpose elements in square batten forming networks of articulated parallels nailed on two layers that can be more-or-less unfolded depending on the surface to be covered. This type of manufacturing, for which there was a large demand, constituted for the peasants a complementary activity during the bad season and provided them with a little extra money, when they could make more than what they needed for their own use.

Close to these uses of wood—that include neither carpentry nor joining, but only tying—is the manufacturing of brooms; these were made of birch or broom. The Bretons even obtained—from King Louis XII, called the Father of the People, who, after Charles VIII, had married Anne de Bretagne—a special privilege that allowed them to cut broom in all the forests of the kingdom and sell their brooms there. One might surmise that Queen Anne wished to find for her household, throughout the kingdom, the brooms that she was used to. One should mostly imagine that this queen (who popularized clogs) tried to favor her fellow countrymen—to the extent that, throughout her life, she prevented the reformers of the *Eaux et Forêts* to operate in Brittany as they did in the rest of the Kingdom[7] in order to repress the abuses in matters of forest exploitation—and wanted in this manner to ensure them a market for the brooms.

The requirements of wickerwork influenced the exploitation of woodlands. Certain trees were specialized; they were pruned so it would be easier to periodically cut the shoots suitable for these products. In countries of *bocage*, hedges and riverbanks are still used for that purpose; the traditional "tadpole" willows, whose heads are hypertrophied by this treatment, constitute a characteristic feature of certain landscapes.

Fences were sometimes reinforced by thorns to increase their effectiveness. "The Jewish thornbush," writes Pierre de Crescence, "is the best of all to make hedges, because at each leaf it has two thorns,

"Bramble," he writes elsewhere, "is suitable for hedges because it makes them strong, thick and prickly, but because it is weak, it would not be sufficient alone; thus one must add other trees that maintain it and that are so strong and firm that they cannot be harmed." Some forests, such as border hedges, were lined by *plessis*, constituted of felled trees and thorn bushes interlaced and entangled to form a deep obstacle, difficult to pass.

From the Bowl to the Barrel

For household utensils, wood was largely used for everything that didn't go on the fire: knife, spoon and fork handles; ladles, cutting boards, as well as the usual containers; cups, churns, plates, dishes, troughs, bowls; boxes and containers for salt, spices, flour, butter, etc., were made of wood. It was less fragile than ceramics and less expensive than metal. This tradition is maintained nowadays in certain regions, as with olive wood in southern France and other species in mountainous countries and also in central and eastern Europe. Bushel-, spoon-, case-, jug-, trunk-, and bowl-makers as well as turners, are cited among the specialists of these manufactures.

Pierre de Crescence cites maple and alder among the species suitable for "bowls and cutting boards"; he also cites hawthorn as "good for plates, bowls and spoons," and *axerus* of which "goblets, bowls and trays" are made. "Boxwood," he says, "is a little tree with a firm yellow stem, nice wood at all times, covered with nice green leaves and of which young ladies make hats. . . . Good for combs, spoons, knife handles, wax tablets and counters and all other little things that must be carved in nice wood."

Traditional attributes of women, the instruments used to spin and weave—spindles, distaffs, spinning wheels, looms, netting needles, and reeds—were also made of wood. So traditional were these attributes that the queens of France, Jeanne de Bourgogne, wife of Philippe VI de Valois, and Jeanne de Bourbon, wife of Charles V, were buried with their distaff and their spindle, articles that were found in 1793 when their tombs were opened.

Most vessels meant to contain liquids were also made of wood. Apart from the coatings with which big containers were caulked, two methods were used to ensure watertightness. Small containers

—bowls, jugs, pails, cups, basins, pots, and deep dishes—were carved out of the mass, while bigger elements—vats, tubs, barrels, kegs, and large casks—were made by joining and clamping joined boards, adjusted and generally curved, called staves. (This invention is attributed to the Gauls.) The manufacturing of barrels had great importance during a period when fermented wine and drinks were essential elements of food for hygienic and cultural reasons.

Specific names, varying from region to region, designated the different specialists who contributed to these manufactured goods. Wet coopers were called *cuveliers, tonneliers, futaillers*, and *barilliers*. They obtained the necessary accessories for the clamping from the hoop-makers who carved in elm, birch, ash, chestnut or hazel hoops of flexible wood, split, half round or formed of thin stems. They were tightened by tying them around the staves.

Pierre de Crescence wrote about ash that "the wood is good for heating and also very good for making hoops for barrels and other containers." In 1215, the Premonstrants of Lieu-Restauré in the Valois were authorized by the king of France, Philippe Auguste, to take one thousand hoops of hazel and hornbeam each year, from the forest of Retz, to make barrels and also seventy rings of birch that served for the vats and the big barrels.[9] Saint Louis had three coopers in his service. They were fed at the court and "maintained the casks, hogsheads, buckets and barrels of the king."[10]

Barrels were made in all sizes. Common barrels in the region of Bordeaux contained eight hundred to nine hundred liters (one liter = 1.057 quarts). Bigger barrels, especially if they were standardized, were easier to stow in the ships. Except for small kegs, which in hilly countries were transported by donkeys or mules, the transport of barrels was invariably done via water. The hoisting and moving necessary to place big barrels in the ships did not create any special problems because, at that period, there were efficient means of hoisting and gearing down, including cranes, tackles, and pulley-blocks.

The manufacturing of barrel staves was similar in its techniques—including the precision required for its assembly—to the construction of ships, of which the planking, which had to be watertight, was made of boards assembled side by side or lapped and maintained by midship frames. In addition, the planking was caulked with tar, a forest product obtained by distilling certain woods. Food containers, however, could not include anything other than wood, as even wood contributed its taste to wines and, especially, alcohol.

All the big wine regions had to have a sufficient forested domain so as to avoid the costly importation of wood. The forests of the Limousin and Périgord supplied the vineyards of the Bordelais. The vineyard of the Auxerrois and the one in the Parisian region were favored by the possibility of finding wood nearby. The transportation of wine was done mostly via rivers or by sea; the risks of shocks and losses were less than on bad roads, with horse-drawn carts that had no suspension system; and the capacity of the ships was much superior to that of the biggest land vehicles. So, the conditions of development of vineyards were, in addition to the close proximity of the forests producing wood, the possibility of river or maritime service.

The most favorable position was, as in Bordeaux or in Paris, the one where the forests were upstream—providing the wood necessary for the containers and all the vineyard's accessories—and where the customers' regions, toward which the wine was exported, were downstream.

Wine had a considerable importance in the maritime trade; the occupation of Aquitaine by the English at the time of the Hundred Years War, as well as the taste they acquired for Bordeaux wine, contributed to its reputation. It is illustrated by the fact that the capacity of the ships began to be calculated in barrels, because wine was their main cargo.

9 · pRoduction, exploitation, and paRceling ·

Exploitation and Parceling

FROM THE EARLIEST TIMES, forests close to inhabited sites were
exploited by man, and modified through specialization based
on different objectives: wood production for fuel, for construction,
for tools, etc. and food production. Gradually, especially in mountain areas, it became apparent that the forest also played a role as
regulator of the water regime, as an agent of soil fixation, and barrier
against erosion, land slides, and avalanches.

Man preferred certain species and also certain kinds of forests,
and so organized their exploitation, and parceled them out. But the
needs were often contradictory. When a thought-out organization
replaced the random cuttings, this exploitation had to be done in
a way that fulfilled the various needs without breaking into the
capital assets of the forest. A balance had to be struck between
population figures and the surface of the woodlands, meadows, and

cultivated fields. Forest exploitation had to be organized by a power capable of imposing, in the general interest, a long-term management that guaranteed the preservation of the forest estate and its transmission to the following generations.

The Romans divided the forests into three types. Those intended to produce firewood were subjected to annual cuts and were called *sylva caedua* (forests to cut) or *sylvae minutae*. These woods also provided props for the vines and, according to Pliny, were cut every eight years for the chestnut tree, and every eleven years for oak. Other forests served as pastureland for the domestic animals, mostly pigs: it was the *sylva glandifera* (providing acorns) or *sylva saginacia* (intended to feed domestic animals). Construction timber was found in the second category. In the third category were huge forests, that belonged to the state and were not regularly exploited.

During the Middle Ages, the woodlands generally included three large categories. The first was constituted by the coppice, called *bois revenants* or *bois de vente*, cut at regular intervals (eight, ten or fifteen years), that supplied firewood, wood for charcoal, and timbers for stakes, fences, basket weaving, tool handles, etc. In those woods, pasturing was authorized only after several years of growth following the cut.

During the Early Middle Ages, some coppices were cut at longer intervals than those that were used essentially for firewood. They were intended to provide the stakes for the fences and stockades, which enclosed gardens, villages, and even castles (often built entirely with wood during that period). Those *sylvae palariae* (wood for stakes) are frequently mentioned, especially during the first part of the Middle Ages.

The second category included the forests of timber trees (*futaies*), also called *bois de garde* or *de reserve*, that supplied construction timber and where usage rights were exercised. These included the exceptional right, under the control of forest agents, to take the timber necessary for personal use, for repairs, or for construction, with strict prohibitions against trading. Several other rights—such as the one to take bee swarms, barks, leaves, etc., or to cut certain species of woods considered secondary—were specified in the customs.

The third category of woodlands included the warrens (*garennes*), which were game preserves, often surrounded by ditches, embankments or even walls, where only hunting, reserved for the beneficiary of the warren, was practiced.

The *sylva caedua* of the Romans, which was called in the Early Middle Ages *sylva concida* (forest to cut), corresponds to the coppice called *taillis* in French. The word *taillis* began to be used during the eleventh century—with the general meaning that it has today—of a forest regularly cut, of a "pruned" (*tailliée*) forest. The Latin word, used in the Early Middle Ages to designate this category of woodland—*talea*—was opposed to *bannum* or to *foresta*, designating the reserved forest (which was called *banbois* in eastern France).

Since the early part of the nineteenth century, following what Huffel—a forest ranger—denounced as a "denaturation" of the original meaning,[1] the forest rangers have reserved the name of *taillis* exclusively for trees coming from shoots on stumps, in opposition to woods raised from seed. But in the Middle Ages, it was the age and the size of the trees that distinguished the coppices from the timber forests. The latter were composed of trees over thirty years old (sometimes even fifty for certain customs), corresponding to a minimum of three "revolutions" of the coppice; that is, the periodicity of the cutting, or, in other words, the maximum age of the trees.

It would appear that, in the Middle Ages, the growth period for the firewood coppice was even shorter than under the Romans. Pierre de Crescence—an Italian—advised cutting the coppices at least every five or six years, which corresponds to a rather luxuriant vegetation, and seems very short in the French environment. In fact, customs varied considerably from one place to another, considering the diversity of the local situations—soil, climate, etc. When, in 1563, the king of France imposed a ten-year minimum, it was a rule inspired by the periodicity practiced in northern France, and a reaction against unreasonably short terms. In some cases, and for some coppices, one could cut every six years. In case of repurchase, the lord could even in regions cut the coppices at four years and four months. In the Grand Perche, Clermontois, and Beauvaisis the duration was seven years. In other regions, the periodicity was longer; ten or even twelve years in Burgundy. Sometimes, quite rationally, the duration depended on the quality of the soil. Thus, the custom of Lorraine prescribes that the user cannot cut his woods just any place, but has to do it by *lizières*; in other words, by sectors in which one can come back only after a certain number of years "sufficient for the growth of the wood according to the fertility or sterility of the site; the rule is applied to coppices that generally grow in twelve year in fertile places and in eighteen in sterile places."[2]

The French word *recrue*, used to describe young soldiers (recruits) was, originally, a forest term designating the new growth of trees. The foresters used to talk of a twelve-year *recrue*, eighteen-year *recrue*, etc. By analogy, an age group of the human population was designated, and is precisely the one that reaches the age to bear arms, that is, to be sent to "fire."

Keeping mature trees for seeding at the time of the cuttings is an ancient custom; those trees are seed-bearers, *balivaux*. The forest ordinance of September 1376, an edict by Charles V, called "the Wise," recalled this ancient custom too often neglected: "It is ordered that, from now on, all cuttings will maintain seed-bearers, eight or ten per arpent." Some seed-bearers, preserved for a very long time, became famous trees that were given proper names and were sometimes even the object of borderline pagan cults.

The above-mentioned 1376 ordinance, which seems to indicate that the custom to preserve seed-bearers had been long extant, ordered the maintainance of eight or ten per arpent. The arpent varied according to the regions, from two-fifths (about an acre) to half a hectare, so the law requested keeping sixteen to twenty-five seed-bearers per hectare. This rule was included in all the later forest ordinances. Seed-bearers had to be left in the forest as well as in the coppice. In principle, these seed-bearers, as soon as they had gone beyond three "revolutions" of the coppice, were protected the same as the timber trees, but it was extremely difficult to protect them at the time of the cutting. There are many allusions to abuses in this matter. Furthermore, with the system of overly frequent cuttings of the coppice, the seed-bearers, even if they were effectively preserved, were seldom nice trees, "but, on the contrary, remain always stunted, twisted and humped, and cannot go up . . . , as they are not pressed."[3]

The same rule was generally adopted in private forests, especially in northern France. The edicts revealed that forest users had to respect the seed-bearers when they made cuttings.

A Progress: The Forest in Periodic Cuttings

The ordinances of Charles V marked a date in the methods of exploiting the French forest, not so much because they were innovative but because they attempted to make mandatory the methods that were already used in the best cases, but were too often neglected in most when immediate interest prevailed over the long-term perspective that was indispensable for any rational management of the forest estate.

Traditionally (and the example of the abbot Suger looking for the twelve beams he needed for the Saint-Denis basilica is characteristic) the exploitation of timber (*merrain*) was done by "rummaging"; in other words, by choosing trees here and there, depending on what was found. During that period (at the end of the fourteenth century), what today is called the *coupes par assiette* were inaugurated; their capacity and place had to be determined by the forest agents. But, in the previous centuries, this system had already been used in the royal forests, sometimes regularly and sometimes only for what were called extraordinary cuttings.

Charles V, in his ordinance of July 1376, concerning the forest of Roumare, indicated that the cuttings had to include the equivalent of five to six hectares (a hectare equals 2.47 acres) in one piece. This did not mean that everything was cut; on the contrary, it was recommended that only the trees which met the current needs and caused the least waste be felled. The principle of choosing the trees according to the size needed was maintained, so as to avoid unnecessary sawing and waste. "It is forbidden to fell any tree bigger or higher than the required lumber."[4] This agreed with the techniques of the period. The cuttings had to be done with a lot of care, the stumps could not protrude, which was easier for the loggers, but had to be cut at ground level and very neatly so the woods could "come back." On this subject, it can be recalled that even at the beginning of the present century a logger was considered to have done his work well if, after the cutting, a liter of wine could stand firmly on the cut stump; this instrument of verification was not in short supply at a time when loggers normally required—by contract—five to six liters of wine a day.

By a new ordinance, promulgated in Melun in September 1376, that constituted a true statute of forest exploitation in fifty-two articles, Charles V prescribed again the continuance of the cuttings in lots totaling ten to fifteen arpents in one sector, so as to avoid random cutting, that is, taking wood here and there. Article 34 once again recommended cutting the trees with care so as to facilitate their regeneration. In the sixteenth century, the rules still insisted on this point, imposing the use of well-sharpened tools, excluding the saw for cutting trees, forbidding cutting the coppices at the time of the sap rising, and debarking standing trunks.

The organization of the cutting by sector, what is called today in French the *coupe réglée*, the periodic cutting, was the opposite of the random cuttings, called *"forer."* The term *coupe réglée* has, in the common language, been diverted from its original meaning of organized, regular cutting; it should be used only metaphorically to designate systematic exploitation and not disordered and devastating plundering. In the same way, the expression *coupe sombre* (dark cut), about which many people and even encyclopedias are mistaken, designated, in reality, a cutting that preserved a great quantity of tall trees, so that the young seedlings of shade species could develop in favorable conditions; a *coupe claire* (light cut) is, by contrast, one that largely lets the sun through (thinning) and encourages the development of grasses and of light species.

The system of cuts made successively in predetermined sectors (*parquets de coupe*) to which one came back at regular intervals, was reminiscent of the old system of itinerant farming described earlier. Although there was, of course, no alternation between crops and wood, the system followed the same principle of succession between cultivation, new growth and harvest and the same principle of exploited ranges, of which the number had to correspond to the number of years of the rotation.

The limits of the cutting enclosures that were successively exploited were indicated by marker-trees (*arbres de laie* or *de laye*). The trees situated at the angle of the lots were called *pieds corniers* (of the same root as "corner" in English). In the thirteenth century, the word *laie* could designate a specific forest range, a *vente* (area of cut timber for sale) or, sometimes, even a whole forest divided in that manner—as the forest of Laye near Saint Germain.

In the early sixteenth century, when the authorities decided to assemble and complete the existing forest rules, they repeated that the trees used to mark the limits (*laies, pieds corniers*) should be chosen among the best subjects so that they could also play the role of seed-bearers, and should be in sufficient number; this rule introduced the notion of adaptation to different terrains and to specific cases.

The wood merchants, mentioned in the acts and the judgments, appear to have often been without scruples; it was thus necessary to take a certain number of measures to avoid abuses—such as cutting the seed-bearers. The merchant who had acquired the wood, before cutting it, had to have it blazed (*marteler*) by the forester who indicated which seed-bearers to respect. If the merchant started to fell the trees before this operation he was fined.

Furthermore, before cutting, the purchaser of a timber lot had to fence in the range where the cutting was to be done (*hayer*) to protect it from animals. It was a precaution that was already applied in the thirteenth century in, among other places, the forest of Orléans; it was recalled in 1376 in the ordinances of Charles V. There were two reasons for the fence; first, the authorities were concerned that if the sector wasn't specifically delimited by a barrier that couldn't be moved in a few minutes, the merchant would fell trees outside the lot; second, they were afraid that if he wasn't obligated to erect the fence before starting to cut, he would neglect this obligation when he finished his work, and take the wood away— without bothering to build the fence. This fence was sold after a few years, when the shoots were strong enough to allow cattle in the area.

Timber Trees

The production of construction timber of big sizes, of *merrain* suitable for frameworks, floors, shipbuilding or war devices, required tall trees, trees older than several generations of men.

For that purpose, large areas could be set "in defense"; in other words, be forbidden to exploit for sixty, one hundred or even two hundred years, depending on the species. Little by little the undergrowth was thinned out to allow the most beautiful specimens to develop. Another method was to leave, in exploited ranges, a certain number of protected subjects. Both methods presumed a concern for the future, and for long-term planning that went far beyond the average life expectancy of man; they both had to be regulated to ensure the protection of the trees.

For centuries, the extremely large size of some forests—or the difficulty of access—had been sufficient to protect many trees from the loggers, but it was no longer the case. Consequently, provision had to be made for future generations, with an awareness of the long-term aspects, and of the duties toward distant successors. Only human beings with a sense of history, groups of people who could count on a certain stability in time, who were devoted to the public good, interested as members of a family in guaranteeing the perpetuity of the estate and of its resources for their successors, could take such measures: religious communities, dynasties of kings or high lords, noble families, high ecclesiastical dignitaries or rural communities.

Commoners rarely had that concern for the future. Since, as simple holders, grantees of the lord, they didn't own the land, they generally had no assurance of being able to maintain the place for their descendants. Above all, the poor farmer attempted to ensure his everyday livelihood and didn't look further than the following year. Gradually his position became more stable and this encouraged him to manage with the medium-term in mind: not to exhaust the soil, to renew the fruit trees, guarantee wood for fuel, and miscellaneous common uses. But he could not, as an individual, worry about protecting trees for the use of future generations; that preoccupation belonged to other levels of society and to those who made the laws.

In the coppices, given the frequency of the cuttings, the protected seed-bearers rarely became good-looking trees; as Froidour remarked in the seventeenth century, "As they are not pressed, instead of growing nice and straight without knots or branches, they grow like apple trees."[5] The author of this text concluded that the coppice had to grow for fifteen to twenty years; today it is known that even that length of time is not sufficient.

Thus, the method of exploitation of the coppices, which was gradually changed only after the Middle Ages, was not favorable for the development of "nice" trees. To a certain extent, these existed only by chance; when the conditions favorable to their development happened to be met during their first years and when they had then been respected long enough to reach their full maturity. Under these circumstances, it was logical and rational not to count too much on big, straight timber but to base construction methods on what was readily available: timbers of small section, that is, small diameters.

The timber forest must have offered better conditions for the development of the trees. It would appear that during the Early

Middle Ages, when the forests were not overexploited, one could still find, when needed, timber pieces that were big, long, and straight. But the situation rapidly changed from the eleventh and twelfth centuries on.

Because of the difficulty and cost of transportation during the Middle Ages, distance was an efficient deterrent, so it was recommended that ranges of timber trees be placed at the center of the large wooded areas. It was estimated that it was possible to obtain full-grown trees only in forest ranges that were out of the reach of thieves and animal herds. The peripheral zones used as coppice served as defense banks for the center, which was treated as a timber forest. Huffel states that all the ancient rules support this point of view.[6]

The timber forests themselves had to be regularly maintained so that the trees could grow straight and healthy. The rules of this maintenance were more-or-less codified in the sixteenth and seventeenth centuries. During the Middle Ages they were already observed in a certain number of forests—and at least in the royal forests—to the extent that the pressure to cut the forests wasn't too strong. Because the kings needed timber for naval uses, military engineering, and construction, provisions for the parceling-out and management of the forests were necessary so that it would not be too difficult or unusual to find the particular pieces—sometimes extremely big—that were requisitioned.

In the areas reserved to grow as timber forests, supplementary seedings were done among the seed-bearers responsible for the repopulation, and about every ten years the forest was thinned out— what was called in the language of the time "to garden" (*jardiner*) —by cutting the seed-bearers that were too old and were dying and other trees, poorly started, that might hinder the development of the small oaks. Pierre de Crescence described and justified those practices in the fourteenth century: "The woods and forests, where there are beautiful and noble trees suitable for construction and monuments . . . if the nice trees are too close to each other, the second choice ones will be cut and the best ones will be left with more space so they have more food." This technique, consisting of thinning in a rational way to allow better development of the remaining trees, is still used today.

The exploitation age of the timber forest was at least one hundred years, because it was believed, as Olivier de Serres relates, that the oak grows for a hundred years, maintains itself for another hundred years, then dies for a hundred years. The periodicity of the cuttings was based on this concept. "The cutting will be started in the oldest timber forest or the one in the worst state and proportioned so in a hundred years and no less, it will return to timber forest," prescribed an ordinance of 1573 that reproduced a similar rule from an edict of 1544, that had referred to the forests of Brittany.[7]

After the timber trees were cut, respecting the designated trees, the natural seeding was done by the seed-bearers; if there was a shortage in certain areas it was prescribed to till those parts and to plant selected acorns. These areas had to be surrounded by ditches to prevent animals from entering them during the first few years of the new growth. These methods recommended in the ordinances of the sixteenth century (such as the one of 1573) had been perfected through the centuries, and particularly since the 1376 ordinances of Charles V, which, Huffel wrote, constituted the foundation of all future forest laws.[8]

The coppice with standards is a system that was used most everywhere in France, although it was not indigenous to this country. It was also used in England where—after having been criticized from the point of view of sylviculture—it is now considered very rational from an ecological point of view. This system tried to satisfy both the needs for firewood and for timber while maintaining the coppices as places favorable for game. The more systematic Germans, who have very nice forests, recommend the simple open forest composed of trees that are all about the same age. This gives their forests a monumental—but sometimes monotonous—aspect. However, it is not a good solution for the ecological balance required, because it creates a quasi-monoculture of greater fragility. Indeed, exported to Africa by the Germans early in the twentieth century, this method produced disastrous results in the equatorial forest, where the relations and interdependencies between the countless elements of an extremely rich environment are particularly complex.

Consequences of the Exploitation of Firewood

Man's exploitation of the forest, even when his aim is to preserve it and not to replace it by crops, entails deep modifications that depend on the modalities of this exploitation; since in the Middle

Ages the production of fuel was one of the main functions of the forest, a lot of importance was given to the coppices—which were formed mainly by shoots of stumps and which were frequently cut—when compared to today's methods. Coppices were cut every ten years, on average, sometimes less, sometimes more, to obtain bundles of wood and small logs that were burned directly or used to make charcoal. In young woods, the proportion of live tissues is much larger than in older woods; as a result the use of woods eight, ten, twelve or fifteen years old, rather than woods fifty, one hundred or two hundred years old converted to obtain smaller elements, results in more important losses of mineral elements. The exploitation as timber forest, whatever the use of the wood, is less impoverishing for the forest than the exploitation as coppice, and the coppice of short revolution more impoverishing than one of which the revolution is longer, especially when the bark is left on the tree. This was the case for firewood and for timber that was better preserved and ran less risk of being damaged during its transport, when it was barked and squared only on the site of its use.

But to use timbers of big section and cut them into small elements for firewood would have meant a huge work of conversion, very labor-intensive and lengthy with the tools that were available during the Middle Ages; so, people used the timbers most suitable to the different uses, as they were, with the minimum of preparation. According to the needs, people chose and cut according to the size: small wood for firewood, larger wood for pickets and stakes, medium-size timber for light framing, and rafters and large-size timber for beams—the biggest for large balks.

As most of the wood was used for fuel, either directly or through the intermediacy of charcoal (which, for an equal amount of calories produced, consumed much more wood than the direct use of the latter), the coppice dominated. In the long run these modalities of parceling (all the more since it was a coppice of short revolution), impoverished the forest which, little by little, provided less wood in all the categories. In addition, the method of felling also had its importance; indeed, when the entire wooded cover is cut on a large area, what is called a *coupe rase*, and when water is not very deep, it comes up and can asphyxiate the roots, which increases the degradation.

Thus the combination of the needs of the period, with the available means and resources in material, tools, and men led to an exploitation that, by impoverishing the forest, progressively reduced the production of wood, not only for fuel but for other uses as well.

Forests and Transportation

Forests played an essential role in transportation. All vehicles, whether meant for roadways or waterways, were essentially built with wood and, as long as iron remained costly and hard to get, they were operated with very few metal parts. Waterways could even be used directly to transport cheaply the timber and logs, just after the cutting and conversion. The physical environment of the area, particularly the natural links by rivers, was an essential element in the exploitation of the forest. Only small amounts of wood could be exported overland to any distant place, because of the difficulty and costs of land transportation.

One of the reasons for the development of the use of charcoal (which leads to consuming a considerable part of the calories contained in wood to obtain a fuel with a higher caloric power), was the reduced weight under which the same quantity of calories was transported. In mountainous areas, transportation was by mules or donkeys from the sites of charcoal manufacturing to the nearest river or road, where larger loads could be organized for further transport. The Rhône and Durance rivers were used for transportating the loads of charcoal and wood that supplied the areas to the south, which were poor in forests; but all rivers were used for the transportation of wood.

Wood wasn't consumed only on site by the local people; owners of certain large forest estates, especially in the mountains, traded it. Construction timber was even the object of a long-distance trade with the Moslem countries situated around the shores of the Mediterranean Sea, all of which were poor in wood. To make shipbuilding more difficult for the Saracens, the authorities tried to prohibit the exportation of wood, then considered a strategic material.

In 972, the doge of Venice had enacted this prohibition at the request of the then-emperor of the Byzantine Empire, and in 1123 the Christians, after the victory of the Venetian fleet over the Egyptians, reinstated the embargo. But this measure wasn't very effective and trade continued in spite of the prohibitions. In 1154, the

Pisans—from the city of Pisa—delivered forbidden material to the sultan of Egypt, and from the middle of the thirteenth century, the mameluke sultans, who didn't have a fleet, obtained the raw materials they needed—such as iron and wood—thanks to regular trade relations with certain western nations: Genoa, Venice, Pisa, Catalonia, and Marseilles, among others.

From the point of view of the forests' conservation, their geographical location, their relief and their service by roadways or waterways were very important factors; the feasibility of floating the logs on small watercourses, and the rough timber on bigger rivers made the exploitation and the commercialization easier and sometimes led to overexploitation. The possibility of installing hydraulic sawmills in the immediate vicinity of the forests producing the wood also led to overexploitation, to such an extent that, in certain cases, the authorities destroyed the sawmills—as the consuls of the town of Colmars did at the end of the thirteenth century.

Early in the twelfth century, in the region of Toulouse, a great forest (*grandis sylva*) existed on the left bank of the Garonne River; even taking into account the propensity of southerners to exaggerate, it must have been quite large. That is where the famous monastery that took the name of Grand'Selve was established. The Daire, a tributary of the Garonne, ran through the forest. All of the central part of the woods, on each side of the river, disappeared, exported by floating, and the "great forest" was reduced to a wood, called the forest of Verdun, and a few woods on the other side of the Daire. Whether or not the friars were the main actors of the clearing, it was the transportation facilities that precipitated the deforestation.

Aware of the dissuasive effect of distance, the authorities tried to locate the timber trees deep in the forests. In the peripheral zones, near the edges of the forests, it was difficult to preserve timber trees, whether as seed-bearers in the coppices or in full timber woods. Too close to the towns, these trees were exposed to being cut and removed, secretly or even with the complicity of the foresters. Several practical measures were taken to avoid these thefts as much as possible.

Besides the fines and miscellaneous penalties to which the offenders exposed themselves (and which we will examine in the chapter about legislation, usage rights, and penalties), besides the measures aimed at preventing the cutting work from going unnoticed, the elementary precaution that the authorities took for any forest of a certain size was to keep the timber woods as far as possible from the edges of the forest.

So, it was generally the center of the large forests that were set "in defense"; in other words, forbidden to the users who farmed at the limits of the forests, to make it more difficult to fell, convert, and transport the rough timber without the knowledge of the authorities. The exploitation, and often even access, was forbidden to commoners.

Transporting cut wood through the forest, especially long pieces for construction, was often very difficult and sometimes neither carts nor bar wheels could be used. Except where a sufficiently sharp slope permitted sliding the timber along pathways cut through the trees, the only resource was portage, by one or several men, or by animals, oxen, horses, or donkeys. This method of transportation could be used on narrow trails, bad roads, sharp slopes, and has remained traditional in many countries; it was available even to the poorest. It could be used only for small loads of wood—or charcoal—although in some mountainous countries important quantities of fuel were transported by troops of mules or donkeys in caravans, as is still done with those animals and with camels in North Africa and in other countries where wood is rare in some places.

The images, which were still traditional in the seventeenth century and are found in Boileau or La Fontaine, of portage on the backs of men (the poor logger, "the back loaded with wood and the body all in water,") and of portage by animal (the donkey with sponges and the donkey loaded with salt; the miller, his son and the donkey; the donkey loaded with relics), corresponded to an everyday reality, a common method of transportation for centuries, not only in mountainous areas, but all around the countryside.

Transport on the backs of men is often mentioned in the customs; it was a usual method. In some customs, to prevent the users from being able to gather dead wood too easily, the load was limited to what "women or young boys" can carry, or the "choirboy" (when it was wood for the priest). But for heavy loads and large-size elements, particularly for construction timber that had to remain whole, portage was suitable only for short distances and didn't have the necessary capacity; a donkey or a mule cannot carry more than two pieces of rough timber, and not very big pieces. So, in the absence of waterways, wheeled vehicles were necessary.

From the Tree to the Wheel

In the Middle Ages all vehicles were made almost exclusively of wood. Sliding vehicles, on wooden skates or sledges, were not only used on snow or ice, but also on grass, particularly in the mountains, where they were used to transport hay. Although there are no traces of the use of skis in the West during the Middle Ages, sledges were often used. The *schlitte* was a sort of sled used in the Vosges Mountains to bring down the wood, generally on wooden roads, of which the crossbars were perpendicular to the motion and formed steps, on which the man who held onto the load could find a foothold and on which the sled's skates slid easily.*

But sliding wasn't a solution when the ground was flat and resistant, or sticky, or rocky and uneven. The wheel was invented; the initial idea came from the rollers, which, originally simple pieces of trunks, were an easy way to move big objects, and were used since ancient times. The wheel must have come out of the forest; it's the tree that, by developing in concentric layers, introduced in nature the circular shape, of which man made considerable use once he discovered the properties of the center of the circle, and combined the axle with the wheel.

The invention of the axle, fixed to the vehicle, constituted important progress but considerably increased the forces of friction, which were much less with the rollers. It was only with the invention of ball bearings, and their application to the wheel, that the latter would have the same advantages of low friction as the primitive roller system.

The old wooden wheels, because of the difficulties of assembling multiple spokes on a central hub, were often solid, composed of elements of joined wood. When they had openings, wheels were made of elements that were assembled according to two perpendicular directions, not by radiating elements. Two systems were used. In one, a strong piece of wood was placed diametrically, pierced in its center to let the wooden or metal axle through; it maintained

♦ ♦ ♦

* According to Dauzat, the French word *luge* might be one of the oldest words of the French language, preceding even the Gauls; *luge*, sledge, slip and slide, *schlitten* (to slide in German), all derive from a common root *slodia* or *sleudia*.

the rim at its extremities. Two smaller perpendicular pieces were assembled at their center to the main piece and maintained the rim at four other points. Until 1940, this type of wheel was still used in the Asturias in Spain. In the other system, four pieces, symmetrical two by two in relation to the center of the wheel, were assembled according to two perpendicular directions, leaving a hole in the center for the axle and maintaining the rim on eight points regularly distributed; this system is visible on certain antique bas-reliefs.

It was only during the Middle Ages that the system of the hub, to which the spokes were attached, was perfected for the wooden wheel. The rim of that type of wheel was made of split, curved wood; the rolling band was reinforced by supplementary layers of wood that had to be replaced as they wore out, or by a flat iron circling the wheel, which then wore out less quickly.

As soon as the joining techniques had developed—thanks to the increasing availability of iron and to the perfecting and dissemination of new specialized tools in frameworking and other wood techniques—the art of the wheelwright, and especially the production of wheels, evolved. That was when the wheel with spokes developed (more balanced and rational, considering the forces to bear). The spokes were assembled, on one side, to the circle of the rim, and on the other side, to a strong piece of wood—cylindrical or cylindrical/conical shaped—the hub. This was pierced in its center to make a hole for the axle, sometimes in metal, and equipped with a system of locking or keying that prevented the wheel from breaking loose. This type of wheel existed already in ancient times; for example in Mesopotamia and Egypt, where the light war chariots of the Pharaohs were equipped with iron wheels, each with four or six spokes.

The development of this type of wheel—in which the pressure received by the rim is transmitted longitudinally to spokes that are compressed in the sense of their greatest resistance—caused the wheelwright's art to progress; now he had to be able to work both wood and iron, used for the circling of the wheel and often for the axle. Different species, depending on their various characteristics of hardness, resistance, and flexibility were used to make different parts of the wheels; harder wood for the hub, more flexible for the spokes, more elastic and split for the rim, which was made of successive thin layers of wood, glued to each other.

One of the most important applications of the wheel, developed during the Middle Ages, was the wheelbarrow, which appeared in the thirteenth century. Miniatures illustrating construction sites show both wheelbarrows and handbarrows; the wheelbarrow looks like a handbarrow in which one of the porters has been replaced by a wheel. Gradually the characteristics of the wheelbarrow differed from those of the handbarrow and it took the functional shape that it still has today.

Forests and Roads

For transporting heavy weights a certain distance with wheeled vehicles, roads were necessary. The wheel, to receive all its advantages, must be complemented by a rolling way, one that should be as smooth as possible—what today we call a "road." The French term *route* was originally purely related to the forest and meant a breach made through the woods (*rupta*), from which derives the French word *roturier* (commoner). Thus, if the wheel is the child of the tree, the road was born from the forest. However, networks of roads—tamped or paved—existed also among civilizations that didn't know the wheel, because they facilitated traffic on foot or by horse. Pre-Columbian America knew neither wheel nor horse, and had, as did the Roman Empire, a network of carefully maintained paved roads.

As one evokes the relationship between the road and the forest, it is interesting to note the considerable amount of wood used in building roads, not only for bridges but for the roads themselves. Wood was used, either—as in certain Roman ways—to establish substructures for foundations in marshy or unstable grounds; or, for creating specialized ways for sliding sledges, such as those on which, just a few years ago, wood was brought down in the Vosges Mountains, or even for constituting the surface of roads. In the crossing of the Hautes Fagnes in Belgium, the *via mansuerisca* was built by the Romans with trunks of resin trees of very large diameter, that have been identified as being spruce—of a specie that has since disappeared in that region (*picea excelsa*).

In several countries, wood roadways have been built for a long time on marshy grounds or on fragile soils, such as sand dunes. Many examples exist in northern Germany, Holland and Denmark.

Devèze mentions the use of boards in northern Germany to cover muddy roads and the use of branches to fill potholes.[9] This system is found in several countries.

An interesting case, because it was an attempt in the Middle Ages to combine the advantages of waterways and roadways—well before the system of locks allowed the raising and lowering of vessels—is given by what the Russians call the *volokis* (singular, *volok*). The existence of these paths, that allowed loaded boats to pass from one river system to another, above the division line of the waters, appears to be very ancient.[10] Eventually, the tracks were grooved in their center by a deep furrow marking the passage of the boats. Wood rollers facilitated the difficult passages. The Normans probably used them in their southern expansion which, from Novgorod, led them to the shores of the Black Sea, from where a Norman fleet left to lay seige to Byzantium.

In France, the Normans used the same system when they couldn't pass a fortified bridge or to pass from one river basin to the next. In 886, when the Parisians—who had resisted the assaults of the Normans since November of 885, and had finally concluded a truce at an exorbitant price—refused to let them sail up the Seine River, the Vikings transported all of their fleet upstream by building a road with wooden rollers over which they pulled their drakkars. However, this use of roads to move boats was exceptional.

Another use of wood for roads, particularly common in the Middle Ages, were bridges—indispensable for the highways. But there were also ditches, streams, and little rivers that needed to be passed; fording them was no problem, but slowed down traffic and could damage the vehicles or their loads. Sometimes, the ditches were merely filled with branches or logs; elsewhere, when the flow of water had to be respected, culverts were built with tree trunks set side by side and covered with dirt, as is still done today in forest drives, and especially on mountain roads.

Nevertheless, roads were less than perfect in the Middle Ages; they were maintained at the initiative of the local lay or ecclesiastical lords in the measure of their needs until, as the royal central authority developed, the king found advantages in improving certain highways. Some of these had remained almost in the same state in which the Romans—great road builders—had left them. Furthermore, the carts had no suspension system and were difficult to handle, as the pivoting front-axle unit appeared only at the end of the Middle

Ages. Until then, the vehicles pulled by animals were manageable only if they were limited to two wheels, which transferred part of the load to the draft animals; the four-wheel vehicles turned with a lot of difficulty, exercising lateral forces on the axles and the wheels that forced the draft animals to work harder. In fact, loaded four-wheel carts turned only by skidding; this was helped by the bumps in the roads, that made the carts jump and so reduced the friction of the wheels on the ground.

Under these conditions—roads in bad condition, lack of bridges, lack of traffic safety, defective carts and wheeled vehicles, inefficient harnessing systems, poorly fed and not very vigorous draft animals, frequent road tolls and, sometimes, highway robbers—the best solution was to avoid the roads and use the waterways, whenever it was possible.

Wood and Waterways

Although wood can be used as fuel just after being cut, it is not recommended because a great part of the energy is then lost in eliminating the water; it is better to allow wood to dry for a while. However, for the timber used for framings, naval construction or furniture, it is imperative to eliminate the miscellaneous organic substances transported by the sap; they prevent good conservation by constituting an environment favorable to parasites.

"Floating" the timber contributed to this elimination by the exchanges that occurred between the agitated and perpetually renewed water and wood. Today this function is assumed more quickly, but perhaps not more effectively, by steaming. In northern countries that are important producers (Canada, Scandinavia) and of which the woods are famous for their qualities (not merely due to the slowness of their growth), floating is still used systematically before drying and treating the wood in the factories. Making use of a necessary phase in the treatment of wood in order to transport it cheaply is interesting; it is "killing two birds with one stone." Floating is an important step in the preparation of oak.

For firewood, of which the sensitivity to parasites is less important, floating presents no disadvantages; in any case, it is advantageous for this fuel to be stocked for a year or two after the cut to enable it to dry out.

But floating timber along a river presupposed a certain number of conditions of a geographical and political nature. On one hand, even when the relief, the slope, and the profile of the river lent themselves to it, the river, unless it was extremely large, had to be organized so that the timber would not get stuck and create a dam, with sometimes disastrous consequences for the borderers. Specialized laborers, skillful and daring men—for it is a dangerous profession—had to supervise the proper flow of timber and intervene whenever necessary. The wood had to be directed either by men who convoyed it or who were posted at the places where it might stop, so that they could push it back into the current.

Rivers had to be planned—and changed—to permit the traffic of timber; shallow sections were dredged or the depth was increased by well-placed dams; the shores had to be graded, as well as the bed of the river where the timber or even the logs might run aground. The mill canals had to be modified so that the timber could topple over the dam and not plunge into some side channel; the irrigation canals had to be protected to prevent the timber from entering.

Dikes had to be built to maintain a sufficient minimum water level or to allow for a surge of water to free the timber float if it ran aground. Spillways had to be made in all the dams. Because of the lack of political unity in the river basins and the impossibility of continuous supervision of the riverbanks in the Early Middle Ages, none of these fittings could be realized, except on relatively short runs, such as in the mountain areas where they used a system, called "à bûches perdues." One also had to prevent the borderers from taking—secretly or ostensibly—overly large quantities of the merchandise during the trip on the river.

In the feudal system, the occupation of the land at the different levels was only a holding, a sort of grant from the level above, with the king as the superior authority. As a consequence, the king could, in principle, establish collective rules limiting certain aspects of land tenure; he could impose measures of general interest or grant privileges or write patent letters authorizing certain activities, limited to certain professional categories or to certain areas. In reality, his jurisdiction was limited by the influence and power of the local lords and by the existing customs.

Starting in the thirteenth century, a certain number of ordinances and edicts regulated the use of waterways, the trade and traffic of timber, as well as fishing activity that can be considerably damaged by the floating if there are no controls. On one hand, the passage of the logs, timber and rafts perturbed the fauna, could hamper the access to the shores and destroy them, and damage the plants; on the other hand, the sap, that got mixed with the water, was not good for the fish.

The ordinance, issued in August 1291 by Philippe IV le Bel, codified the relations between users and borderers. The ordinance of May 1302 was concerned with cutting wood and fishing in the ponds. The ordinances of 1326, issued by Charles IV le Bel, and the ones issued by Philippe VI de Valois in 1333 were relative to the fisheries in the ponds and the rivers. The ordinance of 1350, by King Jean le Bon, included articles on the exploitation and the sale of wood. The edict of 1411 gave jurisdiction over traffic to the trade provost (*prévôt des marchands*) of Paris, who controlled the exploitation and the transport of wood and established the prices of the tolls that would be paid.

According to G. Guillot-Chêne, wood floating has always been used, not only on large waterways but on any river with a sufficient flow to transport wood from the site of felling to the site of its use. The wood of the Cévennes—which was used, among other things, for shipbuilding in the Mediterranean ports and for the mines of the region—was dispatched on the Hérault River to Agde. The wood of the Pyrénées and of the region of Sault went down on the local streams, and then by the Ariège River and the Haute Garonne, toward Toulouse and by the Aude River to Quillan and Narbonne. The wood of the Massif Central was thrown in the Loire River and followed the higher part of its course until Saint-Rambert, where large barges were built for transporting the timber. The barges were sold as firewood upon their arrival in Nantes. The Var, the Doubs River, and the rivers of the Vosges Mountains rendered the same service in their respective regions.

In the Ile-de-France, all the rivers of the basin of the Seine River participated in supplying Paris. The Ourcq, a subsidiary of the Marne River, transported the wood from the forest of Retz. On the Marne, from Saint-Dizier, came mostly navy and framework timbers; on the Yonne River, mostly firewood. In Saint-Dizier, boats, similar to those of the Loire, were built. Among the waterways that were navigable or "floatable," the Seine and its subsidiary, the Yonne, were the most important. The Yonne basin collects many streams from the Morvan Mountains, that form a navigable river from Clamecy on. As soon as the forests closest to the city had been exhausted or appropriated, Paris took the considerable quantities of wood that it needed mostly from the Morvan. This explains why Paris and the kings of France attached so much importance to that area, and would not allow nearby Burgundy to annex it.

A timber float is represented in a Breughel painting (fifteenth century) showing the construction of the tower of Babel. But it seems that in France it was only by the sixteenth century that the transportation of wood was revolutionized by perfecting the "float" method.

Of Words and Things: Forêts and Forer—Parcs and Parquets Haies and Laies—Baillis and Baliveaux

In a 1376 ordinance, in Rouen, concerning the management of the forest of Roumare that supplied the naval dockyards, Charles V forbade from then on, to "forer" in the forest—that is, to pillage, to degrade. This word comes from the Latin *fur*, "thief," which gave in French *furtif* (furtive, stealthy) and *furoncle* (furuncle, boil), which designated a little bud on the branches of the vine. *Fureter* (to rummage) which comes from *furet* (ferret), (low Latin *furritus*, other derivative of *fur*), meant to take wood, particularly timber, in a disorganized way, here and there. Nowadays, in the foresters' vocabulary, the *taillis "fureté"* is a coppice in which all the shoots are not cut at the same time, but only some of them so that pieces of different sizes can be found on the same stump.

By an ordinance of September 1376, Charles V prescribed that the cuttings of timber should be done by successively exploited forest ranges. The foresters today call these ranges *"parquets,"* which means parcels or little parks (the word means a fenced area); the term was used later to designate a combination of wooden boards of which the design is reminiscent of the aspect of a land divided into geometrically shaped lots. In England, the term "park" designated the fenced-in forest areas reserved for game—what in France was called *garennes*.

To indicate the limits of the *parquets*, marked trees were preserved: the *arbres de laie*. In addition, to facilitate the surveying, a narrow passage was left, the *layon*, a word now used to designate a forest path. When trees were cut successively in two neighboring *parquets*, the marker-trees remained and formed a *haye* or *haie* (hedge), a word that was derived from an old Germanic word, from which comes in German, *Hag* (hedge) and also *Hecke*, which has the same meaning and is perhaps related to *Ecke* (angle). In some cases, if two neighboring lots were cultivated instead of being returned to coppice, the hedge remained; in time, a woodland could thus be transformed into a *bocage*. However, many forest species do not do well when they are isolated and subjected to the wind; gradually, the hedges' trees were replaced by better-adapted species.

The vocabulary of the forest is rich in specific expressions but all forest agents are not purists and confusion occurs, such as between *haie* and *laie*.

The word *laye* (which, in the Latin of the Middle Ages in France was generally written *laia* or, sometimes, *leia*), meant the mark made on a tree to delimit a zone or to indicate a tree to be cut. An edict in Latin, of the Early Middle Ages (the second half of the seventh century), cited by Huffel, mentions an incision on the trees commonly called *lachus* (*"quae vulgo lachus appelatur"*). This word of Germanic origin gave in French, the word *laye* and in German, *Lache*, that still means a cut in a tree trunk. This word is related to the verb *lachen*, which means in German to laugh. It is interesting to note that this idea of an analogy between a split, a cut on a rounded object, and the mimic of laugh is found in vulgar expressions of colloquial French ("se fendre la gueule": literally, to split one's face) and in English ("to split one's sides laughing").

In the thirteenth century, the word *laie* was used to designate a forest divided into cutting areas by marker-trees. The verb *layer* was even used in the sense of exploiting, cutting wood (found in texts of the fourteenth and seventeenth centuries). The forest of Saint-German (en Laye) used to be called the forest of Laye. It seems that some confusion occurred in the spoken language between *laie* and *haie*, which are phonetically very close. A similar confusion occurred between *l'évier* (the sink, derived from *eau*-water) and laver (to wash: in Latin, *lavare*) and created in some regions the colloquial word *le lévier*.

The term *haie* acquired the general meaning of alignment of trees and bushes; and it has retained that meaning. But, in the Middle Ages, it also designated forests that were along a limit, or a border between two territories or two provinces. People have wondered if the word *baliveau* (which in the ordinances is also spelled: *baiviaulz bayveaulx, boiveau*, etc.) was derived from *bailli—balivus* in the Latin of that period—and is a parent of the words *bail* and *bailleur*, meaning a lease, a lessor. The *baliveaux* would thus be the most eminent trees, the ones that dominate the others, unless the term means "trees chosen and designated under the authority of the *bailli*. . . ." But nothing has been found to confirm this etymological hypothesis.

The *baliveaux*, which were also called *estallons* (*étalons*, stallions), had different names in different provinces to indicate if they had survived one, two or several cuttings. Foresters still distinguish them but the names have changed. What was called in the north of the Parisian basin, *père* or *pérot* is now called *moderne*; what was called *tayon* (grandfather) is now called *ancient*. In certain places, those reserved trees were called *mariens*. In a forest near Nancy, there is a place called "Marie Chanois"; people believe it to be the name of a girl but actually it is the ancient site of a "marien chesnois," that is, an oak seed-bearer. *Marien* is a form of the word *merrain*. This indicates that, in addition to their role of reproduction, the seed-bearers were intended to supply timber.

10 · USERS' RIGHTS, LEGISLATION, AND ADMINISTRATION ·

The Rights

h AVING ACCESS TO WOOD was considered such a vital necessity that, during the Early Middle Ages, a law of the Burgondes authorized the inhabitants of one estate to take firewood in the neighboring estate if there were no forests where they lived.

There was a distinction between the important rights (*gros usages*) and the small rights (*menus usages*). Both were exercised by the inhabitants of the agglomerations close to the woodlands by virtue of the "customs," oral laws transmitted by tradition. Investigations were sometimes undertaken to determine, with the help of reliable witnesses, the existence of a specific right, or the beneficiary of certain dues. The inevitable imprecision and the opposing interests gave rise to frequent difficult-to-resolve litigation; it is one of the reasons why, under the reign of Louis XII, many customs were finally written down, in order to bring some rigor and clarity to the customs and to determine the usage rights in a manner that would be less subject to discussions and conflicts.

Among the rights concerning the forests the most important were those linked to the supply of wood and those aimed at the pasturing of animals. Other rights might be regulated and might or might not be granted, depending on the cases; but all rights could be exercised only by the beneficiaries, who were not entitled to cede them. Their list is long and the denominations varied, of course, with the regions. We will use the terminology most usual in the northern half of today's France.

The main rights (*gros* or *grands usages*) were not legal everywhere; they were sometimes founded on conventions derived originally from verbal agreements or immemorial rights. However, more and more often, on the occasion of cessions or lawsuits, or sometimes more systematically, the verbal conventions were replaced by written acts. These, in turn, throughout the centuries became more precise, especially regarding the territorial application of each right. These rights included, first of all, those concerned with the feeding of animals.

The *faucillage*, the right to cut grass and carry it away, was sometimes also called *herbage*. The *champiage, champoyage* or *champéage*, the right to "bring big and small animals to graze in areas of common pastures,"[1] was sometimes limited more specifically to horses. The term *paisson* or *pacage* (grazing rights) was the most commonly used for all sorts of animals. That right was frequently limited or forbidden for certain animals, such as sheep and goats, as we saw in the chapter on breeding. The term *haras* (stud), the right to place horse herds in freedom in a predetermined part of the forest, referred to a form of pasturing right that was not restricted to the nobles; ecclesiasts and commoners sometimes exercised it too. It was the object of a special concession. Sometimes, horses belonging to different owners cohabited on the same territory.

The *glandée* or *faugne* (acorn or beechnut harvest) included the right to pick up the oak acorns or beechnuts that fell naturally. Different from the *glandée* or *faugne*, the right of *panage* or *pasnage* (pannage) did not allow one to pick up the fruits and carry them away, but only to let the pigs to graze on the site. It was also forbidden to cause fruits to fall from the trees.

There were also rights relative to wood under its different aspects. Among these, the *ramage* was the right to take branches and boughs for fences. The right to the *rémanents*, that is, the right to take away what is left after the cuttings (stumps, treetops, branches, etc.), was called in some regions (as in the Orléanais), the right to the *remoisons*. It authorized the beneficiary to take, and even cut, the secondary shoots remaining on a stump after the main stem (*raigeau*) had been cut. The right to live wood was rare, except for the *morbois*; its exercise was controlled by the forest officer. But the beneficiaries often had the right to the ". . . green wood felled or broken by storm or wind." The *caâbles*, called today *chablis*, that is, the trees knocked down by a storm, were subject to a special regulation; the landowners generally were the beneficiaries.

The timber that was used by the different trades could be felled only under the control of the forest officer. The right to "splitting wood" concerned the different species used to make barrel staves, props, laths, stakes, and roofing shingles. The right to "working wood" was reserved for the professionals (carpenters, trunk-makers, cabinetmakers, wheelwrights, wet coopers, clog-makers, etc.) in the coppice and the timber-tree forest. The right to "service wood" (*maronage, marenage* or *marnage*) was the right to cut the timber necessary for the repair (and sometimes the construction) of buildings; it was generally done under the control of an agent and was meant only for the households of the beneficiaries. Reselling the *merrain* was strictly forbidden. The *affouage* was the right to take firewood. The word could also designate the quantity of wood to which each user was entitled. Firewood was taken among the *morts-bois* or *morbis* (trees of the second category, giving neither fruits nor timber), and not to be confused with *bois morts* (dead wood).

The little or small rights included the gathering of dead wood for fuel (fallen wood and sometimes still on the tree) and the *ramas*, collecting of litter (leaves, needles, cones) for the cattle.

Until the twelfth-thirteenth centuries, all users were entitled to gather dead wood and cut the *morbois*. The *faucillage*, consisting of cutting grass for the animals' feed, was sometimes included among the small rights.

Special rights existed and were sometimes codified in certain provinces. There were, for example, the *effeuillage* (thinning out of leaves) and the *abranchage* (cutting away of branches) for the animals' fodder, practices described in the chapter on breeding. The harvesting of bee swarms was also submitted to special rules and was often reserved; it has already been mentioned as being among the miscellaneous food products of the forests.

Usage rights could be transferred only with the consent of the lord, who took advantage of every transfer—cession or inheritance —to levy a supplementary tax. But they could be exercised only by the inhabitants of the territory in which the forest was located. The transfer of usage rights always remained a way for the lords to obtain cash or to increase the value of the forests. Controversies occurred when they also tried to sell rights that the beneficiaries considered they already had—and had been exercising for a long time. In such cases, the king's arbitration could be requested.

Sometimes, too, the nobles or the king repurchased usage rights. The repurchases multiplied from the late twelfth century on. This repurchase, practiced by mutual agreement, gave birth to the practice of *cantonnement* (dividing into sections), by which the nobles, sometimes against the will of the other party, granted to the beneficiaries of the usage rights—in exchange for renouncing all these rights in one-third of the forest—the free use of the rest of it. This process will be examined in the next section.

Ownership of the Forests

In the feudal system, at all levels of society, below the supreme suzerain—the king—individuals only had a sort of usufruct of the land. This usufruct was revocable if they didn't fulfill all kinds of obligations towards their suzerain (or, in the case of the commoners, to their lord) but they could transmit it to their heirs if they had respected and attended to their obligations, and had not been dispossessed, banished or condemned. The nobles owed to their suzerain armed service (*"l'ost et la chevauchée"*). The symbol of the dependence of the commoners was the dues to the lords, whatever their form; they were sometimes linked to the man, but more often to the land, and could be in cash, in kind or in work; they indicated that the land was only granted to the commoner, that he did not own it.

It was thus, within the framework of the usage rights, that the majority of the population took advantage of all the forest products except in the *défens, haies* and *garennes* (and, in the early days, in what was called more specifically, the "forests"). The lords had to respect those usage rights; if necessary, the king was called upon to arbitrate any differences among the nobles and the users. Nonetheless, some communities or mere commoners had properties free of those dues that indicated the dependence on a lord; those were lands held in *franc alleu*. They could be small or large and resulted either from a grant or a sale at a price fixed by the lord, or from a very old tradition. Also, for centuries, collective properties had existed in certain regions, especially in mountain areas where, because of the climatic and geographical conditions, activities had to move from one altitude to another—according to the seasons—to make rational use of the land. However, even when the exploitation system was a collective one, the community, whose members cultivated the land or exploited the forest, only exceptionally possessed full ownership, as we understand it today.

On the plains, too, there were lands, fields or forests that belonged collectively to the free men of certain villages. For that matter, Huffel remarks that nowhere in the charts of the town of Cluny studied for over a century (tenth-eleventh century), is there any mention of sales or exchanges, as if the lands were incapable of being sold or transferred. Among these lands were woods qualified as *nemus francorum hominum* (*franc*, meaning free), and in the dependencies of Cluny, there were even lands belonging to a local Jewish community, mentioned in two cartularies, dated 1005, under the name of *"Terra Hebreorum."*[2]

The customs inherited from the Germanic people had, for a time, set up collective farming systems on the plains. Gradually, however, the ownership of the assigned lots became permanent as each tried to benefit from the fruit of his own labor and of the improvements that he could bring to the lots that he farmed. In the forest, where the system of itinerant farming was still practiced, there still was collective use of the lots, since everyone's lot moved every two or three years within the frame of the temporary clearing, which was a form of right of usage. But, in return, everyone received the use of a lot that had been reoccupied for twenty years or more by the woods, which was meant to refertilize the soil.

Without waiting for the modern economists to finally notice that the soil's fertility is not a free, permanent gift from nature, but "the result of a process of production and reproduction"[3] in which man's labor has a considerable role, the peasants of the Middle Ages attempted to stabilize the land they farmed. For their part, the owners of the land saw that it was to their advantage and resulted in increased productivity.

The frequent existence of perpetual rentals or uses of the forests and cultivated lands, in the framework of the feudal system, complicated the judicial situation. The passage, from the Roman system of ownership, directly to the feudal system of granting "holds" and, later, what can be seen as a progressive return to Roman law and private property, from the Early Middle Ages to the eighteenth century, created great confusion. In addition, all regions did not change at the same time and there were considerable differences in the evolution of habits, customs, statutes, and rules. The fact that certain provinces passed into other jurisdictions following wars, inheritances, family alliances, treaties, and exchanges further complicated the complex maze surrounding the ownership and use of the land.

But little by little, following a movement that started during the twelfth-thirteenth centuries and reappeared after the Hundred Years War, peasants and burghers became landowners. A certain number of woodlands came into their hands by different processes. One of the oldest, which didn't involve any payment in cash, was the contract, that could be called *"à mi-fruit,"* of *complant (ad medium plantum)*, applied in the east, in Burgundy, and in the Alps. A farmer cleared a piece of land and a few years later, after he had developed it, gave back half to the original owner and kept the difference either for his lifetime or, as became more and more often the case, forever. A few examples conforming to this outline are cited by Huffel; in 976, the bishop of Grenoble ceded a forest range to the peasants of the town; in 1003, the abbot of Cluny ceded a piece of land *ad medium plantum*. In both cases, it was after five years that the half had to be returned to the original owner.

As the quantity of circulating cash increased, and as the lords needed money—either to go to war or to join the Crusades or to make important profitable investments, in a common bake house or a mill, for example—other systems developed. Commoners could become owners by simple purchase. However, that required an important sum of money so it was, rather, the townsmen, the merchants, artisans or lawyers who became owners in that way, from the thirteenth century on. In the Orléanais, a great number of burghers had acquired before the Hundred Years War large areas of woods, sometimes reaching three hundred arpents. Among the owners was Jacques Coeur—a tradesman who became Charles VII's treasurer—who owned woods near Boiscommun.

The peasants generally didn't have the means to buy important pieces of land but they were often willing to pay annual rents to be master on their land and do as they pleased. For their part, many nobles wanted land that brought in more income. In this case, the system used was the *acensement*. A lot, sometimes quite small, was granted against perpetual payment of a *cens*, quitrent; that is, a rent payable in cash. Thus, the lord was guaranteed a fixed revenue and the peasant, who had stability on his land for himself and his heirs, was encouraged to increase his production in order to improve his standard of living. In addition, the lord levied taxes in case of transfer or inheritance. Forests were often included in lands subjected to quitrent because it was a way for the lord to spread out the cultivated area and thus increase his revenues. But sometimes peasants also maintained woodlands in order to have free access to a part of forest. Indeed, certain concessions specifically mentioned that they were meant to be used as pastureland or to supply fuel or timber.

Following a peculiar rule linked to the feudal system, once lands had become common by being subject to rent, they could not become noble again because nobles could not own any land that was subject to rent. Thus, until at least the sixteenth century, nobles could not own a piece of "common" land. As a result, a not-insignificant portion of land gradually passed into the hands of the commoners because, although the process was slow, it went only in one direction. The value of the rents paid by the common owners slowly depreciated due to inflation and because of currency devaluations—which had not been foreseen when the contracts were signed. Consequently, after a few centuries, these rents ended up representing a purely symbolic amount; the commoner was then a quasi-owner with extremely minimal rent charges.

Another process used for the transfer of ownership to the commoners was the transfer or sale to a community. Once the *villeneuves* started to develop, they frequently became owners of forests. When the *villeneuves* were founded in the twelfth and thirteenth centuries, they received forests to attract colonists. These donations were made not only for the purpose of clearing the land, but also so that the inhabitants would have the woodlands that were indispensable for any rural community to provide for its needs.

The "law of Beaumont," which was granted to more than five hundred towns, provided for the free use of woodlands for the beneficiary towns; the limits of those forests were specified in the charters. This free use of the woods (*liber usus nemoris*) amounted to full ownership. However, in most cases, the nobles remained users of the forest and could take wood for the common bake house, the maintenance of ponds, drives, locks, bridges, mills, and buildings that belonged to them; they could also pasture their animals without paying any rent. But the right of organizing the police and dispensing justice in the woods was exercised by the town.

The community's rights were more restricted in the towns under the "law of Lorris" (over three hundred in the east and south of the Parisian basin). Under this regime, the townspeople had the benefit only of the usage rights. In a few cases, the ownership of the forests was acquired by the towns by prescription; in this way, the *bailli* (magistrate) of Dijon recognized, for the town of Auxonne, the ownership of the woods of Crochères, of which until then it had had only the use. In 1362 King Jean le Bon acknowledged the privilege by qualifying these woods as "communal woods." This was noticed because this term had apparently never been used before in an official act.

Generally, the towns, burgs, and villages had only the perpetual usufruct (use) of the forests and not the freehold; the kings and lords recalled it several times, as a matter of principle, after the Middle Ages and especially during the seventeenth century, at the time of the forest reforms. The rights acquired by the communities during this period have left their mark to our day. Recently, citizens invoked some Middle Ages texts to request from the commune their portion of firewood, a rule that had fallen into disuse, but to which the increased price of fuel again gives an economic interest.

There was still another way for commoners to acquire forests or any other kind of land: the practice of *cantonnement* (dividing into sections). Basing themselves on the fact that one-third of the production of the land was for the lords, the latter, to get rid of the constraints of the usage rights that encumbered their forests, tried to reduce those rights by granting a corresponding part of the forest in freehold (or at least free tenure) to the village community; the access to the rest of the forest was then forbidden, and the traditional rights could no longer be exercised. It is evident that the villagers were swindled by this arrangement—which completely undermined the foundations of the economic system of the period—suppressing, among other things, many pasturelands, a condition particularly damaging to the poorest farmers. The mere fact that the lord ceded his rights on the part of the forest given to the community did not compensate in any way for the loss of the countless usage rights that the peasants had exercised on the whole until then. This evolution corresponded to the frequent tendency of appropriation and specialization of the lands, which was premature considering the period's technical means and social organization. So, the economic situation of the peasants did not improve; it led to increasing difficulties for them in the seventeenth and eighteenth centuries, right up to the Revolution. Later, when the pressure on the forests diminished during the middle of the nineteenth century, as mineral coal superseded wood, the earlier practice of dividing the forest resulted in giving a certain number of rural communities the ownership of forests that, today, constitute a rather important proportion of the forests in France and represent, sometimes, an appreciable resource for certain *"communes."*

The forests belonging to the Church presented special cases. The Church did not have the right to sell its properties; it could only grant their use; numerous reminders of this prohibition (against the sale of property) were made by the popes and the councils.

Throughout the centuries, the monasteries as well as the churches of the big cities had received by donation or legacy, or had acquired, a great number of forests. In the eleventh century, there were about 1,100 monasteries in France; at the end of the thirteenth century, there more than twice that number. Very few were founded later. For example, between 900 and 1300, there were over 5,300 charters of donation just to the monastery of Cluny, 3,100 of which were between 948 and 1109. As for the "white" Benedictines—the Cistercians—whose order was founded in 1098, the main abbey of Cîteaux owned, at the end of the fifteenth century, over 8,000 arpents of forests in the dioceses of Châlon, Autun, and Besançon (that is over 4,000 hectares, if we are talking of a forest arpent that represented a little more than half a hectare).

Bequeathing lands to the Church was almost a duty for any well-to-do person, and even peasants bequeathed to it, at their death, a few *"journaux"* [T.N.: the measure of land that could be plowed in one day]. The period of the Crusades, especially at the beginning, led to a great many transfers of land. This period corresponds to the two centuries during which many monasteries were created. In the donations many woods were included.

But the vast domain of the Church was a tempting prey; there were numerous spoliations, confiscations, fiscal measures, and *pariages* (by which the protection of the king or a lord was given to the Church, in exchange for joint ownership of the forests). Sometimes the Church was the victim of retaliatory measures. Thus, after Richard Coeur de Lion looted the abbey of Saint-Martin-de-Tours, Philippe Auguste seized the ecclesiastical assets in part of the French estates of the king of England.

Nonetheless, according to Huffel, at the end of the fifteenth century the Church owned more than half of the kingdom's forests.[4] But they were not always well maintained, and when they temporarily came under the management of a king who was the beneficiary of the revenues during the vacancies of the episcopal seats by virtue of the *droit de régale*, the forests were often subjected to abusive cuts.

Forest Legislation

There are numerous and excellent studies on the different periods of forest legislation. Originally, it was merged with the prescriptions relative to the management of the royal domain. Slowly, with the increase of the possessions of the king of France in different provinces, it acquired a general value and tended to be applied even to private forests. This involved a propensity on the part of the representatives of the central power to exercise a right of inspection and control on the forest estates of the whole country justified by the economic and even strategic importance of the forests and of the wood; it was officially confirmed in the sixteenth century by the edicts of François I and Charles IX.

The role of the foresters (*forestiers*) is closely linked to the successive provisions made by the kings to define their attributions and organize their hierarchy and functioning; that is, to the legislation. This legislation was initiated in the form of capitularies, then ordinances concerning certain woodlands, then, later, as texts relative to the "fact" of forests in general—first, the combined forests of the king, then all the forests. The appearance in these texts of the foresters (*forestarii*), especially those in charge of that part of the royal estates, goes back to the Carolingians; the latter were trying to regulate the usage rights of the woods, to prevent the abuses that provoked damage, and to prevent uncontrolled clearings; by creating "forests" (*forestae*), which were reserves, they tried to limit to certain parts of the wooded areas those usage rights that were indispensable to the population.

In a capitulary dated 818, Louis le Débonnaire forbade the lords to create new "forests"; it was a privilege that the king was trying to keep for himself, and the creation of these reserves was done to the detriment of the users. Later, what corresponded to the initial denomination of "forest" was generally called *garenne* (guarded area) and the word "forest" took on, at least in France, a wider meaning. These *garennes* (warrens) were forbidden of access to all users, and reserved for hunting.

The king and the dukes were not the only ones who had foresters; the other forest owners, including the collective owners, generally had "guards" who were in charge of the police in the woods and also the supervision of their exploitation.

The role and the importance of the foresters varied according to the period; this variation is reflected in the forest legislation through which we retrace the ups and downs of this institution, which, of course, was always thwarted by all those in whose interest it was not to have a good forest police, from the small poachers, to the parliaments and the highest lords.

During the period when the royal power was weak within the feudal system, between the ninth and the twelfth century, foresters were no longer mentioned. All-purpose civil servants, such as the provosts, the mayors, then the *baillis* took care of the forests, among their other functions of management and supervision of the royal estates. The fact that these agents were not particularly competent in forest matters, which require special knowledge, might be linked, if not to the reduction of the wooded areas—unavoidable under the pressure of the population increase and its needs for cultivated areas—at least to the deterioration and impoverishment of the woods that remained, because of their anarchistic methods and loose management. This must have convinced the king to reinstate, in the thirteenth century, the functions of the foresters, and to give them precedence over other civil servants in their area of competence.

Of course, the various agents in charge of the administration of the royal domain contested the prerogatives of the agents who were especially in charge of the forests when, in the thirteenth century, these *forestarii* reappeared or, at least, were once again mentioned in the texts, receiving missions that placed them in the foreground. Simultaneously, regulations were undertaken by the kings to oppose the deterioration of the forests and its consequences, among which was the shortage of timber.

By an ordinance of 1219, taken at Gisors, and relative to the forest of Villers-Cotterêts—or the forest of Retz—Philippe Auguste entrusted to the foresters all matters concerning wood and the sale of its production. The bitter struggle that he had led against Richard Coeur de Lion, had ended with the conquest of Normandy, following which the king of France appropriated a large number of forests belonging to English partisans. The knowledge which Philippe Auguste acquired, in all areas, about his adversary, about his available means, and his organization, indicated to him the importance given to the forests by the king of England, and the development of forest legislation in Normandy—mostly for the benefit of the king.

The conquest of Normandy marked a turning point in the forest policies of France, as shown by the title of the *"Charte aux Normands,"* promulgated a century later by Louis X to specify and codify earlier uses, and which was often referred to for several centuries afterward. For a century and a half after the conquest of Normandy, the Capétiens, then the Valois, attended seriously to the forest; they manifested their interest by a series of ordinances—all of which were not followed by effective results—and also by investigations and penalties taken against numerous guilty agents.

As early as 1223, Louis VIII issued in Montargis a new ordinance —concerning the forest of Retz—that forbade ordinary judges to deal in the courts with matters involving the forests; all affairs concerning the latter were to be treated by the *forestarii*. In 1280, Philippe III le Hardi specified that the supplies, which the beneficiaries could pretend to obtain in the king's forests, had to be delivered by the intervention and under the control of the foresters. In 1283, an act mentions the *justiciarii forestarum*, judges specialized in the cases concerning forests, and the functions of *baillis*. The famous *"Charte aux Normands"* was enacted in March 1314 and in July 1315 by Louis X; among other things, it established the basis of the tax deducted by the king on the cuttings made in private woods; it is the *tiers et danger* of Norman origin, the name of which signifies on one hand, for the benefit of the king, a deduction of one-third (*tiers*) of the sale price; and on the other hand, a complementary right, the right of the lord (*dominus*), the *domigerium*, a term translated by the French word *danger*. This right included several taxes for the wax, paper, etc., that could be compared to what today we call the stamp duty or the deed fees. In total, the deductions came to about half of the sale price.

In 1317 and 1318, Louis X took measures relative to the officers of the *Eaux et Forêts*. In February 1319, and again in February 1346—probably because the first ordinance had not been effective —identical ordinances were imposed and, twice again, almost without changes, in 1355 and 1357. Some prescriptions concerning specific forests were assembled in little codes. One of these ordinances, the one called "of Brunoy," taken by Philippe VI de Valois on May 29, 1346, is of special importance because it followed a long investigation, what was called a "reform" (*réformation*), undertaken in 1341 by two *chargés de mission*: Guillaume de Fontaine and Regnault de Givry. The first was a jurist, counselor of the king; the second, a technician belonging to the corps of the *Eaux et Forêts*. The ordinance of Brunoy included rules that continued to be reused until 1789. The doctrine of the conservation of the forest estates is clearly established. The agents of the *Eaux et Forêts* are, in particular, in charge of visiting all the wooded areas, of investigating and having them exploited with the purpose that "the said forests may remain perpetually in good condition."

This preoccupation with conservation appeared during the same period in England; an inventory document of 1356 mentions a "certain wood called Hayley wood, estimated to be 80 acres, in which one can sell each year without creating any degradation nor destruction 11 acres of coppice worth 55 shillings at 5 shilling the acre."[5]

But at a time when the dissemination of information was very sparse and when feudalism broke up the territory and diluted political responsibilities, the simple users who gathered their firewood or timber were not in a good position to realize that the forests were in a state of general impoverishment.

The kings of France might have realized the importance of the forests for the country as a whole, and might have been trying to prevent all the forests and not just part of the royal domain from being poorly managed or overexploited for a purpose of immediate interest, which caused the users to put more pressure on the royal forests. The royal officers, who either wanted to defend the general interest, or quite often saw their own interest when intruding upon the management of private forests, had thus a tendency to meddle with everything having to do with the forests—and, whoever the owners were—a tendency about which the landowners and the beneficiaries complained.

For a long time, the authority of the king over the territory as a whole and his right to legislate on matters of forests outside his own domains, were contested; all the attempts to impose a policy of general protection, from the thirteenth century to the sixteenth century, ran into constant opposition from those who owned forests or who benefited from the existing laxity. In particular, the creation of a specialized administration in charge of the forest was unceasingly countered by the nobles, the ecclesiastical owners, the Parliament and—starting with the reign of Philippe VI in the fourteenth century—by the States General. Every time the king convoked the States General to ask them to vote subsidies so that he could levy taxes, this assembly tried to intervene and attempted to control the use of the funds and the royal policy, in particular, the policy concerning the forests. Thus, in 1355, King Jean le Bon, in a hurry to obtain the agreement of the States General to levy taxes to support the war against the English, had to prescribe to the foresters not to deal with the forests that were not part of the royal estates.

In the ordinance of Brunoy in 1346, the king specifically stated that no new forest rights would be granted. This ordinance was fully developed thirty years later (meanwhile, the first defeats of the Hundred Years War and the "Black Death" had suspended application of all the measures taken by Philippe VI). Charles V, by his ordinance of 1376 taken in Melun, set the foundations of a real forest code. In its preamble, he recalled the malversations to which for centuries the forests had been subjected: "In the past, we have been, by the fault or negligence of the masters and investigators of the *Eaux et Forêts*, or otherwise, deprived of our right, to the great reduction and destruction of our domain."[6] The fifty-two articles of this ordinance were repeated and completed by the later ordinances that, in 1389 and 1402, reproduced with few changes the one of 1376. The articles by then reached a total of seventy-five.

Then, for nearly a century, no new important provisions were made. This interruption in the legislative and regulatory activity of the kings of France can be explained by converging motives. First, and this appears to be the main reason, as the war and the Black Death had depopulated the country, the forests had recovered and the risk of wood shortage had disappeared.

A certain lack of interest in the forests on the part of the kings of France can also be explained—in addition to the fact that they were preoccupied with other problems—by the fact that during the first half of the fifteenth century, the three richest provinces in forests of their domain, Ile-de-France, Normandy, and Champagne, were ruled by the king of England. Furthermore, since the establishment of permanent taxes, the revenues from the domain—and, in particular, those of the forest—no longer represented an essential resource for the royal treasure, all the more since the king had granted the benefit of many forests to high lords.[7]

Last but not least, the fifteenth century kings had little interest in hunting so, contrary to several of their successors, they seldom saw the state of the forest and thus didn't worry about it.

During this period of legislative void with regard to the forests, one must nonetheless mention—although it was never applied— an ordinance taken in 1413 during the bloody Parisian uprising led by the butcher, Caboche. This ordinance includes no less than 258 articles, a certain number of which are concerned with the reform of the *Eaux et Forêts*. Indeed, it bears witness to the very great interest expressed by the townspeople about the problems of exploitation and use of the forests, on which depended in great part the urban economy, a by-product of wood in its different and numerous forms.

At the end of the Middle Ages, which roughly coincides with the end of the fifteenth century, when the population started to increase again, there was no shortage of land for whomever wanted to clear it without having to touch the forests, because there were abandoned estates everywhere. The pleasant memories left by Louis XII, "the father of the people," should be related to this period of relative relaxation in the countryside, with this "certain balance between the needs in wood of the population and the surface of the forests," that Devèze mentions about this king's reign. This balance did not last; by the end of the fifteenth century, the price of wood and the value of a hectare of forest land had clearly gone up.[8]

In the early sixteenth century, the same causes as five centuries earlier—increasing population and relative peace in the country-side—produced the same effects: the pressure was once more exerted on the forests. As the negligence and the abuse of trust of the forest administration augumented, the forests were in a very bad state, which led François I to take a series of measures to eliminate the abuses, reorganize the forest administration, and complete these measures by applying severe penalties.

In 1515, perfecting the work started three centuries earlier by Philippe Auguste, and announcing the measures that would be taken under Louis XIV by Colbert, François I promulgated an ordinance with ninety-two articles, that also included special provisions about hunting—unlike those who had reigned in the fourteenth and fif-teenth centuries, François I was an avid hunter. Because of the religious wars and the ensuing devastation that took place no attempt to apply and develop these measures was undertaken before the end of the century.

In 1583, Henri III attempted to renew the prohibitions against cutting timber trees, forbidding users even to fell seed-bearers, which grew in the coppice and were assimilated to timber trees. This regulation gave rise to the opposition of the private owners, especially of the Church and the religious orders who were the biggest forest owners. In 1589, a Dominican, Jacques Clément, assassinated Henri III and the reform was never put into effect.

His successor, Henri IV, wanted to complete the work of his predecessors. The elaboration of the regulations of 1597 was en-trusted to the most knowledgeable foresters of the time and not—as had been done until then—to jurists. This remarkable document was the first complete project of rational organization for the ex-ploitation of the French forests, providing parceling plans and mis-cellaneous measures to prevent abuse and fraud. It encountered strong opposition and, in particular, once again, from the ecclesiastical owners. Opposing interest groups delayed its application. It was only in January 1610 that the ordinance was registered at the headquarters of the *Eaux et Forêts*, but these delays then prevented it from being registered by the Parliament. As a consequence of the king's murder, the project remained a dead letter (cf. Appendix 1, Chronological and Synoptical Table).

The Administration of the Eaux et Forêts

It is difficult to devote a book to the forest, without mentioning several times the administration of the forests, which became the administration of the *Eaux et Forêts*. Entire books have retraced the history of this organization; our only purpose is to retrace its creation, phases, and development within the context of the Middle Ages, and in its relation to other factors. The kings of France appear to have realized early on the value of certain special agents for the administration of the royal forests. In the beginning, the forests were a very important source of revenue in the royal budget and, later, the site of a material too necessary for the army and navy to be neglected; so, the kings realized the necessity of protecting the forests and managing them on a rational basis.

The mission, function, and role of the foresters, whatever their level or title, included the police and the administration of the woodlands in the largest sense, including the choice of the trees to cut and of those which the users could take, the marking of the different categories of trees, the establishment of drives, the organization of the cuttings, and the sale of wood.

The forest administration—which had had a "forest prefect" under Charlemagne—was organized in a hierarchy that went from people who were among the highest officials in the kingdom to modest sergeants in charge of the relations on site with the countless guests of the forests, and the exploitation areas.

The 1291 ordinance of Philippe le Bel mentions for the first time the existence of great masters (*grand maîtres*) of the *Eaux et Forêts*. At the head of the royal administration of the *Eaux et Forêts* were those great masters who controlled districts of quite different sizes. At the beginning of the fifteenth century, there were seven great masters. Later, this number increased, and they were called "special masters" (*maîtres particuliers*) during the fifteenth century, to distin-

guish them from the sovereign master and general reformer of the
Eaux et Forêts (*souverain maître et général réformateur des Eaux et Forêts*),
who was entrusted by the king, toward the end of the fourteenth
century, with the supervision of the forests in the whole kingdom.
Early in the sixteenth century, when François I acceded to the
throne, there were about twenty special masters with districts of
different sizes and designated in some cases by local titles, such as:
sénéchal des Eaux et Forêts (Anjou), *bailli des forêts* (Marne), *grand-
gruyer* (Bourges), *garde général* (Dauphiné), *grands maîtres* (Orléans,
Valois), etc.

These positions were generally filled by nobles and, occasionally,
by burghers. They were nominated (or confirmed when the king
changed) by the king, and their nomination agreed to and registered
by the *Chambre des Comptes*. These high-ranking officials were well
paid—1200 livres tournois per year for the sovereign master and
400 for the special masters. The latter benefited from numerous
advantages in kind (wood, etc.) and deducted certain taxes on the
sale of wood. Below the special masters were the essential pillars of
this administration, the masters who were assigned to a particular
forest—what was called a "guard" in the duchy of Orléans, on which
Maulde has gathered considerable information.

To take the example of this province, from the twelfth century
on, there were, depending on the periods, seven or eight positions
at this level—many as "guards." These masters had to reside on
site and could go away only occasionally. So, these positions were
generally filled by members of local noble families or sometimes by
burghers. Some lived in their own castle, others in a castle rented
and equipped by the administration. Called captains of the forest
in certain regions, these masters went on horseback with an armed
escort. Their salaries were considerable for the period: two sous per
day (a little less for smaller forests) plus reimbursement of expenses
for uniforms (*droit de robe*), and several benefits. The positions must
have been lucrative as on several occasions the duke of Orléans
borrowed money from his forest masters. Given the important sums
of money they dealt with, they had to deposit a security of five
hundred livres upon taking office.

In a certain number of provinces, instead of forest masters, there
were *gruyers* (or *verdiers*, depending on the regions) who performed
about the same duties. Quite a few *gruyers* were enfeoffed (*fieffés*),
that is hereditary, owners of part of the revenues that they received,

the difference being for the king. These *gruyers* collected all the fines and the fees for dispensing justice. They sometimes were entitled to dues paid, in proportion to the number of households, by each village using the forest. They benefited from larger hunting and wood-usage rights than the guard masters; but they had to support the personnel that assisted them. The nonhereditary *gruyers*, who were nominated and received a fixed salary, the guard masters, and the enfeoffed *gruyers* were all subordinated to the great masters or special masters.

The foresters exercised justice on cases related to the forest. Judgments could be appealed at the next level of the hierarchy. The sergeants delivered the summonses. The guard masters applied fines up to a certain amount, which in the fifteenth century did not exceed thirty sous parisis. The *gruyers* could impose fines of up to sixty ous, which the great master then judged if it was appealed. The supreme authority was exercised by the Parliament, which had a special chamber, the "Marble Table."

The foresters, at the different levels, had to prepare detailed accounts, generally twice a year. Depending on the regions, these accounts were sent to the ducal or royal *Chambre des Comptes*. The officials of the *chambre* compared the accounts of the different levels of the hierarchy, which included not only the receipts and expenditure for the forests, but also the dues paid, either on a regular basis by the paying users or, for the executed or future operations, by the artisans who used the forest. The foresters could be condemned if they didn't present their accounts or were late in doing so. They could also be condemned for any shortcomings in their service or any breach of the rules that they had to follow or were in charge of applying. These accounts are historical documents of great interest through which one can reconstitute life at the local level.

On the local level, the guard masters were often assisted by a lieutenant (sometimes it might be their son), who normally succeeded them. Auxiliaries helped them: a measurer, that is a land surveyor; a sworn clerk who worked for several guards; finally, and most important, the mounted sergeants (generally one per forest or per guard), the sergeants on foot and the sergeants *"traversiers."* The sergeants wore military uniforms; in some provinces they were called guards.

The *garennes* were supervised and maintained by specialized *garenniers*. Among other functions, they had to make sure that the *garenne* remained stocked with game; they placed barriers and thorns to protect the rabbit holes against the roving dogs and birds of prey. In the thirteenth century, they received a salary of one sou (twelve deniers) per day. In 1423, this salary (identical to that of a mounted sergeant but who also had indemnities) appeared insufficient; in Chateauneuf-sur-Loire, the council decided to pay an additional indemnity to the *garennier*.

In the thirteenth century, the mounted sergeants were paid twelve deniers per day; the sergeants on foot received seven. In addition, they had indemnities, such as for the *robe*—that is, the uniform— and for the horse. Their salaries remained about the same in the fifteenth century. In addition, they could benefit legally from miscellaneous small profits and material advantages—and benefit illegally in many other ways. They had, such as today's customs agents, profits on the catch they made; for example, a cart and its harness (the horses were reserved for the king) or the metal tools belonging to the offenders. But they had to list these articles and income in their reports so that the *gruyers* or guard masters could finally decide what they could keep for themselves, depending on the circumstances.

They could leave the forest only on holidays (the forest was "closed" on those days as well as during the night, and the users were not permitted to be there). They could not trade "wood or any other material," nor could they own "a tavern or an inn." They had to live in the territory of the forest and perform their duties themselves. However, some, especially the enfeoffed sergeants who were noble and liable for damage, had themselves replaced by undersergeant clerks or sergeant lieutenants. As a rule, they were not entitled to any usage rights except what was granted to them by the masters or the *gruyers*.

As they were sworn in, the sergeants' word was taken—without the need for witnesses—for events related to the exercise of their duties. This was specified in the ordinance of 1316 and confirmed in 1402 and 1516, explicating the reason: the procedure required efficiency, as a sergeant seldom had the possibility to get witnesses to verify that an offense had been committed. In the early sixteenth century, their word was taken only, according to the ordinances, within the limits of an offense entailing a fine of sixty sols. The

protections that surrounded the consecrated grounds in the thirteenth and fourteenth centuries and made them shelters for criminals, in the Middle Ages, were lifted by the foresters early in the
sixteenth century.

We know from the inventories of seizures conducted in the homes
of the offenders that some foresters raised animals, which was forbidden. The sergeants weren't poor; the inventory of the furniture
belonging to one of them, demoted for having raised animals, included among other things: six large barrels full of wine, and twelve
kegs (also full), two empty barrels and three big vats, ten beds "well
supplied," five hens, four pigs, etc.—and even a bathtub. Even
nobles, generally squires (that is the youngest of a family without
means) occupied sergeants' posts. In each guard, there was a mounted
sergeant and a variable number of sergeants on foot. The sergeants
traversiers were the men in charge of the summonses. They were paid
on a pro rata basis; in the thirteenth century, they received, during
the day, one-fifth of the fine, and, at night, one-third. They were
also entitled to punish fishing offenses.

All the positions in the *Eaux et Forêts* were in great demand at
all levels; recommendations, "string pulling" and, at the lower
levels, humanitarian considerations sometimes intervened. Favorites
of the queen or of the *bailli*, sons of fathers killed in service to the
king, and veterans were ranked as sergeants. All tried to have their
position transferred (many of which became hereditary) to their sons,
to become enfoeffed. But the forest masters complained that the
system of enfeoffed sergeants often led to the admission of incapable
men to perform these duties, which required real competence. It
might be one of the reasons why the French word, *fieffé*, has retained
its pejorative meaning. Thus, in 1287, following a complaint, the
great master Jean le Bouteiller was granted the right to hire another
suitable sergeant to replace the enfeoffed sergeant, who was transferred (*amotus*).

Enfeoffed or not, some foresters misused their postitions; when they
had an interest in the fines, they imposed heavy ones and sometimes
even managed to put "good people" at fault.[9] Certain official reports,
following complaints concerning the conduct of those agents, ir-
resistibly recall the popular tales (*fabliaux*) of that period and the
truculent inspiration of a Rabelais.

Maulde reports the case of Ragobert, a sergeant in the forest of Orléans during the thirteenth century, who was, in the words of the witnesses, especially "treacherous." He was accused of cutting oaks himself, then coming upon and fining the people who were taking—as they were entitled to—the *"remoisons"* (that is, the secondary branches of the cut tree). In another case, he led valets to believe that they could gather wood, then seized their animals and held them until they had paid a heavy fine. Sometimes he would get a fisherman to treat him to a good meal and then led him to understand that he could go to the forest with his cart to gather wood; there, hidden, he would throw himself on the fisherman and punish him. But the local people (including a few leading citizens: a provost, a *"concierge"* and a priest) finally decided to complain and have him punished. His punishment was not described.

In the same region, people complained of the system used by other foresters. After accepting a good dinner, they would notice a cut log in the fire (proof that the host had gone a little beyond his rights when he gathered his firewood) and immediately would arrest the overhospitable offender. Other sergeants were accused of taking wood—to which they were not entitled—and even cows belonging to the users. Others got paid to close their eyes to an offense. Such examples exist through all the centuries.

A sergeant, Drouan de Mareau, condemned in 1278, was in the habit of permitting many people with no rights to use the forest; he received breeches, shoes, and money as gifts. After he refused to repair the damage he had done, he was imprisoned and his furniture was seized.[10] In 1428, a sergeant of Vitry, who had sold an oak tree, was fined 32 sous parisis. In 1452, a sergeant of the duke of Orléans, who had seized some cattle and summoned their owners —while the administration was not informed and didn't receive any of it—was fined forty sous.

Even the guard masters, cornerstones of all the forest administration, did not always set a worthy example for their subordinates. They accepted money or presents in exchange for the remission of a penalty; or were indulgent with their friends, whose offenses they tolerated. They took advantage of their positions to grant, too frequently, "deliveries" of usage rights, made secret deals for their own benefit, took firewood for themselves or offered it to their parents or to the authorities whom they wanted to win over.[11]

The judiciary chronicle of the time includes a few particularly abusive cases which lead one to believe that, in the timber shortage of the time, dishonest foresters sometimes had a share of responsibility.

The forester of Chaumontois received three pigs as a gift from merchants who bought acorns. He bought a barrel "of the best wine of Chécy," from the prior of Saint-Ladre but refused to pay for it under the pretext that the latter owed him more fines than the value of the barrel of wine. In the twelfth century, Robert de Hupecourt, forest master of the guard of Vitry, offered to his surgeon barber who lived at the Croix-Saint-Michel in Orléans several oaks "because the said barber shaved and bled Robert when he went to Orléans". . . He accepted a white sheet from the abbot of Saint-Yveltre-d'Orléans and shut his eyes to the abbot's abuses of his usage rights. He received forty francs from the people of Rebrechien and Bourgneuf for authorizing them to pasture their animals. He used the twenty sous of a fine to buy a saddle for his horse. One day he saw two monks, one from Saint-Ladre-d'Orléans and the other from Aumosne; he invited them for a drink then left them, asking them to pay the bill, seven sous of wine and food.

All the abbots and priors of the area complained about the bad manners and lack of deference of Robert de Hupecourt, all the more since he was a "foreigner" and was accused of neglecting his duties by too frequently staying in his natal Normandy. They accused him of staying too often at their place . . . sometimes for a long time (as in the old days when the kings of France used their right of *gîte* with their vassals). Once, said a witness, he stayed with three horses, four boys, three dogs and a few birds, and spent on that occasion a lot "in drinks and food."

A forester of the same region, Bertaut de Villers, received a "queue" of wine on which, said a witness, he still owed money. . . . He bought a twenty-two sous barrel of wine with the fines paid, but also included this expense in his accounts. He received a barrel of wine in exchange for exempting an offender of a twenty sous fine. Another time, he received from the bishop of Orléans a saddle to release him from another twenty sous fine. Each time, said the witnesses, that he prepared a cart of charcoal for the bishop, he also prepared one for himself and sold it. Another time, he took six cartloads of palisade wood in the king's forest to fence his own house. . . . Bertaut was also famous as a poacher. Accused of having killed a deer, he pretended having done it for pity as the animal had been driven crazy by one of his dogs. He admitted that he set snares, a venial offense. To win over the bishop, he sent him a wild boar and a pig, saying that they were presents from the king. . . . At the end of the investigation in 1278, Bertaud, faced with the abundance of witnesses, finally confessed and was condemned to several hefty fines. But the judges maintained him in his duties.

Some forest sergeants committed acts of violence: the sergeant Moreau stole clothes and shoes from poor people to dress his family and his servant. The sergeant Taupin hit two poor men so hard that they had to go to the hospital of Aumosne, where the witness found them in such bad state that he "thought it would be better for them to die than to recover." Another time, meeting a poor man carrying his firewood, Taupin threw him to the ground, beat him and cut his finger. . . . In 1398, a sergeant was demoted and condemned to a fine of 100 sous parisis for violence.

It is not astonishing that from time to time a sergeant was man-handled. In 1424, a man who had hit a sergeant and thrown him in the Loire, was condemned to ten francs parisis, but this penalty was reduced to four livres "on account of his poverty and *aussi que les gens d'armes estoient sur le pais*," and because he did not know the forester, and might have taken him for a soldier on the loot. In 1433, a poor fisherman was condemned to twenty sous for hitting a sergeant on the head with a pickaxe: the fine was relatively low because of his time in preventive prison.

Nonetheless, it seems that violence became more rare in the fifteenth and sixteenth centuries, while thefts were frequent. War was often invoked as an excuse for the offenses of the sergeants themselves. In 1444, Jean Coichon, sergeant of the Chaumontois, was condemned for having used three oaks to make barrels. But the duke granted amnesty because of his poverty and because, in the exercise of his duties, he had been imprisoned three times by the English and the Bourgignons, beaten and mutilated . . . .

For the honor of the profession one must say that many foresters were not for sale. Renaud, forester of the Chaumontois, sent back to those who tried to gain his favor "the pig in its rope, the wheat in its cart and the fish and the capons that were sent him and did not want to take them." Later, a certain Plume, guard of the Chaumontois, informed his superiors about a merchant who, despite his refusal to accept anything, had left on his table seventy-eight ecus "for his New Year."

There are many examples of offenses, either by users or by sergeants, in matters of pasturing. We will cite some of the most significant. In 1451, more than 400 pigs belonging to a jeweler in Orléans were caught committing an offense in the forest. In 1453, two merchants from Orléans pastured 180 heads of cattle on the burnt-baited lands of the forest: they bought the silence of the guard Baudichon de Beaurain for two ecus. But the story got out and the guard was fined a total of two hundred sous, the merchants sixty-six.

Thefts of wood were also frequent, but punished in very different ways. The circumstances were taken into account: for example, the offender had been for a long time a prisoner of the English, he had lost his house, he was needy. The fines mostly took into account the value of the timbers cut or stolen: a load of dead wood taken in a forbidden area: five sous; an oak already fallen, taken away: twenty-four sous; elsewhere, a dead oak: sixty sous; an *alizier*: sixty sous. . . . Each offense was added; for example, the fact of having gone through a forbidden coppice with the cart led to a increase of five to fifteen sous for the penalty. Using a saw was an aggravating circumstance. The theft of acorns was severely punished: for simply beating a tree to have the acorns, a user in 1451 was fined five sous. Admittedly, acorns were expensive: in 1420, a barrel full of acorns was confiscated and sold for thirty-two sous—the equivalent of over 160 gold francs at the beginning of the twentieth century.

When the sergeants were not accused of breach of trust, they were taken to task for applying overly heavy fines, which was in their interest since the sergeants *traversiers* who made the summonses were paid a percentage. Appeals were sometimes made against penalties applied or condemnations pronounced by the foresters. Many reports are about legal actions taken by the foresters against religious establishments or ecclesiasts who, according to them, had gone beyond their rights or were not the beneficiaries of certain rights that they claimed to have. Those controversies gave rise to searches to find some old ordinance or some very ancient privilege, more-or-less authentic, according to which the order of *nolle prosequi* was pronounced in favor of the accused. But the commoners, who did not have the means to find archives or old scrawls to present for their defense, complained about the arbitrary treatment and bias of the foresters.

Sometimes the foresters complained of being powerless to face certain protected users. Thus, the priest of Combreux and of Courcy were both accused in the thirteenth century of having taken and even sold wooden shingles (*escaume*), slates (*late*) and timber (*merrain*). Also in 1339, the friars of Sainte-Euverte, who were accused of misuse and abuse of their usage rights, showed an ordinance of Philippe le Bel to lay the blame on the forester.

Many archives disappeared during the wars; witnesses had to be called to determine who was entitled or not entitled to specific rights; this entailed frequent contestations, as the forester always started by denying any usage right for which proof could not produced.

On the whole, many foresters (sworn in and therefore more severely punished in case of fault) did their work properly. Their severity was justified by the number of offenses committed and, sometimes, by their importance. And, of course, the misdeeds of the abusive or thieving foresters are known by the proceedings instituted against them, even if they did not all get caught; the mass of those who did their job honestly without giving rise to litigation has left no traces. The tree should not hide the forest.

Periodically, the central administration requested information on the functioning of all levels of the administration of the *Eaux et Forêts*; it was done during "days" or "assizes" that were held at the time when the timber cuttings and the division of pigs were auctioned; if necessary, legal proceedings were also held. In addition, to maintain the foresters' zeal and note the possible offenses, the king and high lords, such as the duke of Orléans, periodically initiated regular or extraordinary inquiries to check the foresters' accounts, uncover the abuses and irregularities, and take all the necessary actions. In the thirteenth century, temporary investigators were nominated. Later, in the fifteenth century, the great master was in charge of the lawsuits against the agents.

The "reforms," which could also give rise to investigations and to condemnations, were more specially oriented toward the exploitation of the forest; the objective was to take a census of the royal forests, to check their surface and their condition, to define their modalities of exploitation and parceling, and eventually to take the measures necessary to restore the forests; it was a specialist's inspection, not a judicial procedure with witnesses. It was only incidentally that a reform implicated foresters. In 1456, the reform of the forests of the duchy of Orléans led to the removal of the general master and investigator because they found "several big and enormous mistakes, faults and damages . . . to the great charge, fault and shame of the master and guards and other officers of our forests. . . ."

The kings had the feeling that they were not always well served; it is apparent in the reasons for the fourteenth century ordinances. Too often the most important positions in the *Eaux at Forêts* were given to high lords who didn't have any special competence, and, at the different levels, it was the same for a certain number of posts, particularly for the enfeoffed officers, *gruyers*, masters or mounted sergeants. The profits that the foresters could make in the exercise of their duties, especially at the high levels of the hierarchy, were a permanent temptation. That is why as long as this system existed—until recruitment by examination, and training for the foresters were established in the nineteenth century—those defects would periodically appear, unceasingly noticed, deplored, and opposed, and always come back, to the detriment of the state's finances, and of the forests themselves—the main victims.

Forest Offenses and Penalties

According to Salic law each holder of a domain could choose the trees that he needed, subject to marking the tree and allowing sufficient time for the forest officer to recognize it and request him to pay the tax, he could then cut it. He had to remove the trees within a year; otherwise the tree fell back into the public domain. Anyone who took a marked tree had to pay a hefty fine (three gold ecus) as well as anyone who secretly cut a tree; the fines for this offense varied depending on the place; they were generally doubled if the cut tree was fraudulently removed. Moreover, certain laws allowed the person who lacked wood for his personal use to get it in the neighboring forest, restricting himself to the fallen trees and to those bearing no fruit.

During the Middle Ages, the justice revenues represented for the beneficiary—church, abbey, lord or king—not just a detail but an interesting profit, in great demand, that completed the taxes paid for the different usage rights. According to Deveze, in Brittany, the value of a forest was estimated by the yield from the taxes and fines or, sometimes, by the remuneration of the foresters, much more than by the yield of the wood cuttings.

The rules in matters of offenses, fines, confiscations, and damages were established by the customs transmitted by word of mouth from one generation to the next. Under Louis XII, many customs were written down—the customs published in the early fifteenth century can be considered to represent the rules in effect during the Middle Ages.

What stands out first of all is that, generally, during that period the penalties for forest offenses were much lighter in the south of France than in the north.[12] This is odd, because at the time of the "Barbarians" the penalties were, on the contrary, harsher in the south. The Barbarians apparently placed a higher value on trees when they were scarcer, which seems to make sense. Sainct Yon explains the opposite situation in the Middle Ages by the more-or-less great need for fuel according to the climate: "One must consider the different situation of the provinces. As the inhabitants of the southern regions do not need wood for heating, as they are rather inconvenienced by the extreme heat, they have less interest in preserving their forests than the inhabitants of northern regions where wood is like a half-life because of the long winters and extreme cold that we endure."[13]

The offenses committed in the forests were, up to a certain seriousness, penalized by the so-called "customary" fine, that is, one whose amount was established in advance and not "arbitrarily" by an arbitrator, lord or judge. In addition to this fine, damages that were aimed at repairing or compensating for the material damage done had to be paid to the owner of the property. Sometimes, as in the custom of the Nivernais, the users, quite logically, were entitled to part of the damages. Normally, as in the north and east of France, the amount of the damage was not linked to the fine. But in the south, the damage was double the fine, which was neither logical nor deterring, since the latter was usually moderate.

To ensure that the offender would pay his fine, not only was what he had taken illegally sometimes confiscated, but also his tools, sometimes even an animal or a carriage, or one of these objects was kept as security. The loss of a saw or an axe was actually considerable damage for a peasant who generally owned very few iron tools; for some, their axe (which they even took when they plowed because it often necessary to cut a few stumps left after the clearing) was a tool that they could not easily replace.

During the fifteenth century, a sergeant who came upon a man taking wood was moved by his supplications and left him his axe "with which he was working," against the promise to bring it back later. Because he didn't keep his promise the logger was fined thirteen sous and four deniers.[14]

To lose an animal or a carriage was certainly even more serious; during the fifteenth century, a "nasty" horse was estimated to be worth sixty to sixty-five sous, a donkey fifteen to twenty and a carriage, according to the case, between twelve sous and four livres.* In the east of France, confiscation was practiced only against "strangers" (*étrangers*) when the offender was caught during the night. The word "*étranger*," such as still in Brittany today, simply meant the inhabitant of another village.

To take an object as security, for example, a tool—or even an animal if it was a pasturing offense—belonging to the offender, was allowed to the forester or to the injured owner. But within a given period of delay, sometimes twenty-four hours or less, sometimes eight days, depending on the customs, they had to refer the matter to the lord who exercised the right to dispense justice. During that time the two parties could settle out of court. If the security was an animal—what was called an "eating security"—it was entrusted to an inhabitant for a certain time, after which the later could sell it on the condition of certain obligatory formalities of publicity announcing the sale.[15] The delay during which, in the absence of security, the victim of the offense could sue was extremely variable. In a region where people apparently wanted to conclude their business quickly and not be encumbered by too many legal actions, for example, in Dax, it was only four days, while in Normandy, where people tended to be litigious, it was one year. Between these two extremes, there were various intermediary delays. Sometimes, the victim of an offense could seize and, after a certain time, kill an animal of each foreign herd caught. This was the rule in the region

◆ ◆ ◆

*Let us recall that a sou represents approximately 5 gold francs of 1914, but as there exists livres tournois and livres parisis, as well as sous, and that they do not have the same value in the two accounting units, comparisons are difficult.

of l'Embrunais; the delay was five days and the animal had to be divided with the "consuls" and the nobles.

The fear of offenders was one of the reasons that justified the prohibition of saws, silent tools, while the axe strokes resonate in the forest and are heard from afar, making secret cutting hazardous. In addition, the foresters considered that sawing was harmful to the shoots on the stump of the tree and that a "clean" cut, favorable to the new growth, could be obtained only with an axe. However, for the conversion of timber legally obtained, there were no restrictions on the use of the saw.

Thus, it is specified in a text of 1402: "Although the use of the saw is generally forbidden to all free users who take wood branded by the forester, they will be able to cut their wood with a saw as long as it was first cut with an axe."[16] In 1404, according to an investigation conducted in Bray, Bonnée, and Les Bordes, cutting down a tree with a saw was, in some cases, fined sixty sous. The same fine penalized the person who used fire, following a method that goes back to the Neolithic period.

Sheep and especially goats, which are dreaded in the forest, were severely fined when they were found in woods that were growing back; in Brittany, for example, twelve deniers for a he-goat, a she-goat or a bovine, but only three deniers for a sheep. Found in a coppice, a bovine was fined two deniers and a horse four.

The fines were generally established by custom; there was the "ordinary" fine of sixty sols while the "little" fine varied from three to ten sols. For example, if you cut in a young, growing coppice (less than three years old), you would be liable to the big fine; but for an older coppice, only to the little fine. For pasturing offenses, "strangers" were liable to the ordinary fine while the local inhabitants paid only the "fine of law" that is, the little fine. In the customs of Artois, of Picardy, and of the north, the big fine was applied for cutting oak, while for any other tree, it was only the little fine.

The fines applied by these customs reflect a period preceding the shortage of timber that was felt from the twelfth century on. This shortage led to the use of wood other than oak for the different needs of crafts and even construction. Oak was a specie particularly favored because it supplied both acorns for the pigs and the best timber for construction. This moderation in the penalties, provided for by customs established at a period when the forest still appeared inexhaustible, certainly contributed to worsening the situation.

◆ ◆ ◆

We already talked about hunting as part of the forests' natural resources. Hunting offenses were more severely punished than ones involving wood, pasturing or other usage offenses without, however, reaching the brutality of the early days when lords had poachers executed or the severity of the English forest law from the eleventh to the thirteenth century. Nonetheless, when François I enacted his ordinances, after 1515, he included hanging for certain hunting offenses. What made the offenses frequent and the penalties often arbitrary (in the modern sense of the word) was that, at all levels of the society, the line between authorized hunting and poaching was imprecise and varied according to the individual to whom the rule was applied (because the hunting right was a concession of the lord exercising high justice) and also according to the place. Forests were often poorly marked out; furthermore, the limits of the different ranges varied with the fraudulent help of the merchants and the land surveyors, and also because of the growth of the forests on the edges, the poor organization of the cutting rotations and the secret felling of the marker-trees (*arbres de laie*).

Several customs provided corporal punishment for hunting offenses—flogging, carcan, and public exposure for commoners—and fines that could reach 250 livres. But the penalties were almost always arbitrary; that is, established by the judge and not by custom, because circumstances could vary considerably.

Poachers sometimes included monks and priests and, more often, students; thus, in 1419, two schoolboys of Orléans, Henry Romain and Noël du Bois were fined ten sous parisis each for having trapped a deer in a net and having "hid it at the end of the street with ditches" with the help of two other schoolboys, Perrin Maillet and Jacques de Vaulx. Even some forest sergeants set snares, as we have seen. Sometimes they were only following the example set by the forest master.

Poachers were severely penalized, as were as the resellers—sometimes. Maulde cites several examples. In 1450, Thiercelin Mautardier was fined forty sous parisis for having been caught setting nine traps, exhibits that had been presented to the forest master. In 1411, the base rate of the penalties inflicted in Seichebrières prescribed that whoever had hidden a stag or a deer had to give a cow, and for a wildboar, a pig. In addition, the guilty person paid a fine of forty sous. In the same year, for taking and hiding birds of prey, the poacher was fined forty sous, in addition to the value of the birds. But, generally, there was just a heavy fine of three to four livres (sixty to eighty sous), that was sometimes reduced by the judge.

In the thirteenth century, a poacher was put in prison or had to pay security of 200 livres tournois, while he was waiting for the results of the inquiry. If the animal was caught in a warren the penalty was increased. But for a warren rabbit strangled by a dog and taken away, in the fifteenth century, near Lorris, the two offenders were fined only twenty sous "in view of the case and their poverty." Sometimes the lord released the offenders from their fines; the farmers of Liffermeau, who had killed two stags, were given amnesty in 1459; they were not "in the habit of doing it," as were many hardened poachers.

Receivers, resellers, and restaurateurs were also prosecuted; a fine of forty sous parisis for an individual caught in Lorris with "venison meat" in his bag; a fine of five sous for a tavern-keeper and ten sous for another one, for pieces of deer seized in 1423. But a fine of thirty-two sous for another tavern-keeper of Sury au Bois for having accepted a piece of venison in payment for wine. In 1450 at Chateauneuf, two poachers were fined eighty sous each (a fine of sixty-eight sous and twelve more for the cost of securing information); because they refused to deliver their trapping devices, they were the object of a house search.

According to Maulde, all the examples that he has researched reveal a rather low level of delinquency.

From the Usage Rights to the Revolution

Forest rights were of vital importance for the most deprived part of the population, the people who needed them the most. Thanks to the forest, even the simplest *"brassier,"* a peasant who didn't own any land and rented his arms (in French, *bras*), could manage to make a living and could even own a few animals. In the forest, he obtained the wood that he needed to build or repair his cabin, the fuel for his fire, and fodder, so that his animals could survive the winter; also hundreds of other products, from the bark with which he made his shoes to honey that he sometimes was lucky enough to find on his way, fruits and berries and sometimes venison, authorized or not.

Any attack on these rights was strongly felt by the peasants, and throughout the centuries the nobles attempted to reduce them with the help of rich peasants who wanted to extend private property to the detriment of the commons. Most movements of rebellion against authority included among their reasons, demands concerning the use of the forest. Some examples of these rebellions are: the revolt of the Norman peasants, crushed in blood in 997; the resistance of the Saxons against the Norman conquerors in England in the eleventh and twelfth centuries; the Jacquerie in France and, later, in Germany, the Great Revolt of the peasants in 1525, one of the reasons for which was the lords' attacks on the forest rights.

All classes of society had an interest in the forest; the alliance of the burghers and the barons which, in the thirteenth century in England, led to the imposition of the Magna Carta on King John Lackland (1215), also had as one of its objectives the reduction of the rights that the king had assumed on the forests.

In the *geste des Normands* or *roman de Rou* (1172), the poet Wace describes the insurrection of the Norman peasants in 997; he recalls the vexations and burdens they suffered, including matters involving forests and hunting: "Every day another lawsuit; lawsuit for the canals, the forests, for milling and moneys for the taxes and the roads, and lawsuits for the mill, lawsuits for homage, fealty, for hunting, brawls, or corvées. . . ." Then he evokes the peasants' hope: "So we will be able to go to the woods and take the trees we choose, go to the fish ponds and take fish, and to the forests for game. In everything we will do what we want in the woods, the waterways and the meadows."[17] But, finally, the poor peasants were savagely slaughtered by the lord's troops.

The king of France sometimes set himself up as the defender of the poor people, stating that "nothing was closer to his heart than defending the weakest against the oppression of the most powerful . . ." and recalled that "the lords had easily taken advantage of the weakness of the poorest."[18] But, in fact, the lords had more influence and the king was far away.

Just before the Revolution the people's laments could still be heard, because the situation had become worse with the extension of the practice of *triage*, by which one-third of the forest was subtracted from the woodlands on which the usage rights were exercised.

The grievances sent to the States General, in 1789, showed the unceasing offensive that since the Middle Ages had been exercised against the time-immemorial usage rights of the peasants.

There they complained about the division of the common pastureland. "By breaking up the pastures, you take away grazing land from the cattle, and by distributing it to the day laborers, you are taking away their arms from the farmers."[19] Elsewhere, they deplore the clearings and the cultivation for the sole benefit of the lord. "Clearing increases the lord's revenues and takes away from the villagers their only resource for raising cattle. . . . The cart roads, herbaceous lanes, confines and limits of the cultivated lands . . . produced grass; the herds grazed there and came back at night well fed; the result was that the herd, healthy and fertile, reproduced and made the wealth of the countryside and supplied the towns."[20]

There they indicate that the prohibition to exercise the ancient rights in the forest deprived the poorest of their resources: "The poor of the parish complain that, although they were always entitled to go to the forest and gather dead wood for fuel, and to cut hay where timber had been felled to feed their animals, these resources have been recently forbidden to them, which reduces them to the worst state."[21]

Another grievance was concerned with the right of *faucillage* in the forest: "The forest master prevents the poor women from mowing the hay and grass in the forest to feed their cows under the pretext that they cut a few germinated acorns."[22]

These few examples, taken from among thousands of similar ones, show how strongly the users regretted the constant reduction, over the centuries, of their collective rights to the forest. It was an important factor in starting the Revolution.

But the 1789 Revolution, led by the *classe bourgeoise*, reduced the collective rights of the poorest even more through private ownership of the land, by the parceling out of the great estates sold as national property, and by the protectionism exercised over the national forests by the state, which resulted in the forest code of the early nineteenth century. Furthermore, the extension of hunting rights to all, after centuries of severe restrictions, provoked, for want of serious regulations, a slaughter of game that depopulated the forest, and thereby further reduced the benefits of collective rights to the forest.

11 · strategy, economics, & politics ·

Forest Border—Forest Defense

G OING BACK TO THE TIME when the warmer climate provoked a receding of the grasslands where man used to hunt herbivores, man, more-or-less consciously, remembered the forest as a hereditary enemy that needed to be reduced by iron and fire, but also as the womb from which he came. The forest remained a disturbing and hostile environment but, nevertheless, an indispensable one. Man, as a child who turns toward its mother, turns to the forest to find subsistence and protection in difficult times.

Starting from the natural clearings that existed in the Neolithic period on certain soils, such as loess, man conquered the areas covered by trees. But the forest persisted, not only in hilly areas, but often on the plain as well; it formed separations, barriers, no-man's-lands between colonized areas and also served a function in the agro-sylvo-pastoral economy.

These divisions were often maintained to limit and defend the different territories. Such are the *haies* (hedges), that are particularly numerous in the eastern regions of France; the word has often remained in the name of places. That is the case for the forest of Haye, which served as a border for the region of Toul. Some provinces, such as Champagne, were surrounded by forests. The forest of the Vosges Mountains extended in the "trouée de Saverne" to separate Lorraine from Alsace. The forest of Marchenoir spread between Maine and Beauce. The *"pays au bois"* (woodland) of Belvès was the border between Agenais, Quercy, and Périgord. The forest of Grésigne separated Rouergue, Albigois, Quercy and Languedoc. The forest of Blimard (or Bimard) formed the border between Touraine and Blésois. Blimard comes from *Blesis marca; marca* (in French, *marche*) was a general name for a border region. The forest of Tusson marked the border between Poitou and Angoumois; it was cleared when the abbey of Tusson was built in 1120, and the marche of Blois (forest of Blimard) disappeared almost entirely when the abbey of Fontaine aux Blanches settled there.[1]

Examples also exist outside of France. The Böhmerwald formed a border between Germany and Bohemia. In central and northern Russia, the forests marked the limit between the Slavs and the people of the steppes.

Nonetheless, in western Europe, the forest often occupies mountain regions that are difficult to cultivate. This coincidence is marked in some languages by the confusion between the word for forest and the word for mountain: *sylva* in Latin, *Wald* in German. The mountain is often a natural border; so, the fact that a forest surrounds a territory or a region is not always by deliberate human will to mark a border and constitute a defense.

On a smaller scale, during the Middle Ages, the forests around the hermitages and the monasteries assured an area of protection and isolation that was desired and preserved by the founders.

In the border forests of the plains, passages were organized in the areas of lesser depth or of greater permeability and played a role similar to mountain passes or river fords. The persistence in Wallonia—after the great invasions of the fifth century of a language derived from Latin—has been explained by the fact that the invaders had to go around the immense forest of the Ardennes, which was dense and difficult to penetrate; so, the country situated to the west was protected by the forests and out of the Barbarians' trajectory.

Still in 1944, before the offensive of von Rundstedt's army, it was still believed an impassable barrier.

The role of border and natural defense played by the forests, which, on their own, were already difficult to penetrate, was often completed by man-made works of felled trees, complicated interlacings of trees reinforced with brambles and thorn bushes; in the Middle Ages these were called *plessis*, a word that left many traces in the toponymy.

Those works already existed in ancient times. Caesar described the ones built by the Nervii in northern France. "They pruned and curbed young trees that developed many lateral branches; brambles and thorns grew in between the trees so that those hedges, similar to walls, offered them a protection that even the eyes couldn't violate."[2] In their battles with the Chérusques (a Germanic people that, led by Arminius who remained popular in Germany under the name of Hermann, massacred in 9 A.D., in the forest of Teutoburg, the legions led by Quintilius Varus) the Romans ran into similar works that formed genuine fortifications.

There were many examples, in the Middle Ages, of hedges reinforced by this type of defense. East of central Europe, a huge defensive forest, the "Preseka" covered Silesia. The western shore of the Bober, a subsidiary of the Oder River, was protected in the thirteenth century by the Lowenberger Hag. In France, the *"haies de Brie,"* which, in the twelfth century, extended east of Nangis for about thirty miles, were reinforced by ditches and felled trees.[3]

In the German Rhineland, in Souabe, and in Franconia, the use of defensive breastworks made of thick interlaced bushes remained traditional. In the seventeenth century, such defenses still existed and the nearby villages had to maintain them. They were constituted of trees cut at different heights, of which the shoots were curbed and attached to the ground so that they would produce other shoots, themselves interlaced and reinforced by thorn bushes. This type of fortification called "protection wood" (*Wehrwald*) existed, for example, around Bonn.[4]

In northern and eastern Russia, the peasants harassed by the incursions of the Tatars had long sought refuge in the great forests and settled in permanent clearings. Moscow was founded in a natural clearing. In the sixteenth century, it was decided to create a permanent fortification of felled trees, interrupted in places to allow passage and defended by towers. It was finished under Ivan the

Terrible: twenty to sixty meters deep (one meter = slightly over three feet), it included ditches, palisades, and earth banks. During the Second World War, the forests still played an important part in the Russian strategy against the German armies.

Before 1914, the Germans planted mugho pines in the Vosges Mountains, which is vegetation difficult to cross if it is planted tightly; the barrier was perfected by thornbushes, fascines, pointed stakes, and barbed wire.

In western Europe, all through the period of invasions, the forests offered a shelter that was always available for the population of the countryside, especially at the time of the Norman incursions in the ninth-tenth centuries. The forests, bordering the rivers on which the invaders penetrated, were often maintained because they formed a screen, a rampart, and a "filter," in front of the cultivated and inhabited lands. But, during the first part of the Middle Ages, it would have been difficult to cultivate—with the existing tools— the heavy alluvial soils at the bottom of the valleys. Later, some of these forests were preserved to facilitate the exploitation and trans- portation of wood on the waterways. Measures were taken by the kings of France, particularly in the Parisian basin, that forbade clearing at less than six miles from the main rivers. The ogre of the fairy tales might have had seven-mile boots so that he could step over those six miles of forest.

Forest Shelter—Forest Haunt

Strongholds against erosion, barriers against invasions, forests in every age have also been shelters where the opponents—partisans and banished, as well as thieves—could regroup, where the resis- tance against the invaders who spread on the plains could be or- ganized; and also sanctuaries, difficult to penetrate, where the conspirators or the opponents of those who held the plain assembled. It is not without reason that in *Macbeth* it is a forest that sets itself in motion to overthrow the usurper; it symbolizes this function of the forests throughout the ages.

In the forests of the Middle Ages—and still today—powerful armies could be placed in difficulty by light, very mobile groups who knew the area well and were able to make use of the covered terrain. These small groups could harass and decimate, with a minimum of losses, an enemy that was exposed to surprises, had a hard time moving horses, heavy material and vehicles and was often unable to orient itself, especially at a time when the compass had not been invented.

Contemporaries did not underestimate the difficulties of crossing forests. In Normandy, a 1306 ordinance authorized any stranger—found in the forests off the public road, and under the condition that he swear under oath that he had gotten lost—to have the forester show him his way. The story of the trip, undertaken in 991 by Richer, a monk at Saint-Rémy-de-Reims, to consult a rare book in Chartres shows him riding from abbey to abbey and getting lost in the forest near Meaux. This episode, related in the *History of France* by Richer, and dated from the late tenth century, illustrated not only how difficult it was to orient oneself, but also how poorly the wooden bridges were maintained and how often travelers had to find a boat to cross the rivers.

People also mistrusted, sometimes wrongly, the workmen who for professional reasons lived in the forests; loggers and especially charcoal burners, who with their faces blackened by smoke and soot looked particularly fearsome and were accused of getting along with the highwaymen and even of being regarded, from time to time, as more-or-less brigands themselves. The Italian revolutionaries, who formed secret societies in the nineteenth century to fight against Napoleon and later against the Austrians, called themselves the *carbonari*. The French word *embuscade* (ambush) evokes well the contribution of woodland to surprise attacks and it is the name of a bush formation (the *maquis*), that was given to the type of armed fighting that, by taking advantage of this natural situation, often manages to check regular armies.

Forests were a threat to the established power, traffic, and trade. The expression *"être volé comme au coin d'un bois"* (to be robbed as at the corner of a wood) also recalls this fear of highway robbers. It added itself to the ancestral terror felt by man when his view is obstructed by vegetation and when he feels dominated by vegetation that may hide hostile creatures—not only around him but above him as well.

Already Caesar—describing the strategy of the Nervii, who took shelter in the forest and came out to attack the legionnaires—wrote that his soldiers "did not dare pursue them further than the open land."[5] A sixteenth century author described the strategic advantages of the Burgundy forests in these terms. "The forest serves wonderfully for the safety of the land because from any place you can go under cover to all the regions of the country, from one fortress to another, and you can easily go to the help and supply of the towns, attack the enemies by night, retreat to safety, and reassemble at a convened spot as close or as far as you want."[6]

Throughout the centuries, the authorities paid particular attention to controlling the forests. To do so, they first had to be able to penetrate them with a maximum of security; this was done by cutting roads (*rupta*) through the bushes and the woods, straight roads such as those traced by Haussmann in the menacing and dense Paris of the nineteenth century to be able to fight by canon eventual barricades and charge with the cavalry. Some of these drives existed before the Middle Ages; the Romans had already crisscrossed western Europe with their highways, built as straight as possible, in defiance of the sometimes very sharp slopes that these directions involved and that, as early as the Middle Ages, led to the creation of diversions on certain sections (that can still be noticed a little on the French national roads).

It was not so much to achieve a saving of time and miles or just to facilitate the staking from point to point by the stars but, also and mainly, because in woodland, or even just in terrain with hedges and bushes, the straight line increases security. It is easier to surprise an army or a convoy in a woodland when the road is winding; a roadblock of felled trees can be set up that the arriving army will notice only at the last minute, which facilitates the ambush and also permits blocking the army's retreat. A straight road with large cleared zones on each side makes surprises much more difficult and allows the front and the rear guards of a moving army to communicate continuously. Even today, on the West Bank, in Israel, the government has forbidden the building of structures less than 150 meters (about 150 yards) from each side of the main roads; this is a military precaution as well as a political measure. Along these itineraries, colonist villages have settled. In the same way, the Romans in Gaul established along their roads large agricultural estates to enlarge the open space, and supervise the roads, and distribute land to the veterans of their wars.

Later, mainly for hunting purposes, the kings built through their forests large straight alleys with stars and roundabouts (rotary intersections), deploying through the forests a network like a spiderweb that facilitated following the hunt. But these straight roads were difficult—and often impossible—to build in hilly or mountain forests that remained choice sites for resistance fighters or outlaws of all kinds.

Clearings in the Middle Ages often corresponded to political views. Reducing the forest, enlarging the flatland, was also reducing the permanent danger represented by the uncontrolled: the brigands. It was to ensure the safety of the traffic on the Paris–Orléans axis —most essential commercially and strategically for the domains of the king of France—that the latter encouraged the establishment of a whole series of clearing *villeneuves* along that road. What was left of the forest of Torfou, which the road crossed between Arpajon and Étampes, was cut down in the sixteenth century, says Charles Estienne,[7] because it still sheltered highwaymen who killed travelers and maintained permanent insecurity on the road. Thus the forest, which served as haunt for criminals—and also for wolves—was reduced, pushed away, and reliable people, submissive to the authorities, were settled in the area. They could supervise the moves of outlaw gangs, offer shelter to travelers, and even, if necessary and included in their obligations, help the royal troops with battues or police operations.

Countless chronicles, romances and acts of justice evoke thoughts about the outlaws who lived in the forests. In the novel *Les Quatre fils Aymon*, Renaud and his brothers take to the forest to live as brigands. Tristan and Iseult find shelter in the forest. However, the forests of the Middle Ages should not be imagined as crawling with all kinds of brigands or robbers. This cliché was due as much to the persistence of old fears and ultimately political concerns, as to reality. For example, the judicial chronicle of the forests of the Orléanais notes that for centuries there were many forest offenses and abuses of rights but, in spite of the wars, few truly criminal acts. Of course, in inhabited regions, the forests were far from deserted. On the contrary, a people of basket-weavers, charcoal-burners, hoop-makers, potters, loggers, etc., as well as shepherds, herdsmen, and swineherds circulated or even lived there permanently.

The robbers would have had a hard time finding sufficient regular income in the vicinity of these modest categories of working people who comprised the majority of the forests' hosts. Furthermore, the foresters combed the forests in search of offenders and, when the lords traveled, they had armed escorts and, sometimes, so did the merchants, who traveled in groups. Many travelers' tales do not even mention encountering robbers. But, of course, when they did, it was the talk of the town, which is not the case of travels without problems.

Users in the forest were often caught infringing upon the rules. "Didn't they meet the foresters too often for their taste?" asks Mauld, who adds:

> ♦ *If one imagines the forest as a retreat for criminals inaccessible to all other men, then one could be surprised to see a whole population of basket-makers and other industrialists spending peacefully their entire nomadic life there, the charcoal-burners . . . building every year their pits in the largest and densest woods. . . . It is in vain that one will look in the forest for traces of organized outlaw gangs in the Middle Ages.* ♦

It was during the wars, and later, especially during the religious wars, that the people living near the forests suffered from organized groups, such as the *routiers* that Du Guesclin was charged with destroying during the Hundred Years War.

People during the Middle Ages mentioned more often meetings with ghosts, fairies, wolves, and witches than with bandits. Dom Morin, referring to a place called *Le Château au Chat*, writes that several people went there during the night and saw witches assemble and do their devotions and spells. It is also mentioned that the forest trees, that could be seen from the main road, were also used to hang criminals that had been caught elsewhere.

So it was mainly the rebels, the banished, and outlaws who were found in the forests. But, even as today, they were described as common criminals by their political enemies. However, from time to time, they did not hesitate to make raids. A few centuries later, under the Revolution, the royalist armies held the countryside in some regions and stopped travelers to find and execute known republicans and ransom the others.

In eleventh century England, the unsubdued Saxons took to the forest after the Norman Conquest, among them the legendary Robin Hood (whose name would be a derivation of "wood"). It was in the "New Forest," created by William the Conqueror, that several of his descendants were killed during the twelfth century. The embryo of the confederation of the Swiss cantons was formed in the thirteenth century, in the forest clearing of Rütli, around the three Wald-stätten; it managed to stand up to the Hapsburgs and achieve its independence. Later, in the seventeenth century, in the forest of the Cévennes, the Camisards fought against the dragoons of Louis XIV. In the eighteenth century, popular brigands, such as Mandrin, found shelter in the forests.

The trees, hedges and woods allowed the Vendeans of the late eighteenth century to hold off the republicans longer. In the wooded mountains of the Tyrol, Andréas Hofer organized the resistance against Napoleon's French army. It was mainly in the forests that during World War II, "partisans" and "maquisards" in the Soviet Union, Yugoslavia, Poland, France, and elsewhere, were able to resist against powerful armed forces and cause them to take heavy losses.*

To break down the resisters based in the forests, the armies often had no alternative, other than to destroy this hiding place. The most common method was fire; the most modern one is the use of defoliants. But fire was a risky method that was difficult to control, so often iron was preferred. Deep forests protected Wales; Edward I, in 1277, and again in 1283, hired several thousand professional loggers and *carbonarii* (charcoal-burners) of the nearby regions to cut a road for his soldiers. They were chosen from "among the strongest, most agile and used to this work," and equipped each "with an axe and a hatchet to cut down big and small trees."[8] Edward I and Henry II also set fire to forests in Wales and Ireland in order to dislodge their adversaries. In Spain, in the Middle Ages, many forests were burned during the "Reconquista" because they were shelters and strong points for the fighters. It was the beginning of the deforestation that was later worsened by the flocks of sheep. In Russia, in the fourteenth century, Tamerlane burned forests to chase the Slavs out. At the borders of Greece and Bulgaria, the Turks

◆ ◆ ◆

* As an officer in the French "Resistance" forces of the Vercors in the Alps in 1943–44, I myself experienced this form of war; I survived thanks to the forest when the German alpine troops and S.S. airborne paratroops, outnumbering us five to one, succeeded in finally crushing the four thousand "maquisards" in this sector.

used fire to force rebels out of the forests of the Rhodope Mountains. In the sixteenth century, during the wars between the Swedes and the Danes, the armies started huge forest fires in southern Sweden.

More recently, in Vietnam, despite the fact that the Americans tried to destroy the forest cover with defoliants, it was once again under the cover of the forests that their enemies were able to bring in weapons and ammunition, enter and infiltrate the southern part of the country and finally force the United States, despite its power, to retreat. And it is always in a forest of Latin America, Cuba, the Philippines or Africa that the opponents of established regimes regroup and organize.

So, the forest has never ceased to be a factor of prime importance in strategy and politics and continues to play an important role in history.

Forest Revenues

We examined earlier how important the forest was in the rural and urban economy. At a time when the self-sufficiency of the estates was the main objective and when exchanges and currency circulation, despite a constant increase, were still minimal and often interrupted or hindered by political events, revenue in cash was not really meaningful. Most of the numerous products derived from the forest were consumed without involving any cash transaction.

The forests benefited, in kind, the miscellaneous users, the forest agents, and the owners or holders, who were all entitled to a part, limited or not, controlled or not, of the wood and other products. What these rights represented was far from negligible; it included what was needed to heat and to cook, to repair and build houses and dependencies, to feed the cattle, the horses, and even the pigs, plus many other food products, and the material for most everyday tools and accessories. Venison provided part of the necessary animal proteins.

But the users seldom enjoyed the free use of these rights. Several dues corresponding to forest usage rights were also paid entirely or in part, in kind; for example, pigs, sheep, honey, eggs, part of the hunt, trapping or fishing, bread, oats (or other cereals, more rarely), wine, duties of transportation, tilling or logging, etc.

The forests also provided the beneficiaries with a cash revenue that was important—especially during the period when exchanges were increasing but were still quite limited out in the countryside.

An increasing part and, sometimes, even the totality of the dues for the usage rights was paid in cash to whomever had the ownership (or at least the tenure in the framework of the feudal pyramid).

The lord who exercised the right to dispense justice benefited from an important revenue derived from the fines and penalties that were imposed on the offenders; this revenue, of which a fraction was returned to the foresters who hunted the offenders and issued the summonses, was sometimes greater than the revenues from the sale of wood.

In some regions, for example, in the Parisian region in the forests of Bondy, Sénart and Saint-Germain, the king levied no taxes on the sales of wood but "only justice and fines, misuses and confiscations, pannage and acorn harvest, warren and hunting."[9]

The royal taxes were collected everywhere else. Where the regime of *Tiers et Danger* was applied—Normandy and bordering regions —the king was entitled to one-third of the price of any sale of wood plus supplementary rights representing, under the name of *danger*, one-tenth in addition to the principal right, which made a total of 43.33%. Other small supplementary taxes for wax, registration, and paper were sometimes added. In other regions, the rights levied by the king's agents were called rights of *"gruerie et grairie"*; the two words appear to have different origins and meanings, such as *tiers* and *danger*. The right of *gruerie* collected by the *gruyer* (or *verdier*, a term used in some provinces that confirms the etymology *grün* [German for green] of *gruyer* since *vert* means green in French) was the main right. The *grairie* was a complementary right levied in some places. Sainct Yon suggests, with plausibility, that the origin of the word would be *agrairie* from the Latin *agrarius* designating everything relative to the fields—laws, taxes, etc. He recalls that the dues on cultivated fields, which authorized the lord to deduct a certain proportion of the sheaves, is called *agrière* or *agrier* in the southwest. We can also note that, in the code of Theodose, the tax on the cultivated fields is called *agraticum*. Devèze, for his part, notes with pertinence that the word *gréerie* (from *gré*) designates in Middle Ages French, an authorization, a "leave"; as the spelling *gréerie* is found in several texts, the *gréerie* would thus be the price paid for the royal authorization. But the whimsical spelling of the Middle Ages is not a sufficient argument. There might have been

—it is a frequent unintentional error in the spoken language—the confusion between the *agrairie* or the *grairie* (derived from *agrarium*) and the *gréerie* (derived from *gré*).

Except in Normandy, where the rights of the king of France were established everywhere at the same time when Philippe Auguste reconquered the province, the rate of the taxes on the sales of wood varied considerably, according to the provinces and even to the townships or the forests to which they were applied. There is a striking shortcut of the extreme variety (that the modern historian tends to call confusion) that reigned in the Middle Ages, in rules and regulations that derived from the changes of status of the land through the centuries. This status could change according to privileges, grants or advantages given to one or another physical or moral person, depending on whether they were transmitted or not to heirs, beneficiaries, acquirers or beneficiaries of donations; it could be modified by the revocation of privileges, feudal confiscations or seizures, or the taking back of holdings because of the lack of male heirs. For example, in Beauce, Gâtinais, Hurepoix, and Orléanais the king benefited from half the revenue of the sales. Elsewhere, in Beaugency, or in Chauny, it was one-fifth. Around Senlis, one-third was levied in some woods, half in others, in others still one-fifth plus one-twentieth, and elsewhere one-twentieth in all.

Besides the yield of the taxes levied on the sales of wood in the forests that didn't belong to him, the king also had the revenues of his own forests that included the revenue from the ordinary annual sales of coppice, the sale of charcoal and ashes, the sale of *"chablis"* (fallen trees), the dues paid by the users, the fines, the confiscations and seizures, and also the receipts, called "extraordinary," collected from the sale of timber.

Early in the thirteenth century, the royal accounts of 1202–1203 show that the only circumscriptions that presented an important surplus, which was sent to the treasury in Paris, were those where there were royal forests. For the second half of the thirteenth century, we have the accounts of Saint Louis, king of France from 1226 to 1270; they show that, after payment of the expenses which included the salaries of the foresters (among them the falconers, who took care of the king's hunt, benefited from preferential treatment and even from noncontractual social advantages, such as pensions for their widows and settlements for their heirs), the revenue of the king's forests—60,000 livres per year—represented 25 percent of the total receipts of the budget.

In 1332, the total gross receipts from woods and forests represented 8,708 livres, of which less than 70 percent came from the cuttings in the woods, a little over 6 percent from the revenues derived for dispensing justice and about the same amount from dues (grazing and other rights). The profits from hunting, for rabbits only, represented 1.8 percent; the profits from the "big beasts" were not estimated. Finally, the dues paid by the landowners for the forests that did not belong to the royal domain represented a little less than 17 percent. The low amount of the forests' yield, compared to the previous century, seems to indicate a sharp decrease in forest production; the French population was at its maximum during that period, the clearings had diminished the forests, and the peasants especially, in order to survive, had to develop their herds, which accelerated the degradation of the forests.

Also, the proportion of taxes in the royal budget had increased; this evolution was accelerated by wars that forced the kings to resort more and more frequently and systematically to use their taxing power. In the context of the feudal system, all transactions consisted of exchanges of services, without monetary circulation, among all levels of the pyramid. At all the successive levels up to the king, the nobleman, in exchange for his holding, owed armed service to his lord, just as the commoner owed the lord who granted him a piece of land and gave him protection, work, dues, and part of the fruit of his labor as peasant or artisan.

Even military adventures as important as the Crusades were still organized within this system, because the lords at all levels who, with enthusiasm and often moved by sincere faith, engaged themselves beyond their strict obligations of *ost et chevauchée* toward their lords, could hope to gain in addition to glory, profits, lands, and an establishment beyond anything that little western wars could yield in loot.

As a result of the Crusades—in the eleventh, twelfth and thirteenth centuries—skeletons of regular armies were started by the military religious orders, Hospitalers and Templars. Furthermore, the western world engaged itself increasingly on the irreversible slope of an economy of exchanges that would upset everything. Already, a lesson of efficient organization had been given by the

Normans and had allowed them to extend their empire to several western European countries.

The first part of the Hundred Years War demonstrated that the French feudal system was unable to stand up to the organized Anglo-Norman army, in which the infantrymen played an important role. The final victory of the French came, in addition to the national feeling developed in contact with occupants speaking a foreign language, from the fact that the kings of France learned their lesson and benefiting from the resources of a larger country, more populated and richer than England, organized a regularly paid army—an army of "soldiers"—equipped with the most modern artillery in Europe. In this way, they definitely eliminated the English who, in turn, had let themselves be overtaken by progress.

By allowing the coronation of the king of France Joan of Arc had him regularly invested with the power over the kingdom. This essential but at the same time it was the last example of true chivalry; it marked the end of the great feudal era. The king could no longer limit himself to a family economy, living from the products of his land and particularly of his forests; he began the evolution, toward the organization of a centralized state, with taxes and civil servants, of which Louis XI, in the fifteenth century, set the first foundations.

The forest would find its place in this scheme of things and the forest administration—which the kings of France had felt was necessary—would slowly shed the major defects constituted by the hereditary transmission of the highest posts and their devolution to incompetent people (*fieffés*, in the proper meaning of the term), the venality of the duties, the disastrous methods used for the handling of public finances, and the system consisting of "farming out" certain duties.

The importance of the forest revenues in the royal budget gives us valuable indications about the evolution of the respective weights of the many different posts. But one should not become hypnotized by the official aspect—underlined by many historians—on which we have information for different periods of history. The weight of the forest is more important in the general economy, at all levels of the social ladder. But there, its monetary value cannot be calculated and is, of course, virtually impossible even to estimate. What we have explained about its resources and its place in the everyday economy gives an idea of its value. Rackham, who studied the case of the forests of England, says that the forests, even the coppice, often had during that period more value than equal surface of arable land, while at the same time cost little to maintain. [10] This is also what is indicated by the anonymous author of *Quatre traictés utiles et délectables de l'agriculture*:

> ◆ *One should not think that the land that is cultivated in wood is of less profit than the others cultivated in wheat or vineyards. Although it is true that the beginning is longer and more difficult than for vines or wheat, the reward is double at the end, because once the first expense is made, nature produces woods and coppices without man's help.* [11] ◆

Forests and Freedoms

The creation of *villefranches*, the advantages offered to those who populated the *sauvetés*, the multiplication of *villeneuves* benefiting from "freedoms" contributed, by starting a popular movement, by playing on the aspirations of the peasants, to accelerate the clearings, maybe more than the big enterprises where the lords settled colonists or hospites who did not have such freedoms. But, beyond their impact on the forests, those rural clearing communes, which had collective structures, under the often distant and irregular control of a lord who did not interfere with the administration as long as he collected regular profits, were a school of collective responsibilities and of self-management. They served as "testing benches" for more important enterprises that were no longer "towns in the country" or pioneering villages, but cities living on exchanges, trade, crafts, and emerging industries for which the impetus was the opening of the outside world—inaugurated by the Crusades—and amplified by the great discoveries that marked the end of the Middle Ages.

The "freedoms" sought by the people who settled in the *villeneuves* were essentially constituted by the replacement of the lord's arbitrariness—that weighed on people and things by contractual rules and that established the rights and obligations of the inhabitants and those of the lord. They gave regular bases and limits to the penalties. Unlike the hamlet or village, which were constituted by a group of people who had links and obligations toward the lord, which differed sometimes even within a family, the *villefranche* was a community. This *universitas*, formed by the burghers, had a moral personality, independent of individuals and could, as such, deal with the lord, make decisions, impose obligations on its members, admit new members (sometimes under conditions of the lord's authorization), exercise (up to a certain point) the rights of police and the administration of justice, collect fines and own buildings, treasure, archives, and a town bell.

Everything that characterized the urban cities existed on a smaller scale in the rural *villefranches*. Indeed, nothing allows us to distinguish between the "rural" town and the "urban" town, except the respective proportion between the inhabitants who had occupations not directly related to the land and the farmers, and between the commercial and craft enterprises and rural activities. Any town, whatever its importance, was still closely linked to the surrounding countryside; many inhabitants still worked there daily and exploited, directly or indirectly, fields, meadows, and woods. All towns tried to own or to have the use of forests because that was where the indispensable fuel and the universal material was located.

"One must note," writes Le Goff,[12] "what confirms the character of 'rural town' to the medieval town—the number and the importance of the articles of the franchise charters concerned with the surrounding countryside"; use of the grazing grounds and of the grape harvest, policing of the fields and vineyards, hunting rights, mills, organization of the pastures, and the collective forests are the object of many articles in the charters.

The question has been raised whether the "freedoms" movement started in France in the twelfth century in the urban cities or if it first developed in the countryside. There were differences according to the various regions and there are no extant documents that describe the beginnings of the movement. In the countryside, the "customs," the franchises granted, were not recorded in writing for a long time; the members of the rural communities as well as most lay lords didn't know how to write in this period when oral tradition had as much value as a written act (as is apparent from the investigations relative to customs). It seems that, at least in northern France, there were franchises, in particular the right to elect representatives, the *échevins*, long before these rules were written.

In 1030 and 1140 many rural centers appeared—*villeneuves*, bourgs and *sauvetés*—between the Seine and the Charente rivers, particularly in Anjou, Maine, and Poitou. These *villeneuves* enjoyed certain privileges but were not granted the designation, *"communes,"* a term that evokes freedoms obtained by force, rather than granted.

The movement of *franchises* developed in the later twelfth century. The famous "law" of Lorris (in the Gâtinais) dates back to the years 1108–1137. It did not grant autonomy to the rural collectivity, but it already represented considerable progress on the way to the "freedoms" and spread to all the regions of the Orléanais, Sancerrois, and the southern part of Champagne. The "law" of Beaumont-en-Argonne (1182)—which was very successful and served more than five hundred times as a model—granted to the collectivity not only material advantages but also the right to elect representatives, to levy taxes, and to participate in the lord's administration. Concerning the forests, this charter granted perpetual use to the *villeneuves*, which is the equivalent of full ownership of the woodlands, that are usually precisely delimited in the texts. The texts of other charters were reused many times but were generally applied to agglomerations that were more specifically urban. In any case, historians today seem to agree:

> ◆ *It cannot be denied that the agglomerations the closest to the rural society represented the first models of urban institutions: the* bourgs *and the* villeneuves *were the first to benefit from franchises, which then entered into urban law.*[13] ◆

This anteriority seems to be confirmed by the anomaly that caused urban cities to be called in French, *villes*, from a word that originally designated a rural exploitation, the Gallo-Roman *villa*. In the United States, the pioneering spirit contributed to the winning of democracy; in France, the collective conscience and the institution that provoked the emergence of a new class developed in the forests and in the solidarity required to enlarge the cropland. This new class, the *bourgeoisie*, after being for centuries the support of the central power against the feudal lords, finally took over the power itself by getting rid of the king.

12 · myth and realities of the forest ·

The Cult of Trees

I N MOST ANCIENT CIVILIZATIONS, trees—whose life span is several times that of men—were treated with the same respect as the elders among men. Several generations lived in the shade of the same venerable tree, almost as if it were eternal. Tradition often recalled the circumstances of its planting and all the events that throughout the centuries occurred around it and that it had "witnessed."

In fact, the "memory" of the tree is real and concrete; the tree registers in its flesh, in its concentric layers, all the events that affect its environment. North American trees, several thousand years old, reveal the trace of fires or even of more general phenomena such as volcanic fallouts several centuries old. This memory of the trees had to have impressed the men of past centuries, even if they couldn't read it as precisely as today's scientists. It is not surprising that, in addition, they imagined that the forests, which effectively are full of life and include scores of living creatures, would also shelter supernatural beings in their depths.

During ancient times, in the region of the Mediterranean Sea, the tree was all the more precious in that it was rare. The Bible mentions trees with respect. Wood is considered a choice material, associated with something sacred. Metal torn from the bowels of the earth, treated by fire, has always held a magical, diabolical, and infernal character that is expressed in the magical functions handed down to smiths in all civilizations. Around the Mediterranean there has been, since the times of antiquity, taboos that protect certain trees, certain woodlands, the *lucus* of the Greeks and Romans; very heavy penalties struck the profaners of those woods. In Algeria and Morocco, little sacred woods protect the tombs of the saints (marabouts) and constitute, at the same time, reserves of seed-bearers. In sub-Saharan Africa, little woods with the same functions exist near certain villages; in the lower Congo, it is sometimes parts of untouched virgin forests called "God's forests."[1]

In Europe in the Middle Ages, there were quite a few forests and woods that were especially venerated. In Gaul, the following forests or sacred woods inherited from the Gauls or the Romans are cited, although no conclusive proof can be furnished: Brocéliande, Paimpont, Corne de Lys, Wüstemberg in the Vosges Mountains, Fougères, and Rennes. In Veynes in the Hautes Alpes, when the aldermen took office in the Middle Ages they had to swear to respect and make others respect the integrity of a little wood situated near the torrent of the Gleizettes and considered to have been a Gallic *lucus*.[2] Among the ancients, as among today's primitive peoples, the veneration attached to the tree was often linked to its healing virtues. Its manifestations followed the rhythm of the seasons, was marked by the trees' changes, and essentially ensured the perpetuation of the specie.

The venerated trees were naturally the ones that, originally, had been preserved as seed-bearers and were chosen because they appeared to be the best qualified, in an attempt at eugenic selection, to reproduce the most-wanted characteristics. Some of these "standards" were preserved for a very long time, and after achieving popular reverence and receiving proper names, died of old age. A few of them found particularly good soil and survived for several centuries; they were often believed to have even greater lifetimes.

In fact, several must have reached the millennium. These trees sometimes grew to considerable size. The strange shapes, "personalized," that could be taken by some trees that were forked, warped, leaning, spiraled or battered also struck the imagination.

Guillaume le Breton, in a poem in Latin, related the story of the giant elm of Gisors that eight men could barely embrace by stretching their arms and touching their fingers: "*Vix bis quatuor illud protensis digitis circumdent brachia totum.*"[3] The talks between the king of France and the duke of Normandy, who had become king of England, were traditionally held under this tree. In August 1188, an incident took place between the French and English; the latter had withdrawn within the walls of Gisors and the French, offended, attacked the elm and cut it into pieces. It is said that Philippe Auguste, in rage, cried out: "Did I come here to play the logger?"

Giant trees have frequently been mentioned; in the nineteenth century there were still live trees that certainly went back to the Middle Ages and owed their extraordinary characteristics to the veneration that had surrounded them. Such a tree was the oak of Treignac in Corrèze, of which the trunk had a girth of over eighteen meters (about fifty feet) and that disappeared in the early nineteenth century. The oak of la Mothe, in Lorraine, dated from the twelfth century and had a circumference of seven meters (about 22 feet). The oak of Haguenau, called "the big oak," had a girth of 7.60 meters (about 24 feet) at a height of about five feet from the ground and died just before World War I. The oak of Malachère in the Haute Saône included ten stems of more than thirty centimeters (almost eleven inches) each. In the same region, the lime tree of Oricourt measured more than seven meters of girth; two other lime trees are said to have been planted in the fourteenth century.

Near Châtillon-sur-Seine an oak, which would have been planted around 1070, could still be seen in the nineteenth century. In Béarn, an orange tree called "le Grand Bourbon" was planted in 1411 by a great grandmother of Henry IV. The "Chêne des Partisans" (the Partisans' oak) in the Vosges Mountains goes back to the sixteenth century. In the forest of Montfort, the "Chêne des vendeurs" (the sellers' oak) had a girth of nearly twelve meters.[4]

It is certain that, in the Middle Ages, there were trees just as extraordinary, which have since disappeared and that were the object of a kind of veneration the Church tried to control. Because the

Church knew the strength of tradition and of popular feeling, it tried to attract this veneration by channeling it into respectable cults; many "chênes de Saint Jean" (oaks of St. John) recall, in fact, the old solstice cults that were celebrated at their feet. Many remarkable trees bear statues, votives or crosses. Some, such as the "Chêne Ferré" in the forest of Orléans, were dotted with nails corresponding to wishes or to voodoo practices. Near Anger, the "Chêne Lapalud" was covered with nails to a height of three meters. Carpenters, cabinetmakers, masons or wet coopers, who passed by the tree, traditionally drove a nail into it. Some of these sacred oaks were transformed into chapels such as the one that, near Mailly in the ancient duchy of Bar, shelters in its trunk a niche consecrated to the Virgin Mary.[5] Masses were celebrated in front of the *"arbre aux fées"* (fairies' tree) that existed in Joan of Arc's time near Domrémy. In the forest of Orléans, the "Chêne de l'Evangile" (gospel oak) probably housed a chapel or a niche. In Nieppe an old oak is linked to a pilgrimage. In Flanders, in the forest of Clermontois, pilgrims gathered around a big oak for a traditional mass.[6]

Hunters have always celebrated masses in the forest. Saint Hubert, whose legend integrated the animal world and the Christian world in the forest, is one of those who contributed to changing the pagan veneration for the forests into Christian devotion.

The veneration of trees, the respect inspired by the majestic forests in which the Romantics pretended to find the inspiration of the architects of the Gothic cathedrals, still reveals itself today in many ways, even under a veil of Christian traditions. One can cite the Maypoles, the crowns of leaves, the custom of strewing leaves, the traditional green branches that sometimes constitute votive objects that are periodically replaced. These customs were transmitted on Palm Sunday, the "May" that is celebrated at harvest time, the symbolic plantings of trees, Freedom or Victory trees, Christmas trees, and the green branch that carpenters place on the finished crest of a roof.

One must also note the symbolic meaning maintained through the ages by certain species—laurel, olive tree, oak, myrtle—reproductions of which still decorate the chests of academicians, generals, admirals, prefects. Pines and firs, in regions where resin trees were rare, were the object of a particular kind of respect on the part of the populations used to seeing trees with deciduous leaves. Their foliage, green year-round, unchanging, conferred upon them a mysterious character: they were symbols of eternity. In the romances of the Middle Ages, these trees are often considered to be magical. Thus, the tree that shelters the magical fountain in the adventure of Yvain—the *Chevalier au lion*—is a cedar or fir tree with evergreen leaves. The tradition of decorating a pine with paper flowers and candy, which was mentioned around 1600 in Strasbourg, appears to have come from Germany. The Christmas cake shaped like a log was a reminder of the wood—to which each person was entitled—needed for heat during the winter.

Each year on March 22, the Romans used to cut a pine and transfer it solemnly to the palatin. This feast of the tree became popular during the time of the Roman Empire. It was a spring festival organized by the carpenters; it included, first of all, mourning manifestations in memory of the death of Attis (symbolized by the pine); then, manifestations of joy associated with the triumph of the resurrected god. The commemoration of the Passion and the Christian Easter, preceded by Palm Sunday, quite naturally replaced this celebration.

During the night from Easter Sunday to Monday, the peasants of the Middle Ages in the Moselle region planted as many trees as cattle heads in front of their stables. These trees were sacred and so were the Pentecost firs (*Pfingst tannen*).[7]

During the Early Middle Ages, the priests, hermits and monks fought against the *"dendolâtrie"* (worship of trees). Saint Adalbert, Saint Bérégisse, Saint Maurille, Saint Martin, and Saint Valéry are among those who cut down trees and substituted Christian cults to replace the pagan ones, or at least the practices that remained from them. The provincial councils also enacted prescriptions to support this action. The simplest and most radical way was to suppress the shelter of these satanic spirits, to declare war on the trees.

Destroying the forest was, for the Church, a solution that eliminated that haunt of evil-minded spirits, that nest of diabolical superstitions, and of magical practices. At the same time, the arable land was enlarged, subsistence farming was increased, and the needs of the growing population were met.

Among the countless superstitions that the Church tried to extirpate, the worship of trees and waters was the most resistant. Raoul Glaber writes:

◆ *One should be wary of the varied forms of diabolical and human deceits that abound in the world and that have a predilection for those springs and trees that the sick venerate without discrimination.* ◆

Associating waters and forests in the denomination and functions of a specific administration (*Eaux et Forêts*) followed the logic of an ancient tradition. In this way, too, a whole domain tinted with dreams, eluding official control, and surrounded with the supernatural was brought back to the concrete and the rational in the framework of an exploitation close to the ground, of an economy with its down-to-earth problems; it was a kind of exorcism. Since the forests, indispensable to the economy, could not be destroyed, they had to be controlled, combed, and organized. People trusted the foresters to hunt not only the offenders but the supernatural beings as well.

The sorcerers of the countryside have, as distant ancestors, the priests of those pagan religions attached to nature that left their mark on our way of thinking. The strong renewed interest in nature, ecology, plant medicine, organically grown foods, solar energy, and the influence of the moon and the stars expresses not only a reaction against the abuses of a mechanistic civilization but also that old foundation of pre-Christian thought, which has not disappeared and which still continues to guarantee customers for the healers, sorcerers, spellbinders, and sometimes to maintain—by the worship of the saints and in the continuation of pilgrimages—practices coming from a very ancient pagan past.

In the early eleventh century, the bishop of Worms, Burchard, a well-known jurist, wrote a "penitential," that was extracted from his compilation of canonical legislation, which under the title of *The Healer* was widely disseminated in Germany. It established the rates of the penances for different sins and constitutes for us an often amusing testimony of the customs and mentality of the period. It includes allusions to many magical practices, and Burchard noted that they are "pagan traditions transmitted from father to son as by a right of succession of which the administrator is the devil." One that still exists today and has won widespread recognition is the celebration of the beginning of the year on January 1st; it was considered by Burchard to be a very reprehensible pagan custom. Among these traditions, many practices were attributed to forest people—cowherds, swineherds, and hunters—or included trees, whether to venerate them, pray near one of them rather than in a church, attach or introduce magical objects in it, or burn candles or torches on it. In his penitential, Burchard also alluded to witches and to rides during which a crowd of women, perched on animals, traveled long distances through the night. Burchard did not deny their existence; he simply incriminated the devil and his transformations.

Burchard appeared to find it usual—if not ascertained—that people believed in the existence of "fauns" and "hairy dwarfs" who, when you gained their good will, stole objects in the houses of neighbors and brought them back to you. The use of branches for several magical practices was also mentioned. The Church, in its attempts to divert the people from those pagan practices, found that the best defense was to establish a feast: Palm Sunday.

Thus, at all levels, one finds this veneration of trees, these symbolic palms, these branches, manifestations going far back that attest to the place of the tree, an archetype deeply rooted in human thought. When Saint Bernard declared in the twelfth century, "You will find more in the forests than in books. The trees and the rocks will teach you things that no master will tell you," he started an evolution that admitted nature and announced brotherly love for all living beings, even the wild ones, that would be incarnated by Saint Francis of Assisi.

The Church, after over a thousand years of fighting, was expressing its triumph over the old pagan gods that it considered definitely relegated to myths and good only to inspire the charming fantasies of poets still impregnated with classical culture, but gods that no one believed in any more. Nonetheless, the forest and the trees remained the haunt and shelter of many diabolical beings, but these were now integrated into the Christian mythology and had their hierarchical place and their function in service to the prince of darkness, the Satan of the Christian religion.

The Mythical Beings of the Forest

It is thought today that it is because man came out of the forest, stood up, became a biped, and thus developed his brain and exercised his vision, that, in all advanced civilizations, he associates, to the extent of using the same word, on the one hand, culture and agriculture, and on the other, forest and savagery. This is reflected in the etymology of many languages. In India, the barbarian, the savage, is called *djangli* (inhabitant of the jungles). In German, the word *wild* (savage) is a doublet of the word *Wald* (forest); the same is true in other Germanic languages. In French and Italian, the savage (*sauvage, selvaggio*) is the inhabitant of the *sylva* (*selva* in Italian), the forest. The wild man, who appears in the miniatures and paintings of the Middle Ages—as opposed to the urbane and cultivated knight—is a hairy being who looks like a monkey. It is a symbol of savagery and, before Darwin, seems to remind civilized man that he is the close parent, both reflection and antithesis, of that "abominable man of the forest," still very close to the animal.

The ancients, as today the animists, placed in the forests a whole pantheon of very natural secondary divinities that didn't have the haughtiness of the Olympic gods. They were close to the earth, waters, and woods as well as to the everyday life of the shepherd, the peasant, and the logger. They appeared to live in harmony both with men and with animals and in their physical appearances borrowed traits from one another. These mixed divinities—fauns, sylvans, satyres—were often represented with animal feet, hairy bodies, and horns or, for the Tritons, mermaids and naiads, with attributes of aquatic beings, but they had human faces and the power of speech. They were sometimes confused with the ancient Celtic, Nordic, and Germanic gods who were also representatives of nature's powers.

The toponymy attests that in France the ancient Gallic gods—such as Belen, the solar god, and Gargan, his son, god of the stones, trees, and waters—left durable memories. Names of places, villages, rivers, mountains, hills, and rocks to which the etymology is linked to Belen or to Gargan can be found throughout France. The legend of the giant Gargantua precedes Rabelais, who did not chose his hero's name by chance but because it was a popular figure; this giant still appeared in 1948 in the country tales collected by Henri Dontenville.[8] The Church tried to replace Gargan by a certain Saint Gorgon—introduced in France in 765—whose cult spread in northern France. His worship is attested to in several places; for example, near the Mont-Saint-Michel, which was a sacred place for the Gauls and where, in the nineteenth century, he was still visited by large numbers of Breton and Norman pilgrims.

But the character and attributes of these divinities from the forests, the waters, and the countryside did not always lend themselves to being assimilated into some saint—imagined for the sake of the cause, or presenting some common traits with the mythical being of which he had to take the place—without overly upsetting the habits, traditions, and rites. In that case, their place was in hell and not with the respectable saints. Of the divinities of the Gallo-Roman mythology that sometimes appear as quasi-animal, sometimes dangerously seductive and anthropomorphic, the Church made either devils, borrowing their shape from the fauns and the sylvans, or fairies and nymphs, resurgences of the ancient naiads; the Church did not deny their existence; it made them creatures of the demon that the men of God had to exorcise and hunt.

Thus, while the farmers were busy with clearing—a pious and civilizing activity in the eyes of the Church—the hermits of the forests, the recluse saints, and the monks who were building their abbeys deep in the woods, were in charge of eliminating, or at least neutralizing, the fiendish creatures that populated the forests. The Church's success was very gradual. Those mythical beings, who were presented to the people as horrible demons, seemed sometimes closer and more familiar, nearer to the earth and nature, than the abstract divinities, the Holy Trinity, the Father, the Son, the Holy Ghost, Mary virgin and mother, of which they were told by priests who spoke in a foreign language, by cloistered monks who were also big landowners, by these distant bishops, mitred and bedecked lords. With an old peasant caution that avoids putting all one's eggs in the same basket, they continued to humor these beings while the Church, by qualifying them as diabolical, officially confirmed, in fact, their existence. Closer to them, speaking their language, aware of their problems, smiths, charcoal burners, poachers, peasants, known sorcerers, intermediaries between men and the occult powers continued to exercise their influence on the minds of the people and to offer their services in all kinds of difficult circumstances.

The fight against the sorcerers—sometimes presented by the Church as successors of the pagan druids and priests of Satan—was an activity that motivated permanent vigilance during the Middle Ages and provoked frequent condemnations of innocent victims. This action went on through the Renaissance and even during the Enlightenment of the eighteenth century. The confessions, obtained by torture, "proved" the existence of the diabolical beings and anchored the people in their superstitions.

Among the myths linked to the forest, the ghost hunter was one of the most widely disseminated in Europe; it went from the pagan religions to the Christian tradition, in which it is generally a hunter condemned to hunt eternally because of some grave fault or his immoderate love for hunting. In the legends of the Pyrénées and of southern France, it is King Arthur, who left mass upon seeing a magnificent wild boar go by. Each province had its legend; here the "Comte Thibaut," there the "roi Hugon," elsewhere the "veneur Caïn," in the Vosges Mountains the Hunt of Jean des Baumes (*baum* = tree), the "chasse Gayère" in the Bourbonnais. The merry wives of Shakespeare evoke the hunter Herne, who rides in the forest of Windsor. His name must be compared to the one he has in other regions: Hellequin or Hennequin (that gave Arlequin), a deformation of *Erl-König*, the *roi des Aulnes* (*roi des Elfes* or *des Erles*), who inspired storytellers and poets, Goethe, Hoffmann . . . up to Tournier.

The spirits who, according to the ancients and the peasants of the Middle Ages, haunted the forests were generally nicer and more playful than those savage ghosts; elfs, fauns, trolls, kobolds, and nymphs presented themselves under a more seductive and less-fearsome aspect. They were, nevertheless, considered by the Church to be diabolical but were resistant to the popular beliefs and persist until today in children's tales, and even in comic strips and movies.

Many phenomena, unexplained at the time, that occurred in the forest—"fairy rounds," those regular circles of mushrooms that sometimes grow in the clearings, echoes, trees with spiral trunks, strange rock formations, and also mysterious disappearances, unexplained accidents, deaths without any apparent cause—confirmed the beliefs of the peasants in the existence of those mysterious creatures and contributed to maintaining them both under the wing of the Church and in the fear of the sorcerers.

The pious legends also contributed to the hardening of these beliefs. Christian heroes—saints—replaced the half-gods that were revered under the Romans; some were martyrs, a fact that would not have been understood in ancient times, but others were examplary knights, such as Saint Martin and Saint Hubert, or slayers of dragons, hydras, or serpents such as Saint Michael, Saint Marcel, and Saint George, who evoked Theseus, Hercules or Bellerophon

—whose exploits also occurred in the waters and the forests, in the depths of which can hide fearsome monsters and from which any surprise can be expected.

While some of these monsters haunted distant lands—the dragon that Saint George fought in Libya in the fourth century or the monstrous serpent that Gozon, great master of the Hospitalers, exterminated in the fourteenth century on the island of Rhodes— others were situated in more familiar environments such as the dragon that Saint Marcel, bishop of Paris in the fifth century, hunted in the marshy forest of the lower part of the Bièvre Valley, or the monstrous serpent of which Saint Liphard is said to have delivered the forest of Orléans. The romance of Parthenopex of Blois represents the Ardennes as "crawling" (*fourmillant*) with elephants, lions, serpents, and dragons at the time of Clovis.[9]

◆ *Mais à cel jor dont je vos cant*
I par avoit de forest tant
Que cil qui erroient par mer
Ni ossoient pas ariver
Por elefans, ne por lions
Ne por guivres, ne por dragons
Ne por autres mervelles grans
Dont la forest est formians. ◆

But these dragons, serpents, and other fantastic creatures that ate children, the giant serpents, hydras, and tarasques that appeared in the hagiography, in the chivalric romances, and in the armorial heraldry were generally considered, at least in France, to have disappeared, exterminated by the saints of the Early Middle Ages and by the knights. They were merely sources of inspiration for the writers of novels and for the capitols and gargoyles of the Gothic cathedrals. However, the numerous fiendish creatures of lesser importance—that were said to haunt the forests—truly existed and no one was surprised to learn that some people had met them or that magicians had dealt with them. Thus, the simple people tried to gain their favors and a more-or-less secret worship of these invisible figures went on in the forest, all the more since, despite the Church's effort to depict those forest creatures as diabolical, the people sometimes tended to think that some of them—such as fairies, elfs, etc.—could be benevolent.

Le Goff estimates that, in the Early Middle Ages, Christian authors were more anxious to fight the official paganism (the Greco-Roman religion) than the old superstitions. Le Goff continues, "to a certain extent, this attitude favored the emergence of these ancestral beliefs more or less cleared of their Roman habit and not yet christianized."[10] Thus Saint Augustin mentions in a passage of *De Civitate Dei* (The City of God), "the sylvans and the fauns that the people call incubi." According to Grégoire de Tours, the cult of Diana still existed in Trèves in the fifth century. In Belgium, in the Middle Ages, people still believed in wood genii (called *woudmannen* or *boschgoden*) and in trees that spoke.

The elimination of the superstitions that had been grafted onto ancient official or popular beliefs was made effective not only by the destruction of the temples and of the representations of deities or deified emperors, but also by substituting Christian monuments for the ancient temples, Christian rites for pagan practices, by replacing ancient heroes with saints, by celebrating saints or Christian events on the previously traditional dates of pagan feasts. Furthermore, the Church also tried to change the meaning of folkloric characters and themes—dragons, ghosts, fauns, and nymphs.

Catholicism attempted to firmly categorize the different myths inherited from the past, and still very much alive—especially in the countryside—by placing the evil powers on one side and the good on the other. The evil powers, whose existence was recognized, were found, of course, far from the churches and far from "civilized" places; in other words, in the country and particularly in the forests. There, in the shade of the trees and in the darkness of the coppice, real monsters, human or animal, could easily hide and one could guess about the even more fearsome imaginary monsters, whose existence the inhabitants of the woods liked to confirm; better probably than the real forest creatures, these mythical beings contributed to preserving the independence and peace of the woodsmen.

Thieves, the frequent and truly real guests of the forests, benefited from maintaining around their haunts superstitious fears that kept intruders away. It was probably the case of the castle of Valvert or Vauvert which had the reputation in the thirteenth century of housing dangerous guests. This castle situated near Paris—in a verdant valley, surrounded by woods—"was a retreat of malignant spirits that tormented those who dared to approach," until, in May 1259, the Carthusians, until then living in Gentilly, were given the mansion of Vauvert by Saint Louis. From that time on, no one ever heard of the devil of Vauvert who, nevertheless, remained proverbial in Paris.

The forest, with its traps, secret places, possible ambushes, difficulties of getting oriented and getting out of it, was felt to be a dangerous place—especially by the people from the towns and the castles. Many city folks even today have an instinctive fear of the forest; they don't dare leave the paths and stay fearfully on the outskirts when they cannot find a well-blazed, reassuring trail or pathway.

While recognizing the utility of the forests' production and the importance of the forest in the economic balance of the estates, its role as a sports ground—that is, for hunting—and for military training, the people of the Middle Ages considered that it was a civilizing activity to clear it and reduce it; thus, a cultivated, open, productive, policed, and taxable area replaced the former haunt of demons and monsters.

In the Middle Ages, supernatural creatures could be only angels or demons. For a few forest apparitions that were recognized as commendable and sent by heavenly powers, many more continued to be considered satanical. For Joan of Arc, this dilemma was resolved in an unfavorable way by her political enemies, when they made her a prisoner of the state.

It's almost always in the forest—sometimes in a clearing—that the heroes of popular tales or legends meet these mythical and often ambiguous creatures. When young Perceval, who has been maintained by his mother deep in the *gaste forêt* in ignorance of the ways of the world and of chivalry, meets armed knights, he takes them to be devils or angels. The tale of Edric the Savage (that is, the "woodsman"), as in many tales of the period, depicts a hero who gets lost in the forest. That is where his adventures start—when he meets creatures full of charm but who are really diabolical—as the story later reveals.[11]

In the novel of Mélusine, Jean d'Arras relates that, while hunting in the forest, the king of Albania, Elinas, meets Présine who presents him with three children, especially Mélusine, the serpent woman who inspired a whole series of Middle Ages tales. It is also in the forest during a hunt that Mélusine, who has become a beautiful young woman, meets Raimondin, son of the count of Forez.[12]

Mélusine promises to make his fortune, on the condition that he marry her and never try to see her on Saturday (on that day—which she doesn't tell him—she transforms herself into an aquatic animal). She bears him ten sons and makes a fortune for her husband by "clearing" land and building towns and castles—among others, the castle of Lusignan from which the family gave its last lord, a sacrifice for the free kingdom of Jerusalem. The Lusignans kept in their coat of arms the legendary serpent, the form under which Mélusine disappeared on the day when her husband, breaking his promise, peeked into his wife's bathroom through a hole, out of curiosity or just forgetting that it was a Saturday.

Forests and clearings play a considerable role in this legend which, under various forms, enjoyed considerable success at the end of the Middle Ages. The husband of Mélusine is the count of Forez (a Forez who appears to have very little to do with the region by that name but who evokes mostly the "forest" context). By the action of the fairy, the domain goes from "savagery" to civilization. Indeed, as Mélusine stands in front of them, clearings get bigger, forests become fields, agriculture replaces nature. At the same time, Mélusine is a great builder. This dual role of clearer and builder well evokes the links between construction and the forest that provides the essential material for building as well as the fuel indispensable for life, but also the pastureland and the cropland, which ensure subsistence. Mélusine is "the fairy of the medieval economic rise."[13] But what the legend also symbolizes is that these events arose from the forest, which was its indispensable foundation and quintessential resort.

Of Words and Things: The Tree and Writing

At several levels, under different aspects and at all periods, the tree plays an essential role in human thought and in its communication. The trees' memory inevitably made an impression on men. But this memory is a sort of will because the tree reveals its secrets only after it is cut. This kind of "chiromancy" of the tree permits discovering the past and recognizing cycles and alternations that constitute les-

sons for the present and the future. Writing, which is meant to
constitute an objective and perennial memory, to transmit the messages, to set words in a visible form, has in several languages of
western Europe, relations with the trees, from the alphabet to the
book. The runes, the alphabet used until the tenth century by the
Anglo-Saxons and the Celts of the British Isles, were in use until
the fourteenth century in Scandinavia and disappeared, specifies
Marcel Cohen, only in the twentieth century. [14]

In this alphabet composed of twenty-four signs in groups of
eight—in an order different from that of the Greco-Latin
alphabet—each letter had the name of a thing in which the denomination started by the sound represented. The ogham writing of the
Celts of the British Isles, found in the Irish manuscripts of the Early
Middle Ages, was based on the same principles. Twenty-two runes
of this alphabet had the names of trees: elm, birch, hazel, oak,
poplar, and alder were the names of the first six letters. [15]

The German words *Buch* (book), *Buche* (beech), *Buchsbaum* (boxwood), the English words book, bush, etc., and the French words
bois (wood), *bosquet* (little wood), *buis* (boxtree), *bûche* (log), and
bouquin (slang for book) all have the same root and are derived from
boscus (wood in Latin). In Irish and Gaelic the same word designated
tree and letter.

The letters of the alphabet are called *Buchstabe* in German, which
means branches of beech (or boxwood), and *bokstafr* in Scandinavian
has the same meaning. It is because the fine grain without knots of
these two species of trees lends itself to incision; in our forest today's
lovers still prove it on the smooth bark of beeches. These styles of
writing remind us that the *greffe* (graft) made on the tree, the *gravure*
(engraving), the *greffier* (clerk) as well as the *grammaire* (grammar)
and the *orthographe* (spelling) are closely related words with a common
root and evoke the primitive incision on wood of the beginnings of
writing. For writing as for building, dried or baked clay replaced
wood when the latter was scarce. It is on these materials that people
engraved what the Latins called "characters."

For the support of written thought, for the surface on which
letters can be traced, the tree also had practical uses. Writing follows
"lines" (horizontal or vertical depending on the language); it is also
a word that comes from the tree: *lignum*, in Latin, designated the
material wood, characterized by its parallel fibers and the straightness

of the tree trunks that the heliotropism of the vegetation sets vertically side by side.

In Latin, the word *liber*, which gave the French word *livre* (book), designated the layer between the sapwood and the bark of the tree that was detached to use as writing paper, as bark in other countries. The paper that we use today, for which the manufacturing technique is derived from the one perfected at the end of the Middle Ages, and the papyrus of the Egyptians, which was made with interlaced plant fibers, essentially use wood pulp. Writing has become today the main consumer of wood, the essential outlet of forests, the abyss in which the press each day sends entire forests.

Thus in all western European languages, in the alphabet, the writing and the books, everywhere, the tree and woods have been intimately linked for thousands of years to the development and the expression of human thought.

epilogue ·
flux and reflux
of the forests ·

One of the inescapable characteristics of the trees is to be rooted in the ground: they are monuments. The most beautiful, the most remarkable, the strangest are guide marks in the ocean of the forest, as seamarks are for sailors.

So the idea that trees might move strikes the imagination. Through the centuries—from the Celtic legend about the war of the trees to Tolkien, passing by the *chansons de geste* and later Shakespeare, who shows the forest of Birnam setting itself in motion in the final attack against Macbeth—the forest in motion is an image that reappears in the legends. Hannibal's elephants have been compared to a marching forest: distant memories of mammoths might exist in men's unconscious. As the men who came to throw down Macbeth in Dunsinane, entire armies later also used the camouflage for their soldiers and their vehicles so that they would blend with nature.

But this image reflects the always threatening reality of the forest, when it is not strictly maintained within its limits by the plow; specific legislation had to be written for those extensions of the woodlands that take advantage of the least slack in the maintenance of arable land. The great catastrophes that befell men or that they brought upon themselves—wars, epidemics, and famines—that reduced the number of men and the intensity of the agricultural activity, always led to a strong return of the forest. As a never-discouraged army, the forest comes back to the assault and reconquers the land that it has lost, as soon as man relinquishes his hold. This patient obstinacy of the trees inspired the respect and fear of the populace.

Unceasingly through history, the forests modified their hold during successive periods of flux and reflux. Their localization changes according to the periods and they don't always come back to the same places. That is because, as we have shown, if the natural factors are very important, human factors are even more decisive. On very sloped lands, on the worst soils, in extreme altitudes and climates, man holds tight and manages to farm. But in our temperate climates, in our countries of generally moderate altitude and sufficiently irrigated, these conditions occur only in mountain regions, for which the maintenance is of prime importance for the rest of the territory because of their dominant position.

The ups and downs of the forest in each region followed the movement of populations. But, during these fluctuations, certain forests ended up in other places than in the past, which does not facilitate the work of the historian, who would like to determine the status of the woodlands at different periods.

It is especially to the detriment of the forest that man since the Neolithic period extended his cultivated territory. And, until the period of mechanization, the means to attack the forest progressed very slowly. The action of Neolithic men on the woodlands was naturally limited, since their means were rudimentary and the population sparse. As early as the Gallic period, the great forests that covered the country were deeply penetrated by a population that is estimated at about 8 million inhabitants on the eve of the Roman conquest. The forests still covered two-thirds of the territory (about forty million hectares) in that period. One could go from one side of France to the other without leaving the forest. At the time of Caesar,[1] the largest forest of Gaul, the Ardennes, went from Reims to Cologne and from Dijon to Liège and was probably linked to that of the Vosges Mountains. After the Roman conquest, the inhabited territory was divided into large domains surrounded by forests and exploited for firewood or as timber trees where the pigs fed. The rest of the forests belonged to the state. It was the *saltus publicus*, almost entirely unexploited and difficult to penetrate.

During the period of the later empire and during the great invasions of the fifth century, the forest regained its primacy over cultivated fields; but, from Clovis to Charlemagne, a certain security and stability returned, the population increased and clearings started once again, encouraged by the public authorities and by the Church. It is estimated that during that period the total area of the forests was about the same as under the Roman Empire—30 million hectares for the territory of present-day France. But the cultivated areas and the forests were not everywhere at the same places. In the Parisian basin, some great estates of two to four thousand hectares, which came from the clearings of the Gallo-Roman period, had returned to the forest, while between the Seine and Oise rivers, certain Merovingian sites were four to six times more populated than the Gallo-Roman hamlets had been. The foundations of Gallo-Roman villas have been discovered totally apart from the inhabited areas of the Middle Ages. In Belgium, there are several cases of medieval sites cleared, cultivated, and inhabited that are quite distant from the places occupied by the Gallo-Romans. This makes one reflect on the idea of the "vocation" of soils and the value of the hypotheses based on geology and pedology to reconstitute the hold of the ancient forests.

The Norman incursions on the whole territory, the raids of the Hungarians in the east and of the Saracens in the south caused great insecurity among the people and determined, in the ninth-tenth centuries, a new regression on the part of the population and a tightening of the cultivated territories. It is around the year 1000 that, with the end of the invasions and what appears to have been more favorable climatic conditions, the population started once again to grow.

But society was getting set. At the beginning of the Middle Ages, the nobility was a class open to all those who could arm and equip themselves, fight on horseback, and bound themselves by a personal contract to a chief. They received from the latter a "hold," of land which the yield had to be sufficient to feed the knight and his family and to maintain and renew his equipment. As long as there were lands to distribute, the number of knights was able to increase; but soon there was nothing left. In addition, the families of the knights expanded; their members refused to take care of the land and would exercise only their profession of arms. Nobility reached the point where it was closed to commoners. The establishment of the law of primogeniture—to prevent the division of the hold into pieces of land that would not have been sufficient to support their owner— sent to the "war market" all the younger sons of noble families who were without revenues or domains. They had to find their means of existence elsewhere, on the outside, in the Iberian Peninsula that was being reconquered from the Moslems, in the east of Germany, in Sicily or in the great adventure of the Crusades which began at the end of the eleventh century.

Meanwhile, commoners had no other resource than to extend the arable land because of the lack of progress in the crops' yield; the only land of conquest, the only possibility for development—and even of survival for this part of the population—was the wastelands, forests, humid zones, flood areas or submerged lands. Clearing represented for the peasants what the Crusades and the wars of conquest were for the nobles. In addition, they sometimes were able to acquire the status of "burgher" and, in the milieu of a *villeneuve*, to be a little more autonomous, to benefit more fully from their work, to enjoy certain freedoms.

Numerous famines—almost every other year in the eleventh century—accelerated the clearings. The strongest attack on the forest in the history of France occurred at that time; from 30 million hectares under Charlemagne, the forest fell to about 13 million at the beginning of the fourteenth century. Combined with the methods of forest exploitation, this situation provoked a wood crisis. The first measures attempting to preserve, manage, and better exploit the forest appeared here and there. During the fourteenth century, the Black Death and the Hundred Years War—preceded during the second part of the thirteenth century by a colder period in certain regions and a deterioration of economic conditions—led to a drastic reduction in the population and, consequently, to a strong return of the forest.

When during the following centuries, a certain stability returned, the population started once again to grow and there were new cuts in the forests; the balance, for a time attained between the agricultural and the forest space at the end of the fourteenth century, once again was upset. At the beginning of the sixteenth century, François I and his successors took a series of measures aimed at eliminating the abuses and also rationally organizing the exploitation of the royal forests and controlling the operations of the private ones; unfortunately, these measures remained without effect. The authority of Louis XIV—backed by Colbert—was necessary to take measures, from 1661 to 1669, that were finally effective but entirely turned toward production in the interests of the king and his projects.

The situation of the regular users did not improve because of the constant encroachments by the nobles, who tirelessly tried to reduce the usage rights of the commoners to appropriate this essential wealth—the forest. Many lawsuits as well as the *cahiers de doléances* (list of grievances) established on the eve of the French Revolution for the meeting of the States General in 1789 illustrate this situation. These encroachments were one of the important causes of the Revolution; the latter abolished the privileges, but that did not return the forest to the community. On the contrary, the sale of the national properties accelerated the privatization and the frittering away of the forest. The development of private ownership of the forest led, as a result, to the further reduction and degradation of the woodlands. It was only through a long effort, marked in France in the nineteenth century by the promulgation of the forest code and by a few great enterprises of reforestation (and, especially, favored by the considerable yield increase of the cultivated land and the development of international exchanges), that the forest in France once again progressively spread, to the extent of covering today about a one-quarter of the territory. In general, it is not rationally exploited but this is mostly due to the fact that it is broken up.

The return of the forest, which today occupies about the same proportion of the territory as it did in the early fourteenth century, is, on the whole, positive. But in many places this advance indicates, as it did after the Black Death and the Hundred Years War, a decline in human occupation; it is not always indicative of progress from the point of view of the ecological balance of the territory. In a deserted territory, the forest, whose roots and cover maintain the ground, is incomparably better than erosion that has devastated, often irremediably, so many regions.

In many hilly and mountain regions, where until 1950 the forest was able to be visited and exploited, the roads are now impassable; the forest has become as impenetrable as the *saltus publicus* of Roman Gaul because of the lack of human occupation.

The forest code of 1827, enacted during the Bourbon Restoration, crowned the efforts of the foresters but, followed by the sale of collectively owned lands under Louis Philippe, it had a very unfavorable influence on the maintenance of agriculture in marginal areas, often extremely important from an ecological and economic point of view. The poor farmers were deprived of the usage rights that allowed them to freely obtain firewood and to feed their animals as well as the miscellaneous forest products from which they benefited. These regulations accelerated the rural exodus that the development of industry and communications had stimulated.

Researchers have noticed today, with the refinement of scientific knowledge relative to the interdependence of the natural phenomena and their links with human occupation, the sometimes disastrous consequences of abandoning certain regions—those in high altitudes, hilly territories and terraced cultures. The deterioration and depopulation of entire regions could have been prevented by taking into account the needs of men and, at the same time the requirements for conserving natural elements.

It has been realized, for example, that a sylvo-pastoral balance is possible, and even commendable, in many contexts. Research and experimentation are pursued in that direction in several regions, for example, in southern France and Corsica. With suitable material and new uses, cultivation terraces can often be maintained and remain economically viable. The biological wealth of the "wild" or semiwild plant zones, such as humid zones or forests, is sometimes more important than that of certain cultivated areas. The importance of the hedges, embankments, windbreaks, and small woods is today recognized and integrated into the environment of modern agriculture. Scientists have denounced the risks that intensive farming methods and abuse of chemical products create for cultivated lands, surface waters, and deep waters, the preservation of which is essential for rural and urban life.

The lesson of the past, the study of the advantages of the ancient uses from the point of view of the utilization of the land, the examination of the drawbacks entailed by the loss of the delicate balance among the different activities, particularly when the maintenance of human occupation is discouraged, could have led, in the context of a global and thorough approach to the problems, to solutions that would have taken into account all the elements involved—human, ecological, economical, juridical, etc.—and finally to a better management of the natural estate that would have made room on the territory not only for the forest but for man.

appendices ·
1-4 ·

	10th century	11th century	12th century	13th century	14th century	15th century
SOCIETY Total Population of Europe (M: Millions)		From the 11th century to the beginning of the 12th c.:: Improvement of the peasant status — End of the 11th century: Peasant revolts		From the early 13th century on: — Deterioration of the peasant condition	1358: The Jacquerie (France) 1381: The Great Peasant Rebellion (UK)	
70 M / 60 M / 50 M / 40 M	42	46 48	50 61	69 73		
SUBSISTENCES	Beginning of the clearings	The clearings develop	The big clearing projects	The clearings slow down and stop	At the end of the 14th century: reestablishment of the forests	
COMMUNITIES		Beginning of the urban "communes"	Policy of new villages: franchise charters	Middle of the 13th century: no more "villeneuves"		
		DEVELOPMENT OF TOWNS AND EXCHANGES				
CATASTROPHIES FAMINES + + PLAGUES * *	+941	+1005 +1032 +1043	+1124 +1144	+1224 +1235 +1263 +1280 +1286	1347 THE BLACK DEATH .1315 .1347 .1373 .1373 .1380 .1399	
CONFLICTS WARS INVASIONS	Establishment, end of invasions, expulsion: 911: Normans 955: Hungarians 972: "Saracens"	1095 — 1066: The Normans conquer Britain	— — THE CRUSADES — —	— —1270 — 1241 to 1287 Mongolian invasions (Eastern Europe)	THE HUNDREDYEARS WAR 1357 1302: Courtrai 1314: Bannockburn 1315: Morgarten	1453: The Turks take over Constantinople —1453
	ROMANESQUE ARCHITECTURE — — —	— GOTHIC ARCHITECTURE — —		— GOTHIC ARCHITECTURE — —	— — GOTHIC DECADENCE	

(Extrait de *Les Racines des cathédrales*, R. BECHMANN.)

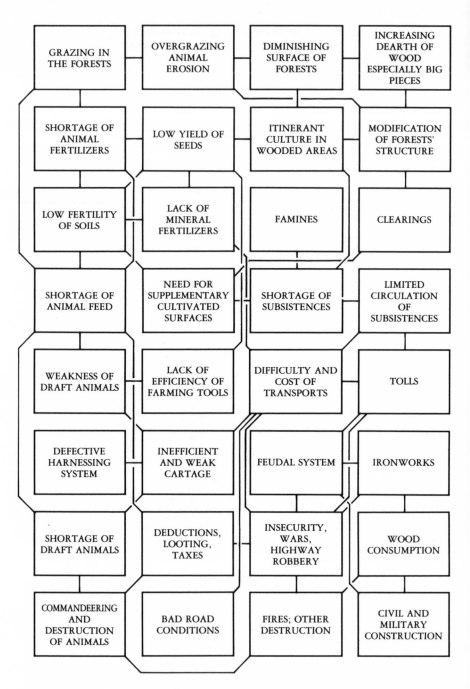

APPENDIX 2: INEXTRICABLE INTERDEPENDENCE OF THE FACTORS

Socio-economical environment 11th-12th century, at start of Gothic era.
(From *Les Racines des cathédrales*, R. Bechmann)

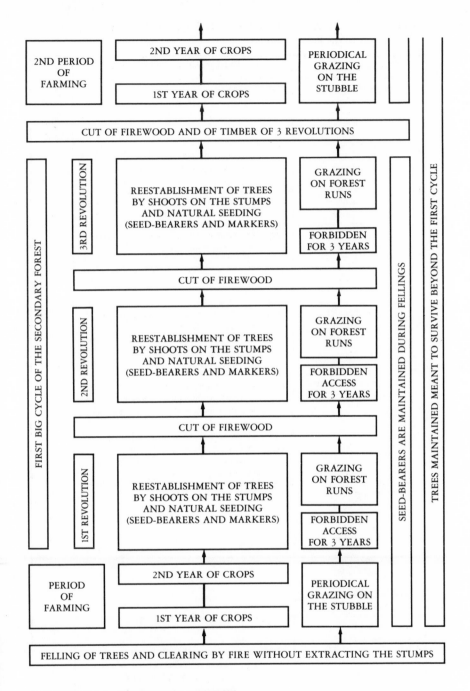

APPENDIX 3: PRIMARY FOREST

Temporary farming in forest clearings. In the case where the operations take place over a period of about 36 years, the complete cycle including 3 revolutions of coppice requires 18 "areas" successively cultivated for two years.

(Copyright Roland Bechmann)

APPENDIX 4: FOREST LEGISLATION IN THE MIDDLE AGES*

(According to the *Revue Forestière*)   *See Chapter 10, p.

PRINCIPAL REIGNS	LEGISLATIVE AND STATUTORY TEXTS	
Philippe II Auguste (1180–1223)	1219—Ordinance of Gisors on the sale of wood	THE CRUSADES (1095–1291)
Louis IX (Saint-Louis) (1226–1270)		
Philippe IV Le Bel (1285–1314)	1291—Ordinance (August 1291) defining the role of the masters of the *Eaux et Forêts*, investigators, inquisitors and reformers	
Louis X Le Hutin (1314–1316)	1315—Louis X specifies the meaning of *morts-bois* in the *charte aux Normands*	
Philippe V Le Long (1316–1322)	1318—Ordinance on the problems of the officers of the *Eaux et Forêts*	
Philippe VI de Valois (1328–1350)	1346—Ordinance of Brunoy organizing the administration of the forests, waterways and fishing	
Charles V Le Sage (1364–1380)	1371—Creation of the "*Souverain Maître des Eaux et Forêts par tout le Royaume*" 1376—Ordinance of Melun (July) on the hammers —Ordinance of September 3, 1376 on the exploitation of navy timber	THE HUNDRED YEARS WAR (1337–1453)
Charles VI Le Bien-Aimé (1380–1422)	1384—Creation of the "Souverain et general maître ordonnateur, dispositeur et reformateur, seul et pour le rout des Eaux et Forêts par tout le royaume" 1396—Ordinance forbidding the poor to hunt 1402—Ordinance on hunting and forests and waterways 1413—Ordinance of Caboche	
Charles VII (1422–1461)		
Louis XI (1461–1483)	One century of legislative void regarding the forests	
Charles VIII (1483–1498)		
Louis XII le Père du peuple (1498–1515)		
François Ier (1515–1547)	1516—Ordinance reviving those of 1346, 1376 and 1402 1518—Ordinance on the forest criminal code 1520—Limitation of the rights of forest owners to guarantee the supply of Paris in wood 1523—Ordinance of June 1523 on seed-bearers 1537—Ordinance on the sales of woods belonging to the Church 1544—Ordinance on the exploitation *à tire et aire* and on the minimum age to cut seed-bearers in the coppice	THE "RENAISSANCE"

notes ·

INTRODUCTION

    1. The titles of the works cited in the notes are given in abbreviated form; for the complete reference consult the bibliography.

CHAPTER 1

    1. P. de Crescence, *Le livre des prouffits champestres et ruraux.*

    2. B. Boullard, *Les arbres aussi se transmettent des messages.*

    3. Stevens, *Le définition agro-économique de la terre.*

    4. *Guide de recherche du groupe d'histoire des forêts françaises*, 1982, p. 34.

    5. Gourou, *Pour une géographie humaine*, p. 93, 114.

CHAPTER 2

    1. Chrétien de Troyes, *Perceval*, p. 35.

    2. Beroul, *Le roman de Tristan.*

    3. For a great part of the following information concerning edible wild plants, I am much indebted to François Couplan, author of *"Plantes sauvages comestibles"* in *Encyclopédie des plantes comestibles de l'Europe*, 1985.

    4. Le Roy-Ladurie, *Postface à l'histoire de la campagne française*, p. 355.

    5. Bechmann, *Les racines des cathédrales*, p. 37–38.

    6. Cited by Huffel, p. 120 and 131.

    7. *Archives du Loiret*, cited by Maulde.

    8. Xenophon, *L'art de la chasse.*

    9. *Compte de Vitry*, 1455, cited by Maulde, p. 472.

    10. *Archives du Loiret, compte des Eaux et Forêts*, cited by Maulde.

    11. D.M. Stenton, *English Society.*

    12. John Manwood, cited by D.M. Stenton.

    13. Perroy, *La féodalité en France.*

    14. Sainct Yon, *Les édits et ordonnances* . . .

    15. Maury, *Les forêts de la France* . . .

    16. *Ordonnances du roi Jean le Bon*, décembre 1355, art. 13.

17. Sainct Yon, *Les édits et ordonnances* . . .
18. *Enquêtes de 1343 à 1416*, cited by Maulde, p. 459.
19. Sainct Yon, *Les édits et ordonnances* . . .
20. Maulde, *Etude sur la condition forestière de l'Orléanais.*
21. *Id.*
22. Chauffourt, *Edits et ordonnances.*
23. Verrier, *Polyptyque du Vieil Rentier d'Audenarde.*
24. Guérin, *La vie rurale en Sologne.*
25. P. de Crescence, *Le livre des prouffits* . . .
26. Caesar, Lib. VI, chap. XXXI.
27. The author warns the readers that the above lists do not allow them to eat or safely use any of the above mentioned plants. Names, characteristics, and properties of similar plants may be very different in different countries and the translation of their names is sometimes approximate.

CHAPTER 3

1. G. Roupnel, *Histoire de la campagne française*, p. 123.
2. G. Sautter, "Terroirs d'Afrique occidentale."
3. M. Le Lannou, *Pâtres et paysans de la Sardaigne.*
4. E. Le Roy Ladurie, *Histoire du climat depuis l'an mil.*
5. G. Duby, *L'économie rurale et la vie des campagnes.*
6. I. Guérin, *La vie rurale en Sologne.*
7. J. Mollin, *Une région de contact.* . . .
8. For the present chapter I am much indebted to Sigaut, *L'agriculture et le feu.*
9. Sigaut, *L'agriculture et le feu.*
10. Métailié, *Le feu pastoral.*
11. Lefèvre, S.H.A.P.I.F., 1977.
12. Le Goff, *La civilisation de l'Occident médiéval.*
13. Sigaut, *L'agriculture et le feu.*
14. Sigaut, *L'agriculture et le feu.*
15. Killian, *L'importance de la scie dans l'histoire.* . . .
16. Bloch, *Les travaux et les jours.*
17. Raban Maur, *De originibus.*
18. Mannerot, *Passages d'outremer.*
19. Ljubomirov, *Istoriceskie Zapiski*, 1941, cited by Devèze.
20. Le Goff, *La civilisation de l'Occident médiéval.*
21. G. Fourquin, *Le premier Moyen Age* . . ., p. 404.
22. B. Gille, *Histoire des techniques.*
23. L. Assier Andrieu, *Aspects économiques.* . . .
24. Killian, *L'importance de la scie dans l'histoire* . . ., p. 133.
25. Chauffourt, *Édits et ordonnances* . . ., p. 103.
26. Legros, cited by Higounet.
27. Sinclair, *Code de l'agriculture.*

CHAPTER 4

1. S. Lefèvre, *La reconstitution des monastères.* . . .
2. Brouillon, *Givry en Argonne.*
3. Barthélémy, *Recueil des chartes de l'abbaye Notre-Dame de Cheminon.*
4. According to Buirette, cited by Maas.
5. Maury, *Les forêts de la France.*
6. Florac, *De modernis francorum regibus.*
7. Lalore, *Collections des principaux cartulaires.*

8. Reinaud, *Invasion des Sarrasins en France*, cited by Maury.
9. Most of the following examples, except for other mentions, are due to S. Lefèvre, *Haies, bois clos, défens et garennes*.
10. Duby, *La société aux XIe et XIIe siècles dans la région mâconnaise*.
11. Rabelais, *Pantaqruel*, chap. XVI, p. 260.
12. Maulde, *Condition forestière de l'Orléanais*, p. 224–50.
13. Buirette, *Histoire de Sainte-Menehould . . .*, cited by Maas.
14. A. Fourquin, *Le temps de la croissance*.
15. Le Goff, *L' apogée de la France Médiévale*.
16. Many of the following examples are due to the study by S. Lefèvre, *Une famille de promoteurs de défrichements . . .*
17. The following examples, if no other source is given, are from Guérard, *Cartulaire de Saint-Père-de Chartres, Cartulaire de Champagne* and have been cited by S. Lefèvre et Georges Duby.
18. Maulde, *La Condition forestière . . .*, p. 115.
19. *Recueil des actes de Philippe Auguste*.
20. Perroy, *La terre et les paysans. . . .*
21. *Archives de Saône-et-Loire*.
22. Barthélémy, *Notice historique sur les communes du canton de Ville-sur-Tourbe*.
23. Duby, *L' économie rurale. . . .*
24. *Archives de la Côte-d'Or*, 3,11476.
25. Duby, *L' économie rurale . . .*, p. 164.
26. Guérard, *Cartulaire de Saint-Père-de-Chartres*.
27. Except for mention to the contrary, most of the examples in this chapter were taken from S. Lefèvre and P. M. Folliot.
28. Lesort, cited by Maas, p. 43.

CHAPTER 5

1. Devèze, *Le pâturage au XVI siècle*.
2. Devèze, *La vie de la forêt française*.
3. cf. Devèze, *Le pâturage au XVI siècle; La vie de la forêt française*; Fourquin, *Les campagnes de la région*; Bézard, *La vie rurale*; Grand et Delatouche, *L' agriculture au Moyen-Âge*.
4. Sainct Yon, *Édits*, p. 533.
5. Roupnel, p. 106.
6. De Barthélémy, *L'ancien diocèse de Souhel*, p. 402.
7. P.M. Folliot, "Les Templiers . . .", *Bulletin de la Société archéologique d'Eure-et-Loire*, p. 119.
8. Maulde, *La condition forestière . . .*, p. 109.
9. Maas, *Les moines défricheurs . . .*, p. 43.
10. Rémy, "L'abbaye de Mautier en Argonne."
11. Maulde, *La condition forestière . . .*, p. 110.
12. Kuhnholtz, *La terre incendiée*, p. 213.
13. Id., p. 22.
14. Soltner, *Les grandes productions végétales*, p. 393.
15. Chauffourt, *Édits et ordonnances . . .*, p. 110.
16. *Coutumier de Saint-Aubin-d'Angers*, p. 262.
17. *Coutume de Folgara* (northern Italy), cited by Duby.
18. Translated into French from the Latin text of 1155.
19. Soltner, *Les grandes productions végétales*.
20. Chauffourt, *Édits et ordonnances . . .*, p. 113.
21. Serres, *Le théâtre d'agriculture et mesnage des champs*.

22. Sclafert, *Déboisements et pâturages au Moyen Âge*.
23. Boutry, *La forêt d'Ardenne*.
24. I. Guérin, *La vie rurale en Sologne aux XIV et XV siècles*.
25. Duby, *L'économie rurale . . .*, p. 708.
26. Aristote, *Histoire naturelle*, Lib. 8.
27. *Assises de 1184*, cited by Duby, *L'économie rurale . . .*, p. 665.
28. Planhol, *Le monde islamique: essai de géographie religieuse*.
29. Polyptique, ed. Longnon.
30. F.L. Ganshof, "Le domaine gantois de l'abbaye Saint-Pierre . . ."
31. Higounet, *Forêts de l'Europe occidentale du V au XI siècle*.
32. Chrétien de Troyes, *Perceval*.
33. F. Rabelais, *Gargantua*, chap. XXI, p. 84.
34. Examples cited by S. Lefèvre, *La défense de la frontière normande . . .*
35. Chrétien de Troyes, *Perceval*.
36. Brooke, *The Twelfth Century . . .*, p. 134.
37. Bautier, *The Economic Development of Medieval Europe*.
38. Id., p. 205.

CHAPTER 6

1. Chauffourt, *Édits et ordonnances . . .*, p. 116.
2. Huffel, *Économie forestière*, p. 115.
3. Bautier, *The Economic Development of Medieval Europe*.
4. Toussaint, *Forêts et forges*, p. 279.
5. Chauffourt, *Les édits et ordonnances . . . .*
6. Sclafert, *Le Haut-Dauphiné au Moyen Age . . . .*
7. Gille, *Histoire des techniques*.
8. James, *Chartres, les constructeurs*.
9. Linnard, *Historical Importance of Charcoal Burning*.
10. Maury, *Les forêts de France*.
11. Guérard, *Cartulaire de l'église de Notre-Dame de Paris*, cited by M. Bloch.

CHAPTER 7

1. Maury, *Les forêts de la France*.
2. Venet, *Les anciennes forêts*, p. 43.
3. Caesar, Lib. V-XL, p. 159.
4. Joinville, *Histoire de Saint Louis*, p. 195.
5. Killian, *L'importance de la scie . . .*, p. 135.
6. Bechmann, *Les racines des cathédrales*, p. 216–224.
7. French text by Gimpel according to Panofsky.
8. Crescence, *Le livre des prouffits champestres . . .*, chap.V.
9. Harvey, *The Medieval Architect*, p. 146.
10. Salzman, *Building in England*.
11. Viollet-le-Duc, *Dictionnaire*, t.3, p. 25.
12. Id., t.3, p. 23.
13. Id., t.2, p. 215.
14. Enlart, *Manuel d'archéologie française*, t1, p. 681.
15. Bechmann, *Les racines des cathédrales*, p. 261.

CHAPTER 8

1. Cicéron, *Philippiques*, 2–76.
2. Pognon, *La vie quotidienne en l'an mille*, p. 265.
3. Villon, *Ballade de la grosse Margot*.

4. Rabelais, *Pantagruel*, Tiers-Livre, ch. XVII, p. 410.
5. Chauffourt, *Édits et ordonnances . . .*, p. 116.
6. Caesar, Lib II, XXXIII, p. 70.
7. Devèze, *La vie de la forêt française*, t.II, p. 104.
8. Crescence, Liv. VII.
9. Peigné-Delatour cited by S. Lefèvre, *Politique forestière . . .*
10. H. Bernard, *Des métiers et des hommes.*

CHAPTER 9
1. Huffel, *Les méthodes de l'aménagement forestier*, p. 14.
2. Id., p. 9.
3. Froidour, *Instructions*, t.I, p. 7.
4. Sainct Yon, *Les édits et ordonnances.*
5. Froidour, *Instruction*, I, p. 7.
6. Huffel, *Économie forestière . . .*, p. 47.
7. Id., p. 47.
8. Id., p. 50.
9. Devèze, "Les forêts d'Allemagne au XVI siècle . . ."
10. Devèze, "Contribution à l'histoire de la forêt rusee."

CHAPTER 10
1. Coustumier général, t.I, p. 210.
2. Huffel, *Économie forestière*, p. 86.
3. Stevens, *La définition agro-économique de la terre.*
4. Huffel, *Économie forestière*, p. 68.
5. Cited by Racham, p. 181.
6. Isambert, *Recueil général . . .*, t. V, p. 451.
7. Geneau de Sainte-Gertrude, *La législation . . .*, p. 72.
8. Bezard, *La vie rurale dans le sud de la région parisienne.*
9. Most of the following examples are taken from Maulde, *La condition forestière . . .*
10. Maulde, op. cit.
11. Maulde. op. cit.
12. Devèze, *La vie de la forêt française.*
13. Sainct Yon, *Coutumes de Lorraine*, XV, 32, p. 418.
14. Account of 1424, cited by Maulde, p. 358.
15. Hanauer, cited by Huffel.
16. Chauffourt, *Édits et ordonnances*, p. 103.
17. *Roman de Rou*, adapted by Pierre Daix.
18. *Édit de Saint-Germain-en-Laye* (April 1667).
19. *Cahier de doléances de Frenelle-la-Grande. Bailliage de Mirecourt.*
20. *Cahier de doléances des bouchers et charcutiers de Troyes.*
21. *Cahier de doléances de Loury. Bailliage d'Orléans.*
22. *Cahier de doléances d'Ingré. Bailliage d'Orléans.*

CHAPTER 11
1. Maury, *Les forêts de la France . . .*, p. 144.
2. Caesar, Lib II, XVII.
3. Higounet, *Les forêts d'Europe . . .*, p. 382.
4. Devèze, *Les forêts d'Allemagne . . .*
5. Caesar, Lib II, XIX, p. 61.
6. Gollut, *Mémoire historique de la république séquanaise*, p. 84.

7. C. Estienne, *L'agriculture et la maison rustique*, p. 93.
8. Linnard, *S.I.H.F.*, p. 207.
9. Sainct Yon, *Les édits et ordonnances*, p. 327.
10. Rackham, *S.I.H.F.*, p. 181.
11. *Quatre traictés utiles et délectables de l'agriculture*, p. 560.
12. Le Goff, *L'apogée de la France urbaine mediévale*, p. 274.
13. Chedeville, *Histoire de la France urbaine*, p. 160.

CHAPTER 12
1. Aug. Chevalier and L. Hedin cited by Kuhnholtz-Lordat.
2. Maury, *Les forêts de la France.*
3. Guillaume Le Breton, *Philippide*, Lib. III, verse 102, cited by Brial, *Historiens de France.*
4. Maury, *Les forêts de la France . . .*, p. 225–227.
5. Maury, *Croyances et légendes.*
6. Maulde, *La condition forestière de l'Orléanais. . . .*
7. Coremans, *L'année de l'ancienne Belgique*, p. 22.
8. H. Dontenville, *La mythologie française*, Paris, 1948.
9. Parthenopex de Blois, cited by Maury, *Les forêts de la France . . .*, p. 39.
10. J. Le Goff, *Pour un autre Moyen Age*, p. 288.
11. According to Walter Map, cited by Le Goff, *Pour un autre Moyen Age*, p. 310.
12. J. d'Arras, *Roman de Mélusine.*
13. Le Goff, *Pour un autre Moyen Age*, p. 326.
14. M. Cohen, *L'écriture.*
15. O'Donovan, *A Grammar of English Language*;
Dumeril, *De l'origine des runes.*

EPILOGUE
1. Caesar, Lib. VI, XXIX, p. 196.

BIBLIOGRAPHY ·

ABBREVIATIONS

SIHF	Symposium International d'Histoire Forestière (Nancy, septembre 1979)
SAEL	Société Archéologique d'Eure-et-Loir
SHAPIF	Sociétés Historiques et Archéologiques de Corbeil, d'Étampes et de Hurepoix
ENGREF	École Nationale du Génie Rural, des Eaux et des Forêts
INRA	Institut National de la Recherche Agronomique
CNRS	Centre National de la Recherche Scientifique

AGRICOLA (Georges), *De re metallica*, Bâle, 1556.

ASSIER-ANDRIEU (Louis), «Aspects économiques de l'organisation et de l'évolution de la forge de village en Haute-Catalogne», *Revue ethnologie française*, n° 3, Paris, 1982.

ANONYME, *Quatre traictés utiles et délectables de l'agriculture*, Paris, 1560.

BADRÉ (Louis), *Histoire de la forêt française*, Paris, 1983.

BARTHÉLEMY (E.), *Recueil des chartes de l'abbaye Notre-Dame de Cheminon*, Paris, 1883.

———*Notice historique sur les communes du canton de Ville-sur-Tourbe*, Paris, 1865.

BAUDOT, *Les Noms des défrichements dans la toponymie de la France*, Bruxelles, 1949.

BARRAU (Jacques), «Culture itinérante et sur brûlis», *Études rurales*, 1972.

BAUER (Erich), «Der spanische Wald in der Geschichte», *Actes du S.I.H.F.*, Nancy, 1982.

BAUTIER (Robert Henri), *The Economic Development of Medieval Europe*, London, 1971.

BAUTIER (A.-M.), «Les plus anciennes mentions de moulins hydrauliques industriels et de moulins à vent», *Bulletin philologique et historique*, 1960.

BECHMANN (Roland), «L'énergie hydraulique», *Aménagement et Nature*, n° 42, Paris, 1976.

————«L'Architecture gothique: une expression des conditions du milieu», *Pour la science,*, n° 4, Paris, 1978.

————«Des forêts à l'architecture», *Aménagement et Nature*, n° 53, Paris, 1979.

————*Les Racines des cathédrales (architecture gothique, expression des conditions du milieu)*, Paris, 1981.

BECK (X. M.), *Les Techniques sidérurgiques.*

BECKER (M.), PICARD (J.-F.) et TIMBAL (J.), *La Forêt*, Paris, 1981.

BECKMANN, *Beiträge zur Geschichte der Erfindungen*, Leipzig, 1780.

BÉROUL, *Le Roman de Tristan* (adapt. Muret), Paris, 1913.

BERTHON (R.), *La Forêt de Saint-Germain-en-Laye* (Collection les Forêts de France), Paris, 1857.

BERTRAND (Georges), «Vers une histoire écologique», *Histoire de la France rurale*, t. l, Paris, 1979.

BETOLAUD (Yves), «Forêt et civilisation urbaine», revue *Aménagement et Nature*, n° 3, Paris, 1966.

BEZARD (Yvonne), *La Vie rurale dans le sud de la région parisienne de 1450 à 1560*, Paris, 1932.

BLAIS (R.), *La Forêt*, Paris, 1938.

BLOCH (Marc), *Rois et serfs* (Thèse), Paris, 1920.

————«Champs et Villages», *Annales d'histoire économique et sociale*, 1934.

————«Avènement et conquête du moulin à eau», *Annales d'histoire économique et sociale*, 1935.

————*Les Travaux et les jours*, Paris, 1939.

————«Les invasions, occupation du sol et peuplement», *Annales d'histoire sociale*, 1945.

————*Les Caractères généraux de l'histoire rurale française*, Paris, 1952.

BOISROUVRAY (F. de), *La Forêt au fil de l'homme*, Paris, 1979.

BOISSIÈRE (J.), «Les forêts de la vallée de la Seine entre Paris et Rouen», *Annales historiques du Mantais*, n° 6, 1979.

BOULLARD (B.), «Les arbres aussi se transmettent des messages», *La Forêt privée*, 1981.

BOURGENOT (L.), «La forêt vierge et la forêt cultivée», *Revue forestière française*, Nancy, 1973.

————«Histoire des forêts feuillues», *Revue forestière française*, Nancy, 1977.

BOUTRY (L.), «La forêt d'Ardenne», *Annales de géographie*, XXIX, 1920.

BRIE (Jehan de), see JEHAN DE BRIE.

BRISEBARRE (A. N.), *Bergers des Cévennes*, Paris, 1978.

BROOKE (C.), *The Twelfth Century Renaissance*, London, 1961.

BROUILLON (J.), *Givry en Argonne*, Châlon-sur-Marne, 1867.

BRUNET, *Structure agraire et économie rurale entre Seine et Oise*, Caen, 1960.

————«Problèmes relatifs aux structures agraires en Basse-Normandie», *Annales de Normandie*, 1955.

BUIRETTE, *Histoire de la ville de Saint-Menehould et de ses environs*, 1837.

BUR (M.), «Le défrichement et le partage de la forêt du Mans, près de Meaux 1150–1250», *Bulletin philologique et historique*, 1963.

CALMETTE (J.) et HIGOUNET (C.), *Le Monde féodal*, Paris, 1951.

CARREZ (J.), *Les Hommes et leur forêt*, Paris, 1973.

CARUS-WILSON (E.-M.), «An industrial revolution of the XIIIth century», *Essays in Economic History*, London, 1954.

C.E.N.E.C.A., *La Forêt dans le monde (Colloque)*, Paris, 1978.

CÉSAR (Caïus, Julius), *Guerre des Gaules* (trad. Constans), Paris, 1926.

CHAMPIER (L.), «Structure des terroirs bourguignons», *Annales de Bourgogne*, 1955.

CHAPELOT (Jean) et FOSSIER (Robert), *Le Village et la Maison au Moyen Âge*, Paris, 1980.

CHAUFFOURT (Jacques de), *Édits et Ordonnances des Eaux et des Forêts*, 1603.

CHAUMEIL (L.), «Origine du bocage en Bretagne», *Mélanges Lucien Febvre*, 1954.

CHAUVET (P.) et PONS (P.), *Les Hautes-Alpes, hier, aujourd'hui, demain*, Gap, 1975.

CHEDEVILLE (André), *Chartres et ses campagnes XIᵉ-XIIᵉ siècles*, Paris, 1973.

———«De la cité à la ville 1000–1150», *Histoire de la France urbaine*, Paris, 1980.

CHILDE (G.), *The Story of Tools*, London, 1944.

CHRÉTIEN DE TROYES, *Yvain ou le Chevalier au lion* (traduction de C. Buridant et J. Trotin), Paris, 1972.

CLEMENT-GRANDCOURT (Michel), *Un étang: pour quoi faire?* Paris, 1982.

CLERS (Bertrand de), *Chasse et nature en Europe*, Nancy, 1959.

C.N.R.S., *Aspects de la recherche sur l'histoire des forêts françaises*, 1980.

COCHET (Pierre), *La Forêt*, Paris, 1963.

COHEN (Marcel), *L'Écriture*, Paris, 1953.

COLVIN (H. M.), *History of King's Works*, London, 1963.

———*Building Accounts of King Henry II*, Oxford, 1971.

CRESCENZI (Pietro dei), dit Pierre de Crescence, *Opus Ruralium Commodium*, 1320. (Translated into French in 1373, under the title: *Le Livre des prouffits champestres et ruraux*, éd. Jean Bonhomme, Paris, 1486.)

DARBY (H. C.), *Domesday Geography of Eastern England*, Cambridge, 1952.

———*Domesday Geography of Midland England*, Cambridge, 1954.

———*The Domesday Geography of South East England*, Cambridge, 1952.

———*The Domesday Geography of Northern England*, Cambridge, 1962.

DAUZAT, *Le Village et le paysan*, Paris, 1942.

DECARREAUX (J.), *Les Moines et la civilisation*, Paris, 1962.

DESCHESNES (Georges), *Législation forestière dans l'antiquité romaine*, Paris, 1883.

DEFFONTAINES (P.), *L'Homme et la forêt*, Paris, 1933.

DEVÈZE (Michel), *La Vie de la forêt française au XVIᵉ siècle*, (2 tomes), Paris, 1961.

———*Histoire des forêts*, Paris, 1965.

———*La Forêt et les communautés rurales, XVIᵉ-XVIIIᵉ siècles*, Paris, 1982.

———«Le pâturage du XVIᵉ siècle dans la moitié Nord de la France d'après les coutumes«, *Bulletin philologique et historique*, 1967, vol. 1, Paris, 1969.

———«Les forêts d'Allemagne au XVIᵉ siècle», *Revue forestière française*.

———*Contribution à l'histoire de la forêt russe*.

DION (R.), *Essai sur la formation du paysage rural français*, Tours, 1934.

———«La part de la géographie et la part de l'histoire dans l'explication de l'habitat du Bassin parisien», *Société géographique de Lille*, 1946.

DOMET (P.), *Histoire de la forêt d'Orléans*, Orléans, 1892.

O'DONOVAN (J.), *A Grammar of Irish Language*, Dublin, 1845.

DONTENVILLE (Henri), *La Mythologie française*, Paris, 1948.

DUBY (Georges), *L'Économie rurale et la vie des campagnes dans l'Occident médiéval*, Paris, 1962, t. I et II.

———*Guerriers et paysans*, Paris, 1976.

———*Saint-Bernard et l'art cistercien*, Paris 1976.

———*La Société aux XIᵉ et XIIᵉ siècles dans la région mâconnaise*, Paris, 1953.

———*Le Temps des cathédrales*, Paris, 1976.

DUBY (G.) et MANDROU (R.), *Histoire de la civilisation française*, Paris, 1958.

DUBY (G.) et WALLON (A.), *Histoire de la France rurale*, t. 1: BERTRAND (Georges), BAILLOUD (G.), BERTRAND (Claude), LE GLAY (M.), FOURQUIN (G.), Paris, 1975.

DUBY (G.), CHEDEVILLE (A.), LE GOFF (J.), ROSSIAUD (J.), *Histoire de la France urbaine*, t. 2, «*La ville médiévale*» (*vol. dirigé par J. Le Goff*), Paris, 1980.

DUHAMEL DU MONCEAU (H.-L.), *Éléments d'agriculture*, Paris, 1762.

DUMERIL (E.), «De l'origine des runes», *Mélanges archéologiques et littéraires*, Paris, 1850.

DUVAL (M.), *Régie seigneuriale et crise forestière en Bretagne au XVIIe siècle*, Rennes, 1978.

EDLIN (H. L.), *Forestry in Great Britain* (Forestry Commission), London, 1969.

EIDSVIK (Harold), «Évolution du rôle des parcs nationaux et des zones protégées par rapport aux populations des écosystèmes», *Études et Recherches, 3e* Assises internationales de l'environnement, vol. 4, Paris, 1981.

ENLART AMILLE *Manuel d'archéologie française*, Paris, 1927.

ESTIENNE (Charles) et LIEBAULT (J.), *L'Agriculture et la maison rustique*, 1590.

FEBVRE (Lucien), *Philippe II et la Franche-Comté*, Paris, 1915.

——«Une enquête: la forge de village», *Annales d'histoire économique et sociale*, 1935.

FEL (A.), «Réflexions sur les paysages agraires des hautes terres du Massif central», *Annales de l'Est*, n° 21, Nancy, 1959.

FELLER (P.) et TOURRER (F.), *L'Outil*, Bruxelles, 1970.

FISCHESSER (B.), *La Vie de la forêt*, Genève, 1970.

FOLLIOT (Pierre Marie), «Les Templiers dans la baillie de Chartres», *Bulletin de la S.A.E.L.*, n°s 96 & 97, Chartres, 1983.

FOSSIER (R.), *La Terre et les hommes en Picardie jusqu'au XIIIe siècle*, Paris, 1968.

FOUQUE (Bertrand), «Pour une économie énergétique spatiale», *Aménagement et Nature*, n° 65, Paris, 1962.

FOURNIER (G.), *Peuplement rural en Basse-Auvergne durant le haut Moyen Âge*, Paris, 1962.

FOURQUIN (G.), *Histoire économique de l'Occident médiéval*, Paris, 1969.

——«Le premier Moyen Âge, Le temps de la croissance», *Histoire de la France rurale*, t. 1, Paris, 1975.

——*Les Campagnes de la région parisienne à la fin du Moyen Âge, du milieu du XIIIe siècle au début du XVIe siècle*, Thèse de lettres, Paris, 1959.

FRAPPIER (J.), *Étude sur Yvain ou le Chevalier au lion*, de Chrétien de Troyes, Paris, 1969.

FROIDOUR (L. de), *Instructions pour la vente des bois du Roy*, Toulouse, 1678.

FRUHAUF (Christian), *Forêt et société: de la forêt paysanne à la forêt capitaliste en pays de Sault sous l'Ancien Régime* (C.N.R.S.), Toulouse, 1980.

GADANT (Jean), *Techniques et matériel d'exploitation forestière*, Meymac, 1951.

GANSHOF (F. L.), «Le domaine gantois de l'abbaye Saint-Pierre au mont Blandin à l'époque carolingienne», *Revue belge de philologie et d'histoire*, 1948.

GENEAU DE SAINTE-GERTRUDE (M.), «La législation forestière sous l'Ancien Régime», *Revue des Eaux et Forêts*, 1942–1943.

GERBAUT (Alain), «Sur le bois de chauffage de Paris du XIIIe siècle à Louis XIV, *Annales forestières*, 1949.

GILLE (Bertrand), «Le moulin à eau, une révolution technique médiévale». *Techniques et civilisations*, III, 1954.

——«L'évolution de la technique sidérurgique. Esquisse d'un schéma», *Revue d'histoire des mines et de la métallurgie*, 1970.

——*Histoire des techniques*, Paris, 1978.

GLESINGER (Egon), *Demain, l'âge du bois*, Paris, 1951.

GOBLET 'ALVIELLA, *Histoire des bois et des forêts de Belgique*, t. 1, Bruxelles, 1927.

GODEFROY (Frédéric), *Dictionnaire de l'ancienne langue française du IXe au XVe siècle*, 10 vol., Paris, 1881-1902.

GOLLUT, *Mémoire historique de la république séquanoise*, Dijon, 1647.

GOODMAN (W. L.), *The History of Wood-Working Tools*, London, 1964.

GOUROU (P.), *Pour une géographie humaine*, Paris, 1973.

GRAND (Roger) et DELATOUCHE (R.), *L'Agriculture au Moyen Âge de la fin de l'empire romain au XVIe siècle*, Paris, 1950.

GRANDMESNIL, «La forêt de Saint-Germain-Laval au Moyen Âge», *Mémoires de la Féd. des S.H.A.P.I.F.*, Paris, 1977.

GROSSETESTE (Robert de), *Housebondrie*, 1240.

Groupe d'histoire des forêts françaises, *Guide de Recherche* (C.N.R.S.—Institut d'histoire moderne et contemporaine), Paris, 1982.

GUÉRARD (Benjamin), *Cartulaire de Saint-Père-de-Chartres*, Paris, 1898.

GUÉRIN (I.), *La Vie rurale en Sologne aux XIVe et XVe siècles*, Paris, 1959.

GUILLOT-CHÊNE (Gérard), *Le Flottage en Morvan du bois pour Paris*, Paris, 1979.

GUINIER (P.), *Technique forestière*, Paris, 1947.

GUINOT (R.), *Plantations et reboisement*, Paris, 1944.

GUYOT (J.) et GIBASSIER, *Les Noms des arbres*, Paris, 1961.

HARVEY (John), *The Medieval Architect*, London, 1972.

———*The Master Builders—Architecture in the Middle Ages*, London, 1971.

HENLEY (Walter of), cf. WALTER.

HENRY (Bernard), *Des métiers et des hommes au village*, Paris, 1975.

HENRY (Simone), «La forêt de Bouconne», *Étude de géographie historique dans les travaux du laboratoire forestier de Toulouse*, Toulouse, 1946.

HENSEL (Witold), Perspectives de la recherche archéologique sur le milieu rural en Europe occidentale du haut Moyen Âge.

HIGOUNET (C.), «Contribution à l'étude de la toponymie du défrichement: artigues du Bordelais et du Bazadais», *3e congrès international de toponymie et d'anthropologie*, 1951.

———«L'occupation du sol du pays entre Tarn et Garonne», *Annales du Midi*, 1953.

———*Hagiotoponymie et Histoire*, 1958.

———«La géo-histoire», *L'Histoire et ses méthodes*, Paris, 1961.

———«Les forêts de l'Europe occidentale du ve siècle à l'an mil» (*XIIIe Settimana di studio del Centro Italiano di Studi sull'alto Medio Evo, 1965*), Spolete, 1966.

———*Paysages et villages neufs du Moyen Âge*, Bordeaux, 1975.

———«Les forêts de l'Europe occidentale», *Agricoltura e mondo rurale in occidente nell'alto medievo*, Gent, 1966.

HUBERT et autres, *Les Terrains boisés* (Institut de développement forestier), Paris, 1978.

HUFFEL (G.), *Économie forestière* (t. l), Paris (1904), 1913.

———*Histoire des forêts françaises de l'origine jusqu'à la suppression des maîtrises des Eaux et Forêts* (*E.N.G.R.E.F.*), *Paris, 1925.*

———*Les Méthodes de l'aménagement forestier en France.* Nancy, 1926.

HUMBERT (R.), *Le Sabotier*, Paris, 1979.

I.N.R.A., *Reboisement des montagnes. Systèmes agraires*, Orléans, 1979.

———Le Reboisement en montagne depuis l'empire ottoman, 1981.

ISAMBERT, *Recueil général des anciennes lois françaises (29 vol.)*, Paris, 1825.

JACQUIOT (C.), *La Forêt*, Paris, 1970.

———*Écologie appliquée à la sylviculture*, Paris, 1983.

JAMES (J.), *Chartres: les constructeurs* (3 tomes), Chartres, 1977–1982.

JANSSEN (W.), *Studien zur wüstungen wüstungsfrage in fränkischen Altsiedelland zwischen Rhein, Mosel und Eifel nordrand*, Bonn, 1975.

JOINVILLE (Jean de), *Histoire de Saint Louis* (1309), éd. de Wailly, Paris, 1874.

JEHAN DE BRIE, *Le Bon Berger*. Traité de bergerie (XIVᵉ siècle), rééd., Paris, 1879.

JUILLARD (E.), Genèse des paysages agraires *(Annales E.S.C.)*, Paris, 1951.

JUILLARD (E.), DE PLANHOL (X.), MEYNIER (A.), SAUTTER (G.), «Les pays d'open-field du Nord et de l'Est», *Structures agraires et paysages ruraux; Annales de l'Est*, 1957.

KEILLING (Jean), «Le sol et l'agronomie», *Encyclopédie de l'écologie*, Paris, 1977.

KILLIAN (Phil. Herbert), «Die Bedeutung der Säge in der Geschichte der Forstnützung (L'importance de la scie dans l'histoire de l'exploitation forestière)», *Actes du S.I.H.F.*, Nancy, 1979, Paris, 1982.

KUHNHOLTZ-LORDAT (G.), *La Terre incendiée*, Nîmes.

LALORE (C.), *Collection des principaux cartulaires de l'ancien diocèse de Troyes*, Paris, 1875–1882.

—Le *Polyptyque de Montier en Der*, Paris, 1878.

LANGLOIS (Émile), *Compagnon du devoir*, Paris, 1983.

LE BOUVIER (Gilles) dit BERRY, *Le Livre de la description des pays*, 1450, Paris, 1908.

LEFÈVRE (Suzanne), «Un entrepreneur de défrichements au XIIᵉ siècle: David de la Forest», *Mémoires de la S.H.A.P.I.F.*, t. 28, Paris, 1977.

————«La défense de la frontière normande et l'aménagement de la forêt d'Yveline», *103ᵉ Congrès des sociétés savantes*, Nancy-Metz, 1978.

————«Les monastères et la rénovation du réseau routier médiéval en Ile-de-France», *104ᵉ Congrès des sociétés savantes*, Bordeaux, 1979.

————«Une grange de l'abbaye des Vaux-de-Cernay», *Bulletin de la S.H.A.C.E.H.*, Corbeil, 1980.

————«Une famille de promoteurs de défrichements au Moyen Âge: la Maison de Châtillon», *La Forêt privée*, n° 132, Paris, 1980.

————«La politique forestière du chapitre de Notre-Dame de Paris au Moyen Âge», *La Forêt privée*, n° 139, Paris, 1981.

————«La reconstitution des monastères après les invasions normandes en Ile-de-France», *Mémoires de la S.H.A.P.I.F.*, t. 32, Paris, 1981.

————«Haies, bois clos, défens et garennes dans la région parisienne, au Moyen Âge», *La Forêt privée*, n° 148, Paris, 1982.

————«Politique forestière des monastères de l'Ile-de-France XIIᵉ-XIIIᵉ siècle», *Actes du S.I.H.F.*, Nancy, 1982.

LE GOFF (Jacques), *La Civilisation de l'Occident médiéval*, Paris, 1964.

————*Marchands et banquiers au Moyen Âge*, Paris, (1950), 1962.

————*Les Intellectuels au Moyen Âge*, Paris, 1957.

————*Pour un autre Moyen Âge*, Paris, 1977.

————«L'apogée de la France urbaine médiévale 1150–1330», *Histoire de la France urbaine*, Paris, 1980.

LE GOFF (H.), et VIDAL-NAQUET (P.), Lévi-Strauss en Brocéliande, *Claude Lévi-Strauss: textes réunis*, Paris, 1979.

LE LANNOU (M.), *Pâtres et paysans de la Sardaigne*, Tours, 1941.

LE RAY (J.), *La Forêt française*, Paris, 1977.

LE ROY LADURIE (Emmanuel), Histoire et climat, *Annales E.S.C.*, 1959.

————Aspects historiques de la nouvelle climatologie, *Revue historique*, 1961.

————*Histoire du climat depuis l'an mille*, Paris, 1967.

LESORT, *Les Chartes du Clermontois (1096–1352) conservées au musée de Condé*, Paris, 1904.

LIEUTAGHI (P.), *Le Livre des arbres, arbustes et arbrisseaux*, Paris, 1969.

LINNARD (W.), Historical importance of charcoal burning in the woodlands of Wales, *Actes du S.I.H.F.*, Nancy, 1982.

LOESETH (E.), *Le Roman en prose de Tristan*, Paris, 1890.

LUCHAIRE (A.), *Études sur les actes de Louis VII*, Paris, 1885.

MAAS (W.), *Les Moines défricheurs (Champagne-Lorraine)*, Moulins, 1954.

MACHUT (R.), «La formation des terroirs et l'évolution de l'habitat dans la région de Somain du haut Moyen Âge à nos jours», *Actes du 8ᵉ Congrès de la Fédération des sociétés savantes du Nord de la France*, 1967.

MARETTE (J.), *Connaissance des primitifs par l'étude du bois*, 1961.

MAULDE LA CLAVIÈRE (René de), *Étude sur la condition forestière de l'Orléanais du Moyen Âge à la Renaissance*, Orléans, 1971.

————*Histoire de Louis XII*, Paris, 1888–1891.

————*Hommes libres de l'Orléanais au XIIᵉ siècle*.

MAURY (Alfred), *Les Forêts de la France dans l'Antiquité et au Moyen Âge*, Paris 1856.

————*Histoire des grandes forêts de la Gaule et de l'ancienne France*, Paris, 1880.

————*Croyances et légendes du Moyen Âge*, Paris, 1896.

————*Les Fées du Moyen Âge*, Paris, 1843.

MAZOYER (L.), *La Vie parisienne à travers les âges. La banlieue parisienne des origines à 1945*.

MESTRE (J.-L.), «Les étapes et les objectifs du droit forestier: du Moyen Âge au code forestier de 1827», *Droit administratif*, n° 5, mai 1979.

MÉTAILIÉ (Jean-Pierre), *Le Feu pastoral dans les Pyrénées centrales (C.N.R.S.)*, Toulouse, 1981.

MEYER (F.), «Législation et politique forestière: onze siècles d'évolution», *Droit administratif*, n° 5, mai 1979.

MEYNIER (A.), Problèmes et structures agraires, *Annales E.S.C.*, 1955.

————*Les Paysages agraires*, Paris, 1958.

MOLINIER (R.), «Les forêts», *Encyclopédie de l'écologie*, Paris, 1977.

MOLLIN (J.), «Une région de contact entre Préalpes et avantpays: la plaine de Saint-Laurent-du-Pont, Les Échelles», *Revue de géographie alpine*, n° XLVIII, Grenoble, 1960.

MONTAGARD (J.) et PICARD (M.), *Guide de la forêt et de ses à-côtés*, Paris, 1977.

MORIN (L.), *La Forêt en France*, 1975.

MORY (P.) et SERVIN (R.), «Une relique forestière en région peu boisée: Howardries en Brunehaut (Belgique)», *Association des ruralistes français*, 1979.

NEEDHAM (Joseph), *Science and Civilisation*, Cambridge (1951), 1965.

O'DONOVAN (J.), *A Grammar of Irish Language*, Dublin, 1845.

PALISSY (Bernard), *Traité des sols divers et de l'agriculture*, Paris, 1953.

PERROY (E.), *Chartes du Forez*, Paris, 1939.

————*La Terre et les paysans aux XIIᵉ et XIIIᵉ siècles*, Paris, 1953.

————*La Féodalité en France (Xᵉ -XIIᵉ siècle)*, Paris, 1956.

PESSON et autres, *Écologies forestières*, 1974.

PICAR (M.) et MONTAGARD (J.), *Le Bûcheron*, Paris, 1979.

PICARD (J.-F.), see BECKER (M.).

PIRENNE (H.), *La Ville et les institutions urbaines* (2 vol.), Paris, Bruxelles, 1939.

PLAISANCE (G.), «Les caractères originaux de l'exploitation ancienne des forêts», *Revue de géographie de Lyon*, n° 1, 1953.

————*Les Formations végétales et les paysages ruraux*, lexique et guide bibliographique, Paris, 1959.

————«L'emprise des forêts françaises et son explication», *Actes du 88ᵉ congrès national des sociétés savantes*.

POGNON (E.), *L'An mille*, Paris, 1949.
———*La Vie quotidienne en l'an mille*, Paris, 1981.
PORTEOUS, *Forêt et folklore*, London.
POUPARDIN (D.) et KALAORA (B.), *Le Statut de la forêt et ses contradictions (I.N.R.A.)*, Orléans, 1979.
———*L'Administration forestière dans ses rapports avec les associations* (1880–1950, C.N.R.S.), Olivet, 1980.
POURTET (J.), *Les Repeuplements artificiels* (E.N.G.R.E.F.), Nancy, 1961.
QUARTIER (A.) et BAUER-BOVET (P.), *Guide des arbres et arbustes d'Europe*, Neuchâtel, 1982.
RABELAIS (F.), *Œuvres complètes*, Bibliothèque de la Pléiade, Paris, 1941.
RACKHAM (Olivier), The Surviving Medieval Woods of Lowland England, *Actes du S.I.H.F.*, Nancy, 1982.
RAMADE (François), «L'agression humaine traditionnelle», *Encyclopédie de l'écologie Larousse*, Paris, 1977.
REINAUD, *Invasions des Sarrasins en France*.
REMY, «L'abbaye de Moutiers en Argonne», *Congrès archéologique de France 1875*, Paris, 1876.
RENOUARD (Y.), «La capacité du tonneau bordelais au Moyen Âge», *Annales du Midi*, n° 21, Bordeaux, 1953.
RICHER, *Histoire de France*, Éd. R. la Touche-Paris, 1930–1937.
ROUPNEL, *Histoire de la campagne française*, Paris, 1932.
SAINCT YON, *Les Édits et Ordonnances des Roys; coustumes des provinces, règlements, arrests et jugements notables des eaues et forests*, Paris, 1610.
SALOMON (M. de), *Traité de l'aménagement des forêts enseigné à l'école royale forestière*, Paris, 1836 et 1837.
SALZMAN (F.), *English Industries of the Middle Ages*, London, Delft, 1964.
———*Building in England down to 1540*, Oxford, 1967.
SAUTTER (Gilles), «Terroirs d'Afrique occidentale», *Études rurales*, Paris, 1962.
SCLAFERT (Thérèse), «Cultures en Haute-Provence. Déboisements et pâturages au Moyen Âge», Paris, 1956.
———«À propos du déboisement dans les Alpes du Sud. Le Haut-Dauphiné au Moyen Âge», *Annales de géographie*, Paris, 1926.
SEGUIN (R.-L.), *L'Équipement de la ferme canadienne aux XVIIͤ et XVIIIͤ siècles*, Montréal, 1959.
SERRES (Olivier de), *Le Théâtre d'agriculture et mesnage des champs* (1600), Paris, 1804.
SIGAUT (F.), *L'Agriculture et le feu*, Paris, 1976.
SINCLAIR (Sir John), *Code of Agriculture*, London (1820–1832).
SIVERY (G.), *Structures agraires et vie rurale dans le Hainaut à la fin du Moyen Âge*, Lille, 1972.
SLICKER VAN BATH (B. H.), «Le climat et les récoltes en Haut Moyen Âge», *XIIͤ settimana di studio del centro italiano di studi sull'alto Medio Evo*, Spolète, 1966.
SOLTNER (Dominique), *L'Arbre et la haie*, Angers, 1980.
———*Les Grandes Productions végétales*, Angers, 1982.
SPRANDEL, «La production du fer au Moyen Âge», *Annales d'histoire économique et sociale*, Paris, 1959.
STENTON (D. M.), *The 1st Century of Feudalism: (1066–1166)*, London, 1950.
———*English Society in the Early Middle Ages (1066–1307)*, London, 1951.
———*Bayeux Tapestry*, London, 1957.
STEVENS (J. F.), «La définition agro-économique de la terre», *Futuribles*, n° 52, Paris, 1982.

STOUFF (L.), *Ravitaillement et alimentation en Provence au XIVe siècle*, Paris, La Haye, 1970.

THEOPHILE, *Traité des divers arts*, Paris, 1924.

THIBAULT (C.), *L'Homme et la forêt ou les métamorphoses* (polycopié).

THIBAULT (Max) «Aménagement et gestion des rivières à saumon atlantique», *Etudes et Recherches, 3e Assises internationales de l'environnement*, vol. 4, 1980.

TIMBAL (J.), see BECKER (M.).

TOUSSAINT, *Forêts et forges*.

VENET (Jean), Les anciennes forêts de l'abbaye de Mont-Sainte-Marie et les forêts communales du Haut-Doubs. Influence de l'histoire sur la structure et le traitement des forêts, *Actes du S.I.H.F.*, Nancy, 1982.

VERHULST (Adrian), «Genèse du régime domanial classique en France au haut Moyen Âge», *XIIIe settimana di studio del Centro italiano di studi sull'alto Medio Evo*, Spolete, 1966.

———*Histoire du paysage rural en Flandres*, Bruxelles, 1966.

VERRIER (L.), *Polyptyque du Viel Rentier d'Audenarde*, Bruxelles, 1950.

VIE (Louis), «Le régime juridique de l'arbre et des forêts en Gaule des temps préhistoriques au Moyen Âge», *Recueil de l'Académie de législation*, 1920–1921.

VIERS (G.), *Géographie des forêts*, Paris, 1970.

VILLON (François), *Œuvres* (Éd. L. Thuasne) Paris, *1923*.

VINAVER (E.), *Étude sur le Tristan en prose*, t. II, Paris, 1925.

VINOGRADOFF (P.), English Society in the XIth century, *Essays in English Medieval History*, Oxford, 1908.

VIOLLET-LE-UC (E.), *Dictionnaire raisonné de l'architecture française du XIe au XVIe siècle* (10 vol.), Paris, 1858–1868.

WALTER OF HENLEY and others, *Treatise on Estate Management and Accounting* (Ed. D. Oschensky), Oxford, 1971.

WHITE (Lynn), *Technologie médiévale et transformations sociales* (trans. M. Lefeuvre), Paris, La Haye, 1969.

XENOPHON, *L'Art de la chasse* (traduction Delebecque), Paris, 1970.

index